Cultural Heritage and Contem
Series VIA, Eastern and Central I
General Editor
George F. McLea

Civil Society,
Pluralism and Universalism

Polish Philosophical Studies, VIII

by

Eugeniusz Górski

The Council for Research in Values and Philosophy

Box 261
Cardinal Station
Washington, D.C. 20064

Printed in the United States of America

Library of Congress Cataloging-in-Publication

Górski, Eugeniusz.
Civil society, pluralism, and universalism / by Eugeniusz Górski.
p. cm. -- (Polish philosopical studies ; 8) (Cultural heritage and contemporary change. Series VIA, Central and Eastern Europe ; v. 34)
Includes bibliographical references and index.
1. Civil society--Case studies. 2. Pluralism (Social sciences)--Case studies. 3. Universalism--Case studies. I. Title. II. Series.
JC337.G667 2007 2006102781
300.1--dc22 CIP

ISBN 978-1-56518-241-7 (pbk.)

Table of Contents

Introduction

The comparative essays and articles gathered and updated in this volume were written in various times and under various occasions. They concentrate on the ideas of civil society, democracy, pluralism and universalism in Poland, Central and Eastern Europe, Spain and Latin America. Although Poland has contributed considerably to the development of the civil society and to other above mentioned ideas, these essays show - against the dominant opinion - that the revival of the idea of civil society that has marked the last 25 years had earlier occurred in Italy and to some extent even in the neighboring Yugoslavia, among authors inspired by Antonio Gramsci, and also in Latin America, but not in Central Europe or the Anglo-Saxon world. The difference in time, however, was not great, so rightly it can be argued that the idea appeared almost simultaneously in various parts of the world (Italy, Latin America and East Central Europe). It is worth noting that the influence of Gramsci in the discourse on civil society was initially greater than that of classical liberalism.

The idea of civil society appeared broadly at the end of 1970s and in the 1980s in the political discourse of the Latin American Left and of the Central European democratic opposition. Both circles quite independently from each other and mutually rather hostile used the idea in repressive contexts as a tool in their struggle for freedom and democracy against military, bureaucratic-authoritarian and totalitarian regimes in the two regions of the world. The idea of civil society presupposed a moral necessity of social defense against dictatorships, and an attempt to create and dominate an independent public opinion. Gramsci and his Western and South American followers saw in that peaceful conquering of the sphere of civil society an illusory chance for a socialism without bloody revolution. Similarly, the Central European dissidents saw in the gradual conquering of the alternative or parallel social sphere a chance for overthrowing without violence, or a deep reform, of communism. The Central European proponents of this kind of society were very ambiguous in their discourse on a third road, a non-political and ethical community. In that discourse it was difficult to differentiate between their personal views and Machiavellian camouflage. The democratic and workers' revolution of Solidarity could not announce at the very beginning the need for a liberal and capitalist revolution.

The spontaneously democratic ideology and phraseology of an independent civil society from Eastern Europe and Latin America, re-elaborated in Western countries, was later used with lesser effect in the struggle against African and Asian dictatorships. Since the end of 1989 the term civil society, repeated like a mantra, has become a name for human dreams, and a key element of the post-totalitarian and post cold war *Zeitgeist*.

There are many definitions and conceptions of civil society. In the Polish scholarly literature civic, liberal, political, and communitarian interpretations have been identified, as well as republican, liberal and normative conceptions. Eclectic interpretations, combining individualism with social solidarity and republican virtues, conflict with cooperation, are also abundant. The most recent research transcends the local or national conception of civil society confined within the boundaries of one state, and refers rather to a general idea of citizenship or globalization from below, to the European, inter-American, global and network civil society. After the collapse of communism the theme of civil society, "a renewed call for the redevelopment of civil society" has come and become fashionable, especially in Central and Eastern Europe.[1]

Manuel Castells has differentiated between two traditions in the interpretation of the concept of civil society: one stemming from John Locke, tradition of Anglo-Saxon liberalism and a Marxist-humanist tradition represented by Antonio Gramsci. They cannot do without the concept of the state, but the state they referred to was a national state. Nowadays, however, in the epoch of globalization (embracing not only free trade, but also a globalization of human rights and a globalization of collective human activities) we are witnessing a crisis of the national state and of national democracy. So the process constituting present-day civil society reaches far beyond the national state. The crisis of the institution of the national state and of its surrounding civil society is a cause of the rise of new cultural identities and of a new civil society not so much connected with statehood. New organizations and alternative movements (ecological or human rights defenders) that are being created have easy access (thanks to the Internet) to information and communication. This gives great possibilities for human mobilization and for acting upon public opinion. According to Castells, a new global civil society is being constituted. Its aim is an affirmation of universal values and of new symbolic codes, as well as an offensive transformation of the state, of which Gramsci dreamt in an earlier epoch. It is interesting to see that the idea of civil society with some references to Gramsci is present in the rebellious movements in Argentina and Latin America. But the Gramscian categories are insufficient nowadays. The key concept of hegemony does not sufficiently take into account the links of a country with the world economy and international politics.

A vision of a new universalism is embraced by the idea of a global civil society. Many authors dream of a new force that would speak for the planetary humankind, that would express the needs and dreams of over six billions of people and which would not act in the egoistic interest of particular nations. Such controlling counterpart against the United States can no longer be exercised by any nation or group of nations. Only the emerging global civic movement identified with the interests of the world community, can oppose US particularism.

The Internet and other interactive media very deeply enter into the world community, they deliver new possibilities for a global communication and universal intercultural dialogue. Thanks to the new electronic links a new consciousness of a planetary humanity is being created, almost a Teilhardian noosphere. According to James F. Moore from Harvard (and even in the opinion of the *New York Times*)[2] such global civil society or world public opinion is becoming a very important political player, a second superpower after the United States, but before the European Union, which is also being named a civil superpower. A natural ally of the global civil society, situated in opposition to a particularistic attitude of the US government is the group of 21 organized and led by Brazil, India, China and South Africa.

Much attention is being paid also to a new formula of civil society, to the structures of Civic Communities via Internet and direct democracy coming soon. The possibility of such direct democracy causes anxiety among the forces exercising an unlimited hegemony today. Even now it is more difficult than in the previous epoch to hide inconvenient facts.

Nowadays, especially in the Americas, quite a lot is being written - both from leftist radical and right wing positions - on the world associational revolution, or the global civil society. Civil Society is becoming a place for the search for a new systemic alternative, a place for liberation from "oppressive" liberalism or the place where a reconciliation and appeasement of contradictions generated by the free market may occur.

The new social movements in Poland and elsewhere enter into contact with the Forum of European Civil Society and with the world alterglobalist movement, which aims at a global civil society. The idea of a global, transnational or international civil society is welcome both by socialists and by liberals inspired by Immanuel Kant, for example by R. Dahrendorf or A. Colas. The latter combines international civil society with universalist principles and with a new „socialist internationalism".

Today in Europe that is unifying, and beyond it various attempts are being made to recover a new, leftist concept of universalism, the concept referring to the European tradition of the rhetoric of liberation, to universal human nature, to Immanuel Kant, the young Marx and radical ecology. Moral and even materialistic universalism is being defended. Very strong, inspiring and unifying, especially in Poland, is the influence of John Paul II's Christian Universalism. This "Polish, Slavic and universal Pope" (George H. Williams from Harvard) has initiated a new stage in the history of dialogue and universalism.

New reflections on civil society are combined in this book with similar considerations on other topics in social philosophy and the history of ideas (pluralism, westernism, universalism, transitions to democracy), are also combined with a more general idea of a dialogue of Eastern Europe with the whole Hispanic world and with universal civilizations of the Americas in the Western hemisphere.

Earlier, usually more complete versions of the essays gathered here had been published in my books in Polish and Spanish,[3] partly also in the scholarly journals: *Dialogue and Universalism*, *Estudios Latinoamericanos*, and *East European Politics and Societies*.

NOTES

1 George F. McLean, "Philosophy and Civil Society: Its Nature, Its Past and Its Future", in G. McLean, ed., *Civil Society and Social Reconstruction*, (Washington: The Council for Research in Values and Philosophy, 1997), 8; Viorca Tighel, "Social Change, Civil Society, and Tolerance: A Challenge for the New Democracies", in *Civil Society: Who Belongs?* (Washington: The Council for Research in Values and Philosophy, 2004), 126.

2 "A New Power in the Streets", *The New York Times*, February 17, 2003.

3 Eugeniusz Górski, *Dependencia y originalidad de la filosofia en Latinoamerica y en la Europa del Este,* (Mexico: UNAM, 1994); *O demokracji w Hiszpanii 1975-1995*, (Warsaw: IFiS Publishers, 1997); *Rozważania o społeczeństwie obywatelskim i inne studia z historii idei,* (Warsaw: IFiS Publishers, 2003).

Part I

Civil Society in Eastern Europe, Latin America and Spain

Chapter 1

Reflections on Civil Society

In the most advanced States civil society has become a very complex structure, one which is resistant to the catastrophic irruptions caused by immediate economic factors (crises, depressions, etc.).

The superstructures of civil society are like trench-systems of modern warfare. -- Antonio Gramsci, *Note sul Machiavelli.*

Lo scandalo del contraddirmi, dell'essere con te e contro te; con te nel cuore, in luce, contro te nelle buie viscere.

-- Pier Paolo Pasolini, *Le ceneri di Gramsci. Poemetti* (Milano: Garzanti, 1963), 77.

This Essay focuses on the reception of the civil society concept, particularly in the political thought of Antonio Gramsci and his followers. I direct attention to the concept's universal importance and its relevance to contemporary political philosophy, especially in Poland, East Europe and Latin America. Intellectuals in these countries (notably Leszek Kołakowski and Adam Michnik), as well as numerous Latin American Gramsci students – and first and foremost the Italians headed by Norberto Bobbio – have markedly contributed to its return from oblivion and new content. Thus, this heretofore rather mythical idea developed into a material force which eventually acquired revolutionary traits and, in the past 25 years, spread throughout the Western world, especially its East European and Latin American peripheries. Lately, however, East Europeans and Latin Americans have lost much of their initial faith in civil society – which for a short time was viewed as a paradise and an *ersatz* form of earlier socialist illusions – as an easy transition path from poverty to well being.

ANTONIO GRAMSCI'S CONCEPT OF CIVIL SOCIETY

Antonio Gramsci (1891-1937) was the first 20th-century thinker to apply the civil society concept to his own ideas, although its presence in European social thought, especially works by representatives of the British Enlightenment (Locke, Hume, Ferguson), Hegel and the young Marx, dates back to the 17th Century. However, contrary to Marx and Engels, who tied civil society to the economy, or the "base", Gramsci rather links it to society's "superstructure" as a category between the economic base and the state's strictly political institutions. Thus, although not everyone appears to be aware of the fact, Gramsci pioneered the trend to revaluate the civil society concept that has been gaining ground in today's social thought.[1]

The first to notice the importance and the reformatory, tradition-belying and innovative creativity of Gramsci's civil society (*società civile*) theory was Norberto Bobbio (1909-2004), the Italian philosopher and lifetime Senator and one of the past century's most outstanding scholars of democracy. Bobbio, an active socialist (for a time even on the Italian Socialist Party's Central Committee) and today a gallant figure for Italy's postcommunists, dreamed of synthesizing socialism and liberalism.[2] Paraphrasing Marx, Bobbio pointed out that for Gramsci civil society encompassed not so much economic as ideological and cultural relations,[3] thus constituting an "upside-down Marxism" inspired largely by specific interpretations of Hegel.

Gramsci distinguished between civil and political society, or state. The distinction, however, was rather abstract as in fact he believed certain elements of the state concept were applicable to civil society. Hence, in *Prison Notebooks*, he outlined an "integrated state" concept which organically incorporated both. For Gramsci civil society was also political society, operating without formal sanction but capable of influencing collective thought and modes of behavior.[4]

An important part of civil society are the institutions of manipulated public opinion. According to Gramsci, "what is called 'public opinion' is closely connected with political hegemony, namely with the point at which civil society makes contact with political society. The state, when it wants to undertake an unpopular action, creates adequate public opinion to protect itself; in other words, it organizes and centralizes certain elements within civil society."[5]

It is said that Gramsci paid more attention to the role of superstructure in the processes making up a ruling class's reign than actual power understood as enforcement and administration. For Lenin hegemony was mainly political, for Gramsci it also had an ideological aspect, and also related to the period before a given class's or group's acquisition of real political power. Seen this way, the revolutions are hegemony conflicts in which the old ruling class' political reign (*dominio*) is separated from society's intellectual and moral leadership (*direzione*).

Joseph Buttigieg, a Notre-Dame-resident U.S. Marxist and today one of the best Gramsci scholars, claims a ruling class's position is stronger when it combines political domination with control over civil society. To achieve this, ruling classes must often sacrifice their own interests and move from mere political and economic control to a moral and intellectual unity model and a milder form of hegemony over subordinated groups. Therefore, governments must rise above immediate class interests. Reiterating Gramsci, Buttigieg says a dominant position in civil society is more important than legal and political control, which, while allowing ruling groups to impose their will, is often lost in coup d'etats. Hegemony, on the other hand, is more resistant to the effects of revolt.[6]

The military terminology Gramsci employs to describe state and social revolution is crucial in understanding his civil society concept. Especially important is the distinction between manoeuvre and positional warfare, one entailing direct combat, the other passive resistance like entrenchment or psychological tactics. State-of-the-art combat science lays more weight on positional tactics than armed combat, and Gramsci too believed that a positional approach aimed at conquering the tall wall bastions of civil society – especially in the cultural sphere – is fundamental in the political battles waged by the developed capitalist states. Social revolution in the countries of the capitalist West cannot be limited to the struggle for political power and state government. It must also penetrate to the complex system of social relations in which the ruling bourgeoisie has entrenched itself. In other words, it must first and foremost win control over "a system of entrenchments and fortifications typical for parts of civil society". In this the western countries' situation was fundamentally different from that of socially backward Russia, where the main goal was political power (and in fact the Winter Palace). Western attempts at proletarian upheaval failed among others because their leaders, in their eagerness to copy Russia's October Revolution, forgot that their societies were structured differently from Russia's. This fact was ignored by west-European revolutionaries, including the Trotskyites, who proposed frontal conflict. According to Gramsci they would have done better with a positional strategy – which he undertook to prove during Italy's almost-successful working-class upsurge.

In his deliberations on the essence of the modern state Gramsci points to statehood's educational functions, e.g. its role in the evolution of a new citizenship model to meet rising production needs. Here the state's influence on the moralities and mentalities of individuals is exercised with the purpose of winning their consent and support, and in such a way as to make them see necessity, and even enforcement, as freedom. State has a tendency to extend its laws onto spheres of life which were once legally neutral domains of civil society, and therefore usually unsanctioned. However, modern civil society does exert some pressure on individual behavior, morality and world outlook. Moreover, civil society is tied to state (political society) by such an intricate web of connections that citizens often feel as if it were actually the state.

In fact, Gramsci's train of thought suggests not so much that the state should be overcome or abolished as assimilated into a regulated society, an ethical organism with a well-rooted hegemony and consensus system.[7] The goal here, therefore, is not state but "regulated society" answering to Gramsci's vision of communism. Gramsci's views on civil society are fundamental in all efforts to reconstruct his quite original political thought.

The essence of civil society is best represented in the functioning of the political parties and other "public" associations which form its tissue and compete for supremacy, hegemony or alliance within its boundaries. In civil society parties that win power do not automatically stifle all rival social and political life, but do their best to maintain a balance between the many interests present in such pluralistic communities. Working-class hegemony in civil society stems from consensus and does not exclude pluralism, subordinated groups engaging in positional warfare to promote new values – and eventually develop new civil society models.[8]

Gramsci's reflections on statehood and society are closely tied to hegemony and the role intellectual elites play in its sustenance. He employs the hegemony concept not only to penetrate past and present social relations, but also to analyze theories involving "new type" parties building "historical blocs"[9] by social classes heretofore subordinated by the bourgeoisie. Hegemony in civil society takes place on various superstructure levels, and often goes beyond mere political commandeering. Superstructure takes on the form of institutions – state-run in political communities and non-governmental in civil societies. In both cases intellectuals – in Gramsci's words the "clerks" or "superstructure functionaries" of the ruling class – play a crucial role in the system.

In describing Gramsci's civil society concept I have tried to set it against the various semantic contexts present in his reflections on the state, hegemony, ideology and superstructure. It is often said that this concept represents a basic and autonomous aspect of superstructure, functioning as a bridge between the base and superstructure's institutional outlets.[10] Gramsci's civil society can take on a variety of forms: it can be a ruling class's ideology propounded by science, art, economy and law, a philosophy supported by social groups striving for closer ties to the ruling class, an element of political ideology, and a factor influencing a ideological information channels like the schooling system, media, libraries etc.[11] These observations led Gramsci to redefine the state as "the equilibrium between political society (i. e., a dictatorship or some other coercive apparatus used to control the masses in conformity with a given type of production and economy)... and civil society (or the hegemony of a social group over the entire nation exercised through so-called private organizations such as the church, the unions, the schools, etc.)"[12] According to Gramsci's notes on Machiavelli, the state consists of political and civil society, it is hegemony "armored by coercion", thanks to which the active consent of the governed is being obtained.

In analyzing relations between state and civil society Gramsci makes frequent historical references with regard to the latter, he also mentions a possible future in which civil society has completely assimilated and eliminated the state.

GRAMSCI IN ITALY AND WORLDWIDE

In the 1970s and 1980s not only orthodox marxists but also maoists, eurocommunists, socialists, social-democrats, and partly also liberals, nationalists and propagators of the "new right", "new evolutionism" and "new thinking" concepts initiated by Gorbatchev and "perestroika",[13] drew heavily on Gramsci's inspiring and often backhanded writings, especially on civil society. Of all these attempts to put Gramsci's thoughts to creative use only Adam Michnik's and his followers' new evolutionism proved itself as a political strategy (discounting the general postulates of broadly understood, classical liberalism). Thus, ironically, Poland, a socialist country, was the only place where Gramsci's theory proved helpful in the mounting of a worker revolution – albeit a pro-capitalist one.

After the war Gramsci's writings were used by almost all political forces in Italy, by the 1960s they already belonged to the pan-European philosophical and political canon. For some years the Gramscian civil society concept, as well as its interpretation by the leftist-croceanist or center-right (liberal) Gramscist Norberto Bobbio, were in the center of debates on the relations between democracy, pluralism and socialism between Italy's socialists and communists. Accompanying this in subsequent years were controversies around the Eurocommunism theory, mainly among Italian and Spanish Marxists. Bobbio's interpretation, which accented ideas and the human free will, postulated a breakaway from Marx' and Engels' economic determinism and the authoritarianism of Lenin.

These questions are a fundamental motif in newer Gramsci studies, which focus on matters like the specifics of his political thought, his views on statehood and the role of intellectuals, his interpretation of "passive revolution" and the emergence and development of freedom. The historical import of Gramsci's philosophy arises from the presence in his writings of concepts like civil and political society, as well as equally important and closely related notions like citizenship, historical bloc, hegemony, jacobinism, organic crisis and consensus.

Many southern-European Marxists saw Gramsci as the pioneer of Eurocommunism, which discarded classical revolution as inappropriate for the countries of the West. According to one of them, by rejecting frontal attack, armed battle and "storming the Winter Palace", Eurocommunism in fact advocated entrenchment and positional warfare.[14] Gramsci, however, athough quoted (and deftly reinterpreted) by Eurocommunists, never claimed positional warfare would eliminate manoeuvre tactics or the possibility, at some point in time, of revolution against the old system. Here (as in many other respects) the Eurocommunist theory showed its weaknesses, illusory character and naivete. Gramsci did not reject classical communism, but merely modified its proletarian rule theory and supplemented it with concepts like moral and political hegemony.

In the 1970s and 80s Gramsci's theories, especially his civil society concept, also exerted a strong influence on the theoreticians of the French and Italian new right (Alain de Benoist, Marco Tarchi), who sought a deeper rooting in culture in a bid to enliven their own conservative revolution projects (*Gramscisme de droite* in France, Cezary Michalski and the young national right in the 1990s in Poland). It is interesting to see that the Gramscian idea of democracy and hegemony has recently been recalled by a neo-conservative author from the powerful foundation Freedom House, which supported in 2004 the Orange Revolution in Ukraine.[15] In fact, the general response to Gramsci by diverse political groupings was marked by a dose of sympathy, which to a degree made him public property (*Gramsci di tutti*, to use Togliatti's expression).

A historical paradox is Gramsci's rapidly rising popularity in the United States and the Anglo-Saxon world,[16] as well as the foundation in 1989 – almost simultaneously with the fall of communism and resulting total discontinuation of all Gramscian studies in East Europe – of the International

Gramsci Society affiliating members on several continents. An interesting case here is Poland, where Gramsci's civil society ideas inspired the forces that toppled communism. However, the new system had no love for this theoretician, although his revolution strategies proved themselves in practice in the case of Solidarity. We can speak of a radical ingratitude of Poland to Gramsci, of the unique country, where Gramscian technology of revolution proved to be effective. Poland remains one of the very few countries in the world whose free press made no mention at all of Gramsci's 1991 centennial (as it failed to note lesser Gramscian anniversaries in 1997 and 2001). Neither Adam Michnik's influential *Gazeta Wyborcza* daily nor the postcommunist *Trybuna* ran a word. Moreover, since 1991 no Polish paper nor popular or scholarly periodical has printed as much as one feature on Gramsci. It appears that, although there have been no official verdicts to this effect, Poland has sentenced Gramsci's ideas to oblivion for at least twenty years – just as he was very quickly and effectively forgotten in all of East Europe after 1989.[17] Nonetheless, it is hardly possible to lie about the source of today's civil society concept – nor the fact that an Italian communist's ideas were fundamental for Solidarity's approach to civil society – even if the truth is embarrassing for many a rightwing politician.

Gramsci's philosophy and civil society theory met with a totally different reception by Latin American followers of the dependency theory and leftist sociology that for over three decades now – in Brazil and Mexico since the mid-1970s and in Argentina since even earlier – have successfully flourished in that part of the world.[18] At the time the corrosion of Brazil's 1964-installed military government was becoming visible. The system's decay was to a large degree hastened by the emergence of new social movements which were oriented towards modern civil society. It was then that Gramsci advanced to one of the icons of Brazilian democracy, his term "civil society" gaining immense popularity. Civil society became a synonym of all that opposed the state's hegemony. Towards the end of the dictatorship period even those public organizations that were close to the country's big capital were timidly moving away from the regime and closer to the opposition. In this situation – and against Gramsci's intentions – the inseparable terminological pair "civil society" and "state" became a radical, almost Manichaean dichotomy in which all that descended from civil society was considered positive and all that related to the state negative. It is impossible here to list all the interpretations of civil society presented by multifarious leftwing factions. However, both in Brazil and the world the approach to Gramsci was soon modified by the social-liberal influence of Norberto Bobbio, thanks to which it not only helped topple dictators but also led to the erosion of leftwing intellectualism, whose representatives in Latin America and elsewhere began to take an increasingly social-democratic and even openly liberal stand.[19]

After the fall of "real socialism" interest in Gramsci waned a little almost everywhere in Latin America. A notable exception is still-communist Cuba, where the downfall of Soviet-style state socialism inspired a search for other leftist solutions. In 1991, the year of Gramsci's 100th birthday, crisis-torn Cuba became the site of the rediscovery of this quite unorthodox Marxist philosopher.[20] While still in the late 1980s the term "civil society" was known only to a handful of Gramsci scholars, in the second half of the following decade a debate on restoring civil society on the island was in full progress, the first to come out with such appeals being the Cuban Catholic Church (in a document in 1994). Recently the idea has also come to the ruling elites, who after 1996[21] also began a debate on civil society, initially adorned with the ritual "socialist". The discussion focused on the role of civil society in Cuba's uncertain future, especially in light of the country's imminent democratization, pluralization and difficult transition to a new political model (although some Cuban leaders still hope for a communist revival, especially in Latin America).[22] The fall of Latin America's rightist and East Europe's leftist dictatorships have encouraged Cuba to consider gradual change and launch a search for a "reconstruction model". However the capitalistic model in neighboring Haiti and the frequently miserable effects of Latin American attempts at economic neo-liberalism are proof that such moves warrant caution.

The breakdown of Latin America's authoritarian regimes and ensuing "conservative" transition to capitalistic democracy (before the fall of communism in East Europe), forced the Latin American left to reset its ideological sights and reconsider its approach to the rules of democracy. The recent bitter experiences under dictatorship, especially the ruthless repression and torture, were among the reasons for Latin America's rejection of revolutionary social models in favor of reevaluating democracy as such[23] and acceptance of general human rights. Today the continent's left values its participation in the institutional structures of official democratic state and civil society. More attention is also being paid to the role of civil society – especially NGOs – in shaping democratic culture.[24] Also, the fall of Marxism-Leninism in East Europe had a natural impact on the Latin American left, which faced globalization and the contemporary world's increasing complexity. An interesting light on this is thrown in the reminiscences of Władysław Dowbor and Alfred Sirkis, two Polish-descended former Brazilian revolutionaries, who recount that they had the impression of actively participating in a global war between imperialism and revolutionary socialism, and conclude wryly: "How naïve we were. We thought we could change something with a few guns". Recounting the revolutionary left's mounting crisis, Dowbor also mentions the Polish anticommunists' inability to understand Brazil's anti-American moods (and frequently huffy stance towards 'third world" Latin America). Here is what he told them: "You were under a communist dictatorship and we under a rightist regime… the 'physical/intellectual type' which in Latin America most often became a Marxist, guerilla or underground leftist, became an anticommunist in Poland; the same type of human who in Poland became a self-gratifying, opportunistic *apparatchik*, wore a military uniform and tortured students in Brazil… Latin America's rightist regimes had the support of the CIA and its agents, U.S. money and U.S. arms. Whether you wanted to or not, your revolution, your struggle for freedom and justice, had to be colored red". Sirkis also claimed that "Solidarity's alliance of the working class with the intelligentsia was more typical for Latin American communists than anticommunist generals". Clearly disappointed with the extreme left, Sirkis expressed content over the fact that it was given no chance to commit crime in the name of Brazilian freedom – and turned to more concrete forms of organizational activity by founding Brazil's Green Party.[25]

Thus, the concept of continental revolution failed to win ground in Latin America, however the leftist – and especially Gramscian – revolutionary model, based on the creation of a historical bloc and winning hegemony over civil society in the course of arduous positional warfare, quite unexpectedly brought fruit in Poland and East Europe.

Andrzej Walicki points to the fascination with Gramsci displayed by post-Stalinist Poland's revisionistic-minded Marxists.[26] One of them, Adam Michnik, came out with a so-called "new evolutionism" program following the anticommunist opposition's failures in 1956, 1968 and 1970. Michnik managed to combine the loose ideas of former Polish Marxists like Leszek Kołakowski and Jacek Kuroń into a coherent strategy for the political opposition.[27] And in this, more or less consciously, he allowed himself to be inspired by Gramsci's civil society concept.[28]

In his program for the opposition Adam Michnik stressed the importance of constant public pressure on the authorities as a means of coercing reform. According to Michnik, "the path of perseverant struggle for reform, the path of evolution towards broader civil and human rights, is the only path for dissidents in East Europe". In Michnik's opinion it was Poland's "revisionist-minded ex-Stalinists" who created and spread to the country's intellectual elites a new opposition model involving the rebirth of civil society. Jacek Kuroń (1934-2004) also saw the opposition's main tasks in the protection of civil rights and the formation of new public movements as a pressure instrument on state government. Kuroń also presented a "program for Polish society's self-organization into independent public movements and the foundation of related institutions" with the aim of creating "a civil Poland". Neither author uses the term "civil society" in his pre-Solidarity works but both appear quite close to it, best evidenced by Kuroń's words, "the program for today is a democratic society organized into trade unions, consumer associations (…), local governments, co-operatives and similar groups".

Like Gramsci before him, Michnik spent much of his prison time ruminating on the failure of the movements he supported.[29] The subsequent action undertaken by the Worker Defense Committee and Solidarity's self-restricting worker revolution had much in common with the Gramscian concept of positional warfare within civil society as war waged by a leftist political opposition against the state.

Andrzej Walicki frequently criticized the original Solidarity's leftist-populist character and evolution into a mass socialist movement striving for public control over the entire economy. Even some Solidarity activists eventually realized, that, "because of its nature, structure and organization, this monstrous movement was ill-suited for democracy, and this mainly for two reasons: it was structured like a factory, but expressed essentially political goals – which is a classical feature of communism – and secondly, it was *per se* an all-embracing movement, which augured badly for any tolerance of pluralism."[30]

Many revisionist-descended members of the democratic opposition strove to refresh Marxism, make it more democratic and humane, and looked to Gramsci for help. Zbigniew A. Pelczynski, a Polish-descended Oxford professor, believes the events in Poland gave Gramsci's theories a new, practical perspective, and uses modified Gramscian categories to analyze the formation and growth of the Solidarity bloc. According to Pelczynski, Gramsci proved useful to the democratic opposition's theoreticians, the ideologues of "new evolutionism", and the "detotalitarianization" of communism.[31] Referring to Gramsci, Pelczynski wrote: "One might say that in Poland on the threshold of the 1980s the Communist Party's political and economic 'domination' was still intact, but its 'hegemony' was already seriously undermined.... During 1981 Solidarity's ideas achieved 'hegemony' over Polish society, but the state's 'domination' over the economy – and, even more, the police and the army – remained intact... The opposition between the Communist Party 'bloc' and the Solidarity 'bloc'... evolved into a struggle for power of the kind Gramsci postulated."[32] The broad-scale character of this short-lived bloc created by Solidarity – which embraced workers, peasants, intellectuals and the Catholic Church – was something unprecedented in the world, and far beyond Gramsci's boldest dreams.

In 1980/81 Lenin's *The State and Revolution*[33] was frequently, if somewhat cautiously quoted in Poland, and the Gramscian civil society concept (which rejected market economy) enjoyed popularity in the 1980s due to its clear juxtaposition of revolting society and state (although, because of his communist roots, direct reference to Gramsci was considered improper in anticommunist circles). Also the moral and psychological pressure applied by Solidarity ran close to the Gramscian method of fighting for hegemony over civil society – fighting without physical violence.

Asked why August 1980 had been a success, one of Solidarity's leaders said: "Because there was an elite, because the atmosphere was right, and because we had mass support. This came together and the Bolshevist revolution theory became reality. Marxism and Leninism were beaten by their own weapons – the working class myth, a working-class leader, and a small group who mapped out goals and knew how to interpret social moods".[34] What is more, Solidarity to a large extent proved Ernesto *Che* Guevaras radical *foco guerrillero* and subcontinental revolution theory, which found adequate expression in Solidarity's famous – and eventually fulfilled – appeal for the liberation of Eastern Europe's "working people".[35] Thus, Lenin, Gramsci, Sorel, Rosa Luxemburg and Che Guevara proved of little help in Latin America despite their quite positive reception. At the same time, selectively and pragmatically applied, their theories proved quite useful in East Europe's political battle against communism – although they were never really very highly valued here.

Poland's "carnival" in 1980/81 can be compared to Italy's *biennio rosso* (two red years), during which Gramsci was active in worker councils and commissions. In Italy's and Poland's case the *biennio rosso* period was followed by respectively Mussolini and Jaruzelski, however in neither country did the regime take on such an openly totalitarian form as it did in the case of Hitler and Stalin. The Italian revolutionary movement of 1919/1920 was in many ways naïve and ultimately failed on a misconceived theory about "the inherent weakness of the industrial bourgeoisie". Similarly during Poland's two "white-red" years, the commissions set up by the working-class Solidarity Union and the later Self-Governed Republic Clubs[36] displayed much naïveté. At the time protests were frequently patterned on variants of the Italian strike model, the working class, prematurely and temporarily included in civil society, successfully fighting against the degenerated worker state in the name of a new collectivist utopia.[37] "Now the people, who were hitherto 'nothing', were to be everything – control everybody and everything – by means of worker self-government bodies and a trade union".[38] This is truly material for a tragicomic epic novel. Even Władysław Frasyniuk, the current leader of the liberal Democratic Party said during a debate marking the 20th anniversary of August 1980: "At the time we really believed we'd own our factories. Not regions or cities, but precisely factories". At a recent Polish Business Council sitting Adam Michnik also recalled how difficult it was to give up illusions of "worker council rule".

FROM MARXISM TO LIBERALISM

Although the distinction between the state and society is crucial for classical and contemporary liberalism, before the fall of the Soviet bloc the term civil society rarely appeared in the western political discourse. Flora Lewis, a longtime *New York Times* correspondent in Poland, once said that, "Americans don't talk about civil society because they take it for granted", triumphantly adding after Gramsci: "The Communist ideal is destroying itself as the century ends because it could not create the 'fortress and earthworks' of civil society, nor accommodate them".[39] From then on the term civil society began to lose its bellicose Gramscian connotations, becoming a synonym of commercial and social privacy – a free market opposed to an omnipresent state. During the transition to democracy in East Europe and Latin America the civil society concept was reinterpreted to serve the interests of liberal democracy rather than proletarian revolution.

Also in Italy the communist party founded by Gramsci (CPI) was found to be redundant. In view of the new realities it was decided to transform it – with the help of Gramsci's universally applicable thought – into a new democratic leftwing party with a classical social-democratic leaning. According to Cecilia Lesgart Italy became a "melting-pot of political ideas" (we might add that the countries of Latin America and East Europe frequently served as convenient "testing-grounds" for diverse social theories and projects), enabling leftwing intellectuals to make the theoretical leap from

Marxism, revolution and socialism to the more liberal and democratic "intellectual and moral reform" model.[40] Also the new, moderate Latin American left, frustrated by its repeated failures (especially in Argentina and Chile), began to oppose revolutionary projects, increasingly turning to parliamentary democracy as a goal in itself, a historical achievement imposing legal restrictions on all authoritarian and arbitrary rule. New interpretations of Gramsci in Italy and some Latin American countries made acceptance of democracy *per se* easier, enabling a distancing from Marxism's orthodoxy and dogma towards liberalism. The introduction of new terminology led to the gradual "secularization" and dismantling of Marxism. In this new situation building hegemonies was conducive to the emergence of civic culture and democratic change strategies much different from political transformation through an insurgency against the state. Also adopted at the time was the Gramscian concept of state enriched by, and not opposed to, civil society.[41]

Bolshevist armed combat methods proved ineffective in Latin America, bringing the continent's more moderate leftists to the conclusion that Brazil and the rest of Latin America are to a large degree western and not oriental like Russia, and therefore frontal attacks on the dictatorial state should be replaced by positional warfare conducted by a young and dynamic civil society.[42]

Studies of Latin America's transition from dictatorship to democracy again made mention of the civil society concept, also noting the lack of independent civil society traditions in the region (as in East Europe). As we know, the civil society concept appeared almost simultaneously in the opposition-launched political discourse in both regions towards the end of the 1970s, and especially in the following decade. The difference was that in Latin America Gramsci and his followers were quite evidently the only driving force behind the term's resurrection, while in East Europe this role fell to post-Marxist revisionists (once quite fascinated by Gramsci) and liberals (at first reluctant to call themselves that, either out of shame or tactics).

Also pointed out was the fact that Latin America's military *juntas* had failed to entirely destroy civil society, eliminating only those of its segments which were closely linked to the revolutionary left and the poorest proletariat. Economically stronger groups managed to retain considerable autonomy from their regimes.

The above-quoted Brazilian Marxist Carlos Nelson Coutinho concluded that the replacement of the Gramscian civil society concept by a liberal one in the course of Latin America's conservative transition to democracy helped cover up social conflict, bringing hegemony to liberal forces.[43] Coutinho suggests a return to the original Gramscian civil society concept. In his belief "correct definition of civil society's and the state's theoretical status is one of the most important and most actual topics in the ideological-political debate. Showing Gramscian civil society's purely political dimension, revealing its dialectical bond with the struggle for hegemony and winning of power by the subordinated classes is an inherent part of the battle for the deconstruction of one of neo-liberal ideology's most treacherous aspects, in which the seemingly 'leftist' terminology inherited from our battles with dictatorship focuses on this new, apolitical and aseptic 'civil society' concept. A concept which, as we have tried to show, has nothing in common with Antonio Gramsci's revolutionary ideas".[44]

Since 1980s the question of broad enlargement of civil society and democracy has become a central theme in the critical thought of Latin America.[45] Some Latin American authors argue, however, that using the term civil society masks social classes and class antagonisms, that civil society is incapable of negotiation between polarized sectors of society, that the term has been appropriated by privileged classes, who perceive popular class as not citizens, but "mobs" threatening property and security.[46]

The most recent Latin American and global reflections on civil society attempt to combine this approach with solidarity (with reference to Lech Wałęsa, Vaclav Havel and John Paul II)[47], an apolitical "third sector"[48], the search for a new state social policy, and even a total lack of trust in all statehood and existing political parties. Here, civil society is presented as a partner of government in building legitimate statehood and a defender of historical and cultural values in a world in which commercial ties are fast becoming the most universal human bond. Civil society has also been associated with the quest for social peace and justice in Latin America, with church communities organized by liberation-minded theologians, and with the post-modern search for a new liberation utopia. Today, however, the multithreaded civil society discourse is usually connected with neo-liberalism, market economy, constitutionalism[49], and inter-American integration.[50]

Interestingly, reference to civil society is increasingly frequently made by authors focusing on aggression, frustration, civil protest movements and the failure of neo-liberal economy in some countries, notably Argentina, where civil disobedience has increased.[51] Many of the authors who wrote about the recent events in Argentina and its "stalemate" situation (among others J. C. Portantiero), applied Gramscian categories to describe Argentinian realities: the organic crisis, the crisis of hegemony and domination, the crisis of the state, of bourgeois democracy, and even the very idea of representation.[52] Some see Argentina as a new "civil hegemony", hear the sounds of civil society amongst the clatter of pots and pans, in sauce pan-banging protests and visualize neighborhood gatherings as the nucleus of a "people's democracy", in opposition to bourgeois rule. Argentinian civil society appears to be quite chaotic, disintegrated, and divided into classes far removed from classical social theory. Even the so-called dominating class is disintegrated, is a "conglomerate of corporations dividing between themselves the various spheres of power and competing for hegemony, with each corporation primarily defending its own interests and privileges. The functioning of this social class in Argentinian society is pre-modern, almost medieval, in character", wrote a famous philosopher from Santa Fe.[53]

Also pointed out is the insufficiency of Gramsci's categories in the contemporary world. The hegemony concept, fundamental for Gramsci, takes only scant notice of an analyzed country's ties to global economy and politics, both of which play a deciding role today. Visible in the events in Latin America – from revolting Argentina and president Lula's populistic Brazil to Colombia, long since half-ruled by guerillas, and Chavez's Venezuela with its not-only-geographic closeness to Cuba – is the strong influence of Latin America's gigantic northern neighbor. In an era of prevailing liberalism and "the end of history" the United States are very concerned about mounting revolutionary and populist trends in Latin America, seeing in them a multiple specter of Vietnam.

THE IDEA OF CIVIL SOCIETY IN POLAND AND EAST CENTRAL EUROPE

Generally speaking, almost all countries of Central and Eastern Europe had no important traditions of democratic civil society. A special case is that of Poland, where social traditions of citizenship, although they were absent for some time, are relatively strong in Polish political culture. Poland has a rich libertarian tradition, dating from its famous constitution of May 3, 1791.

However, the Polish fear of absolute rule and the absolute supremacy of social self-organization over state organization was an obstacle to the country's modernization and facilitated Poland's partition by its neighbors at the end of the 18th century. In the 19th century the Polish state did not exist, but there existed numerous forms of independent associational life, of civil society directed against the oppressive rules of Russia, Germany and Austria. After regaining its independence in 1918, Poland was very unstable, characterized by ultra-pluralism, economic crisis and political fragmentation.

After the Second World War a communist regime was installed in Poland by Soviet troops. Communist Regimes in Central and Eastern Europe soon after their installation made virulent attacks on all signs of civil society. During Stalinism all aspects of independent civil society and associational life were suppressed. The idea of civil society appeared with the emergence of democratic opposition after 1976.

Before the Solidarity trade Union was born the term "civil society" could be encountered in the writings of Polish authors quite seldom and rather accidentally, mostly in emigré papers (Leszek Kołakowski, Zygmunt Bauman and Aleksander Smolar);[54] it often appeared either as a loan translation of a corresponding word in English, French or Italian or as a conscious reference to then magically sounding need for civil courage in combating the dictatorial regime.[55] Later this term turned to be a quite effective though symbolic counterweight to the so called civil militia (communist state police).

The first Polish author to use the term civil society was Leszek Kołakowski in his text published in 1974.[56] The term is also used in his well-known text written in English in 1975 and published in a joint publication entitled *Stalinism* in New York in 1976. In the article entitled the "Marxist Roots of Stalinism" which was first published in German in 1977 and later, in 1984, in Polish, Kołakowski uses the term civil society to discuss strivings for the "nationalization" of all citizens, to describe the undeniable advantage of the state over society in the Russian tradition and especially under the Stalinism regime. The author characterizes the omnipotent apparatus of the Stalinist state in confrontation with which the isolated individual becomes powerless which leads to almost total destruction of the civil society. Kołakowski describes the process of destruction of the remains of this society hidden even within the party factions.

The author ponders how the Marxist tradition was used to strengthen Stalinism and sees the seeds of the Stalinist totalitarianism in the Marxist utopia according to which the liberated humanity was in general to remove the difference between the civil society and the state in the future and was to eliminate all antagonisms between private interests. In Marx's interpretation proposed by Kołakowski the introduction of the unity of the political and civil society and in general the introduction of a harmonious social unity would be possible via the elimination of private property and, actually, via the destruction of civil society by the state.[57]

According to Andrew Arato (a long time U.S. resident from Hungary) the idea of civil society has been revived by the neo-Marxist critics of socialistic authoritarianism who, with this notion, invalidated one of the Marx's assumptions thereby paving the way to post-Marxism. Arato names such authors as Kołakowski, Mlynar, Vajda and Michnik in the East; Habermas, Lefort, Bobbio in the West, Weffort, Cardoso and O'Donnell in the South or, in Latin America. They were deep in the tradition of the western, neo-Marxist discourse. Some referred to Hegel, young Marx, Gramsci and Croce to renew the old dichotomy between civil society and the state which was largely forgotten in the 20th century.[58]

In my opinion, it was exactly this Gramsci-coined notion of civil society which was interpreted in the social-liberal spirit by Norberto Bobbio as early as 1967 which later was widely in the West. It was next adjusted by Adam Michnik and Solidarity to the conditions of the peaceful revolution in Poland.

It is fair to add that scholars from Central and Eastern Europe participated in 1967 in the famous Congress devoted to Gramsci in Cagliari in Sardinia[59] where civil society aroused heated debates. In truth only the Italian philosophers and French Jacques Texier[60] discusseed with Norberto Bobbio, but papers were read out by Markovic, Vranicki and Mikecin from Yugoslavia, famous Czech philosopher Karel Kosik (*Gramsci e la filosofia della "praxis"*) and Tibor Huszar from Hungary (*Gramsci e la vita intellectuale ungherese*). They all underlined the huge influence of Gramsci on the intellectual life in their countries.[61]

At a successive congress devoted to Gramsci and organized by the Gramsci Institute in Rome in 1989 scholars from Central and Eastern Europe pointed to the dependence between the degree of a system democratization and the interest in the philosophy of Gramsci in their countries. In Czechoslovakia the of author of *Quaderni del carcere* was the most popular during the Prague Spring. However, certain groups of intellectuals were still interested in his philosophy even during the "normalization" under the Husak regime. Many used the society-related ideas of Gramsci to wage a long, perilous but not entirely fruitless war on Brezhnev's orthodoxy in Czechoslovakia.[62]

Together with the formation of the Solidarity trade union the term "civil society" (at the beginning used in quotation marks) began to play increasingly important role in the process of fundamental systemic changes carried out in Poland and in other Central and East European countries. The famous entry in the August 1981 Accords from Gdańsk recognized that the "leading role" of Polish United Worker's (communist) Party may be limited to the state and should not affect the (civil) society. In the article *Minął Rok* (A Year Has Gone By) written by Adam Michnik in August of 1981 the author mentioned the signing of the agreement with the organized society, asserting that "self-organization which ensured the protection of professional, civil and national rights" was the essence of the nascent Solidarity trade union. For the first time in the history of the communist system "civil society" was reconstructed in Poland. Adam Michnik's writings and activities contributed considerably to the development of democratic civil society in Poland and in the region. In *The New Evolutionism* Michnik presented a program of struggle for civil liberties and human rights in Poland, which was "addressed to independent public opinion and not just to the authorities. Instead of telling the government how to improve itself, the program should tell the society how to act. As far as the government is concerned, it can have no clearer counsel than that provided by the social pressure from below."[63]

The emergence of the Labor Union Solidarity has been defined as the regaining of a public social sphere and as the self-organization of civil society against the communist state in the project of self-governing Poland. The civil Society that emerged during the Solidarity period was the first to appear in the peaceful and self-limiting revolution in a one-party Soviet-type regime.[64]

In August 1981 Adam Michnik wrote that the main task of the Labor Union Solidarity was the restoration of social ties and self-organization aimed at the defense of various human rights.[65] In a posterior interview Michnik credited Vaclav Havel with being one of the first to use the term civil society in communist Europe.[66] Michnik, however, and his friends from Solidarity have given this concept new meaning, rather collectivist or communitarian, articulating the democratic, anti-totalitarian feelings of the Polish society.

The imposition of martial law by General Jaruzelski was calculated to destroy independent civil society in Poland. As this attempt failed, the process of development of civil society was not halted, but acquired new forms. The military regime never liquidated the public sphere, which was supported by the underground, unofficial and even the official Catholic press, numerous publications and independent institutions.[67]

Soon in the late 1980s, new concepts of civil society based on liberal economic individualism appeared provoking various discussions, e.g. on the level of democracy in popular movements, on the need of pluralism and of one all-encompassing organization. Also some leftist authors and even the communist party ideologists began to preach the idea of (socialist) civil society.

From that time on the "civil society" appears from time to time in the opposition journalism (which built a model of extreme dualism between the civil society and the still allegedly totalitarian and communist state) as well as in the official press (seeking a model for easing the tension between the two). As time went by the more moderate representatives of the anticommunist opposition admitted that "at present no one can state that the dualism exists exclusively on the state authority – society level as the society itself is diversified holding within it different groups of interest."[68] The question also appeared in foreign publications about Poland[69] and in works related to the history of the idea referring to modern times.

Already mentioned, Zbigniew Pelczynski, who described the struggle of the first, egalitarian Solidarity using terms coined by Gramsci, often received interesting and sometimes "surprising" results. Pelczynski stressed that Gramsci "ruled out the possibility of a quick assault on the state-economy domination system by the radical-social forces developing within civil society. Instead he visualized a slow 'war of position' in which struggle would shift from one sector of the front to another, involved capturing and temporarily losing key positions, but in the long run tilt the balance of power from the state to the civil society."[70] Pelczynski believed that Solidarity – overwhelmed by revolutionary impatience and the will to immediately gain political power – departed from the demands of Gramsci, but these demands became closer to the Catholic Church led at that time by Primate Stefan Wyszyński. He demanded a break in the struggle, the healing of the childish leftist sickness, better organizational preparation and the dealing with the Gramsci-coined sphere of civil society. (The primate did not quote Gramsci and had probably never read his work).[71] Wyszyński recommended that Solidarity leaders should postpone direct political goals for a later date. However, the leaders were afraid that the weary masses may turn their backs on democracy. Pelczynski believed that the leaders were rather keen on developing the political society than on the consolidation of the civil society.

Solidarity soon came out with the neo-communist and anarchist idea of the self-governing Republic of Poland. The country was to be ruled by collective self-government, workers' councils (soviets), workplace councils (*consigli* from Gramsci) and civic committees (at the time, not even in the autumn of 1989, was the need for democratic political parties perceived). Pelczynski believed that the idea of the self-governing Republic of Poland was an original theoretical contribution to the Gramsci strategy of the 'war of positions'. In his work published in 1988, seven years after the imposition of martial law Pelczynski criticized the idea as "hopelessly utopian". He also criticized the resignation from the idea of the gradual path and slow "evolutionism." However in 1989 communism in Poland collapsed largely as a result of Gramsci's idea of the 'war of positions.' According to Pelczynski, Gramsci "was enough of a Marxist to believe that a ruling class never surrenders power voluntarily. A revolution was inevitable to overthrow the system of domination and to give power to the working class and its allies,"[72] as it was authoritatively put by this well-known liberal author from Oxford who thought that the decision not to resort to force was a "liberal and bourgeois fetish." This, without any doubt, would not be welcome by Gramsci who never said that the war of positions excluded the war of maneuvers and the revolutionary breakup with the old order at a certain stage. However, it turned out that Poland and some other countries managed to make a revolution without violence. The theory of "new evolutionism" actually proved to be true after thirteen years. The final act of peaceful transition of power may be quite hard to explain in terms of Gramsci's theory of historic materialism and easier in terms of conspiracy theories but it would be best for us if – as long as the Kremlin archives are blocked – we recall the supernatural factors: on the 10th anniversary of the Round Table agreements Adam Michnik called it a true miracle.[73]

The real career of the term "civil society" in everyday language of press and other mass-media began in 1989 during the Polish transition to democracy. The issue of making citizens more active and revival of civil society was dealt with in a large team of the Round Table talks between the state authorities and Solidarity opposition.

The rate of political evolution was accelerated by the social agreement (pact) concluded at the Round Table, earlier parliamentary elections and the spectacular victory of the Solidarity in the elections. The disorganized senile Polish United Workers' Party (originally Communist Party) soon ceased to be the ruling force, loosing its leading position and becoming nothing more than a small element of the pluralist civil society. After the dissolution of the ruling semi-communist party by its members, its successor the Social-Democratic Party of the Republic of Poland also proclaimed that parliamentary democracy and self-governing civil society were its aims.

In the amended constitution of the Republic of Poland, the word 'socialist' was replaced by civil. The so-called Civic Committees that originated from the Solidarity, the Civic Parliamentary Caucus (OKP), then the Civil Movement – Democratic Union (ROAD) and recently the Civic Platform gained extraordinary importance. At the same time, the crisis of public participation and first symptoms of escape from freedom appeared in the Polish civil society tired of economic difficulties.

Following the interest in civil society regarded as a kind of opposition to the state, the first postulates of creating civil state and theoretical constructions of "civil socialism" appeared in the 1980s. Also the first non-communist premier in his speech on July, 1990 said that Poland is building a modern civil state of law.

Note that as the privatization of Polish economy continued and the sphere of political freedom under post-communism and peripheral capitalism broadened, terms such as "socialist civil society" or "civil society of socialism" disappeared completely in journalism. The term "civil society" with no additional adjectives became popular. One of the authors, who propagated the great socio-economic transformation aiming from socialism to a modern capitalist (civil) society, declared authoritatively that the idea of democratic socialism is an illusion and that the socialist civil society will never become a reality.[74]

In fact, already in the texts written by the ideologists of the late semi-communist party, stress was put on the creation of material basis for civil society in Poland,[75] civil society without additional adjectives became synonymous to participatory democracy, an "attribute of a state of parliamentary democracy."[76]

Initially, the main problem in the discussions on civil society was whether it can exist in "real socialism". Some defended a thesis on the constitutional lack of civil society under communism.[77] Others spoke about distorted, defective or even socialist, as we have seen, civil society, mainly in Poland and Yugoslavia. During the deep crisis of the countries of real socialism civil society was very often identified only with the anticommunist opposition.

After the collapse of socialism in Poland and elsewhere a new discussion began, this time on the nature and functions of civil society in post-communist countries. The problem is in the question how the term can be applied in the description of new transformation processes. The failure of state socialism conformed the thesis on the supremacy of civil society over the state, but nobody knew how the currently defective and passive civil society could form or reproduce its fully developed structure. According to an author, this defect becomes a painful and highly dangerous fact because in its defective shape the civil society is not able to coordinate liberated social life.[78]

In the present-day Poland some observers see in civil society a positive ideal, while others look at it with suspicion. Those who are against it are afraid that the idea of civil society threatens the superior idea of nation. The right wing wave of nationalism that arose after the fall of the old system is upset by the leftist liberal origin of this idea in the Polish context.

Andrzej Siciński, one of the leading Polish sociologists, has argued on numerous occasions for the topicality of the theme of civil society in present-day Poland and presented a broad program of multidisciplinary research both on the ideal of civil society and on the actual changes taking place in Poland and Eastern Europe. He has observed a kind of vicious circle in present-day Poland: "the lack of civil society hinders the creation of representative elites, and the lack of this kind of elites inhibits the creation of civil society."[79] Other obstacles to the formation of real civil society in Poland are: the poor state of Polish economy, a weakness of middle classes, a low level of the institutionalization of political parties, a lack of social bonds and of other mechanisms typical for Western-type civil society. Sicinski has noticed, however, a remarkable increase of grass roots associations, organizations, charitable actions, etc., which would constitute, in his opinion, a new attractive version of civil society.

Another author in her paper presented at a special conference organized by the Civil Institute in Warsaw saw numerous obstacles in forming civil society in Poland, obstacles enlarged by the egoistic attitudes of the majority of politicians, which loose all prestige in embittered Polish society and are left alone in disorientation.[80]

According to Professor Bronisław Geremek, one of the historical leaders of Solidarity, the concept of civil society will retain its validity in post-communist societies. He does not think that Solidarity's hope for creating a civil society was only an illusion, although he admitted that the society has not turned out to be a "strong buttress" upon which democracy could easily be built. Characterizing the initial magic of the word "citizen" under late socialism and the subsequent post-communist letdown, Geremek noticed that "the civil society of 1980 was the projection into the future of a vision that rested upon an awesome emotional unity. The civil society of more than ten years later cannot and should not base itself on emotions, but instead on the building of carefully nurtured institutions: on the practical realization of ethical values; and on the involvement of the greatest possible numbers of people in public life. The main task now is constructing democratic mechanisms of stability, such as constitutional checks and balances; civic education in the spirit of respect for law; and the encouragement of citizen activism. Civil society – he concluded – does not act in opposition to the democratic state, but cooperates with it. It no longer has to be a kind of 'parallel *polis*' but now can simply be part of the *polis*."[81]

It is important to emphasize that the Polish Catholic Church played an important role in forming a contra-system[82] and civil society under communism, but with the advent of democracy, its role has become ambiguous. Its traditional strength may be dangerous for a fully autonomous civil society and may provoke new conflicts in future. The Church in Poland and other countries passing from dictatorship to democracy will have to find its place in pluralist civil society or even to strive for hegemony in such countries like Poland, where it has always been closely associated with national aspirations.[83]

The new situation in Poland requires also an end not only with the fundamentalist myths of social justice and unity of the first Solidarity, but also to end with the paternalistic concept of the state. According to Jadwiga Staniszkis, a brilliant and conspicuous analyst of the East European transitions, the creation of genuine civil society is a complex and painful process that requires both privatization in economy and deep cultural changes.[84]

All efforts to create a significant civil society in Poland failed and a succeeding attempt to mobilize it was made first by the then president Lech Wałęsa in his proclamation to the nation delivered on July 13, 1993, and favoring the so-called Non-Party Bloc of Support for Reforms, since weak and elitist political parties did not arouse social appeal.

The specific feature of Polish situation is the State, however paradoxical it may sound, that is an indispensable tool in building civil society. The invisible hand of the free market has turned out to be insufficient in order to revive the passive and disoriented society in Poland and other East Central European countries.

There is an increasing need to preserve all rules of law in the new society full of egoism, economic abuse and social pathology. Numerous authors consider the law and new constitution (approved with difficulties as late as in

1997) as a precondition for the development of civil society. The law stabilizes and gives dynamics to every civil society.[85]

Besides, the symbolic idea of civil society in Poland draws more inspiration from traditional nationalism and specific communitarian feelings than from truly liberal values.[86] It is also said that the bitter heritage of communism has left a specific type of human mentality, the so-called *homo sovieticus*: a passive man deprived of initiative and imagination.[87]

Polish society after 1989 seemed lost, exhibiting signs of learned helplessness, tended to withdraw from public socio-political life during the economic recession. As a result, the society begun to experience new forms of anomy.[88]

In fact, civil society in Poland is still much more a utopian ideology than a concrete reality. The idea of civil society, however, has lost its initial strength and is now entering into crisis.

It is quite a problem that the real capitalism built in Poland and other countries of the East differs considerably from "utopian-socialist" dreams and "living one's life in truth," a slogan until recently vehemently voiced by the prime movers of the systemic transformation. It is hard to say whether it was an intentional deception or naïveté. Some former Solidarity activists (like Kuroń, Modzelewski, Kowalik, Bugaj and partly Mazowiecki) feel considerable psychological discomfort and express it publicly[89] which attests to their real sensitivity and naïveté. For an impartial observer it was a sad spectacle to see in August 2005 an enormous enthusiasm of the Polish political class and at the same time deep frustration and disenchantment of the working class on the 25th anniversary of the (Workers') Solidarity in Poland. Discussing with Lech Wałęsa who claims to have envisaged the transition to capitalism in Poland as early as 1980, Professor Karol Modzelewski (Solidarity's former spokesperson, who even invented Solidarity's name) declared that for (peripheral) capitalism he would not have spent in prison eight years, or even a month: he would not have considered it worthwhile.[90] The feeling of discomfort is alien, at least to some degree, only to those who had long been convinced that Poland would have to return inevitably for good or bad to the structures of peripheral capitalism which was only prompted by Solidarity. Many authors consider the division of the world into its Centers and peripheries to be a sophisticated reproduction of the 19th century working class dependency on capitalists within one country. They see such model of global economy development, in which strong Centers impose their rules upon peripheries and semi-peripheries, as still valid. Peripherization is being considered as a normal condition in the epoch of globalization. The transition from the position of poor peripheral countries to the Center is extremely difficult; although possible, only few countries from over 200 have succeeded in it. Some propagators point to those few examples of passing from periphery to the Center seen particularly in small or scarcely populated countries, like Ireland, Finland, Taiwan or Singapore. Especially in Poland there is a dominant conviction that with the formal adhesion to the European Union serious financial resources will come that would ensure the advancement from the European margin to the world center, although many Euro-skeptics doubt it and consider fixing of the Latin American model of dependant capitalism. Psychological and social reasons require a faith in one's own capabilities, require a bit of an universalistic optimism to believe in the possibility of escaping a fatalistic determinism of dependency, to believe in the effective action of the role solidarity in the enlarged European Union.

The drastic change of the Solidarity program after 1989 is also a problem and was termed by some as a "huge fraud" of elites or the unforgivable sin of Solidarity. It proved to be a quite useful explanation of the mass transition of disappointed workers, who failed to adjust to the official civil or bourgeois society, to the anti-civil criminal world. The Polish political and socio-economic (r)evolution has undergone a complicated ideological process from the Gramscian idea of the civil society to the liberal idea of open society as seen by Karl Raimund Popper. An expert in the work of the latter said: "Without exaggeration we may say that Popper was the proper idol of the 1989 revolution. The underground printing offices published Popper's *The Open Society* and *The Poverty of Historicism* which were arduously sought in political opposition circles."[91] The democratic and trade union opposition in Poland started to yield to the looming ideas of liberalism and critical rationalism and learned how effectively to use Popper's anti-dogmatic trial and error method in the political struggle in line with the principle that the end justifies the means. Adam Michnik saw different type of ideas and concepts in the Committee for Workers' Defense (KOR): "Being the turning point of the processes of the reconstruction of the independent civil life KOR, at the same time was the crossing point of different ideological currents, the meeting site of people from different generations and circles, a river which absorbed very different streams."[92]

Disputes on who contributed the most to overthrowing communism have been held in Poland and in the world. Often mentioned are the United States (especially the Carter and Reagan administrations), the Catholic Church (especially of Pope John Paul II) and the Afghan Mujahedins; also mentioned are the names of Gorbachev and Yeltsin, Wałęsa, Kuroń and other KOR and Solidarity leaders, and even the names of Edward Gierek and Generals Jaruzelski and Kiszczak, as well as Colonel Kukliński. However, it may be said that in this world-wide war on communism the victory was scored by "Its Excellency The Civil Society."[93] In the peaceful struggle, in the war of positions on the state of real socialism the victory was scored by the civil society, the idea[94] revived and launched into the political struggle (with capitalism) by the Italian communist Gramsci. I believe – and this is one of the main, quite perverse and apparently absurd thesis of the present work —that the group of intellectual prime movers of this epoch-making victory, the event that ended the Cold War and postponed for some time the threat of WW3 includes above all the names of Antonio Gramsci, Norberto Bobbio, Leszek Kołakowski and Adam Michnik.

A number of recent enthusiasts of the systemic changes manifest authentic surprise at the fact that the cheated Polish society lacks "the willingness to protest and to self-organization to exert pressure on the rulers"[95] which generally bring result contrary to intentions. Many manifest naïve surprise that the so called transition to democracy in Poland and Eastern Europe failed to integrate Poland with the capitalist Center but instead was a transition to the oligarchic, dependent and peripheral capitalism quite common in the contemporary world. This should be the explanation to the mass social apathy and 20-percent turnout in the last elections to the European Parliament and below 40-percent to the Polish Parliament in 2005. A bit frightened, politicians have promised to the disappointed people of post-communist peripheral capitalism in Poland a moral revolution against that corrupt system (a bit earlier there had been an orange revolution in Ukraine, the rose revolution in Georgia, tulip revolution in Kyrgyzia, and a bloody revolt in Uzbekistan).

Recently also in Poland there has begun a discussion on relations between the civil society (currently present only on the official political scene) and new social movements. The notion of a Fourth Sector has been introduced to mark organizations protesting the existing socio-economic, political and cultural system.[96] The said organizations condemn market and liberal mechanisms and any type of state coercion and propose drastic changes exceeding the limits set by the intra-systemic Third Sector. These apolitical and anti-institutional movements demand autonomy or even independence from the state sector. They build new utopias of the radical-ecology-oriented type or synthetic-universalistic, democratic-"cosmocratic", neo-communist (M. Hardt and A. Negri) and anarchist-socialist models.

New social movements in Poland strike up contacts with the Forum of the European Civil Society and the world anti-globalist movement (alter-globalists) oriented on a global civil society. This movement wants to turn to a new internationalism, new social Internationale of the 21st century the opposing supranational political and financial institutions of global capitalism. Offensive movements proposing new, global (international) civil society take advantage of the strength of the Internet (and its broad opportunities to create horizontal social ties) and seek ideological sources in the non-submissive, defiant-romantic tradition and in the Gramsci's idea of cultural hegemony and civil society. Could this idea be once again the source of rich inspiration for anti-systemic alternative?

CIVIL SOCIETY AND SOCIAL CAPITAL IN POLAND

Theorizing on the concept of civil society has been quite frequent in the social sciences since the late 1980s, especially in the political discourse of Western and semi-Western countries that aspired to full integration with the capitalist Center. Strong civil society has been considered as a remedy for democratic deficit, social apathy and economic backwardness.

Recently yet another concept, somehow related to the previous one, has entered common discourse--the idea of social capital as formulated by Pierre Bourdieu and James S. Coleman, and further advanced by Robert D. Putnam and Francis Fukuyama[97]. Theoretical and practical considerations on social and cultural capital have appeared in Poland in connection with translations of American and French authors. They demonstrate the importance of social capital as a valuable social resource for the functioning of modern democratic and civil societies in a market economy, undergoing social, economic and political transformations. Social capital as a problem appears as a social and economic category full of cognitive and descriptive value, both as a social commodity and as a peculiar socio-psychological and behavioral fact[98]. Social capital is usually strengthened when dominant elites voluntarily give up a part of their privileges for the common social good. The term is used to describe the mechanisms of conversion of social and cultural capital into material capital, and in analyzing the dynamics of social and structural changes in Polish society, especially in its local communities[99]. Consciously creating and managing social capital and increasing its quality is understood as an ability to bond individuals in an affluent society and to develop their potential. The social capital concept appears also as a criterion for social development and modernization[100].

Social capital is often considered as a fragment of a general cultural competence, of economic culture, and therefore is strongly correlated with some religious and ethical systems, especially with Protestantism and Confucianism, where cultural, immaterial values in organizing economy really do matter[101].

A specific case is that of Catholicism. Max Weber associated the development of capitalism rather with Protestant ethics than with Catholicism, but much has been changed since the publication of his famous book. Religion, especially the Catholic religion, can play an important role in improving social capital in post-communist Poland. It can allegedly guarantee social cohesion, cultural unification and durable ethical system. It can be a substitute for other, more modern institutions existing in Western world, and can prevent negative consequences of modernization[102]. Even Robert Putnam, far from glorifying civic spirit of the Catholic Church in Italy, highly appreciated some associations closely related to the Church. Polish bishops, including the former primate Stefan Wyszyński, were originally afraid of the spirit of capitalism, but after 1989 they accepted with a "moderate goodwill" or with limited consent the Polish transformation. It is rather generally accepted now that the Catholic Church with its moral strength and effective incentives for human cooperation may be an institution favoring pro-capitalist economic modernization, and may be a potential source of social capital[103].

Putnam's theory of social capital has met with considerable interest in Poland. Even the question whether it is possible to emulate his Italian research has been posed. Observers demonstrate analogies and differences between Poland and Italy[104]. In an epilogue to the Polish edition of Putnam's work Rychard indicates that Poland could learn from his analysis. According to Rychard, Putnam's book has filled a blank in Polish discussions on democracy. It has shown a new perspective in looking on democracy, in which a network of social ties and institutions matters more than political actors. Especially important is the neglected space between individual and the state.

Rychard pointed to the historic role of Solidarity, but its conception of civil society born in a protest accentuated more unity that diversity. Civil society in the twenty first century could take more normal forms, according to Rychard. In the early 1980's it was an ideology of civil society without civil society proper, while in the mid 1990's it was a beginning of real civil society and social capital no longer with an ideology[105].

Others have seen serious methodological shortcomings in Putnam's concept: it is tautological, it gives new meanings to capital and ignores market failures coming from various interest groups. It is a nostalgic attempt of return to a natural state of man, in which staying in nature ensures stable and mutually beneficial interactions. Putnam perceives norms of reciprocity and trust as the invisible hand of the market, what has not been demonstrated. In modern economies and societies the principle of reciprocity is a necessary but not sufficient condition of an economic order, argues a Polish critic of Putnam[106].

Polish authors regard social capital as a metaphor or a stylistic figure, as a mere concept of one or few theories, or they treat it as a category of an attractive, well-grounded theory in the making. It turned out that there is a need to differentiate between various kinds of social capital. The concept gains popularity as a result of a fashion coming from the United States (and partly from France), from the Center of economic, cultural and scientific world[107]. The old concept of economic capital had been negatively charged with Karl Marx's (and his leftist followers) critique, while the concept or watchword of social capital (with its strong rhetorical force) has spread quickly all over the world, since it can easily enter into various theories and political programs (the need for social capital is accepted by liberals, conservatives, republicans and socialists) and be regarded as a remedy for all troubles[108]. It was present, among others, in the famous manifesto by Tony Blair and Gerhard Schröder, in the US Democratic Party platform, and in the leftist ideas propagated by Bourdieu and his followers.

One of the first and unusual definitions of social capital presented in Poland differed greatly from that of Putnam. It was rather similar to Bourdieu's views and conceived of social capital as all general informal ties (or acquaintances) thanks to which an individual raises its probability for entering an elite or to preserve his or her place in it[109]. Some critics, however, call into question the usefulness of social capital as a theoretical tool for broader, macro-social analysis, since it serves to explain various and even opposed phenomena. It is regarded as unclear and poorer than other theoretical approaches, for example the basic values of the European Union or the Social Teaching of the Catholic Church (with its primacy of common good, subsidiarity and solidarity principles). In the Polish Government document, issued in September 2005, it was stressed that the subsidiarity principle will be a fundamental value accompanying the Operational Civil Society Program and all its activities.

One of the critics wonders if the ambiguous concept of social capital covers only a network of social ties supporting existing order or if it can cover also those ties that arouse resistance against the extant order and express a will to change it radically. Without answering this question it is impossible to classify factors favoring the social capital development[110].

On the one hand, social capital is regarded as a means for realization of a goal such as social development, but on the other hand it is regarded as a goal for itself, because trust, loyalty, solidarity and ability to cooperate introduce positive values in human life. Besides, empirical data from various countries show that economic growth is not always accompanied by high or growing social capital; sometimes the growth is possible only in the conditions of calming excessive social tensions.

Polish and Central European authors have paid much attention to the role of civil society and associational life in the transition and consolidation of democratic order. However Polish democracy, civil society and their discontents require new tools for grasping the monstrous reality of post-communist or, better, peripheral capitalism. The importance of social capital understood as a common tendency or ability to cooperate effectively is often stressed nowadays. Many Poles disillusioned with the new reality see it as still post-communist, pre-capitalist or incompletely capitalist, lacking in social capital and in other goods. The new reality cannot be described only with the help of the civil society concept, which in the new political context of neo-liberal reforms had to change or renounce its originally communitarian, patriotic and even nationalistic meaning.

The metaphorical concept of social capital is unclear and rather intangible as compared with physical (material or productive) capital and human (individual and educational) capital[111]. The present popularity of the social capital concept is now probably more intensive than the human capital concept introduced in 1960s by Theodore William Schultz and Gary Stanley Becker. The term came from economies to other social sciences (sociology, psychology, political science, ethics, theory of management, theories of culture) and is considered a sign of economic imperialism. In the realm of economies social capital coordinates individual and group activities, and contributes to the economic development of local communities, regions and nations, but in sociology it refers to interpersonal norms of trust and reciprocity in a historical process of human relations. It reflects durable institutions, cultural norms or codes and social networks. Social capital favors human solidarity and a high quality of life. Some authors consider civic associations as the most important element of social capital or even as its main source (apart from religion, formal institutions and family ties)[112], others derive civic engagement energy just from social capital.

According to many Polish authors, the broad concept of social capital is the essence of civil society, especially of civil society that is effective in its development. It contains everything that determines sound social relations, the common good and cooperation[113]. According to Piotr Sztompka, the President of International Sociological Association, "the key to rebuilding robust civil society is the restoration of trust in public institutions, public roles, and political elites, as well as in the viability of a new political and economic order"[114]. However, the link or correlation between the density of civil society organizations and the degree of interpersonal trust (associated with social capital) is rather complicated. In the majority of Western and/or rich countries high civil society indexes are accompanied by high interpersonal trust and socioeconomic wellbeing. However, for Japan and Spain, low civil society density and high interpersonal trust are characteristic. By contrast in Brazil, strong civil society and associational life lies behind unconsolidated democracy and low social capital[115]. Poland, although it has contributed considerably to the rebirth of the civil society idea and to the East European transitions to democracy, is still lacking in both robust civil society[116] and social capital, as we shall see later on. Poor countries, like Poland and Brazil, usually show lower levels of interpersonal trust than more affluent democracies. The World Bank and other institutions believe that strengthening social capital by investing in it may improve the situation in underdeveloped countries.

Bronislaw Misztal in his work presents a different approach, by putting the concept of civil society in the wider context of the "good society" debate. He argues that what is crucial for constructing a good society is how dead capital (social capital) can be mobilized and put to work. Thus, his approach suggests that civil society can be built even in societies where people have relatively less subjectivity, authenticity and subsidiarity, but that it requires extensive measures of social mobilization. This approach is consistent with the more economically oriented work of De Soto.[117]

The present widespread discussion on social capital in Poland and elsewhere is not only an intellectual fashion, but is connected with a further development of democracy and market economy in the whole world. The concept is considered a useful tool for researchers and for practical social engineering. It is mysterious glue that makes good society out of separate individuals. Some Polish authors believe that the category of social capital allows a better understanding of public life in new post-communist democracies than the civil society perspective which was very fashionable till recent days. Doing research into the causes of progress or stagnation in small Polish towns and local communities Trutkowski and Mandes, two young authors, have gone beyond the civil society and social participation theories and made use of other theoretical tools, more sensitive to cultural and historical context, such as social capital concept[118]. This is often considered a value in itself, as a virtue necessary for capitalist development.

The social capital concept has usually positive or neutral (Coleman) connotations, but some American and Polish authors speak also about dark, unsocial, negative capital (F. Fukuyama, M.E. Warren, Alejandro Portes, Margaret Levi), perverse and unproductive capital present in criminal or terrorist groups and even in some corrupt political elites. The dark social capital in Poland is made possible and facilitated by high level corruption, symptoms of crony and political capitalism, by erasing the distinction between the private and public spheres, and by formal, institutional and financial barriers hindering the civic and political activity of Polish citizens[119].

Present-day Polish political culture is full of distrust, especially towards state institutions. Poles belong to the least trusting societies of Europe.

According to the European Value Survey from 1999 Denmark, Sweden and Holland are the countries where the trust is highest. In those societies over 60% of the citizens put trust in their fellow countrymen, whereas in Poland only 18, 4%. Moreover in Poland there has been, at least since the 1970s, a vacuum between family and nation. This void has not yet disappeared; under the post-communist peripheral capitalism it has not been filled with much desired civil society. According to Janusz Czapiński, who established criteria for strong civil society in high social capital, present-day Poland does not fulfill any criteria of civil society[120]. From the point of view of general interpersonal trust Poland has occupied the last place in the European Social Survey in 2002 and in later years. In Poland the opinion according to which one can trust the majority of people is shared only by 10, 5%, whereas in very affluent Norway by over 70%. Also recently a tendency to enter voluntary associations has decreased rapidly. In this we hold the last place in Europe. Also intolerance towards homosexuals is displayed more frequently in Poland than in other countries. The high level of interpersonal trust, active participation in voluntary organizations and tolerant attitudes towards homosexuals are strongly correlated with material prosperity and with general satisfaction with life. One can conclude that material wealth paves the way towards social capital and that it is very difficult to build social capital under economic misery and profound political disappointment with the post-communist reality and its democratic leaders. Mass migration of young Poles from formally democratic Poland, even more intensive than under foreign occupation, is a sign of great dissatisfaction and distrust. Perhaps only the rapidly increasing level of education can give a slight hope for a possibly higher degree of social capital in Poland in the future.

The weakness of Polish civil society consists in a low engagement of citizens both in public affairs and in non-governmental organizations. Equally low is civic honesty[121]. Social apathy has led to the fact that the percentage of Poles participating in legal and illegal demonstrations (or even contacts with politicians) is the lowest in Europe. At the beginning of 1980s the most frequent demonstrations and strikes in Europe were precisely in Poland. Now, high unemployment and the widespread awareness that after 25 years of protests some problems (inequality, social exclusion, injustice, corruption) are more acute than ever prevents people from violent protests. Tadeusz Kowalik, a leftist scholar, one of the first Solidarity advisers, declared recently that in Poland, after a dozen or so years of radical changes, there has been established one of the most unjust political systems known in the history of the European continent[122]. Another scholar, Andrzej Zawiślak, a former minister coming from Solidarity, declared that even in his darkest projections forecasts he could not imagine a political system of so low quality as has been created out of Solidarity's dreams for Poland[123].

Zdzisław Krasnodębski, an intellectual guru of the ruling Law and Justice Party, along with Rafał Matyja, points at a deep distrust existing in public and social life of Poland, a distrust in Polish politics, a distrust of post-communists and of neo-liberals coming from the former democratic opposition, a mistrust of liberals towards Catholic traditionalists and of liberals towards the ruling conservative party accused of preparing a dictatorship, which is a sign of Polish abnormality[124].

Poles do not trust in them and do not participate in political life; usually they do not show real interest in public affairs. The turnout at polls is very low, in 2005 at parliamentary elections about 40%, at local authorities elections in 2002 about 44% and for the European Parliament in 2004 only about 20%. Relatively the highest turnout in recent years, about 50%, was for the presidential election in 2005. The low turnout at the polls comes from a widespread popular disappointment with politicians of all tendencies who have never kept their promises when they came to power. Now only 40% of Poles accept democratic rules.

A lot of distrust towards its citizens is shown also by the authorities of the Polish state. Distrust is present even within the ruling coalition. The state restricts individual choices, multiplies regulations, prohibitions and bans, and does not support NGO's. A generally frightening atmosphere of distrust and suspicion is also fostered by the official policy of persecution and distrust towards possible "agents", people who might ever have had any contacts (even unconsciously) with the former communist rulers, and especially with its secrete police. Besides, crucial decisions are usually taken beyond any real dialogue by isolated political leaders who distrust the common sense of their fellow countrymen[125].

The research Institute for National Memory, full of young inexperienced historians, has been transformed into a political police and a kind of inquisition. Only young people, below 35 years and former emigrants, seem to be free from political suspicion. Afraid of the recently prevailing excessive cult of former communist dissidents, those historians now eagerly discover and exaggerate ambiguities in their behavior under communism. The former finance minister and deputy prime minister under the Law and Justice party government, professor at the Catholic University of Lublin, unjustly accused of collaboration with the former communist secret police, has recently declared with indignation: "The epoch of solidarity and liberty has ended; the epoch of squalidity has begun".

Distrust in legendary leaders of Solidarity (Lech Wałęsa, Tadeusz Mazowiecki, Jacek Kuroń, and Adam Michnik) and of some famous Catholic priests is widespread. Also the most important neighbors of Poland (Germany and Russia) are treated with mistrust. Even some foreign ministers in the Third Republic were accused of having been Soviet agents. Other politicians were accused of having been children of the pre-war Communist Party of Poland members or grandchildren of Wehrmacht soldiers. A well-known fact is a mutual mistrust of all presidents of independent Poland; recently, at the end of August 2006, Lech Wałęsa and Lech Kaczyński celebrated separately the anniversary of Solidarity.

Other sociologists are less pessimistic in their estimation of the condition of civil society and trust in Poland. They are still impressed by the spontaneous self-organization of the first Solidarity, although they acknowledge that civil society is still weak and in the making[126], and that we have had problems in the transition from rebellious civil society in opposition to a civil society which after 1989 somehow participation in local and central authority[127]. Even those who are rather pessimistic in their estimation of the present condition of civil society and social capital in Poland believe in a kind of neo-socialistic equalization, in a European Solidarity that eliminates regional differences; they are convinced that in the long run Poland will become very close to the material wellbeing, social and organizational rules of other countries of the European Union.

After the fall 2005 parliamentary and presidential elections Poland is strongly led and governed by twin brothers, who have managed to form a right wing coalition of semi-authoritarian, populist and conservative forces. The victorious forces have taken advantage of widespread discontent, the acute crisis of the leftist parties, and the popular frustration caused by the corrupt democracy installed during the transition from authoritarian socialism to peripheral capitalism in the preceding 16 years. They have focused their critique on liberal and post-communist elites blaming them for egoism, for all the evil and especially for unrealized utopian dreams of the initial communitarian and egalitarian Solidarity movement; its aim, as we know, was to combine freedom with social equality.

The leading conservative and "republican" Law and Justice party is trying to strengthen state power, to consider it as a superior aim, and to embrace with its rule all independent spheres of life. It shows therefore a deep distrust towards the ideas of self-management, civic communities, independent initiatives and civil society in general. Jarosław Kaczyński, the leader of the ruling party and now the prime minister of the right-wing government declared that the idea of civil society, promoted by the former communist dissidents, is a Western liberal invention, alien to the Polish political culture. Although in subsequent declarations his reservations towards the idea of civil society have been slightly diminished, his emphasis is still being put on a strong solidary state, on an exclusive concept of the Polish nation, on suspiciousness and mistrust towards the majority of citizens. The ruling coalition is promoting only patriotic education, not civic education.

Jarosław Kaczyński's project of a moral revolution and of the Fourth Republic, overcoming the first 16-17 years of the unsuccessful Third Republic after the 1989 breakthrough, is criticized by neo-liberal and post-communist intellectuals: it brings a danger of centralization, of weakening civil society and of unrealistic expectations[128]; it favors the feeling of instability and even of a disaster[129]. This deepens a neurotic complex of victim, revives the old Polish romantic, messianic myths and other prejudices. The whole conception of twin brothers Kaczyński is being considered as archaic and provincial, it generates chaos on the political scene and anti-modern traditionalism, it curtails competence of independent institutions, promotes general incompetence and contempt for intellectual elites[130]. Polish liberals are afraid of the excessive, anachronistic cult of the state directed against civil society that limits the state power[131]. It seems that the new Polish political tendency to connect politics with moral infallibility, with the ideas of sovereign state and of sovereign democracy, and looking for an absolute enemy (something similar is present today also in Russia) is inspired by Carl Schmitt's ill-famed political thought, by the conservative revolution theory in Weimar Republic[132] and by the tradition of Polish and European authoritarianism (Franco, Salazar, Dollfus, Pétain, Piłsudski, Dmowski). Robert Krasowski, the Editor-in-chief of the semi-official Polish daily *Dziennik* has recently (9 September 2006) announced in his Editorial the demise of Western liberalism and its gradual replacement by neo-conservatism: "The neo-conservative *Realpolitik* is being executed today, and its classics – Strauss and Schmitt – are being studied today by the Prince advisers. Not only Bush's, but also Blair's, Putin's, Sarkozy's, Olmert's or Kaczyński's advisers. What is more, no alternative is seen for the new, more rigid, and for some less sympathetic, face of the West".

According to Krasnodębski and other ideologues of the Fourth Republic, the Third Republic has been a sick state that badly needed deep reconstruction. His book *Demokracja peryferii* (Democracy of Periphery), published in 2003[133], met with great interest. It was a balance of the Third Republic disaster, not of successful transformation, which imitated in a mindless way Western liberal solutions which in fact are unattainable, and forgot about the originally Polish tradition of moral and rather collectivist republicanism, romanticism and even the participatory and republican Solidarity movement. According to Krasnodębski in Poland after communism a façade democracy without values and a new oligarchic system has been introduced, which will not allow building a genuine market economy and a fully democratic system. The former socialist utopia has been replaced by a new liberal utopia[134]. He has criticized the popular modernization theory present in the new Polish capitalism in a manner similar to the dependency school. Much to his surprise no significant leftist critique (almost all post-communists have become liberals) of the new social and political order has appeared in a country of huge fortunes and public misery. Besides, he noticed that new hegemonic relations are rising in a united Europe, in which Poland with its weakened state and shaky economy may become a vassal subject or peripheral to the European Empire.

Unlike liberals and post-communists, Krasnodębski suggests that there had been a viable alternative to the dependent development model chosen in 1989 by liberal elites or imposed on Poland (although supported for a time also by the Polish society fascinated with Western dependency when the Soviet socialism collapsed[135]), and that even now the communitarian, anti-individualistic project of the Fourth Republic may change substantially the disastrous situation of Poland.

The conservative revolt against the pathological democracy of the periphery or better against the peripheral capitalism in Poland, the revolt against all kinds of foreign interference fired up intellectually by Krasnodębski and continued in practice by the twin leaders, is a noble and naive attempt to avoid the evils of capitalism present in all underdeveloped and dependent countries. Such revolts usually end in failure, as did the leftist indignation at a false democracy in the so called Third World countries. The ideologues of Polish Solidarity and of the Law and Justice party have never read texts by Raúl Prebisch and by the dependency school, so they are not aware of universal, rather permanent defects of peripheral capitalism, present in the existing world system. Some, however, have noticed a similarity between the specific case of Poland and of Latin American countries; unfortunately this superficial observation was accompanied by a nationalist feeling of superiority, what appalled the Mexican ambassador to Poland, among others.

The watchwords of a Fourth Republic, of moral revolution and of a "new distribution of trust"[136] suggest that the utopian ideals of Solidarity were betrayed after 1989. They call for a new state, for moral sanitation of the national reality, for political purges and extraordinary tribunals, for breaking corrupt business cliques, for a more radical breaking off with communism, for toughening laws on former Communist collaborators, and for the elimination from public life of post-communists treated as scapegoats. The calling for a breaking from communism has turned out to be very difficult in the specific situation of Poland, where the majority of post-communists have turned out to be much more pro-capitalist than have the members of Solidarity. Those mythic watchwords have rather turned out to be a skillful and efficient maneuver warning the political class of a possible danger, of a forthcoming leftist revolt against corrupt capitalism; eventually, the watchwords turned out to be an efficient maneuver helping to absorb both populists and nationalists, populist Left and Right wing forces into a conservative, allegedly anti-systemic, coalition promising the disappointed people a morally decent capitalism with social sensitivity and human face[137]. However, the expectation that only morally decent people will rule, will overcome the corrupt system in a poor country, and will introduce justice in peripheral capitalism is a new and extravagantly quixotic utopia or simple naiveté.

Official spokesmen and intellectuals associated with the rightist ruling party stress the need to preserve national sovereignty and a strong national state in the European Union. They have opposed the till now dominant tendency to prefer civil society newspeak to national identity discourse. They say that after 16 years of transformation Poland is still a post-communist country with a weak state, a corrupt, regulated economy, and a weak civil society. They say, similarly to extreme leftists, that the process of modernization in Poland is limited to few great cities, that it consists in inner colonization. Only a tiny middle class draws profit from this modernization, while the overwhelming majority of people is marginalized and treated as the "rubbish" of civilizational change. This reality is perceived by a considerable part of society as an unjust social and political order[138]. This reality is defined in Poland as a monster of post-communism (Jarosław Kaczyński), as incomplete capitalism (Jadwiga Staniszkis) or savage capitalism. Only a few authors treat it as (normal) capitalism or better peripheral capitalism, which exists in greater part of the world[139], especially in Latin American countries, which, except for Cuba, have never had communism.

Dariusz Gawin interprets the post-communist situation in Poland also as a second *trahison des clercs*, when the Solidarity leaders betrayed workers, the people of Solidarity, leaving them alone while changing into a middle class. Behind this project stood an ideology of Polish liberalism (pop-liberalism) or lumpen-liberalism (Jarosław Kaczyński), which easily and derisively stigmatized those who could not cope with the new reality, and considered them therefore as a redundant mob. In such a situation the watchword of Fourth Republic has been whole-heartedly accepted by the poor, less educated and Catholic people living in the provinces as a promise of a just, more inclusive and transparent modernization.

The spokesmen of the Law and Justice party opt for a noble republicanism in which the people prevails over false liberal elites and becomes a chief political player. One of them has posed the question of how the areas of trust could be extended and areas of distrust reduced in Polish politics[140]. The sources of distrust, in his words, do not lie in superficial, subjective reasons, but in fundamental differences between the conservative Law and Justice and liberal Civic Platform, which allegedly feels contempt for the democratic decisions of the people. The first party is interested in a deep reform, renovation of the Polish state, and in the creation of the Fourth Republic, whereas the second party would presumably like to preserve existing social and economic structures. Andrzej Nowak sees the obstacle to fundamental change in the independent spheres of mass media, banks and courts. But the care for civil society, for the third sector organization and social capital is clearly seen precisely in the above mentioned institutions, especially in the independent press[141], quite often criticized by the present government of Poland.

The Law and Justice rule is interpreted as a playing with authoritarianism, with a gradual retreat and dissolution of democracy[142]. This is a dangerous tendency, since the number of people willing to participate in political decisions is decreasing. The citizens do not believe in the value of democracy, but retreat to privacy; they do not trust courts, political parties and other institutions; they are convinced that all decisions usually are undertaken beyond any control. Polish citizens conceive of democracy not in terms of political liberty and free market, but in terms of controlling the market, and in terms of social and economic equality. It seems that in Poland and elsewhere after a wave of democratization a new period of a democracy outflow and its implosion is oncoming. Perhaps the only guarantee that democracy in Poland will not collapse easily lies in the impact of foreign public opinion and in the participation of our country in the European Union and in NATO structures. In Europe Poland is now perceived with distrust as a country that ceased to be a leader in post-communist transformation; it is rather an isolated *enfant terrible* trying to find a dangerous solution to its illness.

Liberal elites, who are rather excessively fascinated with the "great success" of the Polish transformation, announce a forthcoming defeat for the conservative, rather mythical revolution: "The most important fault that will probably be found with the 'anti-systemic coalition', when it loses its power, are lost chances. Attached to it is a growing provincialism of Poland, an atmosphere of permanent cold war, growing isolation in foreign policy, and pushing a part of Poland down towards its worse part: towards obsessions, pathological distrust, paranoid threat of strangers, grandiloquence on dignity"[143].

Liberals and left-wingers are trying to interpret the complicated Polish reality of 2006 as a situation in which the old opposition between the communist state and civil society is coming back, and being reproduced in new circumstances. They argue that "once again it is necessary to build an *alternative polis* based on knowledge, freedom, debate, pluralism and friendship", that Poland should be proud of its civic tradition based on cultural values, and not of the authoritarian tradition of a repressive state[144].

NOTES

1 Gramsci's enormous role in the rebirth of the civic society concept is generally acknowledged in the near and "far" (Latin America) West. In Poland, however, where Gramsci is completely forgotten, publishers offer voluminous editions on civil society which do not even mention his name.

2 Interestingly, some orthodox Marxists in their comparisons of class society and civil society theories saw precisely Gramsci's concept as a clumsy syncretism of liberalism and Marxism, G. Hunt, "Gramsci, Civil Society and Bureaucracy", *Praxis International* 2 (1986), 207.

3 N. Bobbio, *Gramsci e la concezione della società civile*, in: *Gramsci e la cultura contemporanea. Atti del Convegno internazionale de studi gramsciani tenuto a Cagliari il 23-27 aprile 1967*, a cura di P. Rossi, Roma 1969 (2nd edition 1975, expanded book editions 1976, 1977); also among others in *Civil Society and the State. New European Perspectives*, J. Keane, ed. (London: Verso 1988), 83. Norberto Bobbio's writings about Gramsci were widely discussed in Italy and worldwide and appeared in several Italian editions and foreign translation (in Spanish in Argentina and Spain, in Portuguese in Brazil, in English in Great Britain and the U.S., also in Polish and Turkish – the latter while Turkey and Poland were still under military rule), among others in numerous collective works. Since the late 1960s Bobbio contributed greatly to the civil society concept's penetration of contemporary philosophy and everyday language.

4 Marcus A. Green, "Gramsci no puede hablar", in: *Hegemonia, etado y sociedad civil en la globalización*, ed. D. Kanoussi (México: Plaza y Valdés 2001), 82-86.

5 Quoted after W. Adamson, *Hegemony and Revolution. A Study of Antonio Gramsci's Political and Cultural Theory* (Berkeley: University of California Press, 1980), 219-220.

6 J. A. Buttigieg, *Gramsci y la sociedad civil*, 73-75.

7 N. Bobbio, "Gramsci and the Concept of Civil Society", in: *Civil Society and the State*, 76.

8 Marcus A. Green, *Gramsci no puede hablar*, 105.

9 Hughues Portelli (*Gramsci et le bloc historique*, Paris 1972, 8), claims that this key concept expresses the basic aspects of Gramsci's political

thought. In his characteristic of the "historical bloc's" superstructure Portelli – with pronounced help from Bobbio – starts out with a detailed analysis of the Gramscian civil society concept.

10 Cf.: N. Bobbio, *Gramsci and the Concept of Civil Society*, 82-86; Gramsci's thoughts on civil society are contained in *Gramsci und die Theorie der Zivilgesellschaft*, the first part of a special issue of *Das Argument* (July-October 1994) entitled, *Ethik und Staat: Zivilgesellschaft*; also see: "Società civile e riforma intellecttuale e morale", *Critica marxista* 2-3 (1987).

11 H. Portelli, *Gramsci et le bloc historique* (Paris: PUF, 1972), 17-18.

12 A. Gramsci, *Letters from Prison* (New York: Harper and Row, 1973), 204.

13 Interesting information and comments about the influence of Gramsci's civil self-government illusions on the allegedly genuine "intellectual and moral reform" of the Soviet perestroika can be found in W. F. Haug, *Gorbatschow. Versuch über den Zusammenhang seiner Gedanken* (Hamburg 1989); especially chapter 4 entitled, *Die Entdeckung der Zivilgesellschaft*, 331-451. See also E. Novikov, P. Bascio, *Gorbachev and the Collapse of the Soviet Communist Party* (New York: Peter Lang Publishing, Inc., 1994); M. Martin, *The Keys of This Blood. The Struggle for World Dominion Between Pope John Paul II, Mikhail Gorbachov, and the Capitalist West* (New York: Simon and Schuster, 1990), 265-274.

14 J. Sempere, "Eurocomunismo, guerra de posiciones y alternativa de sociedad", *Nuestra Bandera,* 103 (1980).

15 A. Karatnycky, "The Democratic Imperative", *The National Interest*, 76 (2004), 111. Nowadays more and more authors are convinced that men are not ruled by force alone, but also by ideas. See T. Bates, "Gramsci and the Theory of Hegemony", in: *Antonio Gramsci. Critical Assessment of Leading Political Philosophers,* ed. J. Martin, vol. II (London and New York, 2002), 245; Sun Jing, *Wen hua ba quan li lun yan jiu* (On the theoretical study of cultural hegemony), Beijing 2004.

16 This was recorded quite early on and with some concern by, among others, Michael Novak, a U.S. rightwing Catholic liberal quite well known in Poland, in "The Gramscists Are Coming", *Forbes*, March 20, 1989. In a late-September 1992 interview for the Russian daily *Komsomolskaya Pravda*, Chilean strongman Augusto Pinochet also warned Russian readers against the communist Gramsci and his "dangerous" influence despite the fall of Marxism-Leninism in that country, especially on intellectuals. In a book and article entitled *Fatal Fiction – Bolshevism's New Face and Old Mechanisms* (*Antyk* 13-14 (2003), Polish ultraconservative Dariusz Rohnka goes much further in his exaggerated, perhaps even obsessive unease about the presence of Gramsci's ideas in the world, especially in the U.S.: according to Rohnka and other conservatives (notably R. Scruton), Gramsci's strategies are used in the U.S. to "wreak havoc" in social and political relations, education systems, religion and customs, the outcome of this radical political and cultural revolution best evident in the emergence of Bill Clinton, moral relativism

and political correctness, frequently described as "cultural Marxism". Rohnka believes America is going through a cultural revolution patterned on Gramsci's ideas and concludes that, "Antonio Gramsci has no reason to turn in his grave. At the outset of the 21st century cultural hegemony is certainly in the hands of his followers". Another Polish conservative, Stanisław Michałkiewicz, stated that today's "eurosocialistic" and over-bureaucratized European Union was striving to embrace Gramsci's "anti-Christian" ideology.

17 T. Vostos, *Der Begriff der Zivilgesellschaft bei Antonio Gramsci. Ein Beitrag zur Geschichte und Gegenwart politischer Theorie* (Hamburg: Argument Verlag, 2001), 28.

18 Mention of this is made among others by E. Garcia Méndez in, *La teoria del Estado en Marica Latina: modelo para armar*, *Sistema* 61 (1984). In the 19th century the term civil society was already used by Simón Bolivar. One of the first 20th-century works to use "civil society" in its title and to describe socio-historical phenomena concerned Argentina and was published in Mexico: L. Allub, *Estado y sociedad civil: patron de emergencia y desarrollo del Estado Argentino* (México, 1974) In Argentina the term civil society was used in opposition to military society already in 1928 by the famous Marxist Aníbal Ponce in his writings on tyranny, military dictatorship and the leadership system (*caudillismo*). Argentina was also relatively quick to assimilate Gramsci's works. See J. Aricó, *La cola del diablo. Itinerario de Gramsci en América Latina* (Buenos Aires 1988). It is worth adding that the first translation of N. Bobbio's famous text on Gramsci and civil society first appeared in Argentina in 1972, a decade earlier than in Poland.

19 For more on this see: C. N. Coutinho, *El concepto de sociedad civil en Gramsci y la lucha ideológica en Brasil hoy*, in: D. Kanoussi (ed.), *Gramsci y América* (Ciudad de México - Puebla 2001), and Coutinho's short essay, *A recepção de Gramsci no Brasil* in his book, *Gramsci. Um estudo sobre seu pensamento politico* (Rio de Janeiro 1999); also see: A. Squella Narducci, *La influencia de Bobbio en Iberoamérica*, in: *La figura y el pensamiento de Norberto Bobbio* (Madrid 1994).

20 J. L. Acanda, *La contemporaneidad de Antonio Gramsci* (La Habana 1991). It must be noted, however, that Gramsci, Althusser and other western Marxists were quite popular in the young Cuban socialist state before the country's sovietization around 1970.

21 Still in January 1996 the party daily *Granma* called civil society a "U.S.-inspired fifth column", a "Trojan horse sent by the enemy" and an "alien neoliberal intrusion". However, already in March of that year a communist party document and Raúl Castro made cautious mention of a "socialist" or "Cuban" civil society model. A study by the Institute of Philosophy in Havana showed that the civil society concept played a major role in the devaluation of marxism and socialism in the USSR and its satellites and their transition from communism to reform and, eventually, full liberalism. A wide range of Cuban opinions about civil society can be found in a debate entitled, "*Sociedad civil en los 90: El debate cubano*" at http://www.geocities .com/catedragramsci/; M. Limia David, "*Retomando el debate sobre la sociedad civil*" at http//

www.filosofia.cu/contemp. and in J.L. Acanda, *Sociedad civil y hegemonía* (La Habana: Centro de Investigación y Desarrollo de la Cultura Cubana Juan Marinello, 2002). Also cf.: M. Vázquez Montalbán, *Y Dios entró en la Habana*, (Madrid: El País, 1999), 386-391.

22 H. Dilla Alfonso, P. Oxhorn, "Cuba: virtudes e infortunios de la sociedad civil", *Revisita Mexicana de Sociologia* 4 (1999).

23 S. Mainwaring, G. O'Donnell, J. Samuel Valenzuela, eds., *Issues in Democratic Consolidation: The New South American Democracies in Comparative Perspective* (Notre Dame 1992), 294, 311, 333.

24 Manfred Max Neef, Antonio Elizalde y otros, *Sociedad civil y cultura democrática* (Santiago de Chile 1989).

25 A. Domosławski offers an interesting account of Dowbor's and Sirkis' lives in "Jesień Partyzantów", in: *Gazeta Wyborcza*, August 19-20, 2000.

26 A. Walicki, *Marxism and the Leap to the Kingdom of Freedom* (Stanford 1995), 426. This is especially true of Kołakowski, Hochfeld, Bauman and Geremek. The latter has an evident tendency to idealize Gramsci, whose utopian theory he respectfully sets apart from other socialist and communist programs: "In his prison notes Antonio Gramsci outlined a vision of an 'ordered' society easily capable of managing without state institutions, and hence without oppression instruments. In this way the state was to be marginalized and the main political weight shifted from rivalry for state government to positional warfare for hegemony over civil society", B. Geremek, "Społeczeństwo obywatelskie a współczesność", in: *Europa i społeczeństwo obywatelskie. Rozmowy w Castel Gandolfo*, K. Michalski, ed. (Cracow: Znak, 1994), 249.

27 Cf.: David Ost, *Solidarity and the Politics of Anti-Politics. Opposition and Reform in Poland since 1968*, (Philadelphia: Temple University Press 1990), 31, 67. David Ost points to a paradox: "despite the fact that the Marxist tradition devastated civil society in Eastern Europe, it is the Marxist tradition that is largely responsible for reintroducing the concept of civil society in Western Europe". Here, Ost mentions Habermas from the Frankfurt School and Gramsci from the Marxist "old left". Ost fails to notice Gramsci's influence in East Europe, especially on communist revisionists, and overestimates Tocqueville's and Hannah Arendt's role in shaping the opposition's civil society aspirations. The here-quoted W. Adamson pointed to Gramsci's superiority over those social theoreticians and social movement mentors, who, like Alain Touraine, feel a need to bring politics into civil society.

28 In a conversation with me Adam Michnik admitted that he had "learnt a lot" from Gramsci. In his famous conversation with Tischner and Żakowski he even stated, that he had been a "Gramsci-type communist", *Między Panem a Plebanem* (Cracow: Znak, 1995), 80.

29 A comparison of both authors' prison writings would be quite interesting. Both displayed a strong sense of intellectual and moral resistance, both felt alone in their struggle, both had the courage to fight for their dignity, and both rejected freedom offers extended by the official authorities (the fascist

regime in Italy and the communist authorities under martial law in Poland). Cf.: A. Gramsci's *Prison Notebooks* and A. Michnik, *Letters from Prison and Other Essays* (Berkeley: University of California Press, 1985); H. Heintze, "La lecture politique d'un prisonnier solitaire. Antonio Gramsci et les lettres de la prison", in: *La réception de l'oeuvre littéraire* (Wrocław 1983).

30 J. Kaczyński, "Nowa Polska czy jeszcze stara"?, in: T. Torańska, *My* (Warsaw 1994), 118.

31 Z. A. Pelczynski, "Solidarity and the 'Rebirth of Civil Society' in Poland", in: *Civil Society and the State. New European Perspectives*, ed. J. Keane (London: Verso, 1988), 365.

32 Z. A. Pelczynski, "*Solidarity and the 'Rebirth...*", 367, 371.

33 T. Garton Ash (*The Polish Revolution: Solidarity 1980-1982*, London 1983, 9, 15), claims that already before 1980 the Worker Defense Committee operated along the Leninist guidelines of *What Is to Be Done*, with small worker groups instructed by intellectuals in their role as the "avantgarde of the revolution". However, Ash points to a subtle difference: the Committee's goal was evolution, not revolution. Yet the British historian seemed to ignore the Gramscian correction to Leninism and Trotskism when he wrote in 1981: "In sum, the situation in Poland could be, and was, compared of that of Russia in summer 1917. Then the Soviets grew alongside Kerensky's Provisional Government in what Trotsky described as 'Dual Power'. Now Solidarity grew alongside Kania's Soviet-style, Soviet-backed government. The Party leader declared to the Plenum that a state of 'Dual Power' could not be tolerated. Yet it was already there, and Soviet intelligence could see it was there" (*Ibid*, 99).

34 Bogdan Borusewicz, "Dzień jedności", *Gazeta Wyborcza*, August 19-20, 2000.

35 As we know, Che Guevara proposed the creation of "many Vietnams" to force the capitalist world to disperse its forces and ultimately fall. Already in August 1980 *The New York Times* searched for a Baltic Che Guevara among Poland's shipyarders. Here is a fragment of a report on the U.S. press's coverage of the August 1980 events: "The papers usually adorned their articles with large pictures showing workers – all young, bearded and smoking cigarettes, either singing the national anthem or standing next to a cross commemorating social riots that had taken place there a decade earlier, or reading papers, or receiving flowers from children through the shipyard gate. These simple workers were sympathetically portrayed as the new `brave young men` who dared oppose the empire. *The New York Times* called these bearded and frequently bereted workers Baltic versions of Che Guevara", A. Brzezicki, "Polski sierpień w amerykańskiej prasie", *Tygodnik Powszechny*, Aug. 18, 2002.

36 Their founder was proud of the fact that his idea awoke the interest of unionists and socialist party doyens. See: Jacek Kuroń, *Gwiezdny czas* (London: Aneks, 1991), 240.

37 One can say that this was the fulfilment of Gramsci's dreams from his worker council days in Turin. Gramsci saw these councils as an economic-

political and cultural element of an emerging proletarian civil society. Cf.: W. Adamson, "*Gramsci and the Politics of Civil Society*", Praxis International 3-4 (1987/88), 321, 323.

38 L. Mażewski, *W objęciach utopii. Polityczno-ideowa analiza dziejów "Solidarności" 1980-2000* (Toruń 2001), 57.

39 F. Lewis, "*The Rise of 'Civil Society'*", in: *The New York Times*, June 25, 1989. The U. S. Journalist openly admitted something that Poles refuse to accept: that it was none other than the Italian communist Gramsci who introduced the term 'civil society' into contemporary political language.

40 Cecylia N. Lesgart, "El tránsito teórico de la izquierda intelectual en el Cono Sur de América Latina, Reforma moral e intelectual o liberalisto político?", *Revisita Internacional de Filosofia Politica*, 16 (2000). See the Polish left's somewhat similar intellectual transition from Marxism and socialism to liberal-postmodern democracy here in my essay, "From 'Socialist' to Postmodern Pluralism in Poland".

41 Cecylia N. Lesgart, "El tránsito teórico..."; especially important in the article is the part entitled, "Antonio Gramsci y la salida del marxismo" (Antonio Gramsci and the Departure from Marxism).

42 Cf. a short essay by C. Nelson Coutinho, "*A recepção de Gramsci no Brasil*" in his book: *Gramsci. Um estudo sobre seu pensamento politico* (Rio de Janeiro 1999) and a book: Lincoln Secco, *Gramsci e o Brasil. Recepcão e difusão de sus idéias* (São Paulo: Editora Parma, 2002).

43 One liberalism convert is Fernando Henrique Cardoso, an earlier Marxist and until recently President of Brazil. Historical necessity may also force a shift to liberalism by the country's current head of state, leftwing unionist and Labour Party leader Luiz Inacio Lula da Silva (once dubbed Brazil's Lech Wałęsa). Congratulating da Silva on his presidency, Wałęsa repeatedly pointed to the differences between them, Wałęsa representing a typically Polish pro-U.S. stance, Lula a U.S.-hostile attitude typical for Brazil.

44 C. N. Coutinho, "El concepto de sociedad civil en Gramsci y la lucha ideológica en Brasil hoy", in: D. Kanussi ,ed., *Gramsci y América* (Ciudad de México – Puebla 2001). Similarly, a Polish author (J. Tomasiewicz, "Jaki ATTAC?", *Obywatel* 1, 2003, 44) recounts how, "throngs of to-date leftwingers went over to their enemies. Most often it was the former Marxists that became liberals. This resulted not only from their common roots in the Enlightenment, but also their deeply-rooted faith in historical determinism: these people wanted to be always on the side of progress, the winning side, hence when progress turned out to lead to capitalism, they embraced capitalism".

45 Y. Acosta, *Las nuevas referencias del pensamiento crítico en América Latina: ética y ampliación de la sociedad civl* (Montevideo 2003).

46 See *Struggles in the Americas. Hemispheric Civil Society Conference*, R. Boyd, S.J. Noumoff, ed. (Montréal: Mc Gill University, 2003).

47 Cf.: H. F. Gaviria, “El Estado y la Sociedad Civil en la doctrina de la Iglesia”, *Revisita Javeriana*, 1997, October.

48 Cf.: V Encuentro Iberoamericano del Tercer Sector. Colombia 200, *Lo público. Una pregunta desde la sociedad civil. Memorias* (Bogota 2001). Under the term “Third Sector” the authors understand all the various non-governmental organizations speaking up for issues like human rights, justice, solidarity and tolerance. However, Manuel Castells calls so-called NGOs “neo-governmental organizations” due to their significant funding by the state and participation in the emerging “network state”.

49 Cf.: R. Hernández Vega, *La idea de sociedad civil. Avance teórico* (México 1995); E. Peruzzotti, “Constitutionalismo, populismo y sociedad civil. Lecciones del caso argentino”, *Revisita Mexicana de Sociologia,* 4 (1999).

50 G. L. Escobar, “La globalisación y sus efectos en el desarrollo económico”, *Revisita Javeriana*, 1997, October; A. Serbin, “Globalization, the Democracy Deficit and Civil Society in Processes of Integration”, *Pensamiento Propio* 3 (1996).

51 T. Luzzani, “Przebudzenie obywateli” (Civil Awakening), *Gazeta Wyborcza*, February 4 2002. The violent protests launched in December 2001 by the heretofore quite numerous Argentinian middle class (complete with setting fire to buildings and shop looting), were reminiscent of the protests by Poland’s working-class aristocracy in December 1970 and June 1976. The Argentinian riots were the Latin world’s biggest social crisis in the past decades. According to Luzzani the Argentinian middle class had in recent years allowed “its most precious possessions” to be taken away and was now seeking new forms of representation, new leaders and new alliances. The case was somewhat similar with the Polish protesters. It seems that behind the protests in both countries lay the exaggeratedly occidental and false awareness of their citizens, who attempted to deny Argentina’s true position in Latin America and Poland’s in East Europe. An unexpected effect of the Polish and Argentinian protests were the total destruction of an adventurous industrial working class in Poland and a drastic downsizing of Argentina’s wealthy middle class. It is worth adding that society’s poorest, immersed in their usual apathy, hardly ever protested – neither in Argentina and Poland nor elsewhere. The awareness aspects of the Argentinian crisis (the strong influence of illusions) were pointed out by E. Garzón Valdés in his famous article, “Cinco tesis sobre la situación Argentina”, *Claves*, May 2002.

52 M. Romano, R. Sanmartino, “Crisis de dominio burgués: reforma o revolución en Argentina”, *Estrategia Internacional,* February 18 (2002).

53 Julio de Zan, “La sociedad dividida”, (paper at the VII Jornadas Internacionales Interdisciplinarias del ICALA in Rio Cuarto, Argentina 2002).

54 Cf. L. Kołakowski, “Marksistowskie korzenie stalinizmu” (Stalinism’s Marxist Roots), a 1975 paper reprinted in: *Czy diabeł może być zbawiony i 27 innych kazań* (London: Aneks, 1984), 248-249, 251-252, 255-257; See also J. Rupnik, “Dissent in Poland, 1968-1978: The End of Revisionism

and the Rebirth of Civil Society", and Iván Szelényi, "Socialist Opposition in Eastern Europe: Dilemmas and Prospects", in: *Opposition in Eastern Europe*, ed. Rudolf L. Tőkes (Baltimore: The John Hopkins University, 1979).

55 Cf. M. Kusy, "On Civic Courage", *International Journal of Politics*, Spring 1981; a good analysis of the pre-civil-society condition by Czech and Polish authors can be found in: Zbigniew Rau, *From Communism to Liberalism: Essays on the Individual and Civil Society* (Łódź 1998), 92-93.

56 "The Myth of Human Self-Identity: Unity of Civil and Political Society in Socialist Thought", in: *The Socialist Idea. A Reappraisal*, ed. L. Kołakowski & S. Hampshire (New York: Basic Books, Inc. Publishers, 1974).

57 L. Kołakowski, *Czy diabeł może być zbawiony i 27 innych kazań*, (London: Aneks, 1984), 244-259. The term comes forth a whole ten times in the essay. However, Kołakowski fails to see that in many of his writings – especially his early texts – Marx interpreted the 1848 and 1871 uprisings in France as civil society's revolts against the state and therefore gave the term a positive connotation. Years later it was taken over by the Western non-totalitarian left. Cf. C. Gordon, "Governmental Reality: An Introduction", in *The Foucault Effect: Studies in Governmentality*, ed., G. Burchell and P. Miller (London 1991), 29-30.

58 A. Arato, "The Rise, Decline and Reconstruction of the Concept of Civil Society, and Directions for Future Research", in: *Civil Society, Political Society, Democracy,* ed. Adolf Bibič, Gigi Graziano (Ljubljana 1994), 3; see also *Civil Society. A Reader in History, Theory and Global Politics*, Ed. by John A. Hall and Frank Trentmann (New York: Palgrave MacMillan, 2005).

59 Antonio Gramsci was born in 1891 in Ales near Cagliari on Sardinia. Ales, and especially the Congress in Cagliari, was the birthplace of the modern civil society concept which played such an instrumental role in the changes taking place in today's world.

60 Cf.: "Sul Convegno gramsciano di Cagliari", *Critica Marxista,* 2 (1967).

61 Cf.: Gramsci e la cultura contemporanea. Atti del Convegno internazionale di studi gramsciani tenuto a Cagliari il 23-27 aprile 1967, a cura di P. Rossi, vol. 2,2nd edition (Roma 1975); Inside is an essay by Polish author Bogdan Suchodolski. Volume 1 is almost entirely devoted to the Gramscian civil society concept.

62 See G. Liguori, "La fortuna di Gramsci nel mondo", *Critica marxista,* 6 (1989), 82.

63 A. Michnik, "The New Evolutionism" , *Survey*, 3-4 (1976), 263; see also Jeffrey Goldfarb, *Beyond Glasnost. The Post-Totalitarian Mind* (Chicago and London: The University of Chicago Press, 1989).

64 See J. Frentzel-Zagórska, "Civil Society in Poland and Hungary", *Soviet Studies*, 4 (1990).

65 Adam Michnik, "The Promise of Civil Society" in his *book Letters from Prison and other Essays* (Berkeley and Los Angeles: University of California Press, 1985), 124.

66 "Towards a Civil Society: Hopes for a Polish Democracy", *The Times Literary Supplement* 4 (1988).

67 See Hanna M. Fedorowicz, "Civil Society in Poland: Laboratory for Democratization in Central Europe", *Plural Societies*, vol. XXI (1990).

68 An interview with Bronisław Geremek published in *Konfrontacje* 2 (1988), 7.

69 A. Arato, "Civil Society against the State: Poland 1980-1981", *Telos* 1-2 (1981). At the time many western leftists, mostly raised on Gramsci, were thrilled with Solidarity, seeing in it the only really vital working-class movement.

70 Z. Pelczynski, "Solidarity...", 375. A somewhat similar appraisal of the situation was offered in March 1981 by one of the more radical Communist party leaders" "We are in a condition of unarmed rebellion against the political system by most of society, with the state's political structures and the Party and its leading role put in question". Also a study team under A. Touraine pointed to Solidarity's transition from trade union to an openly political organization.

71 However, another author, the above quoted Malachi Martin (*The Keys of This Blood*, 269), who also interprets the recent history of communist Poland with the help of Gramscian terms, deems that "under Wyszynski's canny and guiding hand, the all-pervasive Catholic Church in Poland developed its own anti-Gramsci version of Gramsci process, its own network within which Polish culture could be preserved and developed."

72 Zbigniew Pelczynski, "Solidarity...", 375.

73 A. Michnik, "Cud Okrągłego Stołu" (A Miracle of the Round Table), Gazeta Wyborcza, February 6-7, 1999. Several years earlier the Polish-American sociologist Adam Przeworski called Spain's switch to democracy "a miracle" and "a unique case" not to be repeated elsewhere (*Democracy and the Market: Political and Economic Reforms in Eastern Europe and Latin America* (New York 1991), 8, 187.

74 R. Krawczyk, *Wielka przemiana* (Warsaw: INTERIM, 1990), 19. Also Tomaz Mastnak noticed that civil society was initially conceived as alternative rather than opposition and was first articulated as "socialist civil society", but it "was found very soon that this term was a contradiction in terms." – T. Mastnak, "Civil Society in Slovenia: From Opposition to Power", in *Democracy and Civil Society in Eastern Europe. Selected Papers from the Fourth World Congress for Soviet and East European Studies*, ed. P. Lewis (New York 1992), 134. The former Yugoslavia was one of the first countries where the concept of civil society appeared. See A. Bibić, *Zasebnistswo in skupnost: civilna druzba in drzawa pri Heglu i Marxu* (Ljubljana, 1972); M. Krizan, "Civil Society – A New Paradigm in the Yugoslav Theoretical Discussion", *Praxis International* 1-2 (1989).

75 A. Bodnar, *Społeczeństwo obywatelskie – problemy interpretacyjne* (Warsaw: Wydział Ideologiczny KC PZPR, 1989), 3.

76 W. Markiewicz, "Społeczeństwo obywatelskie a demokracja", *Nowe Drogi,* 7 (1989), 9.

77 J. Staniszkis, *The Ontology of Socialism* (Oxford: Clarendon Press, 1992).

78 P. Ogrodziński, *Pięć tekstów o społeczeństwie obywatelskim* (Warsaw: ISP PAN, 1991), 65.

79 A. Siciński, "Elites and Masses in Post-Communist Countries. The Polish Case", in: *Cultural Dilemmas of Post-Communist Societies,* ed. A. Jawłowska, M. Kempny (Warsaw: IFiS Publishers, 1994), 206.

80 H. Świda –Ziemba, "Społeczeństwo obywatelskie, politycy, życie codzienne", *Więź*, 8 (1992).

81 B. Geremek, "Civil Society Then and Now", *Journal of Democracy* 2 (1992); see also his paper "Die Civil Society gegen den Kommunismus: Polens Botschaft", in: *Europa und die Civil Society*, ed. K. Michalski (Stuttgart 1991).

82 R. Sharlet, "Human Rights and Civil Society" in *Eastern Europe: The Opening Curtain?* (San Francisco -London: Westview Press, 1989).

83 See J. Casanova, *Public Religions in the Modern World* (Chicago and London: The University of Chicago Press, 1994), 92-114 (The chapter "Poland: From Church of the Nation to Civil Society").

84 J. Staniszkis, *The Dynamics of the Breakthrough in Eastern Europe: The Polish Experience* (Berkeley – Los Angeles – Oxford, 1991), 26.

85 See K. Wrzesiński, "Państwo i prawo a społeczeństwo obywatelskie", *Studia Filozoficzne* 4 (1990); J. Zakrzewska, "Prawo w społeceństwie obywatelskim", in *Obywatel. Odrodzenie pojęcia*, ed. B. Markiewicz (Warsaw: IFiS Publishers, 1993), 107-112.

86 See T. Buksiński, "Społeczeństwo obywatelskie a społeczeństwo rynkowe", in *Filozofia w dobie przemian*, ed. T. Buksiński (Poznań: UAM, 1994), 284; T. Buksiński, *Liberalisation and Transformation of Society in Post-Communist Countries. Polish Philosophical Studies V* (Washington, D.C.: The Council for Research in Values and Philosophy, 2003).

87 J. Tischner, *Etyka Solidarności oraz Homo Sovieticus* (Cracow 1992); A. Smolar, "Vom Homo Sovieticus zum Bürger, *Transit* 3 (1993).

88 L. Kolarska-Bobińska, *Aspirations, Values and Interests. Poland 1989 – 1994* (Warsaw: IFiS Publishers 1994).

89 Usually these are meaningless "family feuds" or "safety valves"; nonetheless many post-Solidarity activists unconsciously support and proclaim pre-communist views much more frequently than the post-communists, who today are far removed from all fundamentalism.

90 See the debate on the 25th anniversary of Solidarity, published in *Tygodnik Powszechny*, 36 (2005), 10.

91 A. Chmielewski, "Karl Popper i jego wrogowie" (Karl Popper and His Enemies), *Gazeta Wyborcza*, November 2-3, 2002.

92 A. Michnik, Takie czasy... rzecz o kompromisie (London: Aneks, 1985), 13. In an interesting conversation with Cohn-Bendit, in which he mentioned Hegel, Gramsci, Rosa Luxemburg and Lukacs, Michnik said: "Solidarity proposed civil society, which by nature is an imperfect society. This is what lies closest to my heart. Everything I wrote in prison after December 13, 1981, was a defense of this one thesis: namely that we are fighting not for a perfect, ideal and non-conflictual society, but for a society which resolves its conflicts within a certain set of rules –democratic rules" – A. Michnik, *Diabeł naszego czasu* (Warsaw 1995), 421, 428, 432. Gramsci worked along basically similar lines. Adamson ("Gramsci and the Politics of Civil Society", *Praxis International*, October 1987 – January 1988, 324-325) wrote: "In almost everything Gramsci wrote in *Letters from Prison* one can discern a positional battle for a diversified civil society". Gramsci and Michnik were convinced that revolutions are mainly brought on by political and cultural circumstances, and not economic factors. In their opposition programs both postulated building a civic front in a long march through institutions.

93 In the final period of communist Poland a Communist Party ideologue spoke ironically about "Its Magnificence Civil Society", dubbing the concept "a teacher's pet term". See M. Goliszewski's conversation with L. Krasucki in *Konfrontacje* 2 (1988), 9. Eight years later another leftist, the famous subcomandante Marcos, will bestow greetings and red flowers on "Madame la société civile". See fragments of Marcos' declarations in *Problemes politiques et sociaux*, May 2003 (a special issue entitled "La société civile en question").

94 Commenting the peaceful transition of power in East Europe, T. Garton Ash (*The Magic Lantern. The Revolutions of '89 Witnessed in Warsaw, Budapest, Berlin, and Prague* (New York: Random House, 1990, 135), has present day elites, now reluctant to continue governing the country, declare after King William of Wirtemberg; "Je ne puis pas monter à cheval contre les idées". It seems that some members of the post-communist elite saw the ambiguity inherent in the Hegelian-Marxist civil society concept (*bürgerliche Gesellschaft*) as a historical chance for their own anchoring in a capitalist, bourgeois society. According to Garton Ash in 1989 it was mainly the working class that fought for the simultaneous status of citizens and middle class. The majority's failure to achieve this goal resulted in a chronic "moral hangover" and dangerous frustration bouts which will continue to hamper the country's development for quite some time to come. The problem of expectations running beyond the possibilities of capitalist reform is discussed by Brazilian liberation theologian Frei Betto, who visited Poland in its final communist phase and warned us "not to treat economic reforms as a gift from Santa Claus with each every household receiving a present in the form of a bourgeois lifestyle".

95` I. Krzemiński, "Kryzys państwa – kryzys społeczeństwa", *Rzeczpospolita*, February 17, 2003.

96 P. Żuk, *Społeczeństwo w działaniu* (Warsaw: Scholar, 2001), 118-151; see also John Keane, *Global Civil Society?* (Cambridge: Cambridge

University Press, 2003); *Transnational Civil Society. An Introduction*, Ed. by S. Batliwala and L. David Brown (Bloomfield: Kumaria Press, Inc., 2006), especially the chapter on the rise of civic transnationalism by Sanjeev Khagram.

97 The idea inspired by 18th century authors (Adam Smith, David Hume and Edmund Burke) appeared fleetingly already in 1920 in a text by Lyda Hanifan and in 1977 in a text by Glenn Loury. See Zbigniew Jan Stańczyk, "Dwa rodzaje kapitału społecznego", *Gospodarka Narodowa*, 1-2 (2000), 17; see also *Trust and Civil Society*, Edited by Fran Tonkiss (London: MacMillan Press, 2000).

98 Jerzy Przybysz, Jan Sauś, *Kapitał społeczny. Szkice socjologiczno-ekonomiczne* (Poznań: Wyd. Politechniki Poznańskiej, 2004), 5.

99 The first Polish publications on social capital are summarized by Adam Bartoszek, *Kapitał społeczno-kulturowy młodej inteligencji wobec wymogów rynku* (Katowice: Wyd. UŚ, 2004), 27-32.

100 Tomasz Zarycki, "Kapitał społeczny a trzy polskie drogi do nowoczesności", *Kultura i Społeczeństwo*, 2 (2004). The author shows the main ideological orientations, political discourses and ideal visions of Poland. It is interesting to see that in all cases the social capital concept "can be used to support the arguments both for and against each of the orientations".

101 Halina Zboroń, "Kapitał społeczny w refleksji etycznej", in: *Kapitał społeczny – aspekty teoretyczne i praktyczne*. Edited by Henryk Januszek (Poznań: Wyd. AE, 2004), 59-74.

102 See the quoted above article by Tomasz Zarycki, 59.

103 Mariusz Kwiatkowski, "Kościół katolicki, 'duch kapitalizmu', kapitał społeczny", *Przegląd* Powszechny, 1(2002): 87-89; see also John A. Coleman, S.J., "A Limited State and a Vibrant Society: Christianity and Civil Society", in: *Civil Society and Government*, Ed. by Nancy L. Rosenblum and Robert C. Post (Princeton: Princeton University Press 2002), 223-254.

104 Adrian Cybula, "Making Democracy Work... and Polish (Silesian) Case. An Essay on the Applicability of Putnam`s Research in Polish and Italian Conditions", in: *Eseje socjologiczne*. Edited by Władysław Jacher (Katowice: Wyd. UŚ, 2001).

105 Robert Putnam, *Demokracja w działaniu* (Kraków: Znak, 1995), 319.

106 Bożena Klimczak, "Kapitał społeczny a dobrobyt indywidualny i społeczny", in: *Kapitał społeczny we wspólnotach* (Poznań: Wyd. AE, 2005), 19-21.

107 Andrzej Przymeński, "Kapitał społeczny, pojęcie czy teoria?", in: *Kapitał społeczny*. Edited by Lucyna Frąckiewicz, Andrzej Rączaszek (Katowice: Wyd. AE, 2004), 66.

108 Anna Kiersztyn argues that the ideas which usually enter into social capital conceptions had been known by many philosophers praising the value of social ties, duties and values of trust in good societies. Social capital conceptions may fulfill an ideological function and may want to preserve nice illusions that maximalizing individual profit is in accord with cultivation

of public virtues. See her text, "Kapitał społeczny - ideologiczne konteksty pojęcia", in: *Kapitał społeczny we wspólnotach* (Poznań: Wyd. AE, 2005), 49-50.

109 Edmund Wnuk-Lipiński, *Demokratyczna rekonstrukcja*, (Warszawa: PWN, 1996), 151.

110 Andrzej Przymeński, "Rozwój kapitału społecznego i jego czynniki", in: *Kapitał społeczny – aspekty teoretyczne i praktyczne*. Edited by Henryk Januszek (Poznań: Wyd. AE, 2004), 51-53.

111 See R.W. Jackman, "Social Capital", in: *International Encyclopedia of Social and Behavioral Sciences*, vol. 21, Elsevier 2001, 1416-1419; Mariusz Kwiatkowski, Maria Theiss, "Kapitał społeczny. Od metafory do badań", *Rocznik Lubuski* 2004, vol 30, part II, 13-35.

112 However, E.C. Banfield, E. Tarkowska and J. Tarkowski have shown that the dominant ethos of 'amoral familism', no concern for collective issues, present especially in postwar southern Italy and in Poland of 1980s, led to social disintegration, pathology and very low level of social capital.

113 *Diagnoza społeczna. Warunki i jakość życia Polaków 2005*, Edited by Janusz Czapiński, Tomasz Panek (Warszawa: VIZJA PRESS&IT, 2006), 257.

114 Quoted after Galia Chimiak, *How Individualists Make Solidarity Work* (Warszawa: Ministerstwo Pracy i Polityki Społecznej, 2006), 52. Sztompka has made an attempt to develop his own version of trust, of social and civilizational capital. He saw barriers for progress in the realm of tradition and in generational inertia of some cultural traits.

115 See Omar G. Encarnación, "Tocqueville`s Missionaries: Civil Society and the Promotion of Democracy", *World Policy Journal* 1 (2000): 9-18; id., *The Myth of Civil Society: Social Capital and Democratic Consolidation in Spain and Brazil* (New York: Palgrave Macmillan, 2003); *Funding Virtue. Civil Society Aid and Democracy Promotion*, M. Ottaway and T. Carothers, eds. (Washington, D.C.: Carnegie Endowment for International Peace, 2000).

116 The authors of the above quoted and current *Diagnoza społeczna* say: "We are open, mobile society, but still not civil society", 19.

117 Bronislaw Misztal, "*Tożsamość jako zjawisko społeczne w zderzeniu z procesami globalizacji*", in: *Tożsamość bez granic* (Warsaw: Wyd. UW, 2005): 21-31. See also Bronisław Misztal, "Paul Hanly Furfey as a Theorist of Good Society", in: Bronisław Misztal, ed., *Paul Hanly Furfey's Quest for a Good Society* (Washington: The Council for Research in Values and Philosophy, 2005), 1-21.

118 Cezary Trutkowski, Sławomir Mandes, *Kapitał społeczny w małych miastach* (Warszawa: SCHOLAR, 2005), 49.

119 Daniel Wincenty, "Brudny kapital społeczny – społeczne uwarunkowania i zagrożenia dla demokracji", in: *Obywatel w lokalnej społeczności. Studia i szkice socjologiczne*. Edited by Marek Szczepański and Anna Ślisz, Tychy – Opole 2004.

120 Janusz Czapiński, "Polska – państwo bez społeczeństwa", *Nauka* 1 (2006), 8; see also an interview with Czapiński in *Gazeta Wyborcza*, 18 May, 2006.

121 See *Indeks społeczeństwa obywatelskiego* (Warszawa: Stowarzyszenie Klon/Jawor, 2006), 13.

122 Tadeusz Kowalik, "Mój rok osiemdziesiąty dziewiąty", *Gazeta Wyborcza,* 23-24 March, 2002.

123 "Rozmowa z prof. A. Zawiślakiem", *Obywatel* 5 (2004).

124 Zdzisław Krasnodębski, Granice polityki w Polsce", *Europa,* 24 May, 2006; see also Vladimir Shlapentokh, "Trust in public institutions in Russia: The lowest in the world", *Communist and Post-Communist Studies* 2 (2006).

125 See an interview with Lena Kolarska-Bobińska (*Ozon*, 2006, no. 24, 13), Director of the Institute for Public Affairs.

126 *Civil Society in the Making*, Editors Dariusz Gawin and Piotr Gliński (Warszawa: IFiS Publishers, 2006).

127 See an interview with Piotr Gliński and Tadeusz Szawiel, *Sprawy Nauki*, 2006, vol. XII.

128 The rather ill-famed twin brothers once again have promised the Polish people what had been previously promised and not kept by Lech Wałęsa, by the so-called Electoral Action of Solidarity (AWS) and by the post-communist Democratic Left Alliance (SLD). An independent intellectual Karol Modzelewski (see his article in *Gazeta Wyborcza,* 29-30 May, 2006), associated with the initial Solidarity trade union, has recently written on the cultural cleavage of Poland and posed a difficult question, what would happen in future when the deceived people will ask once again who has stolen their victory.

129 Piotr Sztompka, "O potrzebie wspólnoty obywatelskiej", *Europa,* 24 May, 2006.

130 Andrzej Rychard, "Rewolucja kulturalna?", *Gazeta Wyborcza*, 15 May, 2006.

131 See Aleksander Smolar, "Kaczyńscy atakują społeczeństwo obywatelskie", *Europa*, 4 May, 2006.

132 Jadwiga Staniszkis, "O społeczeństwie bez państwa i polityki. Republika Weimarska, PRL i IV RP", *Europa*, 9 September, 2006.

133 Zdzisław Krasnodębski, *Demokracja peryferii* (Gdańsk: słowo/obraz terytoria, 2003 and 2005). The title is inaccurate, it should rather be *Democracy under Peripheral Capitalism: the Case of Poland*, but Krasnodębski is not acquainted with predominantly Latin American theory and case of peripheral capitalism, and cannot therefore fully understand the Polish case of a similar phenomenon. The perplexing challenge how to modernize a Central European periphery (Poland, Lithuania) in the past and now is also discussed in his recent article "Modernizacja peryferii", *Europa*, 2 September 2006. Krasnodębski, a Polish professor from Bremen University, would arrive at a deeper understanding of the Polish situation, if he read one more German book on his favorite topic: Dorothee Bohle, *Europas neue*

Peripherie: Polens Transformation und transnationale Integration (Münster: Westfäliches Dampfboot, 2002).

134 Zdzisław Krasnodębski, *Drzemka rozsądnych* (Kraków: Ośrodek Myśli Politycznej, 2006), 263. It is interesting to see that also some famous leftwingers, for example Slavoj Zizek, say that after the alleged defeat of all utopias there has come a rule of the last great utopia, of a liberal, capitalist democracy on a global scale.

135 Smolar adds that after 1989 Poles did not want more experiments, fully believed in the market institutions that had been tried out in the West, and wanted to bring their country from the East to the West, they wanted to become the West as quickly as possible. See Aleksander Smolar, "Radykałowie u władzy (2)", *Gazeta Wyborcza*, 9-10 September, 2006.

136 Rafał Matyja, "Za kulisami rewolucji moralnej. Polityczne cele Jarosława Kaczyńskiego", *Europa*, 28 June, 2006.

137 Michał Kamiński, "PiS nie naśladuje metod Gierka, próbuje tylko nadać kapitalizmowi ludzką twarz", *Dziennik*, 20 April, 2006. The wachword of capitaism with human face had been earlier and in vain proposed by the former post-communist president Aleksander Kwaśniewski.

138 Dariusz Gawin, "PiS nie jest wrogi nowoczesności", *Gazeta Wyborcza*, 7 August, 2006.

139 A Polish journalist Marcin Wojciechowski, doubting in Russian capitalism, has asked professor Richard Pipes (*Gazeta Wyborcza,* 22 May, 2006) whether the Russian oligarchic and bureaucratic regime will evolve towards a pure Western-style capitalism and was justly answered that it is still a really existing capitalism, present also in many countries of Asia and South America.

140 Andrzej Nowak, "O sporach, przyjaźni i odnowie polityki", *Europa,* 31 May, 2006.

141 See, for example, Jakub Wygnański, Bogumił Luft, "Szukanie kapitału społecznego", *Rzeczpospolita*, 24 July, 2006. The authors of the inspiring article say that today in Poland there is no conflict between the state and civil society; as both parts are very weak, they strongly need each other. In conclusion, the above well known authors (NGO`s activist and a journalist) firmly insist that a more serious attention to the development of social capital in Poland should be devoted in strategic documents for 2007-2013 years. In the draft project of the so-called Operational Program Civil Society for 2007-2013, issued by the Ministry of Labor and Welfare in September 2005, only marginally it is mentioned a necessity to strengthen social capital and to develop human resources and social economy.

142 Paweł Śpiewak, "Zwijanie demokracji", *Europa*, 2 September 2006.

143 Aleksander Smolar, "Radykałowie u władzy (2)", *Gazeta Wyborcza* , 9-10 September, 2006.

144 See, for example, Magdalena Środa, "Społeczeństwo silniejsze od Kaczyńskich", *Gazeta Wyborcza*, 18 May, 2006.

Chapter 2

The Idea of Civil Society in Russia

Democracy works best where civil society is in a constructive and mutually supportive relationship with the state, and where citizens take their civic responsibilities seriously. This is not easy to secure.

-- *Democracy, Civil Society and Pluralism*, ed. C. Bryant and E. Mokrzycki (Warsaw: IFiS Publishers, 1995), 26.

In this Essay I intend to sketch a brief history of the Russian discourse on civil society. The Essay consists fundamentally of three parts. In the first part I have tried to show the origins of Russian and Soviet totalitarianism, along with a few references to the liberal idea of civil society in Russian intellectual history. The second and a bit larger part shows a theoretical contribution to the questions of civil society and of pluralism during the Gorbachev perestroika, a contribution partly influenced by the Polish experience. The Essay ends with rather pessimistic conclusions concerning the development of democracy and civil society in Russia.

THE RUSSIAN TRADITION

Many observers have paid close attention to a severe lack of genuine democratic tradition in Russian politics and society. Russian society is considered to be of a traditional type of civilization, opposed to modern capitalist society rooted in Mediterranean culture. The opposition can also be expressed in terms of civil society vs. submissive or servile society. In Russia, as in other traditional peasant societies under bureaucratic-authoritarian regimes and with no civil society, only various cliques and fractions struggling for higher offices appeared.[1]

Many Polish and Western authors saw premises for the Soviet totalitarianism in the Russian autocratic and collectivist traditions. Russian authors, however, saw the origin of Soviet despotism erroneously in the ideology of Western Marxist utopias. Jarosław Bratkiewicz noticed that the Russian reception of Marxism appealed first of all to common components of the Russian collectivist and autocratic consciousness. He saw that the Soviet dictatorship was consistent with the popular aspirations of the Russian people marked by oriental passivity.[2] In Russia, the economy and social life were regulated and controlled by the omnipotent State which only occasionally permitted for brief periods of "thaw" and limited, pro-Western liberalization.

So civil, democratic traditions in the Russian society, unlike the Western and even Polish societies, have been very weak. In Russia, soon after the French Revolution censorship forbade using the words "citizen" and even "society."[3] Russia had no important tradition of liberalism, and the inalienable rights of man were never appreciated there. Rather it was claimed that everyone is a servant of the State: the conservative-authoritarian tradition did not tolerate the spirit of citizen independence. "The Russian political culture", wrote the Soviet reformer Fiodor Burlatski, "did not tolerate pluralism of views or the possibility of criticizing state functionaries. Only after 1905 was a small breach made in the wall. But even then it was not allowed in fact to criticize either tsar, tsardom, or the existing political system."[4]

However, the catchword of civil society and the postulates of *glasnost* (openness) appeared relatively early in the tradition of Russian progressive thought. The concept of civil society was used in the eighteenthth century by F. Prokopovich (an adherent of tsar Peter's reforms) and by the representatives of the Enlightenment - Jacob Kozielski and Alexander Radischev. It appears also in the ideology of Decembrists at the beginning of the nineteenth century, in leftist Westernizers (Belinski) and even in some Slavophiles, like Samarin, who in his youth was fascinated by Georg F.W. Hegel no less than Vissarion Belinski.[5] The Slavophiles, however, preferred the typically Russian word *narod* (the people).

The Decembrists used the term "civil society" in striving for political reconstruction of Russia, in their struggle against autocracy of the "old order" and against the tsarist despotism. They were concerned with creating conditions for a rapid development of capitalism in Russia. In their quite revolutionary ideology there co-existed modern bourgeois liberalism (Adam Smith) with the idealization of "old Russian liberties", meaning ancient noble liberties.[6] Struggling against serfdom and all forms of slavery, they wanted to confer a title of citizen on all inhabitants of the State. The constitution projects elaborated by the Decembrists ensured broad civil liberties. In a federalist political structure of the Russian State they followed the example of the newly established United States of America. Many activists linked with Decembrist movement unsuccessfully strove for the transformation of Russia into a state of law and civil liberties. Pavel Pestel (1793-1826), one of the radical republican ideologists of the Southern Association of Decembrists defined the nation as an "association of all these men, who belong to one and the same state and constitute civil society having as its aim the possible existence of the welfare of everybody and for everyone."[7] However, the liberal ideology of Decembrists was unique in Russia and did not sink social roots.

The term 'civil society' was used also by Boris Chicherin (1824-1904), the main ideologist of liberal conservatism in Russia. Chicherin followed the essential points of Hegelian social philosophy. According to Andrzej Walicki, "he conceived of civil society as a sphere of conflicting private interests, that is, as a sphere of economic freedom, individualism and privacy..., he agreed with Hegel on the inseparability of civil society and law, treating civil society as a 'juridical association', situated between the family and the state."[8]

Also the catchword of glasnost appeared relatively early in Russia, convergent with that of civil society. It became well known at the end of Nicolas I's and during the Alexander II's reign, particularly in 1861, when an attempt to carry out some necessary reforms was made. The early changes were termed a "thaw", and censorship was softened in order to allow for public opinion.[9] The political reforms were, however, only of a very limited character. Finally, the tsar Alexander II also sharpened censorship and strengthened the tradition of authoritarian regimes in Russia.

The concept of *glasnost* appeared later in the first years of Soviet power. Lenin used the term in articles on the organization of the socialist state. He favored initially an open, public criticism of economic and bureaucratic inertia. However, the Soviet and Russian tradition conceived *glasnost* as an instrumental action, initiated by the leaders in order temporarily to activate public opinion.[10]

The Russian tradition of an omnipotent state survived and was even intensified after the Bolshevik revolution, chiefly in the Stalinist era. Undoubtedly the lack of a solid, organized civil society hampered the development of democracy, *glasnost* and vice versa. It was Antonio Gramsci, among others, who noticed great differences between Russia and Western Europe in these matters: "In Russia the state was everything and civil society was primordial and gelatinous: in the West there was a proper relation between the state and civil society, and when the state trembled the sturdy section of civil society was at once revealed. The state was only an outer ditch, behind which was a powerful system of fortress and earthworks."[11]

Fiodor Burlatski has recalled that one of the first decrees after the October Revolution "demanded prompt action against the counter-revolutionary press of various tendencies. It was said then that the action is temporary and connected with the sharpening of class struggle. It was also characteristic that immediately after the civil war Lenin returned to the previous view of our Party, which in its successive programs invariably demanded the right for intellectual freedom. Everyday norm of the economic policy (NEP) and an important aspect of its behavior was a pluralism within the Party, trade unions, soviets, peasant associations and especially in realm of culture. It was liquidated along with NEP at the end of twenties. Khruschev did something to restore it again."[12]

In another place while characterizing two models of socialism (war communism and NEP), the tendency towards "barrack communism" and the "social-democratic-bolshevik tendency" that had been shaped in Russia in the 1920s, Burlatski pointed out that the first tendency was unusually strong. During Lenin's reign at least half of the members of the Political Bureau of the Bolshevik party declared for this tendency, which "permanently relied on the backward consciousness of the masses and on their authoritarian-patriarchal political culture."[13]

So the victorious Stalinism buried for many years any idea of democracy and civil society, since the fundamental idea of the "state socialism" remained intact. [14]

THE CONTRIBUTION OF *PERESTROIKA*

The first official effort in the USSR to assimilate the concept of civil society and to adopt it to the conditions of reformed, anti-Stalinist socialism of *perestroika* was made in 1987 by Andranik Migranian from the Soviet Academy of Sciences.[15]

According to Migranian, later Boris Yeltsin's adviser, a genuine *perestroika* required first of all a renewal of society, and presupposed an increase of active citizen initiative. Migranian tried to express these needs with the help of the concept of civil society, then absent in Soviet social sciences. He started from historical analyses and came to the conclusion that capitalism developed best in those eighteenth and nineteenth century countries, in which civil society controlled the state. What is more, he dared to say, and was allowed to do it publicly, that social development goes ahead more quickly and more efficiently wherever individual and social life is free from meticulous regulation by the state and its institutions. He also said that highly advanced civil society was a foundation for political stabilization of nations.

Migranian included into his analyses the tradition of liberal democracy along with that of Marx and Gramsci.[16] He noticed that relations between the State and civil society under socialism depend in great measure on how they had looked before revolution. The author said that the capitalist countries with advanced civil society have a chance for a painless transition to socialism. He did not notice, however, that it was precisely the presence of a mature civil society that was the main obstacle to any revolutionary changes. The only force making revolution in socially and economically underdeveloped countries was the new (socialist) state, complained Migranian. Unfortunately, it has to resort to centralization, which hinders social development. Moreover, the lack of political culture in backward countries magnifies the necessity of the state care over the emerging organization of the new society. In such a situation, the functions of the State and civil society become inverted, the clear separation of their normally distinct functions disappears. In such countries, an additional task of the state should be the formation of a new civil society through gradual limiting of the state intervention in economic and socio-cultural life.

After the October Revolution, the conditions for the emergence of civil society arose during the NEP, but soon were curtailed. Migranian believed that also under socialism civil society should have at its disposal real possibilities of influencing the state power organs and should also control them effectively. According to this innovative author, Mikhail Gorbachev's reforms should consist in reversing the power ratio between bureaucracy and civil society, this time for the benefit of the civilian side, whereas, in the political sphere "the main task of the revolutionary *perestroika* was to achieve a full control of civil society over the State."[17] Migranian advocated a broad institutional extention of civil society in order to avoid the danger of absorbing the individual and broader communities in the State. In order to achieve it, there was a need for radical extention of freedom, so that the human individual could play an essential role in the process of institutionalization of civil society.[18] Migranian expressed his conviction that *perestroika* moved in this direction.

Foreigners commenting on Migranian's innovative views wondered if his deep concern for individual liberties and civil rights was also shared by the Soviet leaders, particularly because the theme of civil society and warrants for the individual did not appear initially in the declarations made by Gorbachev and his closest collaborators. Soon, however, the question of civil society began to appear in the articles written by one of the closest advisors of Gorbachev, the above quoted Professor Burlatski, and even Gorbachev himself declared at the Twenty eighth (the last one) Congress of the Soviet Communist Party, held in July, 1990, that civil society was taking Stalinism's place.

Some Western commentators acknowledged that much of the initiative for change had shifted from the Communist Party to society, that the Soviet Union was becoming step by step a radically different type of society, a civil society. "It might be objected - one observer noticed - that the very idea of civil society is too narrowly Western in origin to be applied appropriately beyond Western Europe and North America...To acknowledge the differentness of Russia's political heritage - he added - does not disqualify it from experiencing evolutionary change."[19]

The term of civil society was also employed by the Democratic Union, opposed to the Communist Party, also by Civil Action, formed in February 1990, and by numerous committees that arose from these parties and organizations.

In the above quoted article on the years of stagnation, Burlatski referred to the idea of socialist pluralism[20] that was earlier unsuccessfully promoted in Poland, looked for the ways out of the crisis of state socialism and began to dream about socialist civil society based on self-managing collectivities and active individuals.

In another article Burlatski proposed a new "more effective model of democratic, humanist socialism" characterized by "the development of civil society and subordination of the state to society."[21] According to Burlatski, "the State should transfer a considerable part of its power, functions, qualifications and prerogatives to society and its institutions. First of all to workers' collectives in factories and cooperatives, to offices, associations and also to social organizations and other, already new social institutions that surely will emerge during the process of *perestroika*. Society should take over much that previously was borne by the state weighed down with overcomplicated tasks and bureaucratization."[22] Burlatski has thus repeated here almost literally everything that had been written on this matter a little earlier in the Polish press.

As is well known, the idea of civil society earlier had emerged in neighboring Poland; it was promoted by the democratic opposition (Jacek Kuroń and Adam Michnik), the Solidarity leaders, and by independent scholars (e. g. Leszek Kołakowski, Jan Szczepański and Tadeusz Płużański). Of special interest is Szczepański's report[23] on the need of deep economic and political reforms in Poland, the report presented to the members of the so-called Consultative Council created at the end of 1986. Szczepański called for independent citizens' initiatives, autonomous from the existing State. His report and the debates of the Council created by Wojciech Jaruzelski turned out to be an important preparatory step towards systemic changes and to the transition to democracy in Poland. It is interesting to notice that the ideas of pluralism, civil society, a kind of socialist personalism[24] and of humanist universalism (see the new journal *Filosofskiie Issledovaniia*) have been promoted in Russia chiefly under Polish influence, especially under Gorbachev, a fact that is not always fully acknowledged.

Burlatski came back to these questions in his remarks at the Soviet Deputy Congress, where he criticized the then-existing model of allegedly omnipotent state, and paid attention to distorted mutual relations between the state and civil society.[25] Everybody should realize, Burlatski continued, that the state power is limited, and is not able to manage directly the economy, and especially the advancement of culture and morality, since these are the tasks for civil society only. This required a rapid farewell to the state-bureaucratic socialism and a transition to a democratic civil society. Burlatski maintained that the state should transfer to society at least two-thirds of its functions previously assumed, should favor decentralization, economic self-dependence of republics, and the development of a federation. According to Burlatski, this does not mean weakening of the state, but rather the other way round, it allows the state to concentrate attention on its fundamental tasks.

Within the structural reforms, Fiodor Burlarski, the leading adviser of Gorbachev, proposed, on the one hand, a liberation of labor and the economy from excessive state care and, on the other hand, a widening of civil rights and political liberties.[26]

Thee ideas of civil society, well grounded in the Anglo-Saxon tradition, were also returned to by Tair Tairov of the Soviet Academy of Sciences. Tairov noted that because of the control of public opinion by the Party-bureaucratic system in the USSR, there were no conditions for the citizen initiative and for the institutional defense of various civil rights. Tairov saw foundations for civil society in the USSR in strengthening the democratic system of councils as representative bodies. De-bureaucratization and de-etatization of social relations as well as elimination of lawlessness born by the administrative command system should contribute to a general democratization of the country. This democratization, Tairov insisted, should also embrace the Communist Party, since the reformed political system should exclude any absolute monopoly of power by the Communist party. Institutions and organizations, public associations forming the tissue of civil society should be liberated from external restraint, and should be granted a legal status. According to Tairov, "a particular importance for the future of the Soviet civil society should include the establishment of the so-called institutions of *glasnost*, among others the elaboration of legal steps on press and television which would ground and deepen the process of ever broader citizens' commitment to public life."[27] It was necessary to elaborate an optimal model of a new socialist statehood "in the shape of Soviet multinational civil society". Tairov wrote that "during perestroika the Party has faced a gigantic task; namely to determine optional proportion between the state and social factors within the political system and also strengthen the position of the individual in the system of moral and political values."[28]

Andranik Migranian returned to the problems and difficulties in forming civil society in the USSR in an atmosphere of a tidal wave of egalitarianism and populism in one of his interviews. The leading ideologist of the *perestroika* was well aware that in comparison with Poland and Hungary, Soviet transformations did not go far. Nevertheless, one should not, in his opinion, speed up and skip stages in the process of ushering in successive reforms. He noted that modernization of Polish and Hungarian societies, the process of forming social institutions independent of the state, had begun over 30 years earlier. "Besides, he added, there existed various forms of property. Peasants still possessed the land. Traditional forms of life were not so much destroyed as in our country in the 1930s. In Hungary and Poland civil society arose as prerequisites to the transition to real democracy. But those who take these countries as an example, Migranian continues, and want also in our country to form at once similar structures, do not understand that for years we entirely eradicated everything - nowhere did totalitarianism go so far."[29] Indeed, Migranian paid attention to the germs of horizontal structures and the few free associations of people in accordance with social and professional interests,[30] but he noted that in fact in the USSR "the whole economic and social sphere still belongs to the state. Only now is the process of weakening these rigid state departments and de-etatization of these spheres taking place. One should throw away all illusions that *perestroika* can quickly be accomplished."[31]

Migranian noted that the Soviet society began to feel more strongly the chains and fetters into which Stalinism had put it. It had once been insensitive thereto, whereas today "human dignity and the sense of civic responsibility are being revived". The process of *perestroika*, according to Migranian, is influenced by the forces proceeding from the ranks, which do not always have enough self-control. In such a specific situation Migranian accepts the idea of gradual transition to democracy through the stage of a so-called authoritarian democracy, "when the state authorities, while limiting freedom to a certain degree, should create indispensable components of civil society, which will be able to assume functions of autonomous management."[33]

Migranian did not say, however, how long the rule of authoritarian system may last and whether the state was able to create civil society that would limit it considerably. Indeed, at the beginning the elements of civil society were not inspired by the state apparatus but emerged as a result of the action of the relatively small faction of Party reformers led by Gorbachev. Migranian recently declared that the social-economic revolution, initiated by Gorbachev, was over in 2004, but the period of transition towards an advanced civil society may last several decades.

Many Russian scholars and even the former Bulgarian president and philosopher Zhelyu Zhelev defend the theory that direct transition from totalitarianism to parliamentary democracy is impossible and that there is a need for a transient, intermediate form of authoritarian dictatorship controlling and preventing social explosions that could lead to chaos and even civil war.[33]

This exposition of views on civil society by perestroika radicals should end with some notes on Mikhail Gorbachev, the initiator of the revolutionary change. Undoubtedly he was a naive man of genius. It is supposed that the main drive for deep economic reform in the USSR and other countries of the so called real socialism, being a failed attempt of extricating it from world peripheries, was a growing distance between those countries and the West (a distance analogous to that existing between the North and the South). Initially it caused a painful shock among leaders and citizens educated in the primitive ideology of the so-called superiority of socialism over capitalism. This refers also to Gorbachev. But his pro-European perestroika and its underlying motive to speed up the development of the USSR ended in disaster (a catastroika, according to Alexander Zinoviev) of the system, of Russia and with dreadful suffering and humiliation for millions of Russians. The vague program of Gorbachev was unrealisable. However Gorbachev's great success, for which the whole world should be indebted to him, was a contribution to a peaceful dismantling of the Soviet Union, what had seemed impossible without the horrors of war. Boris Grushin, a well-known Russian sociologist has said of him: "In my opinion Gorbachev is a man number one in the 20th century world. Although he is a tragic person with no doubt. He has never understood what he was doing. He thought as a Party functionary. He could not imagine how this confusion may end. He had no well-laid plan of perestroika, only illusions. The illusions stayed with him when he presented himself recently as a candidate for presidential elections. He lost them fatally, which has brought an irreparable harm to him and to his few followers."[34]

It seems that great men like Gorbachev (and those unwittingly made by him protagonists, like Wałęsa, Mazowiecki, Gamsahurdia, Sevardnadze) using Hegel's words "blow up the crust of the outer world", express in the history the will of the world spirit and do therefore right and necessary things. Being a tool in the hands of the world spirit they have contributed to the progress of freedom in large parts of the globe. However, they do not achieve calmness and happiness, "they are dropped like the shells of a fruit, die young like Alexander, are murdered like Caesar, are sent to the Saint Helen's island like Napoleon."[35] They obtain 1% votes like Gorbachev and Wałęsa, are blamed by the working people as a cause of their misfortune, they disappear in mysterious circumstances like Gamsahurdia, they avoid with difficulties attempts on their life and incessantly show naivete, like Shevardnadze (forced to leave the presidential post as a result of a velvet rose revolution).

Gorbachev himself, however, found in a deadlock as a result of a self-propelling process and in spite of many other failures, has preserved a steady optimism and in a puzzling way rejected the accusation of ingenuity. At an American University in Turkey he officially declared: "After 2000 there will begin an era of peace and full bloom." What is even more, he declared the following: "The aim of my whole life was the destruction of communism, that unbearable dictatorship against people. My wife, who accepted this necessity even before me, supported me strongly in this effort. In order to achieve this aim I took advantage of my post in the party and in the country. In order to realize this aim my wife pushed me to assume the highest posts in the country. When I got acquainted with the West personally, I was enlightened that I should not give up the aim I had undertaken, and in order to achieve it I had to change the whole leadership of the Communist Party, the Soviet Union, and leaderships in all socialist countries."[36]

PROSPECTS FOR DEMOCRACY

A deep reform of the Communist Party in the Soviet Union turned out to be impossible. Conservative forces stemming from the Party organized in August 1991 a coup d'etat against democracy. The coup, as is well known, failed, and as a result the Soviet Union with its leading communist party ceased to exist.[37] Democratic forces in their initial enthusiasm declared that it was a real victory of civil society over the Soviet state. However, the prospects for genuine civil society in Russia[38] and other post-Soviet countries are still dark and depressing. The societies are passive, tired, and disappointed. *Perestroika* and *glasnost* have been forgotten, the democratic forces that fought so much against communist totalitarianism have been pushed aside, to the margin of the new political scene.[39] New authoritarian states are being shaped in Russia, Belorus, and in Asian, post-Soviet countries. The future is gloomy and insecure. The development of a private market economy, the base of civil society, is extremely difficult in the recent conditions of state-owned land and industry, besides the bad company of social apathy or growing aggressive nationalism. Since the old Soviet ideology disintegrated still there is no economic base for civil society. Instead the new Russian political discourse often resorts to the aggressive and utopian nationalism and to neo-traditionalistic rhetoric.

Many participants of an interesting round table discussion on bureaucracy, authoritarianism, and the future of democracy in Russia deliberated how to build democratic rule in a country that has never experienced it.[40] It was said that authoritarianism was still present and even unavoidable in Russia, the question was only if it will evolve towards parliamentary democracy or towards a severe nationalistic dictatorship. Mezhuiev, for example, did not believe in the victory of democratic rule in the nearest future in Russia. For him, the main cause of the impossibility of a fully democratic system was the absence of civil society which must emerge long before democratic rule can be established.[41]

It was pointed out that the new authoritarian and corruptible bureaucracy in Russia is merging with corporatist economic groups, blocking legal procedures, and it wants to de-politicize society and to subordinate public opinion. Other participants ascertained the absence of democracy in the new Russia and the presence of not more than 10-15% of freedom,[42] as well as the absence of middle class supporting economic progress and civic education.

It was reminded that bureaucracy in Russia, unlike in Western Europe, was not a product of modernization and of the emergence of the state of law, but was a result of legal abuses by the state authorities in the absence of civil society and any democratic control over society.

Still others noted that the need for the state of law has disappeared from the official Russian discourse, and that the real danger for Russia is not authoritarianism promising a state of law, but a sustained transitional period with weak structures of the central state authorities but with strong local *caudillos* and a feeble general will to build a stable democracy. That may lead to a fiercely nationalist rule defending not citizens' rights, but only national rights of the great Russia.[43]

Starting from the mid 1990s the ruling politicians and even some scholars began to refer with a reserve to the till recently fashionable term civil society, though the nationalist and communist opposition never showed much enthusiasm for it. All of a sudden it has begun to be associated with untamed elements, revolts and even with organized crime. Larysa Romanienko from the Russian Academy of Sciences Institute of Sociology wondered why civil society, instead of being a warranty of law and stability, has become a source of social tensions in Russia. She declared that the problem for her country is no more the construction of civil society, but overcoming its destructive and antisocial form, which could have been useful only under the illegal conditions of communism.[44]

In the declarations of Yeltsin and of the ruling party striving for stability there was no reference to this concept, and general Lebed acknowledged that only rich countries of the West could afford that type of society. The idealist construction or pro-Western myth of civil society started to be a drawback in the construction of a strong Russian statehood. Vladimir Putin who replaced the infirm Yeltsin and put forward the slogan of the dictatorship of law (a bit earlier the prime minister Chernomyrdin spoke of economic dictatorship), incessantly returns to the need of strengthening quite traditional "order" and state power, which once again is above the interests of society and citizens. One speaks about a soft authoritarianism and a steered, controlled democracy (political censorship in more important mass media, manipulation in the electoral system and dependent judicial proceedings), is supported in fact by many Russians. A symbol of the new state has become a synthesis of the Byzantine two headed eagle, the three colored flag of Peter I the Great and the Stalinist anthem by Alexandrov. There appears an economic slowdown, political "standstill" and devaluation of Russian reforms.

Putin met at the Kremlin in June 2001 representatives of Russian non-governmental organizations, where everybody spoke of "constructive cooperation" between the institutions of civil society and the State. He said that great Russia is a great society and that Russians are tired with the activity of organizations weakening the State. Some Russians put into the concept of civil society a national pride and love of the fatherland. The Russian interpretation of the concept, however, comes close to the concept of community in its traditional meaning. Many authors wonder whether the concept has a universal meaning and whether it can be equally applied to various countries and civilizations.

Russian scholars still underline that the concept is useful in studying problems of the present-day Russia, in Moscow even the Civil Society European Academy has been established. However a concern is expressed that by now Russians experience only negative aspects of civil society. Besides, capacities of informal civic activities from the first years of democracy have been exhausted and in the consciousness of the masses there have appeared paradoxical ideas and wishes "of socialism without communists, of a dictatorship without repressions, of an authoritarianism while preserving political liberties."[45]

The new rather anti-civic structures of society that are being shaped are deprived of the culture of dialogue, pluralism and tolerance; very often they do not suit the conditions of democracy, so the reform initiatives of deepening democracy must come from narrow elites and state authorities, so that modernization and democratization of society acquires authoritarian forms. Besides, most people do not see any real possibility of influencing the state authorities. The above quoted author maintains that the Russian civil society, still underdeveloped, does not protect against possible antidemocratic regime, but still is not a real base for one.[46]

The Russian society is rather amorphous, fragmentary and atomized; it preserves previous confusion and inertia. The effort to build a tissue of civil society at an accelerated pace, omitting its intermediate stages which generally take some ages and in an unprepared social and cultural milieu could not succeed. The shortage of civil society contributed to the fact that the market acquired forms characteristic of "savage", uncivilized capitalism. As a result the above quoted authors and co-editors have said: "To the Russians there has not been forbidden a movement towards civil society and the rule of law, but at the crossroads, where Russia is now, the question of what social and political forces may lead the movement is very acute. On their choices, initiative and energy depends whether the possibilities will be realized or a new lurch with far-reaching consequences will take place."[47]

Some observers see the question in an apocalyptic way: "In the place of civil society there is a great gaping empty hole."[48] The well-known sociologist Yuri Levada, member of the Presidential Council for cooperation with civil society maintains that "with our passivity and inability for self-organization we are 200 years behind the nations of Western Europe."[49] Yuri Afanasyev, a former adherent of *perestroika* looks at the future as even more dismal: since the present-day economic system ensures not more than one fourth of the population and dooms over a half a degradation to lumpenproletarian, Russia is threatened by police-state dictatorship.[50] The problem is that the deep social-economic transformation caused by the transition from authoritarian socialism to peripheral capitalism paralysed many Russians with a strong cultural shock as a result of which they have lost the will to live, and in reality they live less. The 60 % increase of mortality starting from the early 1990s is unprecedented in peace time since the Middle Ages.

A relatively recent debate on civil society and the state provides a fruitful discussion of: the crisis and topicality of the concept of civil society in Russia and in the West, its place between the state and the market, and a new understanding of the citizenship principle. One of the participants of the round table discussion noted that the intense discussion of civil society owes much "to two Polish scholars (Adam Michnik and Leszek Kołakowski), who advanced the catchword in order to make a theoretical justification of the Solidarity action in relation to the Polish communist authorities. No wonder that the stress was put on the opposition of civil society to the state."[51] Today, however, a different understanding of the concept is needed in Russia. According to Alexeeva, the stress should be put not on opposition, but on social stability, on territorial, national, axiological integration, on community and on integration between the state elites and the masses.

The topicality of Hegel in the present-day Russia has been stressed. Professor Sevcenko highly estimates Hegelian glorification of the State, and Hegel's interpretation of the organic ties existing between the state authorities and civil society. Since radically liberal reforms have failed, the Russian state as an organic whole and a strong presidential authority acquired a greater meaning. In present-day Russia Karl Marx officially is seen in a negative light, but this does not extend to Hegel and Lenin. The attitude towards Antonio Gramsci -- very popular under Khrushchev and Gorbatchev – is now also quite negative.

Russian democrats and reformers have acknowledged that Russia (some years ago considered to be the most progressive country of the world) is backward even in comparison with Latin America as far as the development of political system, democratic culture, and the maturity of civil society is concerned. Latin American civil society is considered to be much more ramified and advanced due to the fact that the right-wing authoritarian regimes of the Latin American past did not destroy large sectors of the private economy, and were much more favorable to the survival and even consolidation of civil society[52] than was Soviet totalitarianism.

Generally, it is assumed that Russia can learn much from the Latin American democratization process and that the so-called Latin American syndrome (a strong economic polarization of society, bureaucratic and corporatist state excessively entangled in the economy, semi-democratic elections, democratic-authoritarian cycles, ethnic rivalries, predominance of the Mafia, army, trade unions and political cliques, a generally weak civil society, and economic dependency on foreign capital) will probably prevail during the nearest 20-40 years of Russia and of some Eastern European countries. For all its cruelty, this variant of Russia's dependent development is considered to be better than the previous totalitarian system.[53]

The Russians, East Europeans and Latin Americans are now beginning to lose their initial faith and hope in the easy possibility of transition from backwardness and the economy of shortage to prosperity and a newly liberated modernization thanks to the formation or reemergence of civil society, conceived for a moment almost as a paradise or an ersatz of the earlier abandoned illusions of socialism. However, there still persists a moderate hope that close cooperation between the state and civil society will permit at least steering and administering the new forms of dependency and interdependency under globalization. In that new epoch of an emerging global civil society Russia still cannot find a proper place for herself, as is the case with some regions shaped by Islamic, Confucian and Buddhist civilizations.

At the beginning of the 21st century post-Soviet Eastern Europe (Georgia, Ukraine and partially Poland) has become an arena of manipulative struggle of right-wing and populist clans and of a new civil society against oligarchic-peripheral capitalism, which had been installed in those countries. It is necessary once again to introduce into practice either the illusions of a democratic socialism or the visions of the flourishing Western capitalism, generally unattainable in the poor countries of the East and the South.

In Russia there still lack the subtle techniques of public relations that strengthen symbolic domination of interest groups. Absent are modern political marketing and non-governmental organizations that efficiently influence the people of Russia and post-Soviet republics. This has led to a defeat of pro-Russian politicians in the Ukraine and Georgia in their clash with pro-American politicians.

After 11 September 2001 Vladimir Putin decided, against the opinion of his closest advisers, to include Russia in the pro-Western antiterrorist coalition. If the coalition and the strategic alliance survives, this may contribute to Russia bringing herself out of the position of a Third World country and modernizing herself significantly. So once again she will become, not the second superpower, but would have an effective place among the world's ten most important countries. Nothing, however, indicates that the steered super-presidential system and the party regime similar to the former Mexican PRI would be abandoned. It is commonly acknowledged that the way of development and modernization "based upon social activity is not easily accepted in Russia, which for historical reasons is not fit for the realization of the citizens' individual initiative.[54]

Many Russian liberals criticize the emerging system of a steered democracy, Putin's slogan for strengthening the state authority and the domination of the state over the individual which is close to the logic of Eastern despotism. Some say: "Our national idea can only be building civil society."[55] But few Russian liberals dream of a realization in Russia the Ukrainian bloodless scenario of a postmodernist upheaval, an orange revolution. Few dream of a birth of civil society spirit with the help of refined Western techniques of propaganda and mobilization.

Alexander Domrin, a Russian lawyer and political scientist considers the discussion on civil society in present-day poor Russia to be artificial and irrelevant, because the concept presupposes relatively high level of welfare: "Destitute people are unable to form a civil society. At the turn of the twenty-first century, the Russian nation must first concentrate on stopping the depopulation and degradation of Russia and on overcoming the disastrous consequences of Yeltsin's regime, rather than on involving the country in another round of radical economic 'reforms' and futile social engineering. Otherwise, there will be no Russia or Russian society, whether civil or uncivil."[56]

NOTES

1 Jarosław Bratkiewicz, *Tradycjonalizm, kolektywizm, despotyzm. Kontynuacyjne ujęcie ewolucji historyczno-politycznej (ze szczególnym uwzględnieniem Rosji)* (Warszawa: INP, 1991), 163.

2 Ibid., 221-232.

3 Thomas G. Masaryk, *The Spirit of Russia* (London 1919), 83.

4 Fiodor Burlatski, *Breżniew - lata zastoju* (Brezhnev - the Years of Stagnation), quoted after *Stalinizm - pieriestrojka,* (Warsaw 1988), 48; see also his interesting book *Novoie myshlenie* (New Thinking) (Moscow 1988).

5 Leonid Kriwuszyn, Stefan Owczarz, "Kategoria 'społeczeństwo obywatelskie' i jej przezwyciężenie w myśli Marksa", *Człowiek i Światopogląd* 12 (1985), 41; L. Kriwuszyn, *Problema gosudarstva i obsčestva v domarksistskoi mysli (Istoriko-sociologiceskie očerki)* (Leningrad 1978); *Filozofia i myśl społeczna rosyjska 1825-1861,* ed. A. Walicki (Warsaw: PWN, 1961), 168, 171, 268.

6 Andrzej Walicki, *Rosyjska filozofia i myśl społeczna od Oświecenia do marksizmu* (Warszawa: Wiedza Powszechna, 1973), 93-112.

7 Quoted after Andrzej Walicki, *Rosyjska filozofia i myśl społeczna,* 105.

8 Andrzej Walicki, *Legal Philosophies of Russian Liberalism* (Oxford 1987), 133-134; see also an article on the topic published by R.A. Poole in *Sociologicheskiie Issledovaniia* 9 (1991).

9 N. Gross, "Glasnost`: Roots and Practice", *Problems of Communism* 6 (1987), 69-70; J. M. Baturin, "Političeskii oscilliator: Novyi Kaprfagen protiv glasnosti (Iz rossiiskoi istorii)", in: *Političeskiie instituty i obnovleniie obsčestva. Jezhegodnik associatsii političeskikh nauk* (Moscow 1989); *Glasnost` in Context: On the Recurrence of Liberalizations in Central and East European Literatures and Cultures*, ed. M. Pavlyshyn, (Oxford 1990); A. Walicki, *Rosyjska filozofia i myśl społeczna,* 167; see also an interesting conversation with Natan Eidelman, *Res Publica* 4 (1989), 44-45.

10 N. Gross, *Glasnost`: Roots...,* 70.

11 A. Gramsci, *Prison Notebooks*, ed. Q. Hoare, G. Nowell Smith (London, 1971), 138.

12 F. Burlatski, *Breżniew - lata zastoju,* 46.

13 Quoted after *Stalinizm - pierestroika...,* fasc. 3, 20.

14 Ibid., 21; previously published in *Literaturnaia Gazieta,* April 20, 1988.

15 A. M. Migranian, "Vzaimootnošeniia individa, obščestva i gosudarstva v političeskoi tieorii marksizma i problemy diemokratizacii socialističeskogo obščestva" (Mutual Relations between the Individual, Society and State in the Political Theory of Marxism and Problems of of the Democratization of Socialist Society), *Voprosy Filosofii* 8 (1987). The contents of of this highly innovative study met vivid echo abroad - see James. P. Scanlan, "Reforms and Civil Society in the USSR", *Problems of Communism* 2 (1988); P. Flaherty, "Perestroika Radicals: The Origins and Ideology of the Soviet New Left",

Monthly Review (1988, September); M. Buckley, *Redefining Russian Society and Polity* (Boulder: Westview Press, 1993).

16 In April 1987, Georgi Smirnov, the director of Marxist-Leninist Institute in Moscow announced that Gramsci is to be considered a key theoretical forefather of *prestroika*. See J. Lester, *The Dialogue of Negation. Debates on Hegemony in Russia and in the West* (London: Pluto Press, 2000), 95.

17 A. M. Migranian, *Vzaimootnošenia...*, 87.

18 Ibid., 91; George Schöpflin ("Political Traditions in Eastern Europe", *Daedalus* 1990, no. 1) rightly noticed that all, in fact, East European modernizers were involved in a contradiction, that of having to construct autonomous civil society from the above, by th State (64).

19 S. Frederick Starr, "Soviet Union: A Civil Society", *Foreign Policy* 70 (1988), 36.

20 Soon came over a huge wave of Soviet publications praising pluralism, not only strictly "socialist" one, e.g.: L.A. Gordon, "Od monolitnosti k pliuralizmu", *Sociologičeskiie Issledovaniia* 3 (1990); S. P. Dudel, "Socialističeskii pliuralizm i uroki leninskoi kritiki empiriokriticizma", *Naučnyi Kommunizm* 2 (1990), V.I. Ilin, A. V. Fiedotov, "Sovremiennyi pliuralizm: niekotoryie razmyšleniia o iego raznovidimostiakh", *Naučnyi Kommunizm* 5 (1989); A. B. Venegov, "Socialističeskii pliuralizm v koncepcii pravovogo gosudarstva", *Sovetskoie Gosudarstvo i Pravo* 6 (1989); L. Jagodowski, "Rehabilitacja pluralizmu", *Nowe Czasy* 46 (1988); It is also interesting to see a round table discussion on "socialist pluralism" published in *Sociologičeskiie Issledovaniia* 5 (1988); see also V. I. Boriev, N. N. Sulgin, "Socialističeskii pliuralizm: podchody k problemie", in: *Političeskiie instituty...*, 151-167; T. I. Oizerman, "Istoričeskiie sud'by pliuralizma filosofskikh učenii", *Voprosy Filosofii* 12 (1991); A. F. Zotov, "Fenomen Filosofii: o čem govorit pliuralizm filosofskikh učenii", *Voprosy Filosofii* 12 (1991).

21 Quoted after *Stalinizm - pierestroika...*, fasc. 3, 22.

22 Ibid., 21; see also Zbysław Rykowski, "Ludzie zamiast mas" (Men Instead of the Masses), *Polityka* 25 (1988).

23 It was broadly commented in Poland and elsewhere. The text entitled "Od diagnoz do działań" was published in a special issue of *Rada Narodowa* 3 (1987) and its Russian translatin was included in *Jan Szczepański o chelovieke i obshchestvie. Refierativnyj sbornik* (Moscow 1990); see also L. Lykoshina, *Grazhdanskoe obshchestvo v Polshe* (Moscow 1998).

24 See Edward M. Swiderski, "From Social Subject to the 'Person'. The Belated Transformatin in Latter-Day Soviet Philosophy", *Philosophy of the Scial Sciences* 3 (1993).

25 F.Burlatski, "Zamietki dieputata. Piervyi, no važnyi šag", *Litieraturnaia Gazieta* 24 (1989).

26 Ibid., 2.

27 T. Tairov, "Gwarancje dla demokracji", *Nowe Czasy* 22 (1988), 29.

28 Ibid., see also M. Głogowski,"Jednostka a pierestroika", *Życie Warszawy*, August 15th, 1988. Also an outstanding Soviet poet declared in

Litieraturnaia Gazieta that the State is not only a 'collective we' but also a 'concrete I'. "I do not care a rap, he added, that the maxim *L'Etat c'est moi* was expressed once by a king, not by a proletary. We should accept the catchword not in royal, but in the most revolutionary and civilian sense" - R. Rozdiestvienski, *Hamulce*, in: *Stalinizm -pierestroika...*, fasc. 1, 42.

29 "Populizm - dobrze czy źle", *Forum* 30 (1989), (translation from *Sovietskaia Kultura*, June 24 (1989).

30 For more information on the emergence of these independent movements, see V.N. Bieriezovski, "Grazhdanskiie dvizheniia", *Sociologičeskiie Issledovaniia* 3 (1989); O.G. Rumiantsev, "Niezależny ruch inicjatyw społecznych i jego rola w przebudowie życia społecznego w ZSRR", *Colloquia Communia* 4-5 (1988). Rumiantsew noted in the article (309-310) that "the practice of non-formal movement proves that the emergence of the elements of socialist civil society appears in the conditions of predominant infantilism of strivings and actions. The infantilism of our society is as if it had two faces and both very arduous: conservatism and extremism. In a word, the illness of infantilism in non-formal groups movement has not yet been cured. From this follows from a general inability to regarding the standpoint of partners and opponents and to correct in time one's own views. From this follows in turn an impatience and inaptitude for dialogue and cooperation as well as a hypertrophy of the representative function. All that is an understandable result of the lack of political culture, of a coerced deficit of civic experience of the society". Rumiantsew in his analyses referred to Hungarian sociologists, especially to E. Hankiss's theory of two parallel societies.

31 *Populizm...*, 3.

32 Ibid., also Andrzej Walicki noticed the process of transition in the USSR from totalitarianism to the authoritarian state of law. A. Walicki, "The Rule of Law in the Russian Intellectual Tradition: Pre-Revolutionary Russia, the Soviet Union and Perestroika", *Dialectics and Humanism* 3-4 (1988), 25; see also V.S. Niersiesiants, "Pravovoie gosudarstvo: istoria i sovremiennost", *Voprosy Filosofii* 2 (1989); K.S. Gadziev, "Kontsepciia grazhdanskogo obščestva: idieinyie istoki i osnovnyie viekhi formirovaniia", *Voprosy Filosofii* 7 (1991); P. Reddaway, "Civil Society and Soviet Psychiatry", *Problems of Communism*, July-August (1991).

33 See the interesting discussion on totalitarianism, authoritarianism and democracy in the global context and particularly in the Soviet Union and Latin America, published in the Moscow journal *América Latina* 4,5,6 (1990); see also the paper by Z. Zhelev on Democracy in Post-Totalitarian Society, delivered at the Warsaw University and published in *Obóz. Problemy narodów byłego obozu komunistycznego* 24 (1992), 109-113.

34 Boris Grushin, "Rosja nie jest racjonalna", *Gazeta Wyborcza*, 28 May, 2001. Gorbachev (and partly Yeltsin) contributed to a peaceful solution of the controversy over the existence of the world among the Russian generals. Similarly like Western pacifists who said better red than dead, Gorbachev was right to acknowledge it was better to be lost than dead.

35 Hegel, *Wykłady z filozofii dziejów*, vol. 1 (Warsaw: PWN, 1958), 47.

36 Quoted after *Brzask,* 4 (2001). Although Gorbachev has never regretted the collapse of communism, the above quoted passage does not seem authentic; see Julian Bartosz, "Apokryf o zdradzie", *Dziś. Przegląd Społeczny*, 6 (2006). It should be added that before Gorbachev and his wife also Alexander Yakovlev, the former poltburo member, claimed a significant contribution to the overthrow of communism. See his book *Predisloviie, abval, posloviie* (Moscow 1992).

37 There is a similarity between the August coup by Yanayev in Russia and an earlier failed coup by colonel Tejero in Spain in february 1981. Both attempts at a coup, provoked by the ruling establishment, finally did not overthrow democracy, but strengthened it somhow. Yeltsin during his visit in Madrid in 1994 compared his role to that of the King Juan Carlos I in the Spanish transition to democracy.

38 The extensive Russian bibliography on the idea of civil society can be found in *Grazhdanskoe obshchestvo v Rossii: zapadnaia paradigma i rossiiskaia realnost,* ed. K.G. Kholodkovskii (Moscow 1996); *Grazhdanskoe obshchestvo v Rossii: struktury i soznanie*, ed. K.G. Kholodkovskii (Moscow 1998); *Grazhdanskoe obshchestvo. Mirovoi opyt i problemy Rossii*, ed. V.G. Khoros (Moscow 1998).

39 Ryszard Kapuściński, *Imperium* (Warszawa: Czytelnik, 1993), 326.

40 "Biurokratiia, avtoritaritarizm i buduščee demokratii v Rosssii (materialy 'kruglogo stola'')", *Voprosy Filosofii* 2 (1993); see also a report from a Warsaw conference organized by Stefan Batory Foundation: *Dokąd zmierza Rosja?* (Whither Is Russia Bound?), *Res Publica* 5 (1993), and a book - *Rosja: Kontynuacja czy punkt zwrotny?*, ed W. Bonusiak, K. Sowa (Rzeszów 1994).

41 *Biurokratiia, avtoritarizm i...,* 6-7.

42 Ibid., 12.

43 Ibid., 25.

44 L.M. Romanienko, "Grazhdanskoie obščestvo uže iest, no...", *Socyologiceskiie issledovaniia* 4 (1994).

45 *Grazhdanskoie obscestvo Rossii: struktury i soznaniie* (Moscow 1998), 211.

46 Ibid., 219.

47 Ibid., 255.

48 Quoted from *Izviestiia*, 20 April, 2001.

49 Quoted from *Gazeta Wyborcza*, 24 December, 2001. Another professor, V. Arzanukhin declared in *Tygodnik Powszechny* (24 February, 2002) that if in Russia in the epoch of globalization there does not arise civil society, so "we will become an inner proletariat in a global system, exploited by advanced postindustrial countries".

50 *Gazeta Wyborcza*, 20 January, 2003.

51 *Gosudarstvo i Pravo*, 1(2002), 22.

52 See the discussion published in *América Latina* 4, 5 (1990); I.V. Danilevich, *Gosudarstvo i instituty grazhdanskgo obshchestva v pieriod pierehoda ot avtoritarizma k diemokratii (Chili, Portugaliia, Ispaniia)* (Moscow 1996).

53 See an article by L. Radzikovski published in *Ogoniok,* 7 (1993).

54 W. Kuwaldin, "Zbudujemy nowy dom", *Gazeta Wyborcza*, 13-14 July (2002), 18.

55 See the words by Mikhail Prusak and Grigori Yavlinsky in *Gazeta Wyborcza*, 18 April and 18 May 2002. The need for the development of civil society in Russia was also perceived by the president Putin in his proclamation of May 2004, but in his proclamation of May 2005 he declared that the break-up of the Soviet Union was the greatest 20th century geopolitical disaster.

56 Alexander Domrin, "Ten Years Later: Society, 'Civil Society', and the Russian State", *The Russian Review* 62 (April 2003), 211.

Chapter 3

Civil Society and Democracy in Spain

La libertad no hace felices a los hombres; los hace simplemente hombres.
-- Manuel Azaña

The aim of this Essay is an analysis of political and intellectual changes that have taken place in Spain after 1975, that is to say from the death of General Francisco Franco almost to the present day. The Spanish transition to democracy, peaceful and abounding in interesting and unknown processes, has met with enormous interest of the worlds of academia and of politics. A very ample bibliography on this topic in many languages has been published. The specific and unique feature of this study that differentiates it from all other historical, sociological and political literature on democratic changes in Spain is its special attention given to the analysis of theoretical and political discourse on the idea of democracy and civil society in present-day Spanish thought.

Although the idea of democracy is based upon universal principles of political representation, its application depends on local conditions and national context. Spain, like Poland is situated on the confines of Europe, and has not had any important tradition of political democracy. Nowadays, it is being said, democracy is well rooted in Spain, but has not sufficiently reached the civic consciousness. Spain has overcome isolationism and historical anachronism, and has overcome also the conflict between its official and real image.

FROM FRANCOISM TO DEMOCRACY

Spain for centuries has suffered from a serious deficit of democratic political culture. The centralist, authoritarian, traditionally Catholic and even Islamic cultural heritage contributed to the fact that the Spanish experience with democracy has been relatively brief.

In the 19th century, in spite of incessant struggles of liberal democrats with monarchic traditionalists and in spite of the proclamation of a short-lived Republic in 1873, Spanish democracy did not attain success. It was equally difficult to achieve a success in the 20th century under conservative monarchy and the military dictatorship of Miguel Primo de Rivera, 1923-1930.

The Second Republic (1931-1936) was characterized by extremism, anticlerical sectarianism, numerous socio-economic and regional conflicts, fragmentarization of the system of political parties, and other weaknesses.[1]

As a result of the cruel civil war (1936-1939) that against the lame, unconsolidated Republic was declared by conservative Spanish generals, the autocratic dictatorship of General Franco was established. The dictatorship shattered for many decades all hopes for liberty and democracy.

On the nature, specific features and the evolution of the Francoist dictatorship much controversy has arisen among historians and political scientists. Some authors[2] emphasize the fascist roots and totalitarian character of the Franco regime, others (first of all Juan J. Linz) rightly noted an early evolution of the dictatorship towards an authoritarian regime without strictly defined ideology, but characterized by certain antidemocratic mentality and a limited pluralism.[3]

Irrespective of the interpretation of the Francoist regime, it is clearly that General Franco and his adherents were opposed to any rule based upon parliamentary democracy. Franco thought liberal democracy to be inconsistent with the character of Spanish society and the spirit of its culture. He deemed that the general voting principle and the political parties system, characteristic of "inorganic democracy" should be replaced by the new system of "organic democracy", based upon corporatist representation of families, municipalities and sindicates. Francoism made use of the organic and anti-liberal conceptions of the Spanish traditionalism from the end of 19th century. The traditionalists opted for "organic unity" in opposition to both individualistic liberalism and particular class conflicts. The organic conception understood this way was in contradiction to the multiparty system.

Franco, like many other dictators, did not reject the word "democracy". On several occasions he repeated: "We do not deny democracy; we want a real and true democracy."[4] He was convinced that his *Movimiento Nacional* and organic democracy gave more natural, just and effective solutions than did communism and liberalism. Some reformers of Francoism were more open on questions of democracy, but it was first of all the democratic opposition to the Franco regime that highly praised the value of democracy. In Spain, however, it was very difficult to distinguish between the liberal democratic opposition to the regime and some liberal representatives of the regime during the last ten years of Franco's life (1965-1975). In Francoist Spain a pluralism of political tendencies was seen not only within the regime's elite, but also in legislative debates of the parliament (*Cortes*), in everyday press and even in the official publications of the *Movimiento* and the government institutions. In Spain, as in Poland under late communism, some institutions created by the regime served as channels of free expression taking advantage of the regime's limited pluralism and limited tolerance. In Spain it was clearly seen after the liberalization of press law, thanks to which there could appear legal publications and debates on constitutionalism, political associations, pluralism within the *Movimiento*, on the idea of democracy and even on the "nationalization" (i.e. legalization) of the opposition.

The Spanish post-fascist organization *Movimiento Nacional* was essentially transformed and became in time isolated within the Franco regime and the society. It had to share power in the limited pluralism of Francoism: the Falange, the army, the Church and conservative monarchists. And it should do so in conditions of increasing complexity of society, namely in the growing political pluralism outside the authoritarian regime. The Franco system of "organic democracy" allowed limited pluralism and various liberalizations, but without legalization of political parties. The exclusion of political parties by the regime that officially permitted only the so-called "legitimate contrast of opinions" led to numerous contradictions within the system.

In the late 1960s and at the beginning of 1970s an interesting discussion on political associations in Spain took place. In 1969 the Minister Secretary-General of the *Movimiento Nacional,* José Solis Ruiz, presented a Statute of Associations that permitted the creation of political associations with no electoral rights that would "formulate and contrast legitimate opinion". This project of "limited pluralism" of Francoist factions or families was totally rejected by the democratic opposition, but even some hard-liners of the regime found it dangerous, so it was postponed. But more or less ambiguous postulates of pluralism began to be formulated by Spanish intellectuals and by the new Spanish press after the abolishment of preventive censorship in 1966. Even some publications of the *Movimiento* and Catholic press called for pluralism and democratization of Spanish life.

In the last years of Francoism its political class was divided into liberal, reformist *aperturistas* or *evolucionistas* and rigid *immobilistas* or *involucionistas*, who wanted to continue the regime without any fundamental change. The first accepted many ideas of the democratic opposition, although sometimes in a restricted or rhetorical form. In 1971 even Ramón Serrano Suñer, one of the founders of the Francoist state, acknowledged the need for a controlled return to a party system. Also Rafael Calvo Serer, the main ideologist of Catholic integrism spoke for a democratic monarchy in Spain. He differentiated between an opposition within the regime and one that was against the regime.

The tendency towards liberalization of the regime and its institutions, towards "political development" and further participation of citizens in political life was present in the majority of publications. Among others the famous monarchist José María Areilza supported a gradual evolution of the Spanish regime towards democracy. Also the Catholic Church moved from supporting the dictatorship to favoring political pluralism.

After Franco's death in 1975 the government of Carlos Arias Navarro wanted to proceed with the gradual opening up of the dictatorship and returned to the idea of political associations (the term "party" officially was still taboo). At that time there no longer existed an alternative of immobilism or reformism, but only an alternative of deep reform or "democratic break" (*ruptura democratica*) with the regime. Eventually the intermediary procedure of "negotiated break" (*ruptura pactada*) was chosen in order to introduce parliamentary democracy.

It is interesting to see that the Francoist regime, especially in its final phase, made great efforts in order to add a democratic mask to its original authoritarianism. The limited pluralism and pseudo-democratic tendencies contributed, however, to the fact that the dictatorship has been transformed into democracy largely by the former Francoists, although the pressure of the democratic opposition also should be taken into account.

›t interesting is the case of the last Secretary General of the *Mov-* Adolfo Suárez, who succeeded Arias Navarro as Prime Minister and made the greatest contribution to the peaceful evolution and transition from authoritarian dictatorship to modern parliamentary democracy. After a series of negotiations and compromises with opposite political forces he submitted to the nation a project of constitutional reform that lead to the establishment of democracy in Spain with the help of Francoist institutions. Its main event was the celebration of general elections on June 15, 1977. In September 1977 the Suárez government legalized the formation of independent unions and business associations which after the dissolution of the *Movimiento* and legalization of parties was considered to be the last step to the creation of a pluralist political system.

Adolfo Suárez, a clever heir of the Francoist authoritarianism and leader of the victorious and eclectic Union of Democratic Center, declared even before the general elections that it was possible for Spain to have a European Social Democracy with important elements of nationalist and conservative sentiments.

The Spanish transition from authoritarianism to pluralist democracy ended with success. This process was observed with attention in Poland both by the communist authorities and semi-official opposition. The Spanish case was recalled a dozen or so years later as a good model for Poland to follow.

The democratic transformation of Spain was not a result of a revolutionary break with the past, nor was it a voluntary self-liquidation of the dictatorship. The transformation was the sum of the crisis and evolution of Francoism, of strong and self-limiting pressure of the democratic opposition, of a series of negotiated pacts, and of an agreement that warranted the rights of the opposition and of the regime forces. Very important were the negotiations not only between the Suárez government and the democratic opposition, but also between the government, military forces and the rightist antidemocratic opposition. Very important also was the respect shown for the Francoist legality and for the institution of monarchy in the process of democratic transformation.

Generational and socio-economic changes that have taken place in the Spanish society since the end of the civil war till the death of Franco were also important for the Spanish transition to democracy.

The trend towards democracy understood in various ways -- towards liberty, consensus, dialogue, agreement, reconciliation and overcoming the historical division into "two Spains" -- was almost generally accepted during the transformation after the Franco death. It was uninterruptedly present in all phases of continuation, reform and democratic breakthrough.

José María Maravall, the eminent sociologist and specialist in social problems of democracy, has paid attention to the fact that in Spain there was a close link between leftist ideas and a support for democracy, stemming from Spanish circumstances. A different situation existed in the majority of Western countries, where the right unequivocally accepted democracy, while in Spain the struggle for democracy implied a sharp division into left and right.[5]

The most painful thing for the democratic opposition was the need to preserve in the new political system the old means of repression (the army, police, security forces) and of the bureaucratic administration which were erected as a result of the Francoist victory in the civil war. It engendered some conflicts and discontent in the Spanish civil society that was formed in the struggle against these forces.[6]

THE PROCESS OF DEMOCRATIC CONSOLIDATION

After the full victory of Socialists in the parliamentary elections of October 1982, there began the process or a stage of democratic consolidation of the young Spanish democracy. This survived the dangers caused by the fragmentarization of political parties, regional separatism, economic crisis, the leftist terrorism and military plots.

The victorious socialists from the PSOE took energetic action in order to restructure the Spanish economy, and to develop privatization and regional economic autonomy. As a result there was an increase in wages, and the economic situation of a significant part of the population touched by the crisis has improved. There appeared also a social consent for a more sharp division of the society into a rich middle class and a poor social strata awaiting a social minimum from the state. The new generation of Spaniards that came to power and took the dominant position in politics, culture and the economy tended towards modernization of the country according to Western patterns and to a greater economic efficiency.

Initially Spanish society was shocked by the excessive material polarization of the citizens as a result of the actions of the Felipe González government, which led for a moment to the loss of his popularity and to less participation in political life. Soon, however, new organizations and associations appeared that have collaborated with local authorities in solving many problems.

The Spain governed by the Socialists or Social-Liberals overcame the economic backwardness (a process which had began, one has to acknowledge, in the early 1960s), created a new and more effective industry, and considerably reduced the state sector after the Francoist etatism. There was a considerable increase in labor productivity and national income.

The precipitated modernization caused also an increase of unemployment, a marginalization of a part of Spanish society and an enlargement of the illegal, untaxed economy that did not guarantee worker security.

The entrance of Spain into the European Economic Community strengthened the condition of Spanish democracy and economy. The government took advantage of this entrance in order to modernize the industrial base, to stimulate technological innovation and to build modern transport and telecommunication infrastructure. Forcing the country to restructure its traditional institutions was not an easy and painless process, but its general balance is undoubtedly positive. Many researchers[7] regard 1985 as a decisive year in the political and economic transformation of Spain. Also the Spanish entrance to NATO made possible democratic reorganization and control of the armed forces, eliminating the danger of a military coup. In March 1986 Spanish citizens accepted in a referendum the pro-Atlantic and pro-American attitude of the Prime Minister Felipe González. The adhesion to the European Community (European Union) and to NATO strengthened pro-European and democratic structures and attitudes in Spain.

The socialist rule in Spain, especially in their first years proved to be very effective, contributing to the consolidation and legitimization of democracy in Spain.

During the transition to democracy in Spain there appeared over two hundred political parties and associations. The majority were so-called "taxi-parties", that is, whose members could enter into one taxi. After the parliamentary election of 1982 their number diminished considerably. The Spanish party system came close to a generally stabile two party system. Two main parties - the Socialist PSOE and the rightist conservative Popular Party (the former Popular Alliance) took advantage of the crisis in the centrist UCD and in the Communist Party of Spain. Besides, in 1983 over 40 parties decided to disappear.

The Socialist Party, thanks to its energetic leader Felipe González, underwent a deep evolution from 1976 when it defined itself at the Barcelona Congress as a Marxist and democratic party, but at its Congress in September 1979, the party gave up Marxism, limiting it to a method and to one of its historical sources. This provoked many controversies and ideological discussions within the party. The relations of Spanish socialists with the Western European Social Democracies, especially with the German SPD have been strengthened since that time.

The stabilization of the Spanish political scene was aided by the fact that since the first democratic elections in 1977 Spain had governments of only three political parties - UCD and later PSOE and *Partido Popular*. The socialists won in 1982, 1986, 1989, and in 1993. The last victory was not an absolute one and required a coalition with Catalan nationalists from the party *Convergencia i Unió*. They lost elections for the first time in March 1996 and regained power in 2004.

Democracy as the principal rule of the new politics has enjoyed the confidence of the Spaniards since the death of Franco and in time ceased to be questioned. Indeed a democratic mentality began to be shaped already at the end of Franco period, but some researchers[8] noted some remnants of authoritarianism in post-Franco Spain, in its public life, even in the socialist rule. It is often recalled that the traditional Spanish political culture - elitist and authoritarian - and many institutions of public life did not support democratic values; therefore democracy was not fully consolidated in the Iberian Peninsula in the 1980s. Quickly getting rid of all authoritarian remnants turned out to be impossible due to the force of the old Catholic tradition, based on the sacred values of a conservative hierarchy which was very important, especially in some provinces.

In spite of some obstacles, Spain has overcome isolationist tendencies, prejudices from the past, nationalist and cultural myths along with psychological complexes. After many historical failures this time, and probably forever, it has united with democracy, Europe and NATO. The authors of a fundamental research into Spanish democracy conclude: "The old advertising slogan, 'Spain is different', may still ring true with regard to the country's many unique and attractive cultural and arquitectural attributes. This exploration of democracy in modern Spain has revealed that, with regard to most aspects of political culture, core government institutions, decision-making processes, the dynamics of partisan competition, and the structure of public-policy outputs, Spain is no longer different. With the single exception of continuing violence and instability in the Basque country, it has taken its place alongside the other stable, consolidated democracies of Western Europe."[9]

THEORIES OF DEMOCRACY

Spain with Portugal have initiated "the third wave of democratization" (Samuel Huntington) in the present-day world. The Spanish process of rapid, evolutionary transformation of an authoritarian regime was very original, evoking much interest abroad, especially in Latin America and Eastern Europe.[10] Equally interesting, although less original (except for the works of Juan J. Linz) turned out to be the Spanish theoretical reflection on the idea of democracy, which accompanied the democratic changes, and the reflections found in the political and scholarly discourse of many actors of the Spanish political scene and in the works by many hispanists and social scientists.

The aspiration towards democracy and its theoretical justification was the principal aim of the Spanish intellectual opposition for many years under the Franco dictatorship. Professor Elías Díaz, for example, since the 1960s is defending democratic values, has struggled for liberty, tolerance, the state of law and ideological pluralism against philosophical and political dogmatism. He contributed significantly in his scholarly works to enlivening Spanish democratic and social-liberal tradition, forgotten and oppressed for many years by the official Francoist propaganda.

In the period when trade and tourist contacts of Spain with foreign countries increased, thereby overcoming isolationism and economic autarchy, the Western tourists brought to Spain also the idea of democracy, which at the moment of Franco's death turned out to be the most powerful political force. The absorbing interest was, of course, in parliamentary democracy, which at the beginning was imagined in a very vague way, with no concern for the role monarchy and other institutions can play. Spaniards associated democracy first of all with the freedom of speech and of political behavior, because mainly in these domains the existing restrictions were heavy.[11]

After Franco's death the Spanish press became a mirror of reality, a privileged place in which the new social and political discourse of democracy was expressed, and thereby co-created the political change. The new political discourse consisted first of all in rejecting "organic democracy". The new concept of democracy appeared in the context of the idea of liberty, equality, dialogue, tolerance, compromise and agreement. The question was how to hold a dialogue between the rulers and the ruled, between the masses and the elites, between the government and opposition, between the central government and local and regional authorities.[12]

Initially the term "democracy", especially in left-wing parties, was closely linked with a definite break (*ruptura*) with the Franco regime, considering it the only possible road leading to the creation of a new and fully democratic system. Democracy was universally accepted. Even Manuel Fraga Iribarne coming from the Francoist side defended the idea of democracy, but did so in the style of liberal authoritarianism searching for a strong leader. Also José María de Areilza suggested that the right-wing forces being a symbol of order and discipline should take the initiative in the process of democratic changes and economic and technological modernization of the country. The Popular Alliance as the main force of the right saw its political vocation in the spirit of a conservative reform and populism, far from any extremism.

The Union for Democratic Center (UCD) presented itself as a party of progressive and reformist Center synthesizing leftist elements of justice and the rightist heritage of patriotism. Uniting various political forces coming both from the *ancien régime* and from the democratic opposition, UCD emphasized in its program that effective functioning of democracy in Spain depends on the existence of a strong non-class party, clearly different from the authoritarian right and the Marxist left.

The most frequent concepts used in Spain during the transition to democracy were consensus (*consenso*) and mutual tolerance, also pluralism and diversity. This diversity has turned out to be possible in the situation of prevalent moderation of political attitudes and while keeping the public order.

The transition from authoritarianism to democracy was accompanied by changes in the usage of political language, which departed from the Francoist new-speak and from the Aesopian style of the semi-official opposition. These changes reflected, but also obfuscated, some social processes in the name of a mutual understanding and agreement.

There appeared various formulas of representative democracy, negotiated democracy, modern, state and party democracy. It was underlined that democracy in Spain could not be rid of qualifiers, since it was still feeble, timid, unconsolidated and consensual. The formulas of social, advanced and guarded democracy have also been advanced. In the first years after the election of 1977 the question was how to democratize the mass media, the educational system, local authorities, international relations, the judiciary system, the state apparatus and all of political life. Initially it was a real obsession, seen in abusing and in inserting of the term democracy and democratization in almost all topics and realms of human life.

The problems of the theory of democracy appeared quite often in the debates of the first democratically elected parliament, especially in the years 1977-1978 when projects of the new constitution were elaborated and discussed. Some authors paid attention to the strong position in the Spanish tradition of definitions of democracy that emphasized not so much civil liberties or the sovereignty of the people as the equality or "equalitarian situation."[13] The presence of such an understanding of democracy was seen also during the debates on the new Constitution, assuming that building new rules of democratic coexistence, and the liquidation of the aristocratic remnants dividing Spaniards were essential. The need to eliminate social marginalization and economic and cultural injustice was also underlined. Others accentuated in the definition of democracy the possibility of changing governments by general voting procedures in regular time intervals and unfettered civil liberties that should be expanded. Finally a compromise was reached, thanks to which the Spanish Constitution speaks at length on freedom, justice and equality.

It is equally important to know how democracy has been conceived, not only by political and intellectual elites, but also by ordinary citizens. In the Spanish case during the transformation at least two thirds of the citizens considered democracy to be the best system of government for their country and in the following years the number of people thinking this way considerably increased.[14]

Nowadays democracy in Spain has gained wide popularity and is conceived more or less in the same way by the elites and by the people. Six out of ten respondents define democracy in close connection with freedom and other liberties, while few associate democracy with the so-called "participative democracy" or "social democracy".

As far as theoretical considerations on democracy are concerned, the most important are works by the most famous Spanish sociologist Juan J. Linz, professor at Columbia and later Yale University in the United States. Spain and the problems of transition from undemocratic to democratic systems have become the main concern for Linz. He often appealed to the spirit of compromise and common sense that eventually prevailed in Spain in recent decades. Professor Linz elaborated a general theory of authoritarian regimes, differentiating them clearly from totalitarian and democratic systems. He paid much attention to the transition to democracy in Spain and in other countries in later years. In the mid 1970s there was no scholarly literature nor any theoretical studies on this topic. Linz is a distinguished pioneer in this domain. He considered the mild transformation of the centralist authoritarian Spain into democracy as an unprecedented political innovation worthy of deep theoretical reflection. He underlined that democratic leaders should hold in high esteem democratic institutions, even above their own goals. The Spanish sociologist was well aware that political democracy does not always ensure the existence of a democratic and egalitarian society with equal opportunities in individual life and in the mobilization of electorate. But it ensures at least freedom and gradual progress towards democratic society, while the acceptance of non-democratic methods, instead of an idealized revolutionary breakthrough, leads to dangerous government crises and to autocratic rule.[15] Linz says that the leaders of new democracies should more effectively persuade the people about the value of conquered liberties, although freedom from arbitrary rule and the possibility of a peaceful change of government is not for everybody the greatest political achievement.[16]

According to Linz, democracy is a political system of governance based upon full liberty of formulation and public articulation of political alternatives in a society characterized by freedom of speech and other fundamental human rights allowing free competition between political leaders.[17] These leaders may obtain the possibility of forming governments only as a result of free, honest and regular elections. Democracy always implies a government *pro tempore* and those who lose elections may regain them in a few years. Linz's procedual and formalist definition of democracy puts much stress on the possibility of holding free and competitive elections to decisive structures of power. He deliberately excludes all rhetorical concepts of people's democracy, plebiscitary or participative democracy that limit the constitutional and representative authority. He deliberatively also excludes all unclear references to social structures and social-economic relations. He rejects definitions of democracy that are excessively burdened with economic declarations and with democratic idealism. Linz is interested rather in empirical clarity than in normative and ideological speculation in his theory and definition of democracy. His minimalist criterion for democracy and his operational definition of democracy turned out to be helpful in understanding the systemic changes in politics in recent decades.

Linz has written much also on the particular forms that democracy can acquire at the end of 20th century and the entrance into the 21st, opting rather for parliamentary democracy than for presidential systems.
His scientific reflection on the fate of democracy in Spain and in the modern world is a valuable and enduring achievement of the social sciences. Also some other, less significant Spanish authors have made remarkable judgements on the value of democracy as a supreme political principle.

Manuel Aragón, considering legal questions and constitutional doubts linked with the idea of democracy, has noticed that the most important theoretical truth about democracy is probably that it has always to be conceived as a problem, as something unfinished and far from absolute. Should democracy cease to be a problem in a country it would probably mean, Aragón continues, the end of democracy.[18]

Also Millet y Bel underlines that democracy is not unchangeable, given once and for all, but it can be improved and perfected.[19] In a similar way Ortega Campos is convinced that democratic forms of coexistence, co-partnership and control of the three powers (legislative, executive and judiciary) can be perfected. This author has written that democracy does not consist only in the formal act of electing, which is only a small part of democracy. The preferential act of choosing may refer to ideologies, but not to fundamental ideas and rules of human life, where long-lasting educational action is necessary. According to Ortega Campos, democracy is not only a doctrine promoting broad participation in political activities, but also an attitude, disposition or frame of mind characteristic of some types of personality.[20]

In Spain the so-called model of *consocional* democracy is popular; it was elaborated by Lijphart in reference to such fragmented societies as Holland, Belgium and Switzerland, but its elements were applied to the analysis of the relatively young democracy in Spain, where centrifugal tendencies were strong, but the political elites succeeded in preserving political balance and collaboration of particular segments and tendencies in the Spanish State, thanks to the integrative style of policy making.[21]

An even greater number of Spanish authors defend democracy as an end in itself, and not only a means of achieving other and supposedly higher aims. According to Ramón Cotarelo, democracy is a system of procedual norms or the whole of the rules of political game. This author understands by democracy a free acceptance of the decisions of the majority, while preserving due respect for the rights of the minority. He maintains that other conceptions of democracy (material, real or participatory) fall into contradiction rejecting formal democracy.[22]

Many interesting reflections on democracy and liberalism can be found in books and papers by the famous philosopher Julián Marías, from the school of Ortega y Gasset. Marías is deeply interested in permanently rooting democracy in Spain, since for a long time it has been the only form of political legitimization in the West.[23] According to Marías, liberalism is an absolute precondition of democracy, the condition ensuring its unfalsified functioning. Democracy has gained great prestige in the present-day world and almost no one dares say publicly that he or she is not a democrat, although many people feel alien to it. According to the Spanish philosopher, democracy and liberalism can and should go hand in hand, but they are totally different and independent one from another. Without liberalism democracy has an oppressive character, while liberalism without democracy is defenseless and short-lived. Marías wanted to make popular in society the conviction that democracy without liberalism becomes an empty word. Liberalism ensures freedom and socially organizes of liberties. Ttherefore, according to Marías, it was good that liberalization and the rise of independent public opinion were earlier in time than the process of democratization in Spain after Franco's death.

Marías very early expressed his wish that Spaniards be drawn by a strong, vital aspiration for democracy.[24] Democracy, in his words, does not give ready solutions; it is, however, the only way of posing political problems which are not always able to be solved. In his words democracy is something excellent; excluding citizens' passivity and marginality, it is the only political system that possesses full legitimization.[25]

Many observers of the Spanish political scene have noticed that a dozen or so years after initiating the democratic breakthrough in Spain other important ideological changes have taken place including some in conceiving the theory of democracy and politics in general. Ingenuous and radical ideals of the nascent Spanish democracy have given way to a more realistic and mature attitude towards democracy in a mass society. The transition to democracy implied in time a transition from utopia to sober reality, a change in the specific political culture born in the years of anti-Francoist struggle. Generally speaking, the transition was from the classic theory of democracy to democracy conceived as a competition between elites over political leadership took place.

In the mid 1970s Spanish political circles and especially the relatively strong Left at that time favored a model of democracy that achieves political decisions through public discussion without much attention to an appropriate choice of individuals who would guide and enforce the decisions. The classic model had profound ethical foundations expressed in the conviction that human dignity and the development of the individual depend on real possibilities of participation in decisions having impact on personal life. The classical theory of democracy presupposed a high level of rationality and citizens' political participation, minimalizing the importance of elites and of political leadership. Spain in a relatively brief time passed an accelerated ideological and institutional evolution from "the people`s will" to the elitarian will of the professional politician.[26] The citizens' role has been reduced to the duty of voting by people who do not participate directly in making decisions, but only vote in general elections. In this conception ethics and politics are separate, morality withdraws to the private sphere and politics is limited to the rules of the game.[27]

The topic of reflections for José María Maravall, a famous professor of sociology and politician, who was minister of education in 1982-1989 years, were the numerous advantages of democracy. He opposed those who hold that market reforms could be carried out more effectively under authoritarian regimes (the case of East Asiatic countries). According to the Spanish sociologist, market reforms and economic increase are more favored by an democratic, not authoritarian, political context; political pluralism gives better information, which can be used in taking optimal decisions. Besides, free press and opposition serve as a system of early monitoring and warn against errors and abuses. Democratic governments turn out to be more stabile in times of economic crisis and provide necessary legitimization of power in periods of arduous reforms suffered by society.[28]

The case of Spain has become a good point of departure for many social and political scientists, and especially for theoreticians and analysts of the transition to democracy. They search for general and particular regularities in the Spanish events from the 1970s, in the events that have led to an official recognition of political pluralism by the authoritarian regime. Analysis of the Spanish road to democracy still inspires many researchers, supplies new facts, ideas and interpretations possibilities for similar historic processes.[29]

Liberalism, especially Popper's political philosophy and closely related to it the so-called "Open Social Democracy" or social-liberalism and social democracy have become the main frame of reference for reflection about democracy in the present-day Spain.[30] This is connected with the rejection of ideals of the welfare state and with the defeat of all projects of real socialism or eurocommunism. A victory has been attained by the elitist theory of democracy which conceives it as a competitive electoral mechanism of ruling elites, being in the service of social stability.

PROBLEMS OF CIVIL SOCIETY

Alexis de Tocqueville acknowledged the capability to associate and its improvement as a fundamental ability making possible the progress of democracy in a given country.

The dominant tradition in Spain, as opposed to Britain and the United States, for example, was characterized by the lack of social bonds between local communities. In the Anglo-Saxon countries a strong civil society integrated by the market was developed, while Spain with its despotic central authorities and provincial "caciques" for centuries has been an example of semi-Asiatic formation, similar to that of Russia. In both cases there was no civil society, but only abnormalities far from the European patterns of modernity, with strong social divisions and conflicts.[31]

The lack of local self-governments, of democratic structures proceeding from the ranks and especially of the middle classes, and of the Enlightenment spirit strengthened the bureaucratic role of central state power. In point of fact, the state was equally as feeble as society, since it could not gain independence from the dominant position of the authoritarian church and the army. These weaknesses of the Spanish state organism led to the state not attaining social prestige, and being being unable to impose its political will and modernize the country.[32]

The lack of identification with the state and even a feeling of alienation was a cause of the conflict and contrast, often described and well-known also from the recent history of Poland, between the real and official Spain.

In the 1940s and 50s it was strictly forbidden to organize any forms of independent associations. In spite of brutal repression, people already in the 1950s began to form such associations and "founded sui generis political organizations and discovered original strategies for extending the boundaries of civil society."[33] It is said that the clear emergence of civil society in Spain took place in the period of crisis of the authoritarian state, during the gradual transition to democracy. This was seen in the years preceding Franco's death, when various opinions and organizations appeared, when the hidden pluralism of the Spanish society became evident. During the anti-Franco struggle and in the initial stage of the transition to democracy, the Spanish democratic opposition unlike the Polish democratic opposition did not use the term civil society, which was not fashionable in the 1960s and at the beginning of the 1970s. One of the first authors who began to write on civil society in the late 1970s was the famous sociologist Víctor Pérez Díaz[34]. It was still the period of great popularity of Marxism in Spain and the book by Pérez Díaz, in the subtitle of which the term civil society appeared, referred in great part to Marx's political theory and its alternatives. Pérez Díaz manifested a liberal and conservative attitude and the writings of Marx were only his point of departure in order to shape his own, quite different political views.

In his famous book on the return of civil society in the post-Franco Spain[35] Pérez Díaz defined this type of society as a heterogenous set of social actors and of social, economic and cultural institutions linked in a complicated way to the state and its political class. The return of civil society was to be a neo-liberal response of the Spanish society to great challenges involved in the real transition to democracy. The quality of liberal democracy in Spain, economic increase, culture and social integration were to follow from the force of this response. Civil society in this view is an expression of the degree of social responsibility, necessary for the realization of the Western system of individual liberties based upon the free market.

Pérez Díaz interprets the 1970s and 1980s as a period of relative predominance of the sphere of civil society over the state. His views were criticized by leftist intellectuals in Spain. They noticed that his opposing of political mechanisms of power to non-political mechanisms of the market does not correspond to the reality of late capitalism, in which, unlike in early liberal capitalism, there no longer exists a clear division between the public sphere and the market.

The problems of civil society were also undertaken by the well-known sociologist Salvador Giner. Initially he paid attention to the desintegration processes and even agony of civil society due to the increase of bureaucracy and of various corporations in capitalism.[36] Collective interests that are formally organized acquired decisive importance. These highly organized interests along with such traditional corporations as banks, the Catholic Church or the army have a privileged place in the state and society. Corporations function often as intermediary in situations of class conflict.

In later works Giner analyzed in a detailed way the changes that have taken place within civil and mass society, and considered the principle of citizenship, democracy and governability in particular countries and in a global perspective.[37] This reflection on society, stretching between corporative reality and citizenship principles, contributed new ideas on the role of democracy and liberty in post-modern civilization.

The term "civil society" began to be broadly used in Spain in the 1980s thanks to Pérez Diaz, and Giner among others. The famous philosopher José Luis Aranguren at a special conference dedicated to the relations between civil society and the state declared that the fashionable word 'civil society' of Anglo-Saxon origin seems to be useful inasmuch as it favors the civic order rather than political, military or ecclesiastical class or *nomenklatura*. It does not embrace, however, those who do not participate in building neo-capitalism (the unemployed or marginalized, ethnic minorities and alternative social movements).[38]

The idea of civil society became popular in Spain in the 1980s in the situation of abrupt decrease of interest in Marxism after equally abrupt increase of its significance in the 1970s. After the "death" of Marxism and other utopias there appeared, along with ecological movements and postmodernism, new ideological tendencies that emphasize the importance of intimate privacy, everyday life, free market and civil society.

Among the Spanish discussants there was no agreement on the fundamental question: are we witnessing a total return of civil society in the situation of highly diminished state interventionism or on the contrary, in spite of the crisis of the welfare state is the realm of state power still increasing while civil society is weakening. How to create a new civil society and deepen the ethical values and quality of democracy have been pregnant topics for consideration.

Some order and optimism was brought to the discussion by Juan Linz in his paper on various forms of state and civil society and on the various relations that can exist between them. According to Linz, a strong state does not imply a feeble civil society and vice versa: strong, active and autonomous civil society can coexist along with an efficient state with high authority. The Spanish sociologist from Yale has also proven that the "corporative egoism" in civil society need not necessarily be negative since corporatist interests constitute a form of defense against state authoritarianism.[39]

The voices of those like Linz were a good counterpart to numerous simplified views expressed in the Spanish press that produced confusion in excessive eulogizing the benign, "spontaneous" and rational civil society, and exaggeratedly exposed excesses of state interventionism. Luis González Seara emphasized that the main task for Spain is not to weaken either the state or society, but the burning need is to revive and modernize society in order to set up an efficient state that could face serious problems.[40]

International comparative research has shown an underdevelopment both of the Spanish state and of voluntary associations that are intermediary between the state and civil society. The shortage of associations and general underorganization of the Spanish society testified not to a lack of social activeness, but only to the predominance of direct and family links.[41]

An important question in Spain is still a search on the border of utopia for a new civil society, a broadening of civic participation and co-partnership if not on the state level, at least in local communities.

Romano Garcia has noted that in spite of the bankruptcy of all utopian attempts to make a new world, the capitalist market does not satisfy fully and the search for utopia is still valid. One should try in a Socratic way to introduce values into social and political life. According to him, society without the Left and without a bit of utopia would mean a triumph of contradictions and of irrationality.[42] Similarly Ramón Cotarelo sees in utopia a motive power, helpful in tending towards further decentralization of power, broadening local self-governments and establishing new relations between work and leisure.[43]

The search for a new cultural identity of Spain under rapidly changing circumstances and the broadening of new citizens' initiatives is still an important theoretical challenge for Spanish intellectuals as we proceed into the 21st century.

THE CRISIS AND RENOVATION OF SOCIAL DEMOCRACY

After the parliamentary elections of 1977 the Spanish Socialist Workers' Party (PSOE) became the main force in opposition with real chances of conquering power in the not very distant future. This situation forced the party to change its policy. First, some actions were undertaken in order to strengthen the organization of Spanish socialists and to unite their various groups. Second, some efforts were made in order to enlarge the Socialist Party's electorate. This aim was to be achieved by gradual getting rid of radical slogans coming from its underground activities period under late Francoism. Felipe González succeeded during the 28th Congress of the party in 1979 to give up its Marxist character which caused for a time crisis within the party since many activists defended Marxist ideology.

During the next party congress in 1981 a great deradicalization was achieved, eliminating from its program almost all postulates of the nationalization of private property. Instead of strictly economic postulates, stress was laid on broadening democracy in industry, on social control and on the public sector. The resolution adopted during the 29th congress presented as a fundamental aim of the party the creation of the Socialist government as a result of elections and obtaining a parliamentary majority. In order to do so, a broad social block embracing a new majority on the left and center was necessary. The socialists succeeded in eliminating the considerable influence of communists and to arrive at a compromise with numerous forces from outside the leftist minority. So in the elections of October 28, 1982, they won a brilliant success which made possible their long-lasting rule in Spain with no need to share power with others.

The new socialist government was faced with great tasks: struggle against the ETA terrorism, elimination of military conspiracy and modernization of the army, and restructuring agriculture and the obsolete industry. Initially the PSOE won an enormous note of confidence and enjoyed an almost general support in preparing a real change (*cambio*), though difficult but necessary reforms that could not be carried out by the Democratic Center Union. Many intellectuals, till then far from the Socialist Party, decided to support its program. Some quite early noted that PSOE was undergoing an evolution towards a typically Western Social Democratic Party, although the party leadership did not for a long time acknowledge its abandonment of socialist dreams.

Socialists achieved undoubted success in economic modernization of the country and in uniting Spain with European and Atlantic structures. But since the late 1980s there have appeared numerous defects in the economy, political behavior and especially the conception of democracy that the Socialists presented. After 1982 PSOE completely dominated the Spanish political scene and began to shape a new political discourse and new political culture, to some extent favoring an "americanization" of Spanish politics. They did not bother to fulfill electoral promises, neglected the value of political programs treated as an empty political rhetoric. They soon gave up the majority of slogans from electoral campaign in 1982 and yet were not punished in several subsequent elections.[44]

Some authors traced the origin of Socialist "flexibility" in the tactics of searching for consensus during the transition to democracy and even in the Francoist tradition, others traced it to the lack of experience or pure opportunism. For many observers the PSOE transformed itself into a powerful voting machine and into an agency of political engagement for its numerous clients.

One of the first authors who attended to the danger for democracy and freedom under the socialist rule was the well-known philosopher Julián Marías. Indeed, the Spanish philosopher acknowledged that it was not democracy that was endangered but its liberal inspiration without which democracy loses its vitality and may degenerate into a new system of oppression.[45] Marías wanted to sensitize his compatriots to the cause of freedom which should be continually guarded and stimulated. In Spain of the 1980s, he added, freedom is still respected, but from 1981 it lacks new inspiring stimuli, since the elections of 1982 civil liberties are endangered by the increasing state interventionism. According to Marías the socialist rule intervenes in almost all spheres of Spanish society, making its accelerating its transformation. It engages economy, education, the system of justice, industry, information policy and even private life. Such a situation leads to diminishing freedom which touches the overwhelming majority of the population. According to Marías, the state authorities intervene too often, transform existing structures too deeply than temporary voting limits permit it, and restrict at the same time possibilities of free citizens activity.

Marías insisted that the important political changes which took place in Spain in 1975/1976 which should not be obfuscated by the continuous propaganda of *cambio* (the change) as happened in 1982.

Another author, coming from the broken UCD, saw a danger for Spanish democracy in the fact that one of its main parties, the ruling PSOE tends towards aims not quite compatible with the Constitution and is able legally alter it into another one, quite different from that in force. Otero Novas maintains that Spanish democracy may perish even without constitutional amendments, if the PSOE still adheres to its collectivist claims and hegemonic control of the social, political and economic power.[46] It may lead to a situation in which the possibilities of replacing a government will disappear. Formally democratic constitution would then defend an undemocratic reality in which the opposition would turn into a façade legitimizing the system of rule.

In the 1990s appeared many publications analyzing the shortcomings of Felipe González' power in Spain as well as a deepening crisis of his Social Democratic rule. Their foundation underlined in a real, but sometimes in a sham and demagogical care for further development of democracy, freedom and the rule of law in Spain.

Seeing signs of democratic crisis in Spain authors who described it generally did not name any sharp warnings. Two authors of an interesting book on this topic strongly marked that no coup d'etat or return to dictatorship is any longer possible. Sinova and Tusell held that the functioning of democracy in Spain does not respond to the previous hopes and to possibilities it usually offers.[47] In their view, democracy is endangered by the hegemony of one political class and by particular features of the ruling party. This "sequestered" democracy functions without critique and under rigid laws which deprive it of flexibility and spontaneity.

Sinova and Tusell pointed to the need for a regeneration of Spanish democracy, and even of a second transition to democracy. This motif soon entered the political discourse of Popular Party opposition leaders.[48]

Starting From 1989 the famous sociologist Amando de Miguel and other critics of Socialists began to nickname their rule "the regime" (*el Régimen*), in much the same way as Francoism was addressed. During the electoral campaign of 1986 the term *felipismo*, analogous to *franquismo*, was coined to name Felipe González' system of rule. This term became popular in the 1990s designating various tendencies and families supporting González.

Many authors maintained that *felipismo* was the embodiment of a style of policy making that favors corrupt behavior. The conception of political power realized by the Spanish socialists tended to limit or control executive authority by other powers and civil society.[49]

Also Angel Cristóbal Montes paid attention to negative aspects of Socialist rule and to the appearance of elements of a personality cult of Felipe González. Spain has always been un lucky when it comes to an harmonious democracy. In recurring periods of democracy and unrestricted political life there soon reappear undemocratic tendencies towards *caciquismo* and clientelism rooted in the traditional political culture of Spaniards. He also reflected upon an interesting phenomenon: the PSOE wins elections, although it does not put its program into practice; this results in many failures and its leaders yield to or tolerate widespread corruption. Montes perceived numerous faults and deformations of Spanish democracy, but underlined that bad democracy is always better than good dictatorship.[50]

After the democratic enthusiasm and excessive optimism of the first years following Franco's death, a typically Spanish *abulia*, indifference and fatalistic glance at public affairs seems to have returned. The socialist party conformed perfectly to that average social mentality and to the lack of public opinion, which helped to prolong its rule in almost a Mexican way, Montes stated with certain exaggeration. He sees the defects of Spanish democracy as deriving from the fact that democracy in Spain has been projected, introduced and enjoyed mainly by the political class of the *ancien régime.* Such a situation was favored by the dominant will of reconciliation, avoiding confrontation and forgetting all horrors of the civil war. Montes expressed conviction that his modern, liberal and progressive conservatism would triumph soon in Spain.

Even more acute charges against the "silent dictatorship" of the socialists and against "totalitarian mechanisms" hidden in the Spanish democracy were formulated by Federico Jiménez Losantos who doubted the democratic character of a regime in which all power is dominated by one political party and held without parliamentary dialogue and judicial control.[51]

A deep crisis of Social Democracy and of its Spanish version of *felipismo* or *socialfelipismo*, related to the Iberian tradition of *caudillismo*,[52] was confirmed also by authors from the Left. Ignacio Sotelo, for example, noticed that when socialists in Spain came to power in Europe their ideas began to lose popularity,[53] and socialists rapidly started to turn right. Sotelo asked why a politics that broke with all ideals of the Left should still be called socialist. However, the fact that socialists threw off the ideological ballast of the past helped them enter into dialogue with the present time, which was more difficult for the conservative Spanish right. For that reason for a long time the conservatives were not an alternative to the socialists. According to Carrascal, Spain passed from authoritarianism to socialism, another form of paternalism. Not having experienced modern conservatism, it stuck for many years in the ambiguities of the left and *felipismo.*

Sotelo defined *felipismo* as a form of socialism that has nothing to do with socialism, but is characterized by the lack of principles, pragmatism, opportunism, personalization of Felipe González' *carisma*, great ability to conform to changing circumstances and of trimming between opposed interests.

In the mid 1990s the socialist rule in Spain was continually shaken by numerous political scandals, crises and common corruption. The political crisis touched also the sphere of morality and citizen consciousness. It was accompanied by economic recession and high unemployment. The socialists lost much prestige in society, as well as the support of Catalan nationalists in parliament. All efforts to renew the bureaucratized party failed, so socialists lost the parliamentary elections of March 3, 1996.

Great corruption in Spain ruled by Socialists in the mid 1990s and the loss of support by Catalan nationalists were a cause of parliamentary election in March 3, 1996, this time won the conservative opposition led by José María Aznar. The victory, however, was not great enough to form a government without support of regional parties. The Socialists were defeated, but preserved much strength and influence on their traditional electorate.

The March election was important for the progress of democracy in Spain, since the victory of opposition did not entail the decomposition of the party hitherto in power, as in 1982. High participation and the lack of any incidents during the elections were a proof of the consolidation of liberal democracy in Spain, of the real possibility of a change of rule through voting procedures. For the first time since 1939 the prime minister in Spain was recalled in fact by voters and not by a Caudillo, the King or his own will. Aznar could hold a limited power, but the voice of the rigid and responsible opposition and of the mature civil society was taken into account. The much discussed and exaggerated danger of the "institutionalization" of PSOE after the example of the Mexican PRI happily had been avoided.

The eight year long conservative rule (1996-2004) was a great economic success. During Aznar's rule Spain achieved an economic boom, even greater than during socialist the rule in the 1990s. Many adherents of neo-liberalism, of privatization and of civil society ("more market, less state") were found in the ruling *Partido Popular*. Victor Pérez Díaz, the above quoted sociologist, stressed the importance of liberal-conservative Spain in the construction of new liberties and of a new Europe (conceived as its American version) and defined as a civil superpower. The defeated left propagated a catchword of republicanism with a new rhetoric of emancipation, civic virtues and the principle of citizenship directed not against the constitutional monarchy, but against the triumphant liberal-conservative tendency.

The democratic Spanish State has affirmed decentralization, the autonomy of provinces and nationalities, and avoided all remnants of Franco's centralist nationalism. But the Franco conception of nation was not replaced with a new one. As a result in Spain there is a lot of the Spanish State, but very little of the Spanish nation. No common political project unites all citizens and nationalities. The Spanish democratic Constitution of 1978 is being questioned by Basques and other nationalities. Peripheral nationalisms have declared a war against the institutions of the Spanish State and according to the Basque premier political sovereignty cannot be stopped. It is difficult to foresee the future. However, the road to the real independence is quite distant. In the influential newspaper *El País* the following opinion recently has been expressed: "Today in Spain horrible ghosts have reawakened that had plunged her into the war of 1936". In recent years there have arisen serious doubts whether the Spanish Constitutional Monarchy based only on the prestige of Juan Carlos I, can in the long run preserve the unity of Spain ("a country without monarchists") as a community in diversity.[54]

In the parliamentary election of March 2004 Spanish citizens refused further support for the conservative *Partido Popular*. Its pro-American attitude, its information policy (concealing the real authors of the terrorist attempts in Madrid several days before the polls) and general style of governing resulted in an unexpected defeat. It was interpreted as a reawakening of civil society in Spain.[55] Aznar sent troops to Iraq against the will of the overwhelming majority of citizens of his country. The Spaniards considered illegitimate the war against terrorism unauthorized by the United Nations. It was an important message for the whole world.[56] As a result a young socialist José Luís Rodríguez Zapatero, who defends a conception of a civic socialism and republicanism, has become a new premier of the government, the fifth chief of the Spanish democratic government. The conservative and post-Francoist forces have shown disappointment with the decision of "an accidental majority"[57] of citizens and with the program of "secular fundamentalism". It is forgotten, however, that in 2002-2003 before the election and before the Islamic attack on Madrid trains, there took place in Spain an intense civic mobilization and self-organization, unconventional protests of the people, altruistic associations, non-governmental organizations, and especially of the youth against government policy in various areas. They were demanding a dialogue between the conservative government and the new civil society, with citizens claiming participation in public life. It was argued that the citizen cannot be a commodity of the ruling class or only voting the class once every four years. In this view politics should be situated in the center of civic activities.[58]

Under the slogan of a new return to Europe socialists achieved once again their success in the election to the European parliament (June 2004). It is a testimony of great stability of the "crowned" democracy and of the political society in Spain 30 years after Franco's death (Poland during only 15 years of democracy had twice that number of prime ministers).

The Spanish PSOE refers now to the enlightenment and republican traditions, tries to build a multicultural society with "polyphonic" morals, makes difficult efforts to reform the statutes of Autonomic Communities, and to establish a dialogue with Islamic civilization. The socialist prime minister strives to transform Spain into a modern, emancipated and truly secular state and civil society. He has drawn his party out of the crisis and lethargy.[59]

NOTES

1 See Stanley G. Payne, *Spain's First Democracy. The Second Republic, 1931 – 1936* (Madison: University of Wisconsin Press, 1993).

2 For example Raul Morodo, *La transición política* (Madrid: Tecnos, 1993), 30.

3 A classical work is here Juan J. Linz, "An Authoritarian Regime: Spain", in E. Allardt, Y. Littunen, eds. *Cleavages, Ideologies and Party Systems* (Helsinki 1964). See also his study "From Falange to Movimiento-Organization. The Spanish Single Party and the Franco Regime, 1936-1968", in: S. Hungtington, C. Moore, *Authoritarian Politics in Modern Society: The Dynamics of One-Party Systems* (New York 1970), 155. More documentation can be found in my Polish books *O demokracji w Hiszpanii (1975-1995*) (Warsaw: IFiS Publishers 1997) and *Rozważania o społeczeństwie obywatelskim i inne studia z historii idei* (Warsaw: IFiS Publishers 2003).

4 *Pensamiento politico de Franco*, vol. II (Madrid 1975), 459-460.

5 J. M. Maravall, *La politica de la transición* (Madrid: Taurus, 1984), 120.

6 A. Guerra, "De la España invertebrada a la politica del cambio. El alcance histórico de la transición española", in: *La transición politica española* (Madrid: Fundación Banesto, 1992), 35-36.

7 See, for example, M. Redero San Roman, ed., *La transición a la democracia en España* (Madrid: Marcial Pons, 1994).

8 For example Howard J. Wiarda, *The Transition to Democracy in Spain and Portugal* (Washington, D.C., 1989).

9 R. Gunther, J.R. Montero, J. Botella, *Democracy in Modern Spain* (New Haven & London: Yale University Press, 2004), 396.

10 See J. Casanova, "Las enseñanzas de la transición democrática en España", in : M. Redero San Román ed., *La transición a la democracia en España* (Madrid: Marcial Pons, 1994), 15-54.

11 S.D. Eaton, *The Forces of Freedom in Spain, 1974-1979. A Personal Account* (Stanford 1981), 6, 11, 29.

12 A detailed analysis of the Spanish political discourse from the period of transition to democracy can be found in R. Del Aguila, R. Montoro, *El discurso politico de la transición española* (Madrid: CIS y Ed. Siglo XXI, 1984) and in J. de Santiago Guervós, *El lexico politico de la transición española* (Salamanca 1992), 144.

13 See M. Ferrol, "Consideraciones sobre la democracia", *Revista de Estudios Politicos*, Nov.-Dec. (1952), 56; M. Bonachela Mesas, "La definición de democracia y el concepto y contenido de la Constitución en algunos debates de las Cortes Constituyentes (1977-1978)", in; *Politica y Sociedad. Estudios en homenaje a F. Murillo Ferrol*, vol. II (Madrid 1987), 916-917.

14 J.R. Montero, "Revisiting Democratic Success and the Meaning of Democracy in Spain", in; R. Gunther, ed., *Essays in Honour of Juan J. Linz. Politics, Society, and Democracy; The Case of Spain* (Boulder: Westview Press, 1993), 145.

15 Juan J. Linz, *The Breakdown of Democratic Regimes. Crisis, Breakdown, and Reequilibration* (Baltimore and London 1991), 97.

16 Juan J. Linz, "Transitions to Democracy", *The Washington Quarterly* 13 (1990), 161.

17 Juan J. Linz, *Los problemas de las democracias y la diversidad de democracias. Discurso de investidura de doctor "honoris causa"* (Madrid: UAM, 1992), 14.

18 M. Aragon, *Constitución y democracia* (Madrid 1989), 137-138.

19 S. Millet y Bel, *Perfeccionamiento de la democracia* (Barcelona 1992), 22-23.

20 P. Ortega Campos, *Filosofia politica de la España immediata* (Madrid 1985), 109.

21 C. Hunneus, *La Unión del Centro Democratico y la transición a la democracia en España* (Madrid: CIS, 1985), 25.

22 R. Cotarelo, *En torno a la teoria de la democracia* (Madrid: CEC, 1990), 86.

23 J. Marias, *La España real. Crónicas de la transformación politica* (Barcelona 1983), 55.

24 J. Marias, *La devolución de España* (Madrid 1977), 131.

25 J. Marias, *La libertad en juego* (Madrid 1986), 125-126.

26 More on this problem can be found in J.M. Gonzalez Garcia, "Critica de la teoria económica de la democracia", in: *Teorias de la democracia* (Barcelona: Anthropos, 1988); see also A. Garcia Santesmases, "Nuevas categorias de entendimiento de la politica", *Anthropos. Suplementos* 28 (1991).

27 On the relations between ethics and politics a lot has been written in Spain, for example: V. Camps, *Etica, retórica, politica* (Madrid 1988); A. Domenech, *De la etica a la politica* (Barcelona 1989); E. Diaz, *Etica contra politica. Los intelectuales y el poder* (Madrid 1990).

28 J.M. Maravall, "The Myth of Authoritarian Advantage", *Journal of Democracy*, October 1990; see also his book *Economic Reforms in New Democracies* (Cambridge University Press 1993), written with Luz Carlos Bresser Pereira and Adam Przeworski.

29 See for instance: A. Domenech, "El juego de la transición democratica", *Arbor* 503-504; A. Fernandez-Miranda, *Lo que el Rey me ha pedido. Torcuato Fernandez-Miranda y la reforma politica* (Barcelona 1995); E. Diaz, La transición a la democracia (Claves ideológicas, 1976-1986),

(Madrid: EUDEMA, 1987); id., Las ideologias de (sobre) la transición, in his book *Etica contra politica*, 214-237; G. Morán, "Universalidad y particularidad del modelo español" in his book *El precio de la transición* (Barcelona 1992), 233-238.

30 See foe example A.J. Perona, *Entre el liberalismo y la socialdemocracia. Popper y la "socialdemocracia abierta"* (Barcelona 1993); V.D. Garcia Marzá, *Teoria de la democracia* (Valencia 1993); I. Sotelo, "Una reflexión histórica sobre la democracia", *in Sociedad civil o estado. Reflujo o retorno de la sociedad civil* (Madrid: Fundación Friedrich Ebert, 1988), 43-54; numerous references to Popper can be found in the former prime minister and leader of *Partido Popular*, Jose Maria Aznar, *Libertad y Solidaridad* (Barcelona 1991), 27, 31, 100).

31 See an interesting comparison of both countries by Angeles Huerta González, *La Europa periférica. Rusia y España ante el fenómeno de la modernidad* (Santiago de Compostela, 2004).

32 J.C. Rubinstein, Sociedad civil y participación ciudadana (Madrid 1994), 70-71; L. González Seara, La década del cambio (Barcelona 1987), 150-152.

33 J. Foweraker, *Making Democracy in Spain. Grass-roots Struggle in the South, 1955-1975* (Cambridge 1989), 2.

34 See his book *Estado, burocracia y sociedad civil* (Madrid 1978).

35 V. Pérez Díaz, *El retorno de la sociedad civil* (Madrid 1987); the version in English: *The Return of Civil Society* (Cambridge: Harvard University Press, 1993).

36 S. Giner, "La agonía de la sociedad civil", *Leviatán,* 5 (1981).

37 Id., "The Withering Away of Civil Society"?, *Praxis International* 3 (1985); *Ensayos civiles* (Barcelona 1987); X. Arbós, S. Giner, *Ciudadanía y democracia en la encrucijada mundial* (Madrid 1993); S. Giner, "Civil Society and its Future", in J.A. Hall, ed., *Civil Society. Theory, History, Comparison* (Cambridge 1995).

38 J.L. Aranguren, "Estado y sociedad civil", in *Sociedad civil o estado*, 17.

39 J. Linz, "Las diversas formas de estado y sociedad civil", in *Sociedad civil o estado*, 31-42.

40 L. González Seara, *La década del cambio* (Barcelona 1987), 153.

41 P. Mc Donough, S.H. Barnes, A. López Piña, "Authority and Association: Spanish Democracy in Comparative Perspective, *The Journal of Politics* 46 (1984), 657-661.

42 R. García, *Entre la justicia y el mercado. Nuevo paradigma para la sociedad civil* (Madrid 1992), 97.

43 R. Cotarelo, *La izquierda: desengaño, resignación y utopia* (Barcelona 1989), 220.

44 D. Share, *Dilemmas of Social Democracy. The Spanish Socialist Workers Party in the 1980's* (New York: Greenwood Publishing Group, 1989), 144.

45 J. Marias, *La libertad en juego* (Madrid 1986), 12.

46 J.M. Otero Novas, *Nuestra democracia puede morir* (Barcelona 1987), 12.

47 J. Sinova, J. Tusell, *El secuestro de la democracia. Como regenerar el sistema politico español* (Barcelona 1990), 10.

48 J.M. Aznar, *España, la segunda transición* (Madrid 1994).

49 M. Miralles, *Dinero sucio. Diccionario de la corrupción en España* (Madrid 1992), 99.

50 A.C. Montes, *La democracia en España, 'sobrevivira'* (Barcelona 1993).

51 F. Jimenez Losantos, *La dictadura silenciosa. Mecanismos totalitarios de nuestra democracia* (Madrid 1993).

52 J.M. Carrascal, *Adiós a la utopia. Ya es siglo XXI* (Madrid 1991), 120.

53 I. Sotelo, *El desplome de la izquierda. Modalidades españolas del fin de una época* (Madrid: Akal, 1994).

54 J. Garcia Abad, *La soledad del Rey. Esta la monarquia consolidada 25 años después de la Constitución?* (Madrid: 2005).

55 P. Ordaz, *Voto de castigo. El despertar de la conciencia ciudadana y la derrota del PP* (Barcelona: Debate, 2004).

56 T. Comin, "14-M: un mensaje para el mundo. Las elecciones españolas suponen un cambio internacional" *El Ciervo* April (2004), 28.

57 See, for example, A. Fontan, "El gobierno en su laberinto", *Nueva revista de politica y arte* 95 (2004), 4.

58 J. Pont Vidal, "Movimientos sociales, socialismo y socialdemocracia en España", January, *Sistema* (2004), 41-70; also of interest is a social-democratic vision of the relations between the state ind civil society presented in the same socialist journal: J. Hernandez Bravo de Laguna, "Relaciones de la sociedad civil con el sector publico", January *Sistema* (2005).

59 See Julia Navarro, *El nuevo socialismo. La visión de J.L. Rodriguez Zapatero* (Barcelona 2001); Oscar Campillo, *Zapatero. Presidente a la primera* (Madrid 2004).

Part II

Parallel Ideas in the Democratic Transitions of Eastern Europe, Latin America and Spain

Chapter 4

Problems of Democratic Transition and Consolidation: Spain and Poland

Me parecía -- y sigue pareciéndomelo - que la amistad entre España y Polonia es algo fundamental.

-- José María Aznar, *Ocho años de gobierno* (Barcelona: Planeta, 2005), 165.

A democratic deficit was characteristic of both Spanish and Polish history. Francoist and communist dictatorships initially had a clearly totalitarian nature and evolved gradually towards an authoritarian rule marked by a limited pluralism. The authoritarian regimes in Spain and in Poland were overthrown in a peaceful way as a result of the pressure of democratic oppositions and by means of negotiations with reformist rulers. Not quite easily a democratic order in both countries has been established. However, both relatively peaceful transitions have universal meaning, and have often been pointed to as a model for Eastern Europe, Latin America and the present-day world.

SPANISH-POLISH PARALLELISM

Many times since the sixteenth century the similarity of historical fate between Spain and Poland has been cited; numerous, political and cultural analogies were drawn between the countries situated on the confines of Catholic Europe, which analogies concerned especially the national characteristics of their inhabitants. Some authors have extended the analogy over the last two centuries, when Spaniards and Poles encountered numerous drawbacks on their road to democracy and liberty.[1] The amazing achievements in this domain beyond the Pyrenees since the mid 1970s revived hopes that also in Poland, despite a less advantageous starting point, analogous success could be attained. "At the beginning there were only dreams and wishes, Jan Kieniewicz wrote when the Polish democracy dawned; now it is being said openly: the transition to democracy in Poland could or should be done in the Spanish way. That is to say, as in Spain after General Francisco Franco's death (November 20, 1975), as a result of an agreement or pact of political forces that decided to dismantle the dictatorship."[2] At the beginning of the Polish transition moderate optimism prevailed, which was later replaced by pessimism.

Adam Michnik was the first political writer from the Polish anticommunist opposition who most often recalled the Spanish experience as a model and pattern to follow in Poland. From the mid 1970s, Michnik was interested in the evolution of Spanish communism, in Workers' Commissions, and then observed from France in detail the last phase of Francoist dictatorship. He also referred to the Spanish experience during the first *Solidarity*, in his book on compromise written in prison in the spring of 1985, during the Roundtable talks, and in numerous essays written during the systemic change and transition to democracy in Poland. Probably the most important ideas in his book are those on the need to compromise, in which interesting and very inspiring considerations on the possibility of a genuine dialogue between society and the communist authorities in Poland are contained. In very unpromising circumstances as early as 1985 Michnik foresaw and proposed that the idea of an agreement and mutual understanding must be revived in future, arguing that Poles - similar to the Spaniards - would be able to elaborate a peaceful and evolutionary road to democracy and compromise. "Such compromise - rightly noted Michnik - succeeded in Spain, its result being the transformation of the Francoist despotism into a system of parliamentary democracy".[3]

In the late 1980s the Spanish example began to be cited with envy and hope by many representatives of the Polish opposition, as well as in official publications controlled by benign censorship, and cited even by Soviet adherents of *perestroika*.

One should acknowledge that some, though rather few, authors from the very beginning emphasized that the Spanish and Polish experience were not comparable; they did not believe that it would be as easy as in Spain to reach a consensus and democracy. Stress was laid on the fact that in contrast to Poland, Spain was a sovereign country, did not have a totalitarian system subordinated to one ideology and that the authoritarian rule did not destroy private property and the market. These differences made the Spanish transition to democracy easier, although strong national and regional differentiation, absent in the Polish case, made it more difficult.

Commenting on the brutality of the Polish political scene after the democratic opposition took over power, Michnik continued to argue: "The Spanish road from dictatorship to democracy proves that it is possible to build a state in which past opponents, often prisoners and their jailers, do not lose their own political identity, but want and can live later together in a common state. They are able to respect the rules of pluralism, tolerance and honest political competition."[4] Michnik's argumentation has been supported by Wojciech Jaruzelski and Aleksander Kwaśniewski.[5] After five years the latter took up the catchword of "the common state" as the main slogan of his successful presidential campaigns.

Michnik pointed to the lack in Poland and East Central Europe of the tradition of democratic coexistence according to rules of democratic order. A similar deficit was characteristic of Spain.

Jan Kieniewicz paid more attention to differences than to similarities between Spanish and Polish transitions to democracy. According to him, The Spanish transition was successful whereas in Poland it was not.[6]

To go farther into the Spanish and Polish transition to democracy and into the quality of democracy established, one should pay more attention to the nature of undemocratic regimes in both countries and to their evolution.

TWO DICTATORSHIPS

The Communist system in Poland was wholly imposed by the Soviet Union, whereas in Spain Franco's dictatorship arose as a result of the Civil War in which alien Nazi and Fascist troops were fighting on the nationalist side. The regimes that were created in Spain after the civil war and in Poland after the Second World War had a clearly totalitarian character for at least the first ten years of their existence. Both regimes brutally eliminated all forms of political opposition and tried to impose an all-embracing ideology upon society. They also tended towards exclusive and unlimited control over society by means of terror and secret political police. Both regimes were in the grip of political unity obsession. In Spain this idea was preponderant in Francoist propaganda till the early 1960s,[7] while in Poland till the end of 1970s the socialist ideology was based on the moral and political unity of the nation.

It is also important to see that both regimes began to loosen their strictly totalitarian traits relatively early - Francoism in the late 1940s and the Polish communism after 1955.[8] Both evolved gradually towards authoritarian rule marked by lame, right-wing, socialist or a limited, but real pluralism.

Cassifying Francoism and Polish communism under the rubric of authoritarian regimes has a great number of opponents, mainly among the radical pro-Communist left in Spain and the stubornly anti-communist right in Poland,[9] who argue that both regimes, for all their evolution, were totalitarian to the very end. Even Adam Michnik wrongly called late Francoism as fascist and Jaruzelski's regime a totalitarianism with broken teeth.[10] By the same token, Raúl Morodo considered both early and late Francoism as "flexible and accommodating totalitarianism."[11] Objective, independent, and unbiased researchers, like Linz and Stepan, argue that both dictatorships were authoritarian, in which opposition by civil society was possible; totalitarian regimes would never have allowed that.

The most interesting description of the Polish communism as a form of an authoritarian regime was done by Andrzej Walicki. He noted that the regime was rather liberal, granting a certain degree of pluralism and relative freedom in social, cultural, religious and academic life.[12]

The best analysis of authoritarianism, with special consideration given to the Spanish case, was done by Juan J. Linz. According to him, in contrast to totalitarian systems, "authoritarian regimes are political systems with limited, not responsible, political pluralism: without an elaborate, guiding ideology (but with distinctive mentalities); without intensive or extensive political mobilization (except at some points in their development); and in which a leader (or occasionally a small group) exercise power within limits which formally are ill-defined, but actually are quite predictable."[13]

According to Linz, the limited pluralism of Franco Spain and of other authoritarian regimes contrasts with the absolute rule by a totalitarian party that grabbed power. Authoritarian pluralism differs also from democratic pluralism in that the latter usually is unlimited, legitimate, and institutionalized through political parties. In authoritarian regimes there is no open competition for power through democratic elections, but only co-optation of leaders by the superior ruler or ruling body. These rulers oppose competitive party system, but under some circumstances, allow limited pluralism and increased liberalization.

The Falange Party of fascist origin remained secondary in Franco regime and later was dissolved in the structure of *Movimiento Nacional* consisting of various right-wing, conservative, authoritarian, and Catholic members. Something similar could have been observed in the case of the Polish United Workers' Party, in which orthodox communists were in the minority at least in the 1970s and 1980s. Sometimes in periods of crisis they played the role of a semi-loyal opposition to the bureaucratic-authoritarian regime.

In authoritarian regimes Linz distinguished between "opponents" within and outside the system, who not necessarily correspond to "legal" and "illegal" critics of the regime. In Spain and in Poland it was difficult to distinguish between the liberal democratic opposition to the regimes and some liberal representatives of the regimes during the last years of both dictatorships. This could be easily seen in the last decade (1980-1989) of the semi-communist regime in Poland, where a million communist party members enrolled in the Solidarity Trade Union and some top party leaders and government officials behaved like a shy and cautious opposition. Linz noticed a strange and peculiar ambivalence of opposition, semi-opposition, and pseudo-opposition in the tolerant stages of authoritarian regimes that lost their ideological strength. This relative "freedom creates a subtle gratitude and dependence on those in power who limit their contestation activities. This in turn transforms them, in the view of many opponents of the system, into a sham opposition that weakens their legitimacy as an alternative. Furthermore, their relative freedom and the soft treatment given them in the case of repression often contrasts with harshness toward less prominent enemies of the regime and the generally difficult condition of life of the masses; the contrast - concludes Linz - weakens their appeal to the common man".[14]

Linz demonstrates that the semi-opposition that has given up hope of transforming the regime from the inside sometimes becomes an a-legal, often tolerated opposition. This a-legal opposition appears also thanks to the autonomy granted by the authoritarian regime to certain social organizations and to relatively broad contacts with other societies.

Linz has shown that limited pluralism emerges sometimes in certain political systems after a period of totalitarian rule. In such post-totalitarian authoritarian regimes the leading position of the party has not ceased, but the party is being modified.

The initial weakness of real totalitarian parties in Spain and in Poland compelled both authoritarian regimes to co-opt political elites from varied social strata with no definite ideological commitments. Later on these authoritarian regimes exhibited broader tolerance and even encouraged a-politicism.

EVOLUTION TOWARDS PLURALISM

In the 1970s the Polish political system underwent a further evolution from a totalitarian regime to the bureaucratic authoritarian regime of Edward Gierek and his team. The process of 'de-totalization' from above was intensified; the authorities tried to build a structure characterized by "lame", irresponsible pluralism that simulates various points of view, correcting thus numerous irrationalities of the decision-making process. At that time new elements, not encountered in other "socialist" countries, appeared in Poland. Such was the development of repressive toleration in which an informal political opposition had a peculiar a-legal status, but with no institutional channels of expression. Characteristic of the decade was also the process of further de-ideologization of the state activity. The communist utopian ideology was ritualized and eroded; it had little impact on the authorities and society, "becoming a mere verbal façade". According to Jadwiga Staniszkis, "In the cultural sphere, this period was marked by stronger and even more frequent references to such traditional values as the nation and the family; a departure from the concept of a separate, socialist culture; and the growing role of elements of mass culture and a pattern of consumption following more developed Western countries."[15] Following Juan Linz's early hints that Poland seemed more authoritarian than totalitarian, Jadwiga Staniszkis described the Polish political system of the late 1970s as a typical authoritarian-bureaucratic regime "that contained limited, not responsible political pluralism, without an elaborated and guiding ideology but with distinctive mentalities."[16]

For historic reasons, mainly due to the existence of private economy in Francoist Spain, the process of pluralization in Spanish society began earlier and was more advanced than in socialist Poland. In Spain the idea of a plurality of opinions and of political pluralism became so popular that it appeared even in the vague language of the official single party-organization *Movimiento Nacional* publications. These publications were trying to reconcile the general postulate of authoritarian and nationalist unity with a pluralism of opinions and critical judgements and to "provide the pluralism that resides in society with adequate channels for expression, for manifestation."[17] At the same time it was stressed that pluralism had nothing to do with political parties (*partidismo politico*). It was acknowledged that pluralism existed in every healthy society and that without plurality there was no political life, yet in the particular case of Spain political parties had allegedly proven to be negative and "disastrous".

The official Spanish *Movimiento Nacional* publications argued that democracy, pluralism and a rich of political life could be guaranteed beyond the system of political parties that usually function only as an electoral machinery and do not care for the welfare of the people. The effort to defend the idea of pluralism without legal political parties was similar, as we shall see, to the conception of the so-called "socialist pluralism" that appeared under late communism. The authors who "defended" pluralism under the late Francoism in Spain or under the late state socialism in Poland and Eastern Europe were taking into account the real existence of ideological pluralism that emerged in spite of, and against, the authoritarian regimes. The defenders of limited pluralism, be it Francoist or "socialist", were broadening step by step their political visions. Manuel Fraga Iribarne, for example, the eminent representative of Francoism, became disappointed after the rejection of the project of political associations and proposed his version of "political development."[18] He was convinced that the process of political reforms, liberalization, pluralism and openness should have been continued because associations were not only a political necessity, but also in accordace with the postulate of human rights. In time he supported the transformation of associations into political parties and their legalization, with the exception of the Communist party.

It is interesting to notice that spokesmen of both authoritarian regimes in their final stages were trying to "defend" the idea of pluralism beyond the system of political parties. The authorities were searching for a model of agreement with the opposition and for a pluralism, initially limited. José Utrera Molina, the General Secretary of the *Movimiento*, in his speech of January 16, 1974, declared that the National Movement should be open to everybody and that it does not combat pluralism.[19] In Poland at the end of 1980s communists leaders began to discuss in a Spanish manner pro-reform coalition, an anti-crisis pact, and obviously the need of social and later of political pluralism. These leaders already consented to the existence of political clubs and independent associations; however they long opposed the legalization of Solidarity. Similarly, the reformed Francoists accepted the existence of political associations; however, they resisted for a relatively long time the legalization of political parties, particularly of the Communist Party. The new political associations could already exist without the need of acknowledging the "leading role of the Polish United Workers' Party" or swearing "fidelity to the Principles of *MovimientoNacional* ".

If the dictatorship in Poland had existed a bit longer, it would not have been led by the declining Party but, as in Spain, by the emerging technocrats, a National Front or PRON, and the army led by General Jaruzelski.

In the last years of Francoism and of the Polish socialism the authorities were deeply divided between the adherents of a liberal-reformist opening and advocates of continuing the regimes without important modifications: the latter represented by the so-called *bunker* in Spain, and the rigid *beton* (concrete) represented by few Polish hard-liners, respectively. The first accepted many ideas of the democratic opposition, although sometimes in a limited form. In 1971 even Ramón Serrano Suñer, one of the founders of the Franco State, saw the need for a controlled return to a party system. Similarly Rafael Calvo Serer, once an ideologist of Catholic integrism, later favoured democratic monarchy and pluralist democracy. Having left the position of Francoist reformism, he declared that regimes intermediate between democracy and totalitarianism are unstable and must opt either for dictatorship or for liberty.[20] Many examples of a similar evolution of views could be noticed among communist power-holders in Poland.

TWO NEGOTIATED TRANSITIONS

Ater Franco's death in November 1975 and after Messner's government downfall in September 1988, the simple continuation or cosmetic reform of both regimes was no longer an alternative to a far-reaching reform of the regime or a democratic, revolutionary breakthrough.[21] Eventually the authoritarian rule was ended as a result of a negotiated break (*ruptura pactada*) or a "refolution" (a Polish combination of reform and peceful revolution, according to Timothy Garton Ash), namely, confidential negotiations of Premier Suárez with the united Spanish democratic opposition, the secret consultations of General Kiszczak with Wałęsa in Magdalenka, and the open Round Table talks between the government and opposition of those days. Those were unique (*sui generis*) and unprecedented events on a world scale in the 20th century.

The most difficult, crucial decision that had to be made by reformist authorities of late Francoism or socialism was legalization of the Spanish Communist Party and of Solidarity, and later their consent to democratic or in the case of Poland semi-democratic parliamentary elections. The problem of legalization of the main opposition forces produced great confusion at the top of authoritarian power in both countries. It was said that the more conservative factions of the state apparatus and of the army were trying to prevent it. This was so especially in Spain, while in Poland what was more important than personal interests or ideological reasons was the widespread awareness that the declining Soviet Union had lost its interest in upholding communism in Poland. Especially General Jaruzelski must have had a direct knowledge of it from Moscow, since he often repeated that his rule had no more "umbrella". Not everyone in the lower echelons of the government and party was fully aware of that and the General's consent for Solidarity legalization was, therefore, treated as a betrayal of the ideals declared on July,[22] 1944, though as President he had tried to defend them in vain in 1990. Similarly in Spain, numerous Francoist generals treated Suárez's consent for the legalization of Communist party and even his project of the decisive "political reform" as treason of the ideals of July 18, the beginning of the famous revolt in 1936. Marginally it should be added that charges of treason have been common in the history of both countries.

It is interesting to notice that the main representatives of the pacted transition (e. g. Adolfo Suárez and Czesław Kiszczak) interpreted it initially as finishing the work started by Franco and by communist reformers. The role played by the King Juan Carlos and by General Jaruzelski was not comparable, but they have preserved a deep mutual sympathy for each other, sympathy derived from their authoritarian mentality.

The first stage of democratic changes in Spain and in Poland was a result of the pressure of democratic opposition on the state authorities who gradually succumbed to it. In time these forces came to an understanding; this was a common feature in both roads to democracy. It was seen also during the time of close cooperation of the communist president Jaruzelski with the first non-communist premier Mazowiecki. This policy of cooperation was called abroad *la démocratisation à l'amiable.*

Starting from 1990, and especially after Jaruzelski resigned as President, initial similarities between the Spanish and Polish road to democracy began to disappear.

In Spain politicians coming from the *ancien régime*, ie. The Premier, the majority of ministers and members of parliament, played a decisive role for seven years after Franco's death, and the King designated by him still reigns. These politicians ruled, this time in a democratic way, till the Socialist victory at the end of 1982. In Poland, however, the representatives of the old regime, ie. President Jaruzelski, the few postcommunist ministers in Mazowiecki's cabinet and numerous postcommunist members of the contractual Diet, ceased to participate in Solidarity's rule quite early, ie. in two years. The parliament elected in October 1991, this time in a fully democratic way, was clearly dominated by the parties coming from the former democratic opposition. But in the elections of September 1993, postcommunist forces won and to a certain degree the situation from the beginning of the democratic breakthrough was reproduced, were the president and the premier coming from opposing camps (this time the president from Solidarity). It resembled somehow the Spanish situation where King Juan Carlos and the socialist premier, Felipe González, were from different political camps. Relations between them were very harmonious, whereas in Poland numerous conflicts broke out between President and Government, although for a time president Wałęsa, it was said, tried to strenghten the Polish political left.

The victory of the postcommunists in parliamentary elections of 1993 and in presidential elections of 1995 and 2000 means that those who saw the main difference between Francoism and the Polish socialism in patriotic and nationalist character of the former and in the anti-national character of the latter, as if leftist, populist and authoritarian traditions and attitudes in Poland had been of no importance, were not quite right. Optimistic predictions of conservative liberals who, being inspired in a way by the Spanish example, thought that their rule would be long-lasting, did not come true: "In Spain the right-wing totalism after a transitional period has resulted in the prolonged, democratically enacted rule of the Spanish Socialist Workers' Party which in fact was is central-leftist. If we assume the existence -- for which there are good reasons -- of see-saw pulsing of political orientations in societies, in Poland leftist totalism after a transitional period should lead to a long-lasting rule of the center and right-wing forces. This forecast may arouse optimism not only among conservative liberals."[23] It turned out, however, that the longing by workers and other employees for earlier social benefits and for a feeling of security led to the victory of Social Democrats five years after the downfall of authoritarian-paternalistic regimes in both countries. It was of no great importance that the Social Democrats in Spain came on the whole from the democratic opposition, while in Poland they came mostly from postcommunist circles.

The September 1997 elections were lost by the Left forces, but over 52% of population did not participate. So the post-communist governments did not last long in Poland, but the Left has preserved its considerable influence in the economy, in the army and strong political structures (the President and SLD Alliance); the Left won once again in 2001, but was defeated four years later.

TWO DEMOCRACIES

After the peaceful systemic change in Spain (the economic system having changed there over a dozen years before the political system), it was not easy to establish a democratic order in both countries. It is common to consider Spanish circumstances as more favourable ones than the Polish situation, but even there serious problems have appeared.

After the self-liquidation of the *Movimiento Nacional* in April 1977 and of the Polish United Workers' Party (PUWP) in January 1990, hundreds of political parties and associations came into being. In spite of the multitude of political parties, pluralist structures were feeble. "Taxi parties" in Spain[24] or "sofa parties" in Poland have turned out to be very small in numbers. In Poland the newly born parties - the Democratic Union (UD) and the Center Alliance (PC) - wanted to become similar at least in their names to the victorious Union of Democratic Center (UCD) in Spain.

In Spain eight years after Franco's death the party system was as tottering and unconsolidated as in Poland at the end of 1990s. In spite of functioning almost three times as long as the young Polish democracy, the Spanish democracy still suffered for many years from corruption and other systemic diseases. Many Spaniards have dreamt of initiating a new, more genuine transition to democracy under the new conservative government of José María Aznar. Many Poles have dreamt of something similar under the new Solidarity led coalition and other anticommunist parties.

In both countries the old political class that got dropped any ideology on the whole did not lose, but often improved its position as a result of systemic change. What is more, one of the main causes that had driven the old elites, especially the economic ones, to change the old regimes was an increasing awareness that authoritarian regimes retard general development and impede their access to consumption on the European level.

Having achieved democracy a serious weakening of promoters and designers of systemic changes became a glaring fact in both countries. In Poland Solidarity recovered for the second time in 1997. In Spain the UCD, initially victorious, split and disintegrated in 1982. The Communist party in Spain and the Catholic Church in Poland found it difficult at first to adapt to the spirit of new times, although they had contributed considerably to erosion and final break-up of old regimes.[25]

A Polish-Spanish parallelism is interesting only for Poles, not for Spaniards. They have never considered it plausible to learn anything important from an unknown Slavic country. Spaniards have dreamt for a long time of coming up to France in standards of democracy and welfare. Such vague dreams were cherished also in Poland, but generally were regarded as unrealistic. The aim of catching up with post-Franco Spain was considered more realistic, especially due to the quite optimistic calculation of economists, according to whom the Polish economy in the pre-war period and in the 1950s and 1960s[26] exhibited a similar or even higher level of economic growth under comparable population, natural resources and political systems. At the turn of 1980s and 1990s Spain clearly outstripped Poland in all figures of economic development. The causes were seen in earlier implementation of political democracy and especially of liberal economic reforms. Looking with envy at Spain, Polish economists saw a key to similar successes in limiting state guaranteed services and pressures on salary increase, in reaching broad consensus in the sphere of market economy and European integration.

It seems that the great economic distance of Poland in relation to Spain that had existed at the turn of 1989 and 1990 has never diminished. Initially President Kwaśniewski and other representatives of the ruling left in Poland set initially the Social Democratic governments of Felipe González as a pattern to be followed, although they were obviously still far behind the Spain dominated by PSOE in the degree of power concentrated by one party, the level of economic modernization of the country, but not in rate of unemployment, corruption and of social inequalities. Also liberal-democratic forces have been refering to Spain as an example to follow (the pattern for the Polish ruling right was José M. Aznar). Once their victorious leader Leszek Balcerowicz set a plan to double the national income in order to place Poland near Spain.[27] As a result of his economic policy, the inflation in Poland in 1998, for the first time since 1980, fell below 10 % (a similar rate was achieved in Spain in 1985 after 11 years).

Till April 1997 Poland did not have a new Constitution, whereas Spaniards ratified their own in a referendum eighteen months after the first democratic elections. Poland is still shaken by numerous political scandals, mutual suspicions of political competition, passionate quarrels about communist Poland, "lustration" and decommunization, whereas the Spaniards did not long focus on the painful wounds from the Civil War and dictatorship.

For all these differences, the general balance of the first years of formation of Polish democracy, as compared to the initial choking with democracy in Spain, is not very disadvantageous to Poland, especially if we take into account the fact that no one in Poland has attempted a coup d'etat or anything similar to the dangerous action of lieutenant colonel Antonio Tejero Molina in February 1981. Moreover, in Poland starting from the Round Table talks at the beginning of 1989 till now almost no politician[28] of the left or right has been assasinated, whereas in Spain the terrorism of the left and of the right-wing forces, nationalist and state terrorism (ETA, GRAPO, Partido Español Nacional-Socialista, Comandos de Lucha Antimarxista, Fuerza Nueva, Guerrilleros de Cristo Rey, GAL, etc.) in 1977-1987 years had almost 800 of victims, many more than the martial law in Poland. These differences occured in spite of similar symptoms of disappointment (*desencanto*) with democracy that became visible in both countries. As is well known, after the period of "revolutionary euphoria" in both countries there appeared a crisis of involvement in political life, decrease of participation in public life and disbelief in its efficiency.[29]

Not fully accomplished the Polish transition to democracy appeared confrontational when compared to Spain. This was not so much with regard to real facts as to isolated and categorical statements made by various political groups and adventurous individuals declaring urgent need for deep decommunization, delegalization of the once victorious Alliance for the Democratic Left (SLD), formal restitution of the pre-communist independent state, collective responsibility and even depriving some people of pensions, including those volunteers who defended the Republic in the Spanish Civil War.[30]

The fact is that the so-called thick line (*gruba kreska*) and excessive role of the secret service forces inherited from the old system have become an essential element of post-authoritarian democracy, although the forgiving "thick line" was applied more willingly and frequently in Spain than in Poland. Moreover, in Spain no use was made of the secret service forces in political struggle, although their role was big. Besides, in Spain the operational documents of police fighting against democratic opposition and records of the *Movimiento Nacional* were destroyed for the sake of national reconciliation, causing much despair among historians.

In Spain the mutual aversion of the camp of conquerors to the conquered in the Civil War has never disappeared, but it was almost unanimously acknowledged that there is no alternative to national reconciliation.The representatives of both factions have made to one other many spectacular and even theatrical gestures of friendship and readiness for cooperation. Close contacts of Adam Michnik with Aleksander Kwaśniewski and Wojciech Jaruzelski have been an example of something similar in Poland, though relatively rare and causing great astonishment.[31]

In both countries the defeated and frustrated right-wing forces severely questioned the morality of leftist winners holding state power - in Poland they questioned it almost since the very beginning of the postcommunist access to power in 1993 and in 2001, in Spain since the second socialist victory in 1986. These assaults were made in spite of good economic results achieved under central-leftist governments. Spanish and Polish critics of the PSOE and SLD rule attended to the fact that these parties had neither a set of ideas nor a program of their own, that holding power was the only important thing for them.[32] In Poland the resistance to the leftist rule took much more violent forms than in Spain to PSOE, but nothing indicated that anyone could ever accept the forms of struggle initiated on July 18, 1936.

In Spain and in Poland attention was paid to the potential but unfounded danger of "mexicanization" of their political systems in which - in spite of the existence of independent public opinion, democratic institutions and certain liberties - the practical possibility of taking over political power from the left-wing forces may disappear for at least twenty years or so -- in Mexico the Revolutionary Institutional Party was ruling interruptedly for over seventy years.[33] The opposition also noted that PSOE and SLD party structures were becoming institutional and tended to be identified with state structures; that the force of PSOE and of the postcommunist coalition in Poland could mean the threat of political one-sidedness and even of monopoly; and that they both introduce legal and structural changes that would protect them against an easy loss of power. Hence, the frequent postulate that the coalition should not fill all government posts even when formally possibilities, the postulates of creating a system of checks and balances and of depolitization of civil service, and vague remarks on the need of politic equilibrium and on more fair competition. Also numerous warnings have been issued against "institutional corruption", clientelism, a corrupt system of parasitic institutions, and excessive economic favouritism by groups that usually vote for the Left.

In Spain and in Poland quite often animated discussions on a crisis of democracy have been conducted; often critical comments have been expressed on "stopped" democracy (*democracia detenida*), "sequestered" democracy, "huchbacked" democracy (*garbata demokracja*) and so on.[34]

The formation of central-rightist governments in Spain and in Poland in 1996 and 1997 respectively, have given rise to new, not very serious waves of publications -- this time by the left-wing forces who lost the elections -- on the alleged limitations to democracy in both countries under new circumstances. For a time Spain and Poland were the only great countries of Europe that had right-wing governments. Some efforts were made to forge a strategic alliance between the two middle-sized, catholic countries of pro-American Europe.[35] José Maria Aznar established very close political relations with the conservative Jerzy Buzek, which were continued during the postcommunist government of Leszek Miller. Both countries defended stubornly, the European treaty of Nice which was favorable for them, but finally rejected (the Spanish catchword *Niza o muerte*, coined by Aznar, was made popular in Poland by Jan Rokita). Aznar was one of the few Western participans at the 20th anniversary of Solidarity in Poland in 2000. He visited Poland also in 2003 and 2004. Polish-Spanish summit conferences were held in Madrid (2003) and in Warsaw (2005). The close relations between Spain and Poland played an important role in the enlarged European Union.[36]

The Socialist Party that won parliamentary elections in 2004 revised the Spanish position on the EU constitution, and drew closer to France and Germany. It has not found therefore much understanding in Catholic Poland either among the ruling Left (for a time Poland was the sole defender of the Nice settlements), or among the Right forces[37] that have come to power in Poland once again at the end of 2005. But the close relations between Poland and Spain continue: Premier Marek Belka participated in an international conference on democracy and struggle against terrorism in Madrid (March, 2005) and at the end of 2005 a spokesman of the new Polish conservative government declared that its economic program was inspired by José Maria Aznar.

Unlike Poland, Spain was connected to the democratic Europe relatively early with a tangled web of close political, economic and military links in order to make impossible a violent breakdown of democracy, while Poland still has many serious problems to resolve. Poland and other "misdeveloped" countries of East Central Europe, with a weak financial and trade infrastructure, will probably have to pass through a more difficult process of adaptation to Europe than had Spain and the south European countries 20 years ago.[38]

NOTES

1 See Janusz Tazbir, "Les Rapports Culturels Polono-Espagnols", *Annali del Dipartimento di Studi dell`Europa Orientale. Sezione storico-politico-soziale*, Instituto Universitario Orientale, Edizioni dell`Ateneo, Estratto, Vol. IV-V, 1982-1983; Alicja Iwańska, *Exiled Governments: Spanish and Polish. An Essay in Political Sociology* (Cambridge: Mass. 1981); Piotr Sawicki, *Polacy a Hiszpanie. Ludzie, podróże, opinie* (Wrocław: Wyd. UWr., 1995); Jan Kieniewicz, "Confines y fronteras. El paralelo histórico a finales del siglo XX", in *Europa del Centro y del Este y el Mundo Hispánico*, Ana I. Blanco Picado y Teresa Eminowicz, eds. (Cracow: ABRYS, 1996); Jan Kieniewicz, "Doświadczenie hiszpańskie w rzeczywistości polskiej", in: *Polska w Europie* (Warsaw, 1996), vol. 21; Jan Kieniewicz, *Hiszpania w zwierciadle polskim* (Gdańsk: Novus Orbis, 2001); Bogusława Dobek-Ostrowska, *Hiszpania i Polska: elity polityczne w okresie przejścia do demokracji. Analiza porównawcza* (Wrocław: Wyd. UWr., 1996); M. Ptaszyński, "Polityka i historia. Historyczna paralela Hiszpanii z Polską", *Przegląd Humanistyczny* 1 (2002); *Democratic Consolidation – The International Dimension: Hungary, Poland and Spain*, G. Mangott, H. Waldrauch, S. Day, eds. (Baden - Baden 2000); Bruno Drweski, "Polska – Hiszpania. Kto wygrał wyścig XX wieku?", *Robotnik Śląski* 10 (2002), 12-13; *Hiszpania – Polska: Spotkania*, ed. E. González Martínez, M. Nalewajko (Warsaw: Neriton, 2003); *Diktaturbewältigung und nationale Selbstvergewisserung. Geschichtskulturen in Polen und Spanien im Vergleich,* ed., K. Ruchniewicz, S. Troebst (Wrocław: Wyd. UWr., 2004); Anna Müller, *Od autorytaryzmu do demokracji. Transformacja ustrojowa na przykładzie Hiszpanii i Polski* (Toruń: Mado, 2004); *Studia polsko-hiszpanskie. Wiek XX*, ed. Jan Kieniewicz (Warsaw: OBTA UW, 2004).

2 Jan Kieniewicz, "Hiszpania - przykład czy wyzwanie?", *Przegląd Powszechny,* 1 (1990), 92; the most penetrating analysis of the changes in Spain and in Poland has been carried out by Bogusława Dobek-Ostrowska, *Hiszpania i Polska: elity polityczne w okresie przejścia do demokracji. Analiza porównawcza* (Wrocław 1996); Few Spanish authors who have related to comparative transition to democracy in Spain and in East Central Europe (especially in Poland) are: Juan J. Linz, "Transitions to Democracy", *The Washington Quaterly,* 3 (1990); Gregorio Morán, *El precio de la transición* (Barcelona 1992), 233-236; José Casanova, *Public Religions in the Modern World* (Chicago and London, 1994), 102-103; José María Maravall, *Los resultados de la democracia: un estudio del sur y el este de Europa* (Madrid, 1995).

3 Adam Michnik, *Takie czasy...rzecz o kompromisi*e (London: Aneks, 1985), 83; earlier hints to the Spanish case can be found in his classical text on

The New Evolutionism (1976); see also K. Grodkowski (K.Dziewanowski), "Komisje robotnicze w Hiszpanii", *Robotnik*, 8 (1978); *Bronisław Geremek en diálogo con Juan Carlos Vidal* (Madrid 1997); K. Maxwell, "Spain's Transition to Democracy: A Model for Eastern Europe?", *Proceedings of the Academy of Political Science*, 1 (1991); *Bronislaw Geremek en diálogo con Juan Carlos Vidal* (Madrid: Anaya & Muchnik, 1997).

4 Adam Michnik, "Etyka a polityka", *Tygodnik Powszechny* 18 (1990).

5 They were the main and constant advocates of a Spanish-style transition to democracy – without memory of the past, without political trials and without de-Francoization or decommunization. See T. Rosenberg, *The Haunted Land. Facing Europe's Ghosts After Communism* (New York: Random House, 1995), 239-240.

6 Jan Kieniewicz, "Polska i Hiszpania: przejście, pojednanie, zapomnienie", *Przegląd Powszechny,* 1 (1997).

7 Interesting remarks on this topic can be found in Piotr Sawicki, "El concepto de unidad de la propaganda franquista. Notas para la historia de una obsesión (1937-1962)", *Romanica Wratislaviensia,* XXVII (1987).

8 Two distinguished scholars argue "that Poland is the only country in Eastern Europe that was always closer to an authoritarian than to a totalitarian regime, even in the 1949-53 period when totalitarian tendencies were strongest". Juan J. Linz & Alfred Stepan, *Problems of Democratic Transition and Consolidation: Southern Europe, South America, and Post-Communist Europe* (Baltimore and London, 1996), 255.

9 Note that the representatives of extreme left in Spain and of the populist right in Poland are similar in rather negatively assessing the road from dictatorship to democracy in their countries, and especially its results. They caracterize the change in the political system as the result of silent conspiracy of the *ancien régime* reformers with moderate factions of democratic opposition in order to continue oligarchic systems of social injustice under a pseudodemocracy.

10 See Michnik's interview: "Towards a Civil Society: Hopes for Polish Democracy", *The Times Literary Supplement,* 4 (1988).

11 Raúl Morodo, *La transición política* (Madrid 1993), 30.

12 Andrzej Walicki, *Zniewolony umysł po latach* (Warsaw: Czytelnik, 1993), 352-353. See also his *Marxism and the Leap to the Kingdom of Freedom: The Rise and Fall of the Communist Utopia* (Stanford 1995); Charles S. Brown, "Civil Society and Dialogue in Post War Poland and its Relevance for a Global Community" *Dialogue and Universalism, 7* (1995).

13 Juan J. Linz, "An Authoritarian Regime: Spain", in *Cleavages, Ideologies and Party Systems*, E. Allardt and Y. Littunen, eds. (Helsinki 1964); and in *Politics and Society in Twentieth-Century Spain,* ed. with an Introduction by Stanley G. Payne (New York - London 1976), 165.

14 Juan J. Linz, "Opposition to and under an Authoritarian Regime: The Case of Spain", in *Regimes and Oppositions,* ed. Robert A. Dahl (New Haven and London 1973), 220.

15 Jadwiga Staniszkis, *Poland's Self-Limiting Revolution* (Princeton 1984), 169.

16 Ibid., 206.

17 *See Concurrencia de pareceres. Coincidencias y discrepancias en el Movimiento Nacional* (Madrid: Ediciones del Movimiento, 1967), 93; see also *Nuevo horizonte del Movimiento Nacional* (Madrid: Ediciones del Movimiento, 1968) and Carlos Iglesias Selgas, *La via española a la democracia* (Madrid: Ediciones del Movimiento, 1968).

18 Manuel Fraga Iribarne, *El desarrollo politico* (Barcelona: Grijalbo 1972).

19 J. Utrera Molina, *Derecho a la esperanza* (Madrid: Ediciones del Movimiento 1974), 18.

20 R. Calvo Serer, *Hacia una tercera república española. En defensa de una monarquía democrática* (Barcelona: Plaza y Janés 1977), 75.

21 See Timothy Garton Ash, "Reform or Revolution?", *The New York Review,* October 27, 1988; José María Bernáldez, *Ruptura o reforma?* (Barcelona 1984).

22 Guy Hermet, "La démocratisation à l'amiable: de l'Espagne à la Pologne", *Commentaire,* 50 (1990).

23 Dariusz Filar, "Polonia es diferente, czyli socjoekonomiczna paralela Polski z Hiszpanią u schyłku wieku totalizmów", *Przegląd Powszechny,* 1 (1990), 116.

24 The term "taxi parties" was created by Joaquín Garrigues Walker, the leader of Spanish conservative liberals, in order to define his own, by no means the smallest, party. See Michael Buse, *La nueva democracia. Sistema de partidos y orientación de voto (1976-1983)* (Madrid 1984), 28.

25 For the role of Catholic church under both authoritarian regimes, see H. Johnston, "Toward an Explanation of Church Opposition to Authoritarian Regimes: Religio-oppositional Subcultures in Poland and Catalonia", *Journal for the Scientific Study of Religion,* 4 (1989); and José Casanova, *Public Religions in the Modern World* (Chicago and London: The University of Chicago Press, 1994), 75-113.

26 A Polish author has written: "Between The Franco Spain and the Gomułka Poland more common features and parallelisms can be drawn than between Jagiellonian Poland and the Empire of Spanish Hapsburgs." Henryk Zieniewicz, "Gospodarki hiszpańskiej przypadek" *Polonia,* Alcalá de Henares, 13 (1994).

27 See his interview in *Gazeta Wyborcza,* September 17, 1997.

28 Perhaps the only exception is the former communist premier Piotr Jaroszewicz, murdered in 1992 together with his wife in very unclear circumstances.

29 In Poland this process has been precisely analysed by Aleksander Smolar and Edmund Wnuk-Lipiński in *Od komunizmu do demokracji* (Cracow: Wyd. Ad Laborem, 1996), 37-38, 50-51.

30 Attempts to take repressive measures by the Solidarity government - and especially by Catholic members of the Polish Parliament - against

the pro-Republican volunteers were met with indignance in Spain, where organizations of veterans, including a nationalist organization of veterans, protested strongly and showed their readiness to take care of Polish veterans. At the beginning of 1996, the Spanish Government granted Spanish citizenship to all those living soldiers of International Brigades who had fought on the Republic's side in 1936-1939.

31 For interesting comments on the fraternization between Michnik and Jaruzelski, see T. Rosenberg, *The Haunted Land,* 243-245.

32 For example Ignacio Sotelo and Francisco Umbral in Spain and Jan M. Rokita in Poland.

33 See Aleksander Hall, "Deklaracje i czyny", *Tygodnik Powszechny*, 9 (1996); Federico Jiménez Losantos, *Contra el felipismo. Crónicas de una década* (Madrid, 1993), 18.

34 See, for example, the following four books published in Barcelona: José Manuel Otero Novas, *Nuestra democracia puede morir* (1987); Justino Sinova, Javier Tusell, *El secuestro de la democracia. Como regenerar el sistema político español* (1990); Francisco Umbral, *El socialfelipismo. La democracia detenida* (1991); Angel Cristóbal Montes, *La democracia en España sobrevivirá?* (1993); and in Poland: Marcin Król, "Democracy in Poland: A Few Skeptical Comments", *Periphery. Journal of Polish Affairs*. 1 (1995); Jacek Żakowski, "Tak gnije demokracja", *Gazeta Wyborcza,* 275 (1994) and a vivid discussion caused by this article; "Garbata demokracja. Dyskusja redakcyjna", *Res Publica Nowa*, 6 (1996).

35 See J.M. Aznar, *Ocho años de gobierno* (Barcelona: Planeta, 2005), 165-166, 187-189.

36 See a common article written by foreign ministers of Spain and Poland: A. Palacio, W. Cimoszewicz, "How to keep the balance in Europe's treaty", *Financial Times*, Sept. 26, 2003; *Polonia – España* (Warsaw: Ministerio de Asuntos Exteriores de la República de Polonia, 2003).

37 A strongly conservative criticism of the ruling Socialist Party of Spain can be found especially in the special issue of *Fronda,* 35 (2005).

38 See Tadeusz Kowalik, "Systemic Diversity of Modern Capitalism", *Dialogue and Universalism* 10-12 (2005), 118.

Chapter 5

Eastern Europe and Latin America in a Comparative and Universalist Perspective

It is a sad paradox that East Europeans and Latin Americans, living as they do within one structure encompassing the whole world and coming across identical or very similar problems and socio-economic structures in the past, know little if anything at all about each other.

-- Henryk Szlajfer (Warsaw, 1987).

The present study is at once a new introduction, a brief supplement (chiefly bibliographical one) and an epilogue to a book of mine on East European and Latin American thought (*Dependencia y originalidad de la filosofía en Latinoamérica y en la Europa del Este,* UNAM), which I published in Mexico City ten years ago. Its aim is an Eastern European - Latin American comparison of ideas. I do not neglect the immense and fairly obvious differences between both regions under consideration. However, here I prefer to look here more attentively at some unexpected similarities and parallels of ideas in the countries of poor capitalism, where not only philosophers and intellectual elites have dreamt of general progress, widespread prosperity, lasting freedom and democracy without the qualifiers of a communist or authoritarian past. The common motifs in philosophical and social theories seen in Latin America and Eastern Europe can be attributed to the dramatic socio-economic events and to the great importance of Christianity, Marxism and Populism. These theories, often permeated with the spirit of messianism, syncretism and utopia, have been developing independently in each region for some time, and with practically no mutual influence.

INTRODUCTORY REMARKS

In recent years much attention was paid to Eastern and Central Europe due to the important political changes taking place there after the collapse of the Soviet system. The interest in Latin America has been rather steady, but was intensified after the collapse of bureaucratic-authoritarian regimes some years before the demise of communism. Also comparative research on political and economic problems of both large regions of the world has been fashionable in the last years. There appeared some innovative books on the topic,[1] many discussions and conferences were held on the difficult transition to democracy, economic underdevelopment, foreign debt crisis, privatization processes and other acute problems of these countries. The participants of the inspiring discussions in Russia,[2] in Poland,[3] in the United States, in Brasil and elsewhere, however, almost never penetrated into the complicated intellectual history of both diversified regions to compare their social consciousness, but often asked whether the tormented reality of Latin America will be the political and economic future of the post-communist Europe.

While in Latin America almost no scholarly research into Eastern European ideas is under way,[4] in our part of Europe many monographs on various currents in Latin American thought have been published recently,[5] but hardly anyone has attempted a comparative research into the philosophy and the history of ideas in both poor, failure-ridden regions of the world.

Some authors, however, noted a similarity in Polish and Latin American identification with Europe, in their self-portrayal as part or extension of Europe, in common problems stemming from the 19th century failures, and in the common search to make up for lost time and to achieve an appriopriate modernization.[6]

Edmund Stephen Urbanski (1909-1996), a Polish Latin Americanist living in the United States, had once occassionally noticed some points of similarity in the remote Indo-Asiatic roots of Eastern European, Slavic and Hispanic American civilization(s) in the remote Indo-Asiatic roots. In particular he saw the following common traits in the Slav and Hispanic character and mentality: a high level of emotionalism, a metaphysical vision of life, a vague sense of practice, a contemplative attitude, enigmatic behaviour, a fatalism and a specific type of passivity in confronting collective dangers.[7]

Witold Gombrowicz (1904-1969), a prominent Polish writer who spent many years in Argentina, saw a fundamental impotence and immaturity in the South American and Polish contemplative, futile search for national originality and genuineness. "Semi-Asiatic" Poles, like Argentinians, were too feeble, lacked individual initiative and were willing to act in accordance with an alien ready-made program. Gombrowicz saw secondary, derivative traits in Argentinian and Polish authors that paralysed and forced them to be in touch with reality only indirectly and with the help of other cultures.[8]

Comparing Eastern Europe and Latin America is frequent nowadays, especially in Poland and Russia, from various political positions, rightist and leftist alike. The Latin American experience is often recalled as a positive example or as a warning for the post-communist Europe. Indeed, both regions of the world have been deprived in their history of independence, political stability and economic welfare. Only the prewar Czechoslovakia and Uruguay were considered for a time as Eastern European and South American Switzerlands, respectively.

Some authors, however, deem that "the realities of Eastern Europe and Latin America are too different to be compared".[9] Admitting some comparison only between concrete societies, Kieniewicz reaffirms, however, a backwardness and joint participation in Christianity of all these societies.

Also the American Richard M. Morse tried to establish a deep contrast between Latin America and Russia.[10] The former, in his words, shared the religion and culture of the backward Iberian part of Europe, whereas the Russians claimed to have their own national culture and a non-European form of Christianity. Ernesto Sábato, a distinguished Argentinian writer, noted, however, that the Iberian inheritance is not fully European: "like all the barbarian outskirts of Europe it did not experience the Renaissance in its strict, rationalist and scientific meaning."[11] In his opinion, Latin Americans share much enlivening barbarism, they grew on a new, boundless, and primitive continent and understood therefore better Dostoevsky, Tolstoy and other north-eastern authors than the purely Latin tradition.

It is very difficult to compare Eastern Europe to Latin America as a whole, since both regions are very diversified. Indeed, Eastern Europe constituted a compulsary, artificially unified bloc for only forty years or so under the Soviet domination, and now has returned to its diversity and pluralism.[12] "In the consciousness of the representatives of the various nationalities in the region under consideration one can hardly note manifestations of uniformity. They feel above all as Lithuanians, Poles, Hungarians, Romanians, and Bulgarians, and not Central-Eastern Europeans. Each of these nationalities has its own rivals and enemies; each of them views its opportunities for the future in a slightly different way."[13] The same can be said about Latin Americans who seldom think of themselves under that rubric, the term Latin America having been used more frequent in Europe and North America than in South and Central American areas of racially and culturally mixed population.[14]

Traditionally, all Eastern Europeans and many Latin Americans, not only stubborn Westerners, rejected the idea of being a part of the Third World. Even among Latin American leftist groups this idea was initially accepted with considerable reservation.[15] In Latin America, opinions began to change a little in the 1970s and in Eastern Europe in the early 1990s.[16] Eastern Europeans no longer looked at Latin America with an air of superiority.

Recently much new literature on Central-Eastern Europe has been published, in which some new specific traits of the region and of its subregions have been discovered. Now everyone is aware that Eastern European countries have been very diverse, but that something common in their histories is also evident: a peasant character with tiny middle classes, a legacy of political and economic dependence on outside powers, and historical force of the ideology of compensatory nationalism used as a means to build fragile nation-states and to struggle against important ethnic minorities.[17]

POLITICAL TRADITIONS

It is well known that almost all countries of Eastern Europe and Latin America lack any important democratic tradition.[18] Many students of Latin America attribute this fact to the predominance of authoritarian centralist tradition of Spanish Catholicism and to the inheritance of other non-democratic Hispanic, pre-Hispanic and even Arabic institutions.[19] Some even claimed that Latin Americans did not in fact aspire to democracy, and that authoritarianism and corporatism were consistent with their traditional cultural practice which had allowed the rejection of free elections, the rule of law, separation of powers and other democratic rules imported from the Anglo-Saxon world.

Until the beginning of the twentieth century it was argued by the representatives of social Darwinism that democratic procedures were irrelevant to and incompatible with ethnic and psychological features of the Latin American people. Also later difficulties in attaining democracy were often explained by the Iberic-Latin patrimonialist tradition, in which there was no clear separation between public and private spheres and where freedom was constrained by ecclesiastical, and military control. The church, like the army, was not conceived to be a mere interest group but was an essential part of Iberian (and Polish) culture and of the state system, bearing a responsibility not only in public education but also for the political realm.

The social and political pluralism that existed in Latin America was usually constrained and controlled by the official state and its numerous bureaucracy. The patrimonial type of Iberian rule did not tolerate any political autonomy of the middle class, civil servants or aristocracy in relation to the central administrative authority. These negative aspects of the Iberian legacy did not allow for the appearance and consolidation of intermediary institutions between the state and its citizens. Any possible germs of civil society were defeated by the centralist state in its formative period. Thus the tradition of Spanish American authoritarianism, including also some features of agrarian authoritarianism, was a serious obstacle to the cause of democracy.[20]

Other authors focussed rather on structural than cultural roots and causes of Latin American patrimonialism and authoritarianism persisting almost to the present day. The new bureaucratic authoritarianism of the 1970s, it was argued, emerged as a consequence of mass mobilization of popular sectors. Its aim was to suppress and control new mass organizations of the people. Whereas populist authoritarianism wanted to regulate the political presence of the masses, modern authoritarianism wanted to exclude them from the political scene.[21]

The opposition by authoritarian regimes to civil society in the form of mass organizations means that in Latin America there exist various political traditions, not only an authoritarian one. Authoritarianism is not necessarily the main current, since there are also liberal and democratic currents of thought and action. "The fact is, as Howard Wiarda rightly saw it, that Latin America remains a mix; an amalgam of a corporatist-authoritarian tradition, a liberal-democratic one, and a newer socialist one. Much of politics centers on the conflict between these contrasting traditions and the various compromises and accomodations used to reconcile them."[22]

But it is necessary to underline that the personalist political tradition of *caudillismo*, *coronelismo* and *caciquismo* has been very strong in Latin America and appeared as a creole response to the crisis of decolonization immediately after independence in the 1820s. This caudillism was dictatorial and oligarchic, based on military force and violence. Such political leadership could be established only in the absence of popular participation in political life.[23]

Modern Latin American dictatorships were rather bureaucratic than caudillistic. The famous sociologist Fernando H. Cardoso, till recently Brasil's President, who along with Guillermo O`Donnell is one of the main analysts of the new type of bureaucratic-authoritarian regimes, named the new bureaucratic sectors in Latin America as "state bourgeoisie", which politically controls state-owned means of production.[24] Authoritarian governments guaranteed these sectors a priviledged position in society, although formally they did not possess private means of production. Their position was compared to that of the Soviet state bureaucracy controlling the production.[25]

In Latin America, it is easy to discern recuring historical cycles of democracy and dictatorship. Some authors argue that "democracy and authoritarian rule have oscillated throughout an extended series of cycles of roughly twenty years' duration and that this pattern of oscillation, sometimes called a 'pendular pattern', is likely to continue. The predominance of authoritarian rule in 1960s and 1970s merely followed the earlier period of democratic rule in the 1940s and 1950s, and is currently being replaced by a cycle of democracy. If this pattern continues, the current cycle has only another fifteen years or so to run before it, too, will be repeated."[26] The recurrence of various repressive periods, thaws and liberalizations has also been noticed in the East European history.[27]

Some say that the relative longevity of the new democracies in Latin America owes much to the unprecedented interest and commitment to democratic ideals shown nowadays by many Latin American intellectuals.[28] The collapse of Marxism and Leninism in Eastern Europe has greatly influenced the Latin American left, which evolved step by step from the neo-colonial, anti-American dependency theories to a re-evaluation of democratic ideals.[29] Participation in real democratic institutions is now much more appreciated by all factions of the Latin American left.

Jadwiga Staniszkis has paid attention to the ideological syndrome of the mixture of neoliberal economic policy with Catholic, populist and corporatist orientation that long haunted Eastern Europe and Latin America. She has noted a formation process of a corporatist state in post-communist Poland, where the executive power is becoming a real power, while pluralism of political parties may function only as an ornament. The disappointed author predicts a rise of centralized authoritarian regimes, taking the form of a corporatist state with pseudo-democratic façade, well-known in the past.[30]

We have observed in the above remarks an acute lack of genuine democratic tradition in Latin America; the same can be said about Eastern European, and especially the Russian-Soviet, tradition.

Eastern Europe was a politically backward region with a predominant state bureaucracy, etatist institutions, and weak societies -- and almost no democratic traditions. As a transitional zone, Eastern Europe only partially participated in the European cultural experience, promoting instead much of its own nationalisms.[31]

It has been noted that "by the end of World War I, social, economic and political retardation were characteristic of most of the region. The largely agrarian, semi-literate societies were politically immature; they were certainly uncommitted to -- and in most cases, unfamiliar with -- democracy. The political culture, such as it was, had its roots in ecclesiastical and monarchic paternalism. This was most evident in the Orthodox and Catholic communities which comprised the majority of the inhabitants of the successor states."[32] This political tradition and the persistence of intolerance even in present conditions do not make for secure democracy in Eastern Europe.

There were great differences between the Eastern European and Western concepts of freedom and nation. While in the West individual freedom was conceived as an unavoidable right and was protected by special institutions, farther east freedom was more precarious and depended much on membership in priviledged groups. Also nationalism was more virulent here, so that it was made a "distinction between the characteristically eastern European-German concept of a nation as a quasi-mystical living body and the more prosaic Western concept of a nation as a political entity."[33]

As it was already mentioned, Eastern Europe and Latin America had no tradition of civil society. Especially under early communism all signs of independent civil society were suppressed. The concept appeared almost simultaneously in the discourse of the democratic opposition during the struggle for freedom and especially during the transition process from dictatorship to democracy in the late 1970s and 1980s. Analyzing the process of liberalization of the military bureaucratic-authoritarian rule in Latin America scholars usually connected the process with the resurrection of a citizenship principle and civil society that culminates in mass mobilization. High mobilization of civil society refers to intellectual groups, middle-class organizations, working class and various associations, and this effort against recent dictatorships attempted to restore the public sphere which previously was state-controlled.[34]

After the initial phase of high level of mobilization, and near popular upsurge (as recently in the Ukraine), there comes the phase of depoliticization and disillusionment in dependent and underdeveloped civil societies of both regions of the world.

It is often said that a pluralistic social order in Latin America and Eastern Europe cannot be taken for granted and that democratic institutions are fragile: "It is unreasonable to expect a future of calm, stable parliamentarism in this part of Europe. Politics will be turbulent, and at times authoritarian, and the Man on the White Horse will probably ride again."[35]

THE IDEA OF CENTRAL EUROPE

Since the end of the communist epoch and even earlier, much effort was exerted to make a distinction between Eastern and Central Europe or East Central Europe and Russia while the Balcan South-Eastern Europe has become a separate problem.[36]

I am going to address briefly only the much debated problem of Central Europe, its identity and its specific thought. Undoubtedly, the relatively new discussion on Central Europe, its rediscovery, a search for a Central European identity began with the well-known work by the Czech Milan Kundera, who put emphasize on vital significance of the region for Europe, and on the area's exaggerated otherness from Russia, the Slavic world and the Soviet Union, which had dominated it after the World War II.[37]

There was noted in Central Europe a sharp and protracted conflict between two ideas of the nation and of culture: "the first, inspired by the ideas of the French revolution, was a democratic, political definition of the nation as a community of citizens. The other was German, romantic, 'blood and soil' concept of the nation. Conversely, two ideas of European culture were at stake: the universalistic, humanist concept of European culture defined by Julien Benda as the 'autonomy of the spirit' versus the concept of culture as identity, or *Volksgeist*, unique to each nation."[38] The rediscovery and reaffirmation of Central European Culture in the 1980s contributed a little to the rejection of ethnic nationalism.

The term Central Europe was first associated with the multinational spirit of the Austro-Hungarian Monarchy whereas later, but before 1945, it reflected the dominant German place in the region of small nations which wanted to be independent from all adjacent powers. After the publication of Kundera's essay the ambiguous concept of Central Europe was included in the anticommunist opposition's political discourse on the region. Now, some years after the collapse of Berlin wall and of the Soviet bloc, it takes on a new, vague meaning.

According to Czeslaw Milosz, the concept of Central Europe has no clear geographic boundaries; it is rather an act of faith, a project for better future of the humiliated nations. He found a specific sensibility in the Central European literary production: "a tinge of nostalgia, of utopianism, and of hope."[39]

Some time ago the Hungarian György Konrad and the Czech Václav Havel put even more stress on the Central European identity, Central European consciousness and mind. According to Timothy Garton Ash, who favoured and promoted the concept of Central Europe in the West, the nostalgic idea of pro-Western Central Europe of the 1980s is still valid and even more real in the 1990s and at the beginning of new century, since these countries, in spite of their great difficulties, are now incomparably closer to the West than some years before.[40]

Also professional philosophers reflected on the unity of Europe and on specific traits of the Central European philosophy stemming from the ancient Greece and the Western tradition.[41] Philosophers of the region used to emphasize in their theories of culture the specific position of their countries situated between the East and the West. Their purely philosophical tradition is not very original, except for the highly innovative common philosophical style of anti-idealistic, empirical analysis, initiated at the end of 19th century.[42] In Central and Eastern Europe, however, as in Latin America, literature very often expressed crucial, existential problems of the human and social conditions

It should be emphasized that many Western and Eastern (mainly Balkan) authors do not like the idea of separating or excluding Central Europe from common Eastern European fate. The Rumanian Andrei Plesu noticed that all Eastern Europeans are united by their historical destiny, common scarcities and sufferings, irrespective of their Slavic or Romanic ethnicity,

Catholic or Orthodox Christianity. He opposed the dangerous tendency of dividing Eastern Europe into first and second class nations or peoples.[43] Also the former Bulgarian president and philosopher Zhelyu Zhelev stated that the future of European space will be decided in the Balkans, and that the democratization of the region conceived as an important element of the European-Byzantine Europe which is willing to be merged into the renovated spirit of a boundless Europe.

COMMON PHILOSOPHICAL AND POLITICAL IDEAS

Eastern European and Latin American thinkers have often asked difficult, "accursed questions" about the historical destinies of particular nations of these distant regions. Russians, like Brazilians, called even their immense Eurasian country a continent in order to set it apart from the rest of Eastern Europe, or from Latin (Spanish) America in the case of Brasil.

Russian, Eastern European and Latin American thought is not very inventive, but instead quite responsive to Western European ideas, treating them often as redeeming and emancipating forces.[44] It is astonishing to see what strange forms Western ideas acquired in the adjacent or more distant peripheries of the West. The thinkers and essayists of the regions under consideration were very sensitive to the philosophy of history, believing that it would elucidate the strange destiny and vague place of their countries in the world.[45]

In recent years, after the East European "autumn of the nations" much attention is being paid to the difficult task of building the foundations of a free society, tolerance, culture of liberty, and to getting rid of aggressive nationalism in this region and elsewhere.[46]

It is also astonishing to see that an oversimplified version of neoliberal ideology, once the myths of Marxism and statism had lost their power, began to triumph in Eastern Europe and Latin America.[47]

In the 1990s postmodernism has spread throughout Eastern Europe and Latin America. Some elements of this philosophical attitude and literary sensibility were present, in fact, in both regions long before the demise of Marxism and communism. Such writers as Jorge Luís Borges and Witold Gombrowicz may be considered forerunners of postmodernism and Zygmunt Bauman and Milan Kundera are almost its classics. The terms 'modernism' and 'postmodernism' had appeared first in the Spanish American literary criticism long before they spread to North America and later to Europe. On the other hand, Central and East European writers contributed to postmodernism *avant la lettre*. Their tragic experience of war, holocaust, concentration camp and gulag favoured the implementation of the following literary genres, motifs and techniques: the grotesque, black humour, paradox, ambivalence, the motifs of labirynth, radical irony and intertextual game.[48]

Postmodern anti-fundamentalism and pluralism, opposed to all political and religious dogmatisms, was widely present in the emigré and underground literatures of Central Europe in the 1980s. This literature played a considerable role in deconstuction and final destruction of the totalitarian ideology of communism and of some other totalising discourses. It happened, however, that the official reception of postmodernism in Eastern Europe coincided in time with the sudden collapse of 'real' and utopian socialism and in Latin America with the loss of faith in progress along with disenchantement with leftist ideas. The phenomenon of postmodernism is, therefore, closely connected with the postcommunist consciousness of crisis, liberation, exhaustion, void and unsuccessful modernization. It has become visible that the post-totalitarian chaos corresponds somehow with fashionable Western ideas of nihilism and deconstruction. Characteristic both for postmodernism -- in which "nothing matters, anything goes" (Carlos Fuentes) -- and for postcommunism is "loosening of forms" and a loosening of official political structures. It is being said, however, that genuine postmodernism is possible only in postindustrial countries abounding in consumer goods. This type of permissive civilization exists neither in Eastern Europe nor in Latin America. So the countries of both regions should not accept uncritically the ideas of modernity, modernization and postmodernism coming from the advanced West.[49]

As we have seen, Eastern European and Latin American cultures and societies can easily be compared. Historically, these still premodern societies had no solid middle classes and their cultures stemmed mainly from landed gentry tradition. These cultures were characterized by a Baroque and neo-Baroque style and devotional Catholicism, humanistic and highly unpractical traits. Later their symbolic and romantic cultural patterns searched for the elaboration or defence of national identity.[50] In this type of predominantly spiritual cultures the abstract manipulation of words and symbols by a community was valued more highly than empirical manipulation of things and forces or competition of economic interests.[51]

Generally, Western culture and philosophy set standards that Latin Americans and Eastern Europeans widely imitated,[52] but many of them did not want to be servile followers of foreign models and developed, with the help of Western thought, national myths and nationalist ideologies. Various kinds of utopian and prophetic nationalism (slavophilism), messianism, *indigenismo* and populism can serve as examples.[53]

These utopian and messianic myths (Slavic, Latin, Hellenic, Byzantine, Eurasian, etc.) and complexes (in particular martyrdom and a cult of martyrs) of underdeveloped countries clashed very often with positivistic programs of progress and organic work (e. g. Polish *praca organiczna*, Czech *malá prace*).

In Mexican history, for example, the myth of indigenous nationalism and messianism was closely associated with the "Indian problem", with the exaltation of the Indian values,[54] whereas in the history of some Eastern European countries it was often associated with the "peasant problem", with the high evaluation of the "simple people" and of traditional religious beliefs opposing modern liberalism. The ideology of nationalism was created by intellectuals, dissatisfied with depressing reality; it favoured economic nationalism and building nation-states, was opposed to real dependency and contributed unwittingly to new underdevelopment. Economic nationalism was predominant in policies of many countries of both regions in the prewar and postwar periods and even in the model of central planning.

It was rightly noted that "in all Latin American countries, the state was founded without the nation's help, whereas in Eastern Europe, certain nations emerged without the blessing of their respective state. This way, nationalism presented itself as an ideology, having nothing to do with either the nation or the state, and as all respective ideologies, it turned out to be unable to distinguish between politics and the economy, and between the economy and society; it proved to be holistic ('totalizante') in nature".[55]

Nationalistic ideologies were supported by numerous thinkers and the search for national identity turned out to be a permanent theme of philosophical reflection for many intellectuals.[56] In recent years, however, nationalism was called in question and rejected by official neoliberal policies and by many intellectuals defending liberal democracy. The Peruvian novelist and essayist Mario Vargas Llosa has recently declared: "Economic nationalism -- which along with cultural nationalism is one of the most tenacious aberrations in our history -- is beginning to show signs of receding at last. Nationalism has contributed substantially to the underdevelopment of Latin America. Yet slowly we are learning that health does not derive from fortifying our borders, but from opening them up wide and going out into the world to capture markets for our products, along with technology and capital and ideas that the world can offer us to develop our resources and create the jobs that we so urgently need".[57] To the most outspoken defenders of the new wave of liberal democracy in Latin America belong also Hernando de Soto, Octavio Paz, Emeterio Gómez, Carlos Rangel and others.[58]

Whereas in Eastern Europe Marxist and populist ideas have lost much of their intellectual force, a considerable part of Latin American intelligentsia is still antiliberal and devoted to the old myths of statist ideologies. Those disenchanted with Marxism and the capacities of the state to improve economic situation, resort to neo-anarchist and neopopulist ideas of citizen's and communal self-management. This new ideology of the so-called *basismo*[59] is democratic, but rejects the formal apparatus and dogmas of liberal democracy. This kind of a new anti-authoritarian and utopian thinking can also be detected in Eastern Europe.

TOWARDS UNIVERSALISM

Also a kind of a broad universalism, rather non-political or embracing various political options, is paving its way in Eastern Europe and Latin America. This type of thinking, not only nationalist and particularist ideas, has deep traditions in both regions.

Latin America is a place where various races and cultural traditions have been present since since the historic encounter of two words in 1492. The encounter has produced a miscegenation of European, native American (Indian) and African population. Many authors, especially the Mexican José

Vasconcelos have reflected much on the creative process of race miscegenation. Leopoldo Zea claims that Vasconcelos' views on the mixture of races become more topical nowadays as a key to a new interpretation of the Spanish enterprise boldly undertaken over 500 years ago, nowadays when the North America and Europe are 'latinoamericanizing' themselves due to active presence there of various races and cultures and when a search for universal solutions of the burning problems of the present-day world is more and more intensive.[60] Now it is not difficult to come across the opinion that "a Latin American synthesis based on patterns of fusion and amalgamation could contribute to a model worthy of global application" in the twenty-first century.[61]

Any brief summary of the recent tendencies in the development of Latin American thought one should underline that the central question of philosophy pursued in Latin America is the question about the very existence, and character of Latin American philosophy and culture. In this debate stretching over a century there have appeared many extreme and conciliatory standpoints. The eminent Peruvian philosopher Francisco Miró Quesada tries to hold an intermediary and somehow conciliary position between an abstract philosophical 'universalism' and regionalism. Some time ago he wrote on the slightly original and 'ex-centric' (directed towards the West) and 'prospective' (looking towards the future) character of Latin American philosophy and on some dangers stemming from it. More recently, however, Miró Quesada has stated that genuine Latin American philosophy *is not so prospective plausibility, but rather is achieved already, being in full blossom topicality*, contributing much new to the storehouse of world, universal ideas.

According to Miró Quesada, an important role in the process of maturation of Latin American philosophy was played by the so-called controversy over its Americanism and universalism. A consequence of a specifically Latin American philosophy (*filosofía de lo americano*) was an increasing awareness of the necessity of obtaining certain independence from the dominant powers in Latin America, and an awareness that the self-realization and full accomplishment of Latin American being requires a just independence and freedom. This philosophy contributed to the creation of a Latin American philosophy of liberation which strove for a real humanism, a universal humanism applicable to all peoples. Such humanism so impossible without prior liberation of all the oppressed of the world.

Miró Quesada maintains that Latin American philosophy is being realized in its double meaning as universal and continental, that "Latin America is today a visible participant of the great Odissey that gives character and meaning to the human history",[62] and that Latin Americans have already achieved security in their philosophizing for themselves and for the rest of the world.

Nowadays a neoliberal universalism, abstract and technocratic, is in vogue and is often considered to be the highest expression of universalism.[63] Its adherents want to change Latin American culture radically, to make it more pragmatic and compatible with requirements of the Western world centers. The politicians introducing neoliberal policies have promised to modernize their countries, bring them to the First World thanks to a common market with the United States.

Latin American intellectuals, however, usually prefer those versions of universalism that throw away all unilaterality, that take broadly into account cultural pluralism and different ways of life, that is the essential component of the 'miscegenated continent'. In fear of being crushed by external powers, they approach the necessary universalism and planetary dimensions of the present-day world from their own particularity.[64]

This dilemma of the division into "Nationals" and more universalist "Europeanizers" is present also in the political ideals of the present-day Poland[65] and other countries of Eastern Europe. It is a rule that countries with a strong complex of dependency[66] and with sustained tradition of the struggle for national liberation[67] may have grave difficulties with European, inter-American and universal integration.

Latin American and North American cultures seem to form two divergent varieties of Western civilization, the obverse and reverse side of one global civilization on the Western hemisphere.[68] Numerous attempts have been made to reconcile them. Filmer S.C. Northrop, a North American philosopher, considered the crucial problem of merging Latin American and Anglo-Saxon cultures. According to him, this task of Pan-Americanism has universal importance, for it would permit the creation of universal philosophy to express world unity: "this task of relating the aesthetic and emotionally immediate religious values to scientific, doctrinal, and pragmatic values is precisely what constitutes the fundamental problem of correctly and safely merging the East with the West".[69]

The search for the inter-American mind[70] and system that have been shaped in spite of politico-economic adversities and behavioral contrasts,[71] reflects a noble effort "to build a world community on the basis of voluntary cooperation of nations and political pluralism".[72] Now, after the collapse of the Soviet System, very influential in Latin America, an actual Pan-American or better Inter-American unity, based on universally accepted values, seems a bit more plausible in the twenty first century.[73] Latin Americans, although still haunted by an obsession with failure (*fracasomanía*),[74] for a moment seemed more than ever favorably disposed to the idea of liberal democracy and economic integration with their northern neighbour. According to Mario Vargas Llosa, "now that growing numbers of Latin Americans finally seem to be learning that highest of political virtues -- common sense -- integration is starting to be understood in its modern sense: as a joining together to speed Latin America`s integration with the rest of humanity. Entering into today`s world with an awareness of possibilities, of risks, and of markets is the best way for poor and backward countries like our own to start being modern -- that is, prosperous. Without prosperity, Vargas Llosa rightly added, there is little freedom, for freedom in poverty is at best a precarious and limited sort of freedom".[75]

The broad-minded ideals of European unity and of universalism have been very influential in the East Central Europe. Works by many writers of the region successfully intended to transcend national barriers and became therefore part of the universal heritage. Such writers as Kafka, Canetti, Čapek, Ionescu, Witkiewicz and Gombrowicz transformed the experience of their native lands into universal symbols.[76] Even the Polish romantics associated their nationalism with a broader vision of universalism, with international brotherhood and the future 'organic humanity'.[77]

The famous Czech president-philosopher Thomas G. Masaryk and his predecessors (Kollár, Palacký) believed in the progress of universal humanitarianism not only in the geographical heart of Europe; they expanded their national views into a universal ideal of mankind. Masaryk with his open-minded views on the world community of nations, on the emerging cosmopolitanism, on the cultural and racial syncretism, is considered to be a representative of a modern type universalism.[78]

Poland and other countries of Central-Eastern Europe and Latin America, all living in the areas of inter-cultural contact, claimed to be the best intermediaries between different civilizations and to fulfill the function of catalyst precipitating the birth of a universalist civilization and a new universalist thinking. Recently, the most serious efforts in this direction have been done by Janusz Kuczyński, the co-founder and honorary President of the International Society for Universalism, established in 1989 in Warsaw, Poland.

This new universalism, according to Kuczyński, has many meanings. First of all, it is a movement of collective consciousness the subject of it is emerging mankind for itself. Kuczyński attaches high importance to this transition from humankind in itself, conceived as a simple collection of nations, to the stage of humankind for itself, humankind as a real, global community.[79] This process is taking place now and is co-created by the International Society for Universalism and International Society for Universal Dialogue. Universalism is also an all-embracing metatheory of mankind, it includes in synthetic form the richness of cultures, individualities and differences, especially in their striving toward all-human unity.

The roads to universalism are multi-level dialogue of cultures and religions, pluralism and reconciliation. Universalism originated from the consciousness of the crisis of all the existing philosophies and ideologies and it offers a kind of metaphilosophy saving their authentic achievements and overcoming nihilism and postmodern "endism".

Universalism is also conceived as an intellectual basis for real tolerance, openness, holistic integration, synergetic cooperation, and as a diagnosis of the emergence of universalist society after the collapse of communism, undermined initially in Poland. It is also a proclamation of the coming age of love, wisdom and *homo universalis*.[80]

The first World Congress of Universalism was held on August 15-20, 1993, in Warsaw and was organized according to three ideas: Dialogue, Solidarity, Covenant. Immediately after the Warsaw Congress the World Congress of Philosophy was held, for the first time in Moscow, and initiated a new stage of universal dialogue in which Russians, East Europeans and Latin Americans could fully participate with no ideological divides. The XIX World

Congress of Philosophy in Moscow (August 22-28, 1993) concentrated on philosophical perspectives of the mankind at a turning point and included the universalist problem of the unity of mankind in Russian philosophy.

Since that time more European and world congresses of universalism have been held, in Britain, the United States, and many similar problems have been seriously discussed in Rio de Janeiro and elsewhere. The last, fourth European Congress of Dialogue and Universalism on "Transmutations of Western Civilization" (the topic precised by Professor George F. McLean from the Catholic University of America) was held at the Warsaw University in June 24-31, 2005. The following problems, among others, were developed and acquired new dimensions: metaphilosophy and the co-creation of the theory of "unifying wisdom"; Science, technology, IT, art, universal society; Pan-human civilization: theory and praxis in everyday life.

The phantom and/or hope of universalism is haunting the present-day world under globalization and the ecological threat.

NOTES

1 Nicos P. Mouzelis, *Politics in the Semi-Periphery. Early Parliamentarism and Late Industrialization in the Balkans and Latin America* (London 1986); *Economic Nationalism in East-Central Europe and South America 1918-1939*, ed. H.Szlajfer (Genève 1990); A. Przeworski, *Democracy and the Market: Political and Economic Reforms in Eastern Europe and Latin America* (Cambridge: Cambridge University Press, 1991); *III Congreso Latinoamericano de la Universidad de Varsovia. Varsovia, 16-18 de junio de 1995. Memorias* (Warsaw: CESLA 1996, t. 1, 2); *América Latina e Europa Centro-Oriental. Perspectivas para o Terceiro Milenio*, ed. M.T. Torribio Brittes Lemos, J. F. Pessoa de Barros, A. Dembicz (Rio de Janeiro: INTERCOM and CESLA, 1996; *Diálogo interregional entre Europa Centro-Oriental y América Latina*, ed. A. Dembicz (Warsaw: CESLA 1997); A. James McAdams (ed.), *Transitional Justice and the Rule of Law in New Demcracies* (Notre Dame and London 1997); B. Greskovits, *The Political Economy of Protest and Patience. East European and Latin American Transformations Compared* (Budapest: CEU, 1998).

2 See T. Vorożeikina, "Latinskaia Amerika i Rossiia (Opyt sravnitielnogo političeskogo analiza)", *Pro et contra* 2 (1997), 90-102; Z. Iwanowski, *Democratization in Latin America and Russia: A Comparative Analysis* (San Diego, 1996); K.A. Khachaturov, *Latinoamerikanskiie uroki dla Rossii* (Moscow 1999); see also *Latinskaia Amerika*, 10 (1999).

3 See *Estudios Latinoamericanos* 14 (1992) and the Proceedings of the 6th Congress of the Federación Internacional de Estudios sobre América Latina y el Caribe, held in June 1993 in Warsaw, especially *Pensamiento ibero y latinoamericano: su percepción en la Europa no-ibera y perspectivas*, ed. J. Wojcieszak (Warsaw: CESLA 1995); *Europa del Centro y del Este y el mundo hispánico. Simposio internacional de hispanistas*, ed. Ana I. Blanco Picado y Teresa Eminowicz (Cracow: ABRYS, 1996).

4 Some abortive efforts in this direction were made by the journal *Aproximações. Europa de Leste em Lingua Portuguesa*, published in Brasil in the 1980s and by the one-time Latin American students in Poland: P. Celso Uchoa, R. C. Fernándes, *José e Józef* (Rio de Janeiro 1985); R. C. Fernándes, "Images de la Passion: Catholiques au Brésil et au Pologne", *Esprit*, Dec. 1987; R. C. Fernándes, *Kościół katolicki w Brazylii i w Polsce* (Warsaw: CESLA, 1996); J. Paucar, "List Latynosa do polskiego intelektualisty" (A Latin American's Letter to a Polish Intellectual), *Res Publica* 12 (1988); for more information on the late Peruvian Julio Paucar and his keen interest in Latin America and Central Europe, see *W Drodze* 12 (1992), and *L'Autre Europe* 26-27 (1993).

5 See, for example, *Teologia wyzwolenia* (Liberation Theology), ed. W. Mysłek, M. Nowaczyk (Warsaw: ANS, 1988); *Iz istorii filozofii Latinskoi Ameriki XX wieka*, ed. A. Zykowa, R. Burguete (Moscow: Nauka, 1988); the two-volume monograph: *Marksizm-leninizm i Latinskaia Amerika,* ed. A.F. Shulgovski (Moscow: Nauka, 1989);); I. Curyło-González, *José Ingenieros i pozytywizm latynoamerykański* (Warsaw: SGH, 1992); N.J. Petiaksheva, *Latinoamerikanskaja filosofiia osvobozdieniia v kontekstie komparativistiki* (Moscow: Unikum-Centr, 2000).

6 J. Paucar, "List Latynosa...", 93; see also M. Kula, "Czy bliżej nam do Europy, czy do Ameryki Łacińskiej", in: *Inni wśród nas*, ed. W. Władyka (Warsaw: IBL PAN, 1994).

7 E. S. Urbanski, *Hispanoameryka i jej cywilizacje* (Warsaw 1981), 9; id., *Breve historia de la literatura polaca* (México 1946), 5; id., *Polonia, los eslavos y Europa* (México - Habana 1943), 11-12.

8 See especially his *Dziennik 1957-1961*, in *Dzieła*, vol. VIII (Cracow: WL, 1986), 117-118, 197, 208.

9 J. Kieniewicz, "Situation, Colonialism, Backwardness. On the Possibilities of Comparative Studies of Eastern Europe and Latin America", *Estudios Latinoamericanos* 14 , part I (1992), 81.

10 R. M. Morse, *El espejo de Próspero. Un estudio de la dialéctica del Nuevo Mundo* (México 1992) 128-130; see also a controversy over a possible parallelism between the Brasilian thinker Tobias Barreto (1839-1889) and Russian democratic revolutionaries; the parallel drawn by J. Bazarian in *Novos Rumbos*, June 19, 1959, and refuted by V. Chacon, *História das ideias socialistas no Brasil* (Rio de Janeiro 1965), 267-272.

11 E. Sábato, *Pisarz i jego zmory*, ed. by R. Kalicki,(Cracow: WL, 1988), 194.

12 See J. Rotschild, *Return to Diversity. A Political History of East Central Europe since World War II* (Oxford 1989); *From Stalinism to Pluralism. A Documentary History of Eastern Europe since 1945,* ed. G. Stokes (New York - Oxford 1991).

13 W. Roszkowski, "Uniformity or Diversity? Central-Eastern Europe before and after 1945", *Estudios Latinoamericanos* 14, part I (1992), 63-64; *Historiografia krajów Europy środkowo-wschodniej*, ed. J. Kłoczowski, P. Kras (Lublin: KUL, 1997).

14 C. Wagley, *The Latin American Tradition: Essays on the Unity and the Diversity of Latin American Culture* (New York - London 1968), 9-10; see also E. Martínez Estrada, *Diferencias y semejanzas entre los paises de la América Latina* (México 1962); I. Roxborough, "Unity and Diversity in Latin American History", *Journal of Latin American Studies,* 16 (1984).

15 See H.C.F. Mansilla, "Latin America within the Third World: The Search for a New Identity, the Acceptance of Old Contents", *Estudios Latinoamericanos* 14, part I (1992); L. Zea, "Latinoamérica y el Tercer Mundo", *Lateinamerika Studien* 6 (1980); C. Rangel, *El tercermundismo* (Caracas, 1982).

16 See the proceedings of the conference "Czy Polska jest krajem Trzeciego Świata ?" (Is Poland a Third World Country ?), in: *Dylematy rozwoju. Porównywalność doświadczeń krajów słabiej rozwiniętych i Polski*, ed E. Butkiewicz (Warsaw 1992).

17 Thomas W. Simons, Jr., *Eastern Europe in the Postwar World* (New York 1991).

18 A time ago Charles Wagley wrote: "There are countries proud of their democratic traditions such as Uruguay and Chile and countries such as Paraguay and Nicaragua where democratic institutions are almost nonexistent". - C. Wagley, *The Latin American Tradition. Essays on the Unity and Diversity of Latin American Culture* (New York 1968), 11. However, soon after the publication of Wagley's book, the relatively democratic tradition of Chile and Uruguay was abruptly broken by very cruel military dictatorship.

19 For a discussion of these theories see Carlos A. Forment, "Socio-Historical Models of Spanish-American Democratization: A Review and Reformulation", *Estudios Latinoamericanos* 14, part I (1992), 213-239; H. Mansilla, "Aspectos antidemocráticos y antipluralistas en la cultura política latinoamericana", *Revista de Estudios Politicos,* 74 (1991).

20 For more information see the following books, written or edited by Howard J. Wiarda, *Politics and Social Change in Latin America: The Distinct Tradition* (Amherst: The University of Massachusetts Press 1974); *The Continuing Struggle for Democracy in Latin America* (Boulder, Colorado 1980); *Democracy and its Discontents. Development, Interdependence, and U.S. Policy in Latin America* (Lanham - New York -London: Rowman &Littlefield Publishers, 1995); *Iberia and Latin America. New Democracies, New Policies, New Models* (Lanham - London: Rowman &Littlefield Publishers, 1995).

21 B. Pollack, "Enfoques sobre los regímenes autoritarios en América Latina", *Sistema* 60-61 (1984).

22 *The Continuing Struggle...*, 4.

23 See "Political Traditions in Latin America", in: *The Cambridge Encyclopedia of Latin America and the Caribbean*, 1989, 302-306; R. Sznepf, "Centrum i peryferie w kulturze politycznej Ameryki Łacińskiej", in: *Kategorie peryferii i centrum w w kształtowaniu się kultur narodowych*, ed. T. Dąbek-Wirgowa, J. Wierzbicki (Warsaw 1986).

24 F.H. Cardoso, *Las contradicciones del desarrollo asociado* (Lima 1975), 15; see also his innovative essay "Associated-Dependent Development and Democratic Theory", in: *Democratizing Brazil*, ed. A. Stepan (New York - Oxford: Oxford University Press 1989), 299-325.

25 See B. Pollack, *Enfoques...*, 47.

26 *Authoritarians and Democrats: Regime Transition in Latin America*, J.M. Malloy and M. A. Seligson, eds. (University of Pittsburgh Press 1987), 3-4.

27 *Glasnost' in Context: On the Recurrence of Liberalizations in Central and East European Literatures and Cultures*, ed. M. Pavlyshyn (Oxford 1990).

28 See Scott Mainwaring, Guillermo O'Donnell, J. Samuel Valenzuela, eds., *Issues in Democratic Consolidation: The New South American Democracies in Comparative Perspective* (Notre Dame 1992), 294, 311, 333.

29 N. See Lechner, "De la révolution à la démocratie. Le débat intellectuel en Amérique du Sud", *Esprit* 116 (1986); Harry E. Vanden, *Latin American Marxism. A Bibliography* (New York 1991); J. Valdés Paz, "La izquierda hoy en América Latina" and the whole discussion on the present-day Left, published in the Mexican journal *Dialéctica* 23-24 (1992-1993). See also G. Vargas Lozano, *Más allá del derrumbe. Socialismo y democracia en la crisis de la civilización contemporánea* (México: siglo veintiuno editores, 1994); J. Rodriguez Elizondo, *La crisis de las izquierdas en América Latina* (Madrid - Caracas 1990); J. G. Castañeda, *La utopia desarmada. Intrigas, dilemas y promesa de la Izquierda en América Latina* (Barcelona 1995); R. Fornet-Betancourt, *O marxismo na América Latina* (São Leopoldo: UNISINOS, 1995); A. Angell, "Incorporating Left into Democratic Politics", in: *Constructing Democratic Governance. Latin America and the Caribbean in the 1990s*, ed. J. Domínguez and A. Loventhal (Baltimore and London 1996); A. Couriel, *Globalización, democracia e izquierda en América Latina* (Montevideo 1996).

30 J. Staniszkis, "Przeszłość jako przyszłość" (The Past as a Future), *Fortuna* 2 (1991); see also T.H. Naylor, "Narcissistic Poland, Europe's Argentina", *New York Times*, July 6, 1989; D. Chirot, "Why East Central Europe is Not Quite Ready for Perón, but May Be One Day", *East European Politics and Societies* 3 (1996); V. Tismaneanu, *Fantasies of Salvation. Democracy, Nationalism and Myth in Post-Communist Europe* (Princeton, 1998); *Between Past and Future. The Revolutions of 1989 and Their Aftermath*, ed S. Antohi and V. Tismaneanu (Budapest: CEU Press, 2000).

31 G. Schöppflin, "The Political Traditions of Eastern Europe", *Daedalus* 1 (1990); a Special Issue: *The Rediscovery of Central Europe*.

32 S. Fischer-Galati, "Eastern Europe in the Twentieth Century: Old Wine in New Bottles", in: *The Columbia History of Eastern Europe in the Twentieth Century*, ed. J. Held (New York 1992), 2-3.

33 V. Mastny, "Eastern Europe and the West in the Perspective of

Time", in: *Central and Eastern Europe: The Opening Curtain?,* ed. William Griffith (San Francisco - London 1989), 13.

34 See J.L. Cohen and A. Arato, *Civil Society and Political Theory* (Cambridge: Mass., 1991), 48-58.

35 N. Ascherson, "1989 in Eastern Europe: Constitutional Representative Democracy as a `Return to Normality`", in: *Democracy: The Unfinished Journey*, ed. J. Dunn (Oxford 1992). V. Tismaneanu, *Fantasies of Salvation. Democracy, Nationalism and Myth in Post-Communist Europe* (Princeton 1998).

36 See Zhelyu Zhelev, "Bałkany a przestrzeń europejska" (Balkans and the European Space), *Obóz. Problemy narodów byłego obozu komunistycznego* 24 (1992); this issue contains a block of materials on the Balkans.

37 M. Kundera, "Un occident kidnappé - ou la tragédie de l'Europe Central", *Le Débat* 27 (1983) and many reimpressions and translations from that time on. See also M. Bobrownicka, "Europa Środkowa Milana Kundery, czyli destrukcja słowiańskiego mitu", in: *Mity narodowe w literaturach słowiańskich* (Cracow 1992), 243-250; *Symbioza kultur słowiańskich i niesłowiańskich w Europie Środkowej*, ed. M. Bobrownicka (Cracow 1996).

38 J. Rupnik, "Central Europe or Mitteleuropa" ? *Daedalus* 1 (1990), 260. Similar opinion was expressed by K. E. Jorgensen: "Two main trends seem to exist in the political-ideological landscape of fin-de-siecle Central Europe. One trend is characterized by populist, introverted and xenophobic ideas, praised in national movements and parties. The opposite trend, liberal 'European' and pluralist, is located on a liberal-social axis. Yet socialist and social-democratic positions are weekly represented, leaving the scene to classic liberalist values and thought'. – "The End of Anti-Politics in Central Europe", in: *Democracy and Civil Society in Eastern Europe*, ed. P. Lewis (New York 1992), 55.

39 C. Milosz, "About our Europe", in: *Between East and West. Writings from Kultura*, ed. by R. Kostrzewa (New York 1990) 106. See also B. Wróblewski, "Europa Środkowa w polskim czasopiśmiennictwie literackim", *Przegląd Powszechny,* 9 (1996).

40 "Nasza Europa" (Our Europe), an interview with Ash, published in *Tygodnik Powszechny* (46) 1991. T. G. Ash is the author of a fundamental, analytic work on the idea of Central Europe: *The Uses of Adversity: Essays on the Fate of Central Europe* (New York 1989); see also Piotr Wandycz, *The Price of Freedom. A History of East Central Europe from the Middle Ages to the Present* (London - New York 1992).

41 A. Jokubaitis, "Druga Europa" (The Other Europe), *Tygodnik Powszechny,* 32 (1991).

42 Peter Simons, *Philosophy and Logic in Central Europe from Bolzano to Tarski. Selected Essays* (Dordrecht: Kluwer, 1992); see also Endre Bojtar, *Slavic Structuralism* (Amsterdam - Philadelphia, 1985); H. Dahm, A. Ignatov (eds.), *Geschichte der philosophischen Traditionen Osteuropas* (Darmstadt 1996); M. Siemek, "Abut a New Europe and the East in Us", *Dialogue and Universalism,* 5-6 (1998).

43 Opinion pronounced in the Polish weekly *Tygodnik Powszechny* 41 (1991), 5.

44 Cf. Marc Raeff, *Russian Intellectual History. An Anthology*, with an Introduction by Isaah Berlin (New York, 1966), 6-9; Leopoldo Zea, *The Latin American Mind* (The University of Oklahoma Press, 1963), 27-33.

45 See, for example, L. Zea, *Filosofia de la historia americana* (México 1978); *Sens polskiej historii* (The Meaning of Polish History), ed. by A. Ajnenkiel, J. Kuczyński and A. Wohl (Warsaw 1990); Jan Patočka, "Filosofie českých dějin" (The Philosophy of Czech History), *Sociologický Časopis* 5 (1969); Józef Żarek, "Czeskie kłopoty z historią" (Czech Troubles with History), in: *Kryzys tożsamości. Slavica* (The Crisis of Identity), Ed. by B. Czapik and E. Tokarz (Katowice 1992); B. Pynsent, *Questions of Identity. Czech and Slovak Ideas of Nationality and Personality* (Budapest: CEU Press, 1994).

46 See A. Michnik, "Myśli wschodnioeuropejskie" (Eastern European Thoughts), *Krytyka* 32-33 (1990); M. Vargas Llosa, "The Culture of Liberty", *Journal of Democracy*, 4 (1991).

47 Critical remarks on this ideology can be found in A. Przeworski, "The Neoliberal Fallacy", *Journal of Democracy* 3 (1992); A. Kukliński, "Latin America and East-Central Europe. The Past - the Present - the Future", *Estudios Latinoamericanos* 14, part II (1992); L.C. Bresser Pereira, J.A. Maravall, A. Przeworski, *Economic Reforms in New Democracies. A Social-Democratic Approach* (Cambridge University Press, 1993).

48 *Postmodernizm w literaturze i kulturze krajow Europy Środkowo-Wschodniej*, ed. H. Janaszek-Ivaničkova, D. Fokkema (Katowice 1995), 5; H. Janaszek-Ivaničkova, "Postmodern Literature and the Cultural Identity of Central and Eastern Europe", *Canadian Review of Comparative Literature* 3-4 (1995); See also *Cultural Dilemmas of Post-Communist Societies*, ed. A. Jawłowska, M. Kempny (Warsaw: IFis Publishers, 1994); M. Szegedy-Maszak, "Postmodernity and Postcommunism", *European Review* 1 (1998) and a Polish discussion "Czy postmodernizm jest dobry na postkomunizm", in *Dialog*, 11 (1991).

49 See J. Ortega, "Postmodernism in Latin America", in: *Postmodern Fiction in Europe and the Americas*, ed. Theo D`haen and Hans Bertens (Amsterdam, 1988); Lecticia J.B. de Vincenzi, "Modernidade, Pós-modernidade e América Latina (Escolhendo o Brasil como caso privilegiado)" and L.O. Cavalcanti Barros, "América Latina na Pós-Modernidade", in: *America Latina em discussão*, vol. ed. M.T. Torribio Brittes Lemos (Rio de Janeiro, 1994); P.Guadarrama González, *América Latina: marxismo y posmodernidad* (Santa Clara-Bogota, 1994); *The Postmodernism Debate in Latin America*, ed. by J. Beverley, M. Aronna, and J. Oviedo (Durham and London, 1995); I. Champi, "Literatura neobarroca ante la postmodernidad", in: *Proceedings of the XIX Congress of the International Federation for Modern Languages and Literatures*, vol. 3 (Brasilia, 1997); J.L. Gómez-Martinez, *Más allá de la posmodernidad. El discurso antrópico y su praxis en la cultura iberoamericana* (Madrid, 1999); P. Lanceros, "Pluralismo consecuente: la teoria politica de la

posmodernidad", *Utopia y praxis latinoamericana,* 9 (2000); I. Gomez y L. Alarcón, "La postmodernidad como un subproducto de la modernidad dominante", *Utopia y praxis latinoamericana,* 10 (2000).

50 John P. Gillin, "Modern Latin American Culture", in: *Man, State and Society in Latin American History*, ed. Sheldon B. Liss and Peggy K. Liss (London, 1972), 328; M. Janion, "Kryzys jednolitego modelu kultury i szanse kultur alternatywnych", in: *Szanse i zagrożenia polskich reform*, ed. P. Łukasiewicz and W. Zaborowski (Warsaw: IFiS Publishers, 1992), 69-71.

51 The case of Russian Orthodox spirituality was different from Catholicism, but it also operated with symbols, lacked pragmatic spirit and yielded later to the Western influence of Roman Catholicism. See A. Walicki, "Catholicism and the Eastern Church in Russian Religious and Philosophical Thought", in: *The Slavs in the Eyes of the Occident, the Occident in the Eyes of the Slavs*, ed. M. Cieśla-Korytowska (Cracow: UJ, 1992).

52 See R. Legutko, *Czasy wielkiej imitacji* (The Times of Great Imitation) (Cracow, 1998); M. Szyszkowska, "Przeciw służalczości" (Against Servilism), *Res Humana* 1 (1993).

53 More information on these problems can be found in: W. Kolarz, *Myths and Realities in Eastern Europe* (London, 1946); *Mity narodowe w literaturach słowiańskich*, ed. M. Bobrownicka (Cracow, 1992); M. Bobrownicka, *Narkotyk mitu. Szkice o świadomości narodowej i kulturowej Słowian Zachodnich i Południowych* (Cracow, 1995); *Współcześni Słowianie wobec własnych tradycji i mitów. Sympozjum w Castel Gandolfo*, Cracow 1997; M. Kula, "Utopie w działaniu", *Twórczość* 1 (1994); V. Tismaneanu, "Resurrecting Utopia: The Search for Myth Under Post-Communism", *Partisan Review* (1997); J. Woleński, "Neomesjanizm", *Koniec wieku* 5 (1993); M.I. Pereira de Queiroz, *O mesianismo no Brasil e no Mundo* (São Paulo, 1965); M. Delgado, "Die Metamorphosen des Messianismus in den iberischen Kulturen", *Neue Zeitschrift für Missionswissenschaft* 1994; F. Ainsa, *Necesidad de la utopia* (Montevideo, 1990); Y. Acosta, "La función utópica en el discurso hispanoamericano sobre lo cultural", *Revista de la Facultad de Derecho* 12 (1997); H. Cerutti Guldberg, *Presagio y tópica del descubrimiento* (México, 1991); E. Montiel, "La condición utópica' *Concordia* 34 (1998). F. Ainsa, *La reconstrucción de la utopía* (México, 1999).

54 See D. Brading, *Prophecy and Myth in Mexican History* (Cambridge, 1984); A. Knight, "Racism, Revolution, and Indigenismo: Mexico, 1910-1940", in: *The Idea of Race in Latin America, 1870-1940,* ed. R. Graham (Austin, 1990).

55 "M. Carmagnani's Some Comments on Economic Nationalism", in: H. Szlajfer, ed., *Economic Nationalism...,*.255.

56 See, for example, the following books that discuss the problem: A.E. Buela, *El sentido de América (Seis ensayos en busca de nuestra identidad)* (Buenos Aires, 1990); J. Ruben Sanabria, "Hay una filosofia latinoamericana?", *Analogía filosófica* 1 (1993); H. Biagini, *La filosofia latinoamericana: su genesis y reconstrucción,* in his book *Historia ideológica y poder social* (Buenos Aires: Centro Editor de América Latina, 1993), vol. 2,. 137-179; H.

Biagini, *Entre la identidad y la globalización* (Buenos Aires: Leviatan, 2000); C.A. Erro, *Que somos los argentinos* (Buenos Aires 1983); E. Martínez Estrada, *Radiografía de la Pampa* (Buenos Aires: DOCENCIA, 1986); C. Astrada, *El mito gaucho. Martin Fierro y el hombre argentino* (Buenos Aires, 1948); M.T. Martínez Blanco, *Identidad cultural de Hispanoamérica. Europeismo y originalidad americana* (Madrid, 1988); Y. Acosta, "Consideraciones sobre la historiografia de historia de las ideas en América Latina", *Cuadernos del CLAEH* 1-2 (1999); *We własnych oczach. XX-wieczny esej zachodnio- i południowosłowiański*, ed. H. Janaszek Ivaničkova (Warsaw, 1977); *W cudzych oczach*, ed. H. Janaszek Ivaničkova (Warsaw, 1983); A. Koyré, *La philosophie et le problème national en Russie* (Paris, 1976); L. Schapiro, *Rationalism and Nationalism in Russian Nineteenth-Century Political Thought* (New Haven and London, 1967); *Russian Thought after Communism.The Rediscovery of a Philosophical Heritage*, ed. J. Scanlan (New York, 1994); *Oblicza polskości*, ed. A. Kłoskowska (Warsaw: UW, 1990); K. Verdery, *National Ideology under Socialism. Identity and Cultural Politics in Ceausescu's Romania* (Berkeley, 1991); A. Marga, "Cultural and Political Trends in Romania before and after 1989", *East European Politics and Societies* 1 (1993).

57 M. Vargas Llosa, "The Culture of Liberty", 10; see also H. de Soto and D. Orsini, "Overcoming Underdevelopment", *Journal of Democracy* 2 (1991); E. Krauze, "Old Paradigms and New Openings in Latin America", *Journal of Democracy* 1 (1992).

58 See O. Paz et al., *Frustraciones de un destino: la democracia en América Latina* (San José, 1985); *Manual del perfecto idiota latinoamericano*, presentación de M. Vargas Llosa (Buenos Aires, 1996); C. Conaghan, J.Malloy, *Unsettling Statecraft: Democracy and Neoliberalism in the Central Andes* (Pittsburg, 1994); Atilio A. Borón, *State, Capitalism, and Democracy in Latin America* (Boulder, 1995); *Liberalism in Modern Times. Essays in Honour of José G. Merquior*, ed. E. Gellner and C. Cansino (Budapest: CEU Press, 1996).

59 D. Lehmann, *Democracy and Development in Latin America: Economics, Politics and Religion in the Post-war Period* (Cambridge-Oxford, 1990), 190-213; see also J. Vergara, "Crítica latinoamericana al liberalismo: acción comunicativa y desarrollo del pensamiento crítico en América Latina", in: *Modernidad y universalismo*, ed. E. Lander (Caracas, 1991).

60 See his comment to the Polish abbreviated and bilingual edition of Vasconcelos' *La raza cósmica* (Warsaw: CESLA, 1992), 38; for more information on the idea of universalism in Latin American thought, see: J. Wojcieszak, *Dylemat uniwersalizmu i partykularyzmu w latynoamerykanskiej filozofii kultury lat 1900-1960* (Warsaw: CESLA, 1989); A. Caturelli, "Filosofías latinoamericanas y filosofía universal", *Convivium. Investigação e cultura,* 4 (1974); F. Schwartzmann, "Singularidad y universalidad de la experiencia y la filosofía americana", *Stromata* 1979; C. Astrada, "Autonomía y universalismo de la cultura latinoamericana", *Revista de Filosofia Latinoamericana y Ciencias Sociales* 14 (1989); R. Fornet-Betancourt, *Estudios de filosofia latinoamericana* (México, 1992).

61 *Understanding Contemporary Latin America*, ed. by R. S. Hillman (Boulder: Colorado, 1997), 346.

62 F. Miró Quesada, "Posibilidad y limites de una filosofia latinoamericana", *Revista de Filosofia de de la Universidad de Costa Rica* 43 (1978), 82; see also his important book *Proyecto y realización del filosofar latinoamericano* (México, 1981) and two minor studies: on his understanding of universalism: "Historicismo y universalismo en la filosofía", in: *Relativismo cultural y filosofía. Perspectivas norteamericana y latinoamericana*, ed. M. Dascal (México, 1992); and on the necessity of serious modification of the liberation philosophy in the present-day political circumstances: "Filosofía de la liberación. Reajuste de categorías", in: *América Latina: historia y destino. Homenaje a Leopoldo Zea*, vol. II (México: UNAM, 1992), 197-205.

63 See Richard N. Gardner, "The Comeback of Liberal Internationalism", *The Washington Quarterly* 3 (1990); F. Fukuyama, *The End of History and the Last Man*, 1992; R.S. Elisaga, "The Development of Contemporary Trends in Latin America", in: *On Social Differentiation*, vol. III, ed. S. Kozyr-Kowalski, M. Chmara and J. Heyman (Poznań, 1992); id., "Las ciencias sociales en America Latina: del diluvio neoliberal al fin del siglo", *Estudios Latinoamericanos* 6 (1996); R. Bernal-Meza, 'La globalización: un proceso o una ideologia ?", in: *Integración solidaria: América Latina en la era de la globalización* (Caracas, 1996).

64 Edgardo Lander, "Retos del pensamiento crítico latinoamericano en la decada de los noventa", in: *Modernidad y universalismo* (Caracas, 1991), 145-177.

65 See J. Jedlicki, "Narodowcy i Europejczycy", in: *Dylematy europejskiej tożsamości* (Dilemmas of the European Identity), ed. E. Skotnicka-Illasiewicz (Warsaw, 1992); E. Skotnicka-Illasiewicz, *Powrót czy droga w nieznane ? Europejskie dylematy Polaków* (Towards Home - Towards the Unknown. Polish-European dilemmas) (Warsaw, 1997).

66 Cf. H. Voisine-Jechova, "Le complexe de la dépendance dans la littérature tchéque", in: *L'Europe Centrale. Realité, mythe, enjeu. XVIII - XIX sičcles*, ed. Beauprêtre (Warsaw: UW, 1991); L. Zea, *Dependencia y liberación en la cultura latinoamericana* (México, 1974).

67 Glaring examples of this motif in Eastern European literatures are given by J. Tomaszewski, "East Central Europe in the 20th Century. An Introduction to the Subject", *Estudios Latinoamericanos* 14, part I, 44-46.

68 Cf. John P. Gillin, *Modern Latin American Culture...*, 326-327; Richard M. Morse, *El espejo...*,.7.

69 P. F. Northrop, *The Meeting of East and West: An Inquiry Concerning World Understanding* (New York, 1946), 436; see also C. García Bauer, *Universalismo y panamericanismo* (Guatemala, 1968); L. Zea, *La esencia de lo americano* (Buenos Aires, 1971), 29-30; Constantin von Barloewen, *Werte in der Kulturphilosophie Nord- und Lateinamerikas. Ein systematischer Beitrag zur Geistesgeschichte des amerikanischen Doppelkontinents* (Frankfurt am Main, 1989).

70 H. Bernstein, *Making an Inter-American Mind* (Gainsville: University of Florida Press, 1961); *Americas. New Interpretative Essays*, ed. Alfred Stepan (New York - Oxford 1992); G. Pope Atkins, *Encyclopedia of the Inter-American System* (Westport: Conn., 1997).

71 Glenn Caudill Dealy, *The Latin Americans: Spirit and Ethos* (San Francisco – Oxford: Westview Press, 1992).

72 L. Ronald Scheman, *The Inter-American Dilemma. The Search for Inter-American Cooperation at the Centennial of the Inter-American System* (New York, 1988), 2. See also interesting comments on the Enterprise for the Americas Initiative and on NAFTA in: W. Dobrzycki, *Dialog międzyamerykanski w latach dziewięćdziesiątych* (Inter-American Dialogue in the 90s) (Warsaw, CESLA 1993); J. Bryła, "Stany Zjednoczone - Ameryka Łacińska; Nowe trendy w polityce regionalnej", *Ameryka Łacińska* 1 (1997), and a discussion on the process of integration in the Americas in *Ameryka Łacińska* 1-2 (1995).

73 Cf. A. Kukliński, "El decenio de tres continentes: América Latina - América del Norte – Europa", in: *500 Años del Encuentro de dos Mundos. Una Perspectiva Polaca*, ed. A. Dembicz, J. Wilkin (Warsaw, 1993), 16.

74 Jorge I. Domínguez, "Latin America's Crisis of Representation", *Foreign Affairs* 1 (1997).

75 M. Vargas Llosa, "The Culture of Liberty", *Journal of Democracy* 1 (1992).

76 J. Tomaszewski, "East Central...", 46; See also L. Thoorens, *Historia universal de la literatura. Rusia, Europa Oriental y del Norte. Literaturas eslavas, balcánicas y escandinavas. Flandes y Paises Bajos* (Madrid - Barcelona – México, 1977).

77 See A. Walicki, "The Idea of European Unity in the Polish Enlightenment and Romanticism", *Dialogue and Humanism* 1993, no. 1; id., "The Idea of Universalism in the Polish Romantic Tradition", *Dialogue and Humanism* 4 (1993); *Uniwersalizm i swoistość kultury polskiej*, ed. J. Kłoczowski (Lublin 1989, 2 vol.); Z. Komorowski, "Universal Values in Polish Culture", in *Values in the Polish Cultural Tradition*, ed. L. Dyczewski (Washington, D.C.: The Council for Research in Values and Philosophy, 2002).

78 K. Čapek, "Thomas G. Masaryk, a Modern Type of Universalism", *The Central European Observer* 1930, no. 8; *The Czechoslovak Contribution to World Culture*, ed. M. Rechcigl (The Hague, 1964); Also the recent Czech President Václav Havel links European unity to universalism. See *Dialogue and Universalism* 5-6 (1996), 10-17, 173-207.

79 J. Kuczyński, *Dialogue and Universalism as a New Way of Thinking*, Warsaw 1989; id., "What is Universalism", *Dialogue and Humanism* 3-4 (1992).

80 J. Kuczyński, "Universalism as the Vision and Proclamation of a New Covenant: Thinking - Wisdom – Love", *Dialogue and Humanism* 2 (1993).

Chapter 6

Philosophy and Westernism in Eastern Europe and Latin America

There is great deal of pessimism and cynicism in Latin America and Eastern Europe today. These are also the sentiments of many popular leaders and human rights advocates. Despite this, I think that there is room for hope.

-- Rachael A. May, in: *(Un)Civil Societies. Human Rights and Democratic Transitions in Eastern Europe and Latin America*, (Lanham, Maryland: Lexington Book, 2005), 9.

So far there have been no, even fragmentary, comparative studies on the nature of philosophy in East European and Latin American countries. Those philosophers who would like to take up this cognitively fertile set of problems should be inspired by the production of representatives of other social scientists and humanists, historians in particular, who already have considerable achievements in the study of peripheral societies. In turn, philosophical investigations can add to the broadly conceived social and historical knowledge.

THE AIM AND OBJECT OF COMPARATIVE STUDIES

Comparative studies of East European and Latin American philosophical thought face many difficulties. First of all, in spite of long controversies, we still do not know whether there is something like Latin American philosophy, even though we already know that there is Latin America ("our America") and a broadly conceived Latin American culture, and literature in particular. If we disregard, for the time being, the multi-motif discussion on the specific features of Latin American philosophy or, more broadly, on the possibility of the existence of national or regional philosophy, we have to admit that everyone agrees that in Latin America there have been for some time professional philosophers and other thinkers who take up genuinely philosophical problems. Moreover, their intellectual production shows many common features.

The situation becomes much more complicated when we look at the eastern, central-eastern, south-eastern, and even north-eastern (Baltic) part of Europe. Political, historical, cultural, and linguistic considerations account for the fact that only few people refer to the existence of "our Europe," and that usually is limited to what is called Central Europe. In spite of interdisciplinary studies of Eastern Europe and on "real socialism", conducted both in the West and in the East for a long time, and in spite of the recently fashionable in Poland problems of Central Europe (being a large part of broadly conceived Eastern Europe), we have not noticed thus far any study that would take up a systematic cross-analysis of the history of philosophy and social thought in East European countries. Thus for the time being we are not in position to state definitely and authoritatively whether the intellectual history of Eastern Europe is marked by permanent and unquestionably common motifs that would authorize us to speak about East European thought in general. We have found no one who would use the term. On the contrary, when it comes to Latin America, in spite of unquestionable internal differentiation of that subcontinent, very many authors use the general term "Latin American philosophy". In particular theologians of liberation say that Latin America forms an indivisible whole. By analogy, terms refering to Latin American theology, thougt, and sociology are in use. People also quite frequently refer to (North) American, African, Australian, and Arabic philosophy, to various Oriental philosophies (Asian philosophy) in the diverse regions of the Asian East, and Western (West European) philosophy, but they almost never do that with reference to East European and Central European philosophy (this though a bit more common). Certainly they are philosophers there, and the traditions of pursuing philosophy are quite rich, and older than in America, Africa, and Australia. Is philosophy pursued in that part of Europe not original or does it lack common elements? It seems that in the history of philosophy and social thought in East European countries we can find not fewer, but much more original ideas than in the case of Latin America, even though, generally speaking, thought in those two regions of the world has been, and still is, dependant upon, and derivative from, West European philosophy. It is true that neither East Europe nor Latin America had a thinker of the format of Descartes, Locke, Hegel, and Heidegger, but only their disciples, popularizers, and epigones.

The lack of systematic comparative studies of the history of philosophy in our part of Europe prevents us from presenting here any readily generalizing conclusions. In this short and introductory paper, we cannot undertake the task, although certain hypotheses on the nature of East European Marxism and populism, are, of course, not alien to us. But when it comes to philosophy in Latin American countries integrated interpretations and generalizing conclusions have very often been formulated, and those conclusions may be in large degree applied also to the description of an equally general but still non-achieved philosophy, if not of Eastern Europe as a whole, then at least in large part.

Before we proceed to analyze relationships between philosophy and society in Eastern Europe and in Latin America, we must pay some attention to the nature of those societies themselves in the regions in which we are interested and which are remote one from another. Exceptionally fruitful in that respect is reference to dependency theory, formulated in Latin America, and also to the conception of world economy and the world systems generalized and modified by Immanuel Wallerstein. Polish historians led by Tadeusz Łepkowski, who as early as in the 1970s began the study of Latin American societies in terms of dependency,[1] fruitfully referred to the works of Wallerstein, and Marian Małowist.[2] Ryszard Stemplowski pointed to the fact that the categories of center, periphery, domination, dependency, *etc.*, were applicable not only in the studies of the history of Latin America and the Third World, but also referred to internally differentiated Europe. "On our continent," he wrote, "we accordingly find not only the center (the craddle) of capitalism. There are there also the peripheries dependent on that center (e.g., Eastern Europe) marked by a dependent type of development (underdevelopment). He was right in pointing to the division into "the center and the peripheries which "obviously not limited to the economy."[3]

The dependent type of development is observable also in Latin American and East European philosophy and culture. While we should avoid the application of mechanical schemata in culture,[4] the sociological and dependency approach seem to be fertile in historical and philosophical research as well. They are largely used by very many students of Latin American philosophy, beginning with Augusto Salazar Bondy and Lepoldo Zea and ending in the latest trends in the philosophy of liberation. But East European historians of philosophy have not yet assimilated that research methodology.[5]

When studying modern and contemporary philosophy we have to confine the center of world philosophy to several countries of Western Europe and perhaps to the present-day United States, disregarding countries occupying a peripheral position. Note, however, that unlike everyday language adopted in this case by Polish philosophers, we use the adjective peripheral in the descriptive and not evaluative sense. Accordingly we note the profound meaning in the philosophical thinking on the periphery, and especially in the effort to think precisely from the point of view of the periphery.

In Central-Eastern Europe philosophical thought started taking shape already in the Middle Ages,[6] generally speaking at first in its Slavic part, which was under the influence of Latin culture. John Hus (1360 -1415) of Bohemia was an outstanding philosopher of that period. An expert on mediaeval philosophy, he was "above all a theologian, reformer and heresiarch, practical thinker and political leader, a theorist of national liberation, head of a state-based national organization, and the struggle against the universalistic German Empire".[7] It seems that one of the characteristic features of East European thought (clearly visible in the case of Hus) and of later Latin American thought consists in the close connection between philosophy and the history of societies in those regions and their struggle for national liberation. It is common knowledge that the nations in Central and Eastern Europe were subject to the domination of the Germans (the Hapsburg dynasty), the Ottoman Empire), and the Russian (and later the Soviet) Empire,[8] while the nations of Mexico and the Central and the South America were dominated by Spain, Portugal, Great Britain and the entire so-called North Atlantic center.

Argentinian Juan Bautista Alberdi (1810-1884), a thinker clearly fascinated by the example of the civilization of the United States, was the first philosopher in Latin America to formulate the problem of Latin American philosophy, its social functions and its role in the civilizational development of the various countries and the entire region. He reflected on whether there was an American philosophy, what it should be like and what was its social mission. He thought that every country and every epoch had its own philosophy. In the early 19th century, he still did not find it in the former Spanish colonies in America. But he had a certain general idea of philosophy which should participate in the consolidation of a nation and in the construction of a new social order. According to Alberdi, America should adopt in practice what would be invented in Europe, and especially in France. In spite of its West European origin Latin American, or, strictly speaking, Hispano - American philosophy should be national rather than purely universal. When looking for a philosophy for the New World Alberdi wrote in 1842: "Pure abstraction, metaphysics in itself, will not take root in America. What are the problems which America is called to formulate and solve at the present moment? They are the problems of freedom, laws and social pleasures, of which man can maximally avail himself only if the socio-poltical order is preserved. They are poblems of public organization best adjusted to the requirements of man in America. Hence American philosophy should be essentially socio-poltical in its goal, fiery and prophetic in its reactions, synthetic and realistic in its conduct, republican in its spirit and destination. We must first of all realize the first necessary condition for the shaping of national philosophy. But that cannot be achieved otherwise than by the investigation of where our country and the world is and what they are heading for, and also of what the country can do for the destiny of mankind.[9]

In Poland in the early 19th century the philosophy practiced was that of common sense, rather eclectic in character ("reasonable eclecticism"). It was on the whole based on experience. The "preparatory" philosophy of the Poles was marked by sobriety, practicality, and political orientation.[10] In the early 19th century Poles were still dominated by many ideas drawn from the Age of Reason in France. Those opinions manifested themselves, among other things, in the belief in the great importance of Western civilization, and in the conviction that one should imitate the French and the British and combat "barbarity."[11] The same motifs were observable in Argentinian thinkers in the 19th century (Alberdi, Sarmiento). It was in particular Domingo Faustino Sarmiento (1811 - 1888) who made the opposition between civilization and barbarity the center of his philosophy.[12] He studied the history of his country and searched for the essence of social and natural conditions which hampered the development of the country. The Russian so-called westernizers or occidentalists also fought the remnants of Tartar and Mongol "barbarity" - in their own country.

The relations between philosophy and society in which it is pursued, issues of cultural identity, and also problems of the philosophy of the history of the various societies and regions of the world were an essential motif in Latin American philosophy (especially as interpreted by Leopoldo Zea)[13] and in East European philosophical culture in the 19th and the 20th century. For instance, in Czech philosophy the sense of Bohemian history was a constant motif. The problem first emerged in the works of František Palacký (1798 - 1876). In the opinion of that historian- philosopher (advocate of the idea of Austro-Slavism) and political leader who presided in 1848 over the first Slavic Congress of Prague, the profound sense of the history of Bohemia and Moravia consisted in the incessant contact and confrontation between the

Slavic and the German elements, manifested by the struggle of the Bohemians against foreign domination. The "Bohemian issue" as interpreted by Masaryk took Palacký's point of departure into consideration, but having the philosopher and politician in one person mitigated considerably the anti-Germanism and the way of thinking of his predecessor. He suggested the creation of a new Bohemian (or Czech) religion, a religion of mankind, in a sense analogous to Polish Roman Catholic Messianism. According to Masaryk, the history of the Slavic nations was the history of the influence exerted upon them by alien neighbouring nations. That idea was even more strongly formulated by Josef Pekař, to whom the sense of Bohemian history meant no conflict and struggle, but incessant reception and imitation of civilizationally more advanced patterns of life. It was for that reason that Pekař rejected the native hussite tradition. In turn leftist thinkers, such as Zdenek Nejedlý (1872 - 1962) referred to Palacký and claimed that the latter thinker's conception could be a foundation of the program of the national and social liberation of the peoples of Czechoslovakia.[14] That permanent motif in the Czech reflection on the history and psycho-social features of their own nation can be observed in other East European nations as well, not necessarily Slavic ones (for instance in the Hungarian, and above all in the Romanian philosophy of culture). In Russia it took the form of the commonly known conflict between the Westernizers and the Slavophiles, who suggested a return to originally Slavic social elements. The idea of Slavophilism, Pan-Slavism, (in Russia also Eurasianism), Austro-Slavism, and Neo-Slavism had numerous adherents in Central and Eastern Europe, perhaps relatively in the least degree in Poland, which more strongly than the other nations in that region stressed its bonds with West European culture.

The same problems and dilemma have troubled and continue to trouble Latin American thought. Many contemporary philosophers (*e.g.*, Leopoldo Zea) refer to 19th century heroes of the struggle for the independence of former Spanish and Portuguese America, in particular to the works of Simon Bolivar and José Martí. The attitude towards the advanced Western civilization and culture, and the resulting search for one's own place in it, is an essential and constant element of their reflections. Some of them suggested an uncritical imitation of Western patterns, others looked for values in their own entire history and suggested the creation of their own national and continental philosophy (Hispano-American, Ibero-American, Latin American, or just American, considering also the pre-Columbian heritage). It can thus be seen that the problem of imitation and even repetition of other people's patterns (and the related, not solely Polish, fear of becoming a parrot of other nations), and on other occasions the striving for authenticity and originality in philosophizing, the striving for shedding alien influence - all that is common to the intellectual history of Eastern Europe and Latin America, and has its roots in the long common struggle for political independence and sovereignty. This is why the problem of dependence and liberation has in Polish, East European (including Russian) and Latin American philosophy its own practical, social and historical dimension, not merely speculative and abstract, as was the case of German idealism and almost entire Western philosophy.

MESSIANISM AND NIHILISM

In the East European and the Latin American tradition there were philosophical and political trends full of Messianic hopes for the liberation and salvation, if not the whole humankind, then at least of a considerable part. There were also pessimistic trends, even nihilistic in character, which manifested a total lack of faith in the creative abilities of mongrel nations, whether they be métises, semi-Asiatic Russians, or other peripheral societies living on the margin of human history. Pyotr Chaadayev (1794-1856), a Russian philosopher, opposed the official ideology stating that Russia was "the anchor of salvation" for humankind while the West was decayng, and expressed a severe opinion on the history of his own nation supposedly forgotten by Providence. According to him Russia belonged neither to the East nor to the West, and had no tradition nor creative power of its own. The Russians were like children born out of wedlock,[15] who must themselves re-establish broken social and historical bonds.[16] M. Mikhailov, a *narodnik*, wrote similar things: to him the Ruusians resembled settlers on new lands.

To some Latin American thinkers America meant also such existence without a past, a land where the culture of the aborigines had been destroyed by the *conquista*. Argentinian Héctor Murena (1924-1975) stressed that the Latin Americans were neither Europeans nor natives and hence could not continue the great tradition of the Incas. The Latin Americans were displaced, exiled Europeans, disherited by history and of the world process of history. Such pessimistic and even racialist conceptions developed in Latin America under the impact of the theories of Gobineau and Gumplowicz. Those conceptions stated that the Latin Americans were marked by an innate inability to develop and to progress, an impossibility conditioned by cultural, geographical, and racial factors. That could be seen in the opinions of the Argentinian Carlos Octavio Bunge and the Bolivian Alcides Arguedas, the author of the book *Un pueblo enfermo* (A Sick People), concerned with South American social psychology.

In Eastern of Europe, too, there were many studies concerned with the psycho-social properties of the various nations in Eastern Europe. Thus the spiritual and civilizational contrast between Russia and Europe, and between Latin America and Western Europe was for a long time an essential philosophical problem.[17] Many authors, for instance representatives of the so-called Bolivian mystique of land and thinkers from Russia and Balkan countries looked for the characteristic features of their native countries in the specific nature of the soil, the landscape, and the climate. They often reflected on the impact upon human psychology of the Argentinian pampa, the Balkan mountain range,[18] and the Russian steppe, and the related dominant way of life of the gaucho, the farmer, and the Tartar nomad.

Various authors tried to deduce the worldview and the properties of the spiritual and philosophical culture of the various peripheral nations from the features dominant in the history and geography of the various regions of the world. For a long time it was believed that the historically young nations in Latin America, Russia, and Eastern Europe (especially Romania) have not created any original and independent system of philosophical thinking. Many historians of ideas still single out specific spheres of interests of the various nations. It is often said that, for instance, Russian philosophy is interested mainly in ethical and historiosophical problems and that it had largely been permeated by the spirit of a Christian, religious interpretation of the the world.[19] Undoubtedly, the knowledge of that philosophy may be useful for the development of universal human nature. It must also be borne in mind that in order to become acquainted with Russian, Polish, Czech, Mexican, and Latin American philosophy in general, one cannot confine oneself to strictly philosophical works because the most abstract philosophical issues usually did not form designated fields of research in peripheral countries. In those countries thinkers concentrated their attention on problems of social, moral, and political philosophy: their religious metaphysics and ethics wanted to analyze the defects of society as it appeared to philosophers. Hence those problems were taken up not only by philosophy but also by literature in the broad sense of the world.

An eminent student of the history of Russian social thought wrote: “In the case of Russia (as in the case of Poland) there are also many additional arguments in favor of a broadened interpretation of the subject matter of the history of philosophy. Philosophy emerged in Russia relatively late and for a very long time it could not develop into an independent and relatively autonomous field of knowledge and creative production. Its autonomization was rendered difficult by the exceptionally hard political conditions, which prevented a free development of philosophy in rigorously supervised politicized state universities (certain symptoms of a change for the better were observable in that sphere only in the second half of the 19th century). Nor was it favored by the intellectual situation of the Russian intelligentsia in the 19th century. The painful consciousness of political oppression, backwardness and the resulting urgent social issues diverted attention from problems not directly related to social praxis. This directed philosophical reflection towards ethical, historiosophical and political problems, often also to religious ones, but, at the same time, it contributed to a certain underestimation and neglect of the classical ontological and epistmological problems. The *narodniki* intelligentsia, which, as is known, was the most influential intellectual formation in the second half of the 19th century, even thought that engaging in ‘pure philosophy’ was something immoral, a betrayal of the holy cause of the people.”[20] Similar opinions were shared by many thinkers in vast Brazil and and smaller Latin American countries.

William Rex Crawford, a North American historian of Latin American thought, holds even that in a young country philosophy must be social philosophy. He maintains, as he does not know the analogous unrest in east and south-east Europe, that it would be difficult to find another region such as Latin America which would so strongly confirm the thesis stating that philosophy draws its new and urgent subject matter from the state of the society in which it develops.[21] Incessant problems following the loss of independence by numerous countries in Eastern Europe and no lesser troubles after its being gained by Latin American countries, make one reflect on the causes of incessant failures and a lack of desired freedom. This gives rise to the question about our identity, about what we really are as Poles, Russians, Argentinians, etc., and how we differ from the rest of the world -- the United States, the West (in the sense of Europe). This is our destiny as a nation and as half of the continent, be it America or Europe which are rather unsuccessful, yet full of hope. Those problems have troubled thinkers in both parts of the world from ancient times to our day. A Hungarian sociologist before the end of communism, said that "the theoreticians of Eastern Europe are frustrated by nowadays with the failure of the Socialist Project, as previously, in the prewar period they were they were frustrated by the experiences of underdeveloped capitalism".[22] After a dozen years or so of the capitalist reconstruction the old frustrations have come back with increased intensity.

Historians of Polish thought have drawn their readers' attention to the special social function of philosophy as a historical component of the development of national culture. This applies in particular to those countries which have not contributed anything important to the history of philosophy as just philosophy. Andrzej Walicki gave several interesting examples in that respect: "The history of Slovak philosophy in the 19th century is of little interest from the point of view of the general history of philosophy, but it is very interesting as a particularly clear example of the 'accelerated development' of national and social consciousness. I do not hesitate to claim that the greatness the universal significance of the philosophy and social thought of Polish Romanticism does not consist in any alleged inauguration of a new epoch in the history of thought (as Polish philosophers of that time used to assert), but in its having an exceptionally rich, internally differentiated, and at the same time clear picture of the formation of the self-knowledge of a modern nation. The Russian *narodniki* movement in the 1870s and 1880s did not give the world any great philosopher and sociologists, but in spite of that its significance is enormous, and not only on the Russian scale. It consists, among other things, in the very sharp and dramatic formulation of those problems of social development with which 'Third World' countries, retarded in their economic development, are faced to this day."[23]

In Eastern Europe and later in Latin America utopian dreams and messianic hopes were connected with the realization of the socialist project or a continental revolution after the victory of Fidel Castro in Cuba. After the collapse of communism a postmodern nihlism was in vogue for a moment, but some elements of a leftist messianism and prophetism are still present in Latin American thought.

It is said that in the Central, established cultures of Europe there is no place for prophetism and messianic utopia, but only for pragmatism and egoism, for national calculus. If so, Central and Eastern Europe would soon produce new utopian prophesies. In this part of the world utopian is not only the search for perfection but also for much desired "normalcy". A protest against miserable social situation and a feeling of special mission seems to be something constant in the countries lacking any stability. Political messianisms, however, are, at present, in retreat.

NATIONS, SOCIETIES, AND THE AUTHENTICITY OF PHILOSOPHY

During recent decades many philosophers in Latin America reflected on the role of philosophy in society and on the problem of its national originality and authenticity. They did that even more intensely and radically than had been the case in Russia and Poland in the past. Augusto Salazar Bondy, a well-known Peruvian philosopher and forerunner of the Latin American philosophy of liberation, tried to demonstrate that in Latin America there had always been a great distance between those who pursue philosophy and the rest of society. That is why, in his opinion, Latin American philosophers cannot be termed national philosophers because society cannot identify itself in them. This is so because those nations have to do with thought transplanted to their respective countries, with products of alien people and alien cultures, which are pursued by élitist minorities. Salazar Bondy does not deny the existence of an universal component in philosophy, nor does he suggest that philosophy must be very popular. He merely claims that philosophy is authentic if it reflects the consciousness of the society in which it develops, and if it finds a profound response in the latter, especially when it comes to its ethical and political consequences. On the contrary, in Latin America philosophy is negative *vis-à -vis* society and is a manifestation of the illusory self-consciousness of the latter. Its imitative character accounts for the fact that it is an expression of an alienated consciousness.[24]

Salazar Bondy sees the cause which determines the present state of philosophy and culture in Latin America in the situation which marks also other nations in the Third World. If we realize that fact, we have to resort to the concept of political and economic domination by developed countries and the related underdevelopment of Latin America. Those countries, which had been dependent in turn on Spain, Britain, and the United States, have become countries of culture dominated by aliens.[25] The socio-cultural effect of that dependence has assumed the shape of deformed society and defective culture, which has been received by philosophy. The latter accordingly has also become imitative and dependent.

Salazar Bondy has formulated his own program of imparting originality and authenticity to Latin american thought. In his opinion it can play an inspiring role in the movement that would put an end to underdevelopment and alien domination.

Yet the Peruvian philosopher does not, as it might seem, postulate a practical philosophy, or an applied or social philosophy, as the model for Latin

American philosophy. Such programs had been suggested in the past. It was argued, for instance, that in the division of philosophical tasks, theory should belong to Europe (Western Europe in fact, because the other parts of that continent were ignored), and its applications to Latin America, which according to Bondy would also mean a form of submission to, and dependence upon, alien powers. The rigorous theoretical character of philosophy is indispensable for its development and fertility. It is also necessary for the discovery of one's own human essence and carrying out the mission of liberation of dependent nations.

Other Latin American authors were on the whole less nihilistically oriented than Salazar Bondy in the assessment of philosophy on their continent to date and of its social functions. Very many philosophers, especially Marxists in Latin America and Eastern Europe, pointed to the ancillary role of philosophy in the task of liberation and the preparation of a social revolution, and the construction of a new political system. Recently, however, as a result of the collapse of many revolutionary projects, illusions, and endeavors to put them in practice, there has been a growing frustration and melancholy, due to the ineffectiveness of all process of liberation, liberation that often leads to new social deformations, subdependency within the periphery, and new captivity.

The social mission of philosophy in Latin America seems now to consist not only in favoring the ambiguous process of liberation in the contemporary world, but also in the search for something new, in the striving for a further integration of the continent, and perhaps also of both Americas. It is similar in Europe: now that sharp political (but unfortunately not economic) divisions are vanishing, it does not suffice to reflect on the liberation and political, and cultural identity of the rather nightmarish Central Europe -- that tortured fragment of Europe suspended between East and West. One has to consider the theoretical possibility of a harmonious co-existence of the entire integrated Europe as a community of fortunes in the changing world system, a system which in order to save itself may have to take up some former socialist slogans. That would require the search for a new and more universal paradigm (as compared with dependency and the present world system) whereby the unity of Europe, the Americas, and the whole world might materialize. Hence the efforts to create intercultural or universalist philosophy. Those newly emerging tasks of philosophy have not been sufficiently profoundly taken up by philosophical thought in Latin America and Eastern Europe, which have been usually social, prospective, and prophetic in character. However, it has become necessary during the 500th anniversary of the encounter of Europe with America and in the following years.

In referring to the fine idea of the reconciliation of America as a whole -- the idea formulated, among others, by Richard Morse and Leopoldo Zea, his colleague on other bank of Río Grande, Morse said: "the whole world must be reconciled, that world which in the course of history was divided into the Center and the Periphery."[26]

The discussion of the specific features of philosophy and its tasks in particular countries of Central and Eastern Europe was revived after the collapse of communism, especially in Russia, partly also in Poland.[27] Leszek Nowak, for example, tried to prove that new interpretations of foreign philosophies have arisen in Poland, but a really new philosophical trend has never arisen here. According to Nowak, great writers and essayists, not professional philosophers, were very close to it. The Polish mind is supposed to be provincial, held captive by the Western thought, and spiritually dependent on the Western Center.

Other discussants (Tadeusz Buksiński) pointed to the need for an activist philosophy that would help to make up for the civilizational backwardness, to overcome the complex of provincialism and imitative attitudes.

The above voices from from East Central Europe and Latin America are testimony to community of creative anxiety and of the "accursed questions" often posed by thinkers in both poor and seemingly distant regions of the world.

WESTERNISM AND THE QUESTION OF RUSSIA

Intellectuals from Slavic countries and also from other parts of Central and Eastern Europe have paid much attention to various relations linking their countries with the West (Western Europe and the United States). In general, the myth of Slavic exceptionalism and singularity was criticized here, because of its negative consequences for the idea of European unity and an all-European integration. But the antithesis of Europe and Slavdom, shaped at the end of 19th century, is still valid in some countries of Eastern and Western Europe.

The antithesis best expressed in Russian Slavophilism, was present to some extent also in Czech, Slovak, and Serbian slavophilism. The Slavophiles opposed the moral health of the Slavs to the spiritual decadence of the "rotten" West. The popular character of Slavic cultures was accentuated and the ancient inheritance was neglected. In the 19th century Russia the Slavophiles also proposed spiritual values of Orhodox Christianity, different from Western Catholicism and Protestantism. In the Polish history, however, the authors critical of Europe underlined not so much the ethnic or linguistic Slavishnes of the Polish nation as its own libertarian tradition, certain psychological traits and other Sarmatian values.

Westernism usually expresses those tendencies which are opposed to Slavophilism and to all ethnic nationalism. It should be noted that in Russia at the turn of the 20th and 21st century more influential than Slavophilism was Eurasianism, the ideology that arose in the 1920s among Russian emigrés, who opposed Russia (Eurasia) to Europe. The Eurasians conceive and fully accept Russia as a semi-Asiatic, not Slavic country with Tartar, Mongol and "Turanian" heritage. So both the Slavophiles and the Eurasians maintain the opposition between the Slavic or "Turanian" Russia and Europe. The strongly pro-European "Westernizers" were opposed to both currents.

Russian Westernism did not form a cohesive, clearly differentiated set of social and philosophical ideas. It was a collection of various democratic and liberal ideas that appeared in the 1840s. The supporters of "Europeanism" were unanimous only in their critical attitude towards the Slavophiles. Belinsky was considered the main figure in the public debate with the Slavophiles and in the controversy over Westernism. He was concerned with the role of Peter the Great in modernizing the ancient Russia, with the antithesis of the pre-reform and post-reform Russian people. Thanks to the Petrine reforms, unreflective approval of stagnant tradition was discarded and people could be raised to the level of society, paving the way toward the modern Russian nation. According to Belinsky, Peter the Great negated the irrational immediacy of the Russian people and stimulated the appearance of the rational thought or individuality represented by universal values of European civilization. These values should appear in their national, Russian form.

Peter's reforms of Westernization, he argued, were historically inevitable, they were the first and decisive step towards modern Russia and should have been continued. Belinsky accepted with some reservations the Western capitalist system. He was convinced of its necessity and superiority over semifeudal Russia. He believed that Russia should adopt deep democratic reforms and should not be afraid of the development of the bourgeoisie as a separate class, bringing civilizational progress. In this he opposed the views of Herzen and Bakunin who set their dreamy hopes on the peasant and the intelligentsia.

According to Andrzej Walicki, Belinsky's Westernism was even more clearly seen in his literary criticism.[28] He was convinced that everything valuable in Russian literature was a result of Westernization and that Russia had no original writing of her own. He did not appreciate those writers who looked for inspiration in folk poetry and popular ballads. Russian culture, in his views, should come closer to the "historical nations" of Europe. The Slavophiles criticized Belinsky's opinions for his alleged contempt for Russia and her autochtonous traditions. He used to answer that he trusted Russia's great potential which could be realized only on the historical background of Western culture. He tried to further the cause of national culture and was convinced that in the future it would be significant in the intellectual life of humankind.

Among the first Russian Westernizers of the 19th century at least two more representatives should be mentioned: Timofey Granovsky and Konstantin Kavelin. Granovsky concentrated on a critique of the Slavophiles' idealization of the common people. According to him, the masses are usually thoughtless, cruel, or apathetically good-natured. One should stir up the process of individualization of the masses through rational, enlightenment education. Granovsky favored the process of shaping the autonomous personality and emancipation from the pressure of immediacy.

Konstantin Kavelin, in turn, in his philosophy of Russian history, emphasized the need for the rule of law in society and paid attention to the gradual process of emancipation of the individual from traditional patriarchal bonds. According to him, development consists in the gradual shaping of the principle of personality, in the negation of community relations founded on kinship and custom. This process began in the 18th century under Petrine reforms.

Kavelin was accused by the Slavophiles of equating personality with Western European individualism, and of seeing the meaning of Russian history in the development of the personality principle.

Most Russian Westernizers believed that progress in Russia consisted in the emancipation of the individual from the fetters of traditionalism and in a rationalization of social relations. They maintained that national development proceeded from the stage of natural immediacy to modern nationalities governed by law and the central state.[29]

Russian liberal and democratic thinkers modelled their vision of Russia's future political and economic order on West European patterns. The need for further Europeanization of their country was something obvious and pressing.

The Decembrists of the beginning of the last century were probably the first Russians to be fascinated by the civilizational progress achieved by the Western Europe. They were strong adherents of Western liberties fighting against Tsarist despotism. Although very pro-Western, they were not without national pride since they claimed their movement to be rooted in the libertarian traditions of Novgorod and Pskov, the ancient free gentry, and even in the 12th century Boyar Duma.[30] In their documents they planned to abolish serfdom and to contribute to the rapid development of capitalism in Russia. They represented Westernized elite of the Russian nobility. One of the Decembrists, Nikita Muraviev in his draft constitution modeled his plan for a social and political system of government on the example of the United States. According to his plan, Russia should become a federation of fourteen states, each one with a separate capital. Each state with a two-chamber parliament might preserve independence in some matters except for legislation. The supreme authority in the whole federation was to be given to a Popular Assembly (the Supreme Duma and a House of Representatives together). The Muraviev's project of constitution guaranteed civil liberties, complete freedom of worship, of assembly and of speech. His constitution was an important step in the history of Russian progressive thought. Although Muraviev was not a republican but a constututional monarchist, his views belong to the first modernizations with a pro-American attitude, called later yankophilia, Westernism or *nordomania* -- these names initially had a depreciatory tint. However, Westernism in Russia has never been so strong as in other countries of Eastern, especially East Central Europe.

The comparison of the Russia and the West is very controversial among scholars. Some present Russia as a country that belongs to an East European or even Asian cultural sphere, distinct or even opposed to Western values. This distinction is based upon historic and religious premises (the lack of democratic tradition, and the dominance of an Eastern Orthodox Church clearly differentiated from the Roman Catholic Church). Others see Russia as generally linked to, and dependent upon, the West. These scholars perceive periods of Russian isolation, but emphasize that Russia and the West have "a common logic of development. Russian culture has no vital existence of its own apart from Europe."[31] Those authors who see similarities rather than differences between Russia and the West are inclined to explain Russian particularism only by her backwardness in relation to Western Europe. Everybody recalls Christian influences and efforts made by Peter the Great and his followers to transform Russia into a Western state. It is said that Peter's reforms split Russian society and consciousness into an educated westernized elite and the common people untouched by modernization. The educated elite felt itself cut off from the people and the barbarian Russian past. In fact, intellectuals were cut off and alienated from both the indigenous past and from Western Europe, which was still distant from them and more advanced. Latin American intellectuals who are alienated both from the Indian masses and from Western elites, who have not fully accepted them, have experienced a similar break. The passionate yearning for Western culture and and a perplexing sense of inferiority was a common feeling of many Russian, East European, and Latin American intellectuals. They often denied that their countries had a civilization and tried to identify themselves with the West European values. This has been a very difficult task. The idealized West did not always conform to their image. Herzen, Bakunin, and other intellectuals rejected their idealized West when they experienced it directly.[32]

The problem of the understanding of Russia's links with the West depends on what we mean by Europe and the West. One concept of Europe limits it to Germanic and Romance nations alone. Polish professor Oscar Halecki excluded from his concept of "European history" only Russia. He put great stress on the close links of the East Central Europe with the Western World and its vivid sympathy with the United States. According Halecki, it was Germany that created a false impression that she was the last country of the West and that east of her, a Semo-Asiatic region begins. Halecki and many others differentiated East Central Europe, strictly connected with the Latin West and North America, from the Russian East. The Polish historian spoke of the East Central Europe or "the eastern part of Central Europe, between Sweden, Germany and Italy, on the one hand, and Turkey and Russia on the other. In the course of European history he emphasized that a great variety of peoples in this region created their own independent states, sometimes quite large and powerful. In connection with Western Europe they developed their individual national cultures and contributed to the general progress of European civilization."[33].

Even Ukrainians used to difference sharply from Russia. Some historians maintain that "at the time of the emergence of Western culture, between the thirteenth and seventeenth centuries, the Ukraine, though of the Orthodox faith, shared components of states of the West European type."[34] Later the development of Ukraine was retarded by Russian despotic tsarism. Ukraine is considered by the above quoted authors as a borderland territory between East and West.

It is interesting to note that all East Europeans (Poles, Lithuanians, Czechs, Romanians, etc.) frequently tried to differentiate themselves from semi-Asiatic or extremely East European Russians. The reasons for this differentiation usually have been political in nature. These small nations were afraid of Russian expansionism and wanted to strengthen their ties with the Western world, except for the equally expansionist Germany. Countries exposed to the Russian frontier and sharing many similarities with this neighbor often wanted to blur them. An objective observer, Henry L. Roberts, is largely correct when he says: "When Poles or Rumanians, despite the presence of linguistic or religious ties with the Russians and a fair measure of common if hardly joyful history, argue that Russia is not the West, whereas their own nations most emphatically are, one feels that this is more than an academic classification, that it is an argument born of fear or desperation, and that the extrusion of Russia from the 'West' is at the same time a call for support and assistance on the part of the Western nations."[35]

Contrary to some Central European scholars or ideologists of Eurasianism, Marc Szeftel argues that it is impossible to see the Russian history and culture as fundamentally different from that of the rest of Europe. Russian economic and cultural life in the past was often based on principles similar to that of Central and Western Europe. From the end of the 18th century Russia, as with almost all of Europe, was inspired by the French Enlightenment. At the beginning of the 19th century Russia shared absolutism, serfdom, and some economic patterns with the Germanic countries. According to Szeftel, who defends a European character of greater part of Russian history, "between 1878 and 1905, among the Christian nations of Europe, Russia was the only one that still preserved an absolute monarchy, but its economic and legal institutions, its social system, and its cultural activity were based on principles common to the rest of Europe of that time."[36] It was the October Revolution that produced a great cleavage in the Russian history.

Westernist elements have occured quite often in the Russian thought and politics from the times of Peter I to Gorbachev and Putin. It is not my aim to analyze them in detail, but it should be noted that at the turn of 80s and 90s of the 20th century even among former Marxists there appeared a group of enthusiastic neophytes, who preached "neoclassical economics as a direct road to Salvation."[37] It was they who at the beginning of the 1990s forcefully propagated Bolshevik monetarism or market Bolshevism. Boris Yeltsin was warned, even by his supporters, that he was introducing privatisation with Stalinist means.[38]

Mikhail Gorbachev in an interview during his first visit to Paris and then in his famous book launched a catchy slogan, that of "the Common European House". Beyond this political catchword and a fairly idealistic vision of the future of Europe, Gorbachev regrettably never thoroughly elaborated the concept. Thus Putin's turn towards the West after September 11, 2001, seemed for a moment to be very spectacular.

Among more recent authors the opinion of Igor Maksymychov from the Russian Academy of Sciences Institute of Europe is especially important.

According to him, Russia practically always has belonged to Europe and to the overall European civilization and did not leave it, even for a moment, from the 17th to the 19th century; today Russia returns to Europe. Thus, he opposed identifying European civilization only with its Western part.

Also Andranik Migranian, the famous political scientist, affirms the European identity of Russia: "Russia for several centuries has been trying to be a European country and simply cannot have other roots. We are a backward Europe, but still Europe. The question is: what tactics will fully introduce Russia to Europe ?"[39] However, the discussion between westernism and eurasianism, that is on the choice of a strategic alliance of Russia either with the West and America or with the great China of Asia drags on in present-day Russia and seems interminable.

POLAND IN EUROPE

Of the countries of East Central Europe probably no one insisted more on its Western and even Latin-Mediterranean profile and character than the writers, thinkers and intellectuals from Poland. For many of them Polish Westernism seemed to be something natural and spontaneous. Although deeply rooted it has not been obvious for everybody and has taken various historical forms. In fact in the history of Polish culture we can notice a struggle of xenophobia with xenophilia. Already in the Baroque era some Poles deemed the foreign influence to be dangerous to its national particularity. As far as Polish relations to the West are concerned they have been both highly positive and highly critical. In this Essay I am concerned with the main features of Polish Westernism, which have been predominant. According to Jerzy Jedlicki, these features can be characterized as follows: "Polish Westernizers thought that the West had created a superior type of civilization, which can be considered as a norm and measure. The values of this civilization have universal validity and will radiate to the most distant countries. The Polish Westernizers were absolutely convinced that Poland belonged to that civilizational circle, but that it was backward in in that regard and characterized by a cultural and economic lag which should be made up. Still Poland was considered to be the most Western Slavic nation and for that reason should serve as a civilizational bridge between the West and the East. This attitude stemmed from the Enlightenment ideology and contributed to the depreciation of vernacular traditions, institutions, and customs. According to this view national traditions were to be disregarded.[40]

Opposite to this Westernism there were various ideas that could be called Sarmatism, Ethnocentrism, Slavophilism and various forms of xenophobic nationalism. It is interesting to see that even anti-Western traditionalists in Poland and Russia borrowed their ideas from Western sources (e.g. German idealism and romanticism) in order to show a contrast or antithesis between Poland, Russia and the West.

Westernism in Poland has always been in vogue, but probably one of the most intensive periods of its practical implementation began after the collapse of communism. Ryszard Legutko, a present-day political philosopher, differentiates between Westernization, economic liberalization, and modernization. According to him, the current process of westernization requires a sober analysis and scrutiny. Ryszard Legutko In Westernization, he discerns a group of imitators who receive from the West something less than the best. He considers himself a Westerner, but at the same time tries to be a critical analyst of the concepts coming to Poland from the West where they are obvious.[41]

There are many contradictions in Polish Westernism. Witold Gombrowicz, among athers, noted that Poles, as "latinized Savs", do not fully recognize themselves in the Western values; they are too Savic in order to be fully Western and too Western in order to be fully Slavic. Recently, Maria Janion added that Poland as a partly Slavic and even postcolonial (but sometimes colonizing) country cannot be fully European.[42]

CZECHS AND HUNGARIANS

Many Czechs used to put a great stress on Western, European sources of their national culture.[43] In Poland it is common to consider the Czech nation as younger and whose culture has predominantly popular elements. Czech authors, however, have shown that their culture is deeply rooted in the European humanistic tradition since the introduction of Christianity in the middle of the 9th century. The heritage of Renaissance and Reformation is of special importance for the Czech spiritual life. Jiři Škvor shows the influence of Western thought on various stages of the national development of his countrymen. According to him, "the cultural works produced by Czech intellectuals under the influence of the modern Western outlook on State, Church, and the people (as described in the works of Voltaire, Montesquieu, Rousseau, Locke, Herder and Kant) received assistance which underlined and stressed the cult of the individual, national and democratic tradition."[44] Deprived for 300 years of their independent state the Czech nation shook off the foreign Hapsburg yoke and tried to preserve its particularity within the Western world.

Many historians have shown universality and receptivity to be characteristics of the Czech culture. Such receptivity enriched Czech thought which was inspired by many Western elements. Czech literature was even overburdened with them and had no time to recreate them quietly in order to express its own values.

After a relatively short period of the influence of Slavophile ideas among the Czech writers of the 19th century, the beginning of the next century is rather pro-Western and pro-American. The greatest intellectual and political figure of the period, Thomas Masaryk turned against the Slavophilism. He said: "I am consciously European in my culture. By that I mean that European and American culture (America is ethnically and culturally a fragment of Europe, transported - though not completely - to America) satisfies me spiritually. As a European I am a Westerner. I say this for the benefit of those Slavophiles who see in Russia and Slavdom something super-European, whereas the best Russians were Westerners too."[45] It has been demonstrated that there are parallels to Masaryk's liberal humanism in American thought. Masaryk himself showed devotion to Lincoln and Woodrow Wilson. On the tenth anniversary of his independent state, Masaryk noted that "in a sense the United States is Czechoslovakia's foster parent. It is upon President Wilson's immortal charter of freedom, as embodied in his famous Fourteen Points, that the foundations of our State are laid. We have tried to pattern our young republic after our great sponsor."[46] He was very critical, in contrast, of Russia - both of the Czarist system and later the Soviet experiment.

At present, a famous Czech writer Milan Kundera has fully and unconditionally associated Czechoslovakia, Hungary and Poland with the Western European culture. His strong Westernism --along with that of Joseph Conrad of Polish origin and George Mikes of Hungarian origin (both quoted by Kundera) -- is a glaringly extreme example of pro-Western, anti-Russian and anti-Slavic pattern of Central European thought. According to Kundera, the so-called Slavic spirit or soul (in fact a purely Russian one) is comic, sentimental, often gloomy and vague; it has nothing to do with the actual Polish or Czech history which has been distant from Russia or outwardly alien to her (in the case of Poland).[47]

Kundera maintains that Hungary loses its identity as soon as it is drawn away from Western Europe, as happened after the Second World War. But for Hungarian intellectuals the question of their relation to the West has always been a complicated problem, and not only under communism. It is said that Hungarian, Polish and Balkan literatures from their earliest history have been literatures of resistance. The first known Hungarian piece of poetry is directed against the Chengis Khan and calls for the help of Christ and Europe in the fight against Tartars. Later on the Turks and Germans superseded them in this role.

In his Essay, *Hungary and Europe* Ivan Boldizsár recalls that Renaissance and humanist ideas reached the Hungarian court earlier than other countries beyond the Alps and that the Hungarian Renaissance humanism still enlivenes the perduring dreams of Hungarian intellectuals who identify themselves fully with the Western tradition.

In later years the political thought of a divided Hungary tried to solve the difficult problem whether the pro-Austrian or pro-Turkish orientation better served the project of the country's reunification.

At the beginning of the 20th century a generation of essayists grouped around the review *Nyugat* (The West) wanted to overcome the barriers of Hungarian provincialism, of the ideology of Eastern or Asiatic Turanism propagated in Hungary, and were willing to join or rather to catch up with Europe. The journal was an important organ of Hungarian pro-Western liberal intellectuals who wanted to synthesize Europeanness with Hungary. The poet Endre Ady and other representatives of the generation condemned the Hungarian archaic provincialism and made strenuous efforts to regenerate their country proposing the idea of the unity of Hungary and Europe. They emphasized that the greatest Hungarians have always been exponents of the European spirit. These essayists also recalled the cultural links with France symbolizing the value of humanism, liberty, and rationalism. At the same time they showed their strong opposition against Nazi Germany and the new nationalistic barbarity which finally came to their country.

Endre Ady compared his country to a rider who came from the distant Eastern steppes, got lost in Europe, and cannot find a place for himself. He wrote about tragic Hungarians who are alone in Europe and roam about it with no definite destination. Some Hungarian intellectuals saw their country as a bridge between East and West, a country tossed by the violent waves of history in both directions. In Ady's vision of his country it possessed both Western (chiefly Austrian) elements and Eastern passivity and helplessness; altogether they produced a rather sad picture of his compatriots.

The problem of what to do in order to equal Europe, to come up to her level has also perplexed Hungarian intellectuals in recent decades. Miklos Jancsó, for example, took up in his famous films and interviews various irrational contradictions and problems stemming from the inferiority complex of a small nation that wants to be European.

THE BALKAN QUESTION

Balkan countries of South Eastern Europe had very few contacts with Western Europe. The Balkan region was influenced by Byzantine culture and then was incorporated into the Ottoman Empire. Oriental and Islamic elements dominated for centuries in the culture of the educated elites, often of Turkish origin. The lack of a common intellectual tradition stemming from the Renaissance humanism created an abyss between Western Europe and the Balkan world that seemed to be isolated from the West.

At the turn of the 18th century cultural contacts between the Balkans and Western Europe enlivened. It was an epoch of national regeneration of the indigenous peoples inhabiting the Balkan Peninsula. The ideas of Enlightenment, of the French Revolution, and of modern democratic nationalism were met with great interest and enthusiastically accepted on the Peninsula. The gradual decay of the Ottoman Empire favored a rebirth of the oppressed peoples. The heralds of new times were first of all the Greeks who fought for their independence and spread revolutionary and rationalistic ideas. France played an important role at the period of national rebirth and shaping modern nations and societies on the Peninsula. Also French culture, thought, literature, and language were in vogue. Some Italians and British influences could also be noticed.

Russia with its Slavophile ideas, played an enormous role on the Balkan Peninsula apart from the Western influences. Russia took advantage of the linguistic, religious, and cultural similarities between her and the many Balkan nations struggling against Turkey for their sovereignty. Russia became their natural ally. The rivalry over influence in the Balkans between Russia and Western powers lasted a long time.

In this Essay I am more interested in Western influences which have been easily noticeable in the 19th and 20th centuries. They resulted in numerous signs of religious indifference and an increase of liberal attitudes among intellectuals. These attitudes tempered the influence of the Russian conservatism and despotism. While organizing their state apparatus, Balkan politicians made use of the administrative and juridical patterns already existing in Western countries. The Western, especially French, cultural influences were strong at the beginning of this century not only in Croatia and Slovenia but also in Bulgaria and Serbia. The Balkan peoples, however, have never found either an appropriate civilizational pattern or an effective path for their national development.

The most important representative of the early Serbian Westernism was Dositej Obradović (1739?-1811). As an enlightened Westerner, he wanted the Serbian people to assimilate fully the rich cultures of the progressive Western nations. According to Serbian Westernism, Europe was a much more enlightened, more progressive, and more civilized model than backward Russia.

The concept of distant, idealized Europe appeared in the Bulgarian consciousness at the beginning of the 19th century. Bulgarian intellectuals had no direct contact with the reality of the West. Both Bulgarian Westernism and search for national identity stem from the tradition of national rebirth. A strong current of Westernism appeared in that country as late as the beginning of the 20th century. The so-called group "Thought" of modernist writers presented themselves as *Kulturträger* in Bulgaria conceived as a cultural province. They were fully conscious of the great distance of Bulgaria from Western culture, but wanted to be included in the future overall European identity. The Bulgarian modernists accepted spiritual absolute values and professed outward Eurocentrism. The so-called young modernists wanted to be a part of universal humanity and their new art sought successfully to combine European culture with elements of their national folklore. Their vague concept of Europe meant universal values, cultural and civilizational progress, and sometimes danger to vernacular tradition. The concepts of Europeanness, Orientalism, and Slavophilism in Bulgarian culture have always been ambiguous. It was very difficult to determine what was vernacular and indigenous, and what alien in Bulgaria and the Balkan Peninsula. The difficult and dramatic dialogue of cultures in Bulgarian thought is a separate problem. The Bulgarian way towards Europe was full of numerous obstacles.. The falling Ottoman Empire that had prevented Bulgarian access to Europe finally accepted its own Westernism. So Bulgarians met with Europe not directly, but in a roundabout way, met with European culture and thought being transmitted to them tardily and often from Turkish, Greek, Serbian, and Russian centers. Many enlightened Bulgars of the 19th century and the beginning of the 20th century did not want want to be identified with Oriental and Islamic culture. The Orient was presented by them as a sphere of misery alien to human dignity. They were ravished by the Western standards and the organizational and technological efficiency of the West.[48]

The slogan of Europeanization of Bulgaria, of her "entrance into Europe" has been very catchy after the fall of communism. Europe is identified with the civilized world, civilized countries and "normalcy". The scope of the concept of Europe is as vague as it has always been in Bulgaria. Generally the concept is associated with human rights and democracy as opposed to violence, despotism, isolationism, and totalism. The first democratic president-philosopher told his countrymen before the elections that they should prove and "demonstrate to themselves, to Europe and the whole world that they are worthy of democracy."[49]

Westernism has also been present in Macedonian literature and thought. It is a widespread phenomenon nowadays. Europe was conceived as a synonymous with the European Economic Community and later with the European Union and as opposite to the East. Europeanness was often associated with civilized states and civilized dialogue in the Macedonian press.[50] This country situated in the center of Balkans wants to be a negation of what is associated with the region, wants to be a real European nation, a factor of stabilization in the Balkans, a symbol of its unifying tendences.

Macedonians also propagated a myth of a good, mild, and noble Slav as an attribute of their nation, to which history and Europe did great harm in accepting its partition. Europe is treated as morally indebted to Macedonians and they claim that this time Europe should compensate for her previous neglect.

LATIN AMERICA AND THE WEST

Westernism has also a predominant current in Latin American thought since the early days of the independence of South and Central American Republics. According to this trend, the paradigm and norm to be followed is a civilization and political culture developed in the most progressive countries of Western Europe (France and Britain) and in the United States of America. Thinkers of this trend looked very often to the United States as the great example and universal norm to be copied in everyday life, politics, and economics. They were thoroughly European in their culture and gave little if any attention to the Indian and other elements of the South American reality. The Spanish tradition was also neglected.

One of the first pro-Western and anti-indigenous thinkers of independent Latin America was the Argentinian Juan Bautista Alberdi (1810-1884). According to him, the European immigration was a synonym of progress as was imitation of the British, Anglo-Saxon pattern of development based on liberalism, industry, and trade.[51] The central idea of his political views was condensed in his phrase "to govern is to populate" in the sense that to populate was to educate, to civilize, to improve first of all after the example of the United States. Alberti argued that in order to educate Latin America in liberty and industry it was necessary to populate it with people from Europe, as it was done in the United States. The root of all Latin American difficulties lies in its poverty, underpopulation, backwardness, shortage of European civilization, and lack of discipline in work.

Alberdi was aware that a pure imitation was inefficient. He noted that South American cities wanted to be little Parises but forgot that Paris had worked hard.[52]

Alberdi's ideas such as his attachment to liberal democracy and civil rights were followed by his countryman, Domingo Faustino Sarmiento (1811-1888). He saw negative elements and heavy obstacles to development in Argentina's *caudillismo*, in the Spanish cultural and political heritage, and in colonial and Indian barbarism. In 1845 he wrote his classic work *Civilization and Barbarism. The Life of Juan Facundo Quiroga.* It was a sharp criticism of barbaric influences in Argentine life derived from the pampa and present in *gaucho* pastoral life and in the interior *caudillos* of his country. Unlike posterior indigenists, he considered the ethnic, genuinely American element (the land, Indians and *gauchos*) to be essentially malignant. His rather simplistic theory equated civilization with Europe and barbarism with the American *pampa*. Harold Eugene Davis maintains that "in some respects Sarmiento anticipated Darwinian social evolutionism and positivist racialism in explaining social reality". His views also express, according to the same historian, "the romantic liberal rebel's concept of a cosmic struggle between the forces of good and evil, one in which the Liberal's understanding of the magnitude of the historic forces that created the social realities drove him to strive to change the course of that history, even while taking his stand upon it."[53]

Sarmiento put great stress on education promoting civilization in Argentina. In his concept of civilization he laid strong emphasis upon technique, and on command over nature by man who wants to achieve physical and moral perfection. He situated the reason of Argentine failures in geography and in racial deficiencies, and rejected Spanish civilization. Latin America should raise herself to a higher level, should correct its aboriginal ideas with modern European races and ideas. In his book entitled *Harmony and Conflict of Races in America* he tried to explain the causes of failure and point out numerous deficiencies in Latin American life. Still, he did not lose his optimistic prospects for the future when he stated: "South America is falling behind and will lose its God-given mission as part of modern civilization. Let us not hold up the United States in its forward march; that is what some are proposing to do. Let us overcome the United States. Let us be America, as the sea is the ocean. Let us be United States."[54]

Sarmiento was typical of the 19th century Argentine and Latin American appreciation of North American progress in welfare and grass-roots democracy. This attitude was widespread among educated elites especially in Argentina and Chile. Among Chileans of note is José Victoriano Lastarría (1817-1888), one of the outstanding intellectuals of his country. He was very favourable to the United States and critical of the Spanish heritage of "gloomy existence without movement". He was a representative of the tendency that saw inspiration in French science, literature, and ideas, on the one hand, and in American political institutions and economic progress, on the other. Lastarría was a great adherent of the American concepts of freedom, liberty, democracy, and the practice of law. He believed in the great future of America and stated that Europe can be saved only if it imitates American democratic patterns. New America, he claimed, should not enter into a federation with European nations clinging to monarchy. He was also strongly opposed to all projects of creating a league of Latin or Hispanic nations to combat Anglo-Saxon civilization. He considered the Spanish civilization outworn, anti-social and out of date. According to him: "The principal cause of our political and social disaster lies in our Spanish task, and we cannot remedy these disasters except by reacting frankly, and energetically against that civilization, in order to free our minds and adapt our society to the new form, democracy."[55]

At the beginning of the 20th century a new kind of Westernism arose in Latin America. It was opposed to the panegyrics completely uncritical of the United States as seen in the pages of Alberdi, Sarmiento, Lastarría, and Bilbao. This reaction against the North American neighbor sought to affirm Latin American culture and is usually associated with the name of the Uruguayan thinker, José Enrique Rodó (1872-1917). He was highly critical of the North American utilitarianism and pragmatism. Rodó maintained that the United States' educational system gave superficial learning and could not produce "aristocracy of merit". According to the Uruguayan critic, the North Americans were unable to comprehend fundamental human values and human destiny. He defended the Latin concept of educated elite and believed that Hispanic Americans could be the best heirs of, and torchbearers for the European, Greco-Roman humanistic tradition in the New World. Martin S. Stabb says that Rodó "felt that the role of Hispanic America's neo-Latins was not simply that of transferring European culture, but of surpassing it, of bringing it to fuller fruition."[56]

In his essay, *Los motivos de Proteo* (1909), a continuation of his famous *Ariel* (1900), Rodó opposed the tendency towards narrow specialization in the present-day technological world and defended Renaissance-like universality and spiritual versatility of man. In his Europeanness and universalism there are present elements of Greek, Hellenic, French, Spanish, and Christian inspiration.

Rodó's humanistic idealism and Prometheanism was directed against the utilitarian North American civilization. The opposition between Hispano America and Anglo America is fundamental to his thought. Rodó was well aware of the admiration that the greatness and material progress of the United States, of the American way of life produced in Latin American minds. He called *Nordomania* the tendency to follow blindly and uncritically the North American patterns of life and thought.

Rodó was one of the first Americans to criticize those 'Yankeephiles' who wanted to imitate North America and at the same time one of the first thinkers who saw in the expansionist tendencies of northern neighbor, the Colossus of he North, a danger for Latin American cultural identity and territorial integrity. The Uruguayan philosopher viewed *yanqui* culture as alien and threatening. Criticizing widespread *Nordomania*, Rodó distrusted the North American pursuit of material success and excessive worship of technological progress at the expense spiritual culture. Nevertheless, the *arielista* movement initiated by Rodó cannot be classified as a typical of Latin America leftist *yanquifobia*. It is almost a slavishly European Westernism aware of some negative aspects of mass culture and utilitarian ideology. Such Westernism limited to classical roots of West European culture was also present in some variants of East European Westernism which criticized the shallowness of North American popular culture and strivings.

The interpretation of historical and cultural ties linking Latin America with Europe has been a constant problem for Hispanic American thought. The adherents of the so-called civilizational project presented the United States as a model to imitate or to copy. According to these thinkers, all Latin American failures and sins such as chaos, anarchy, and so on were due to the colonial, Iberian past still prevailing in its mentality after gaining formal independence.

Civilization or barbarism was the main dilemma generating the need to introduce a new order instead of the chaos inherited from the Iberian colonies. Examples were not only the negative aspects of Iberian heritage, but also Indians, Africans, and *mestizos*, which, it was maintained, true civilization should eradicate.

The pragmatic spirit of the Northern neighbor was deemed very useful for Latin Americans. Such spirit of imitation may follow from an inner conviction that Latin Americans are inferior and that they should take as models more advanced nations. The thinkers who defended an "assumptive model" reacted.[57] These thinkers accepted their reality, such as it was, as starting point. They wanted to assimilate in a critical way all aspects of their proper past.

Two important events in the 19th century contributed to the fact that many Latin American intellectuals reacted violently against both the United States and France which was identified with the essence of European culture. These were the North American invasion of Mexico in 1847 and the French military intervention in that country in 1861. These events forced some thinkers to turn their eyes to their own reality, and not only to foreign models.

Also during the First and Second World War caused by Europeans many Latin American thinkers developed a critical attitude towards the crisis of European culture. Still they maintained that European culture is much more meaningful for them than the pre-Columbian one. According to Leopoldo Zea, Americanity cannot be found in the ancient Aztec and Mayan beliefs. Americanity follows from Europeanness, which all Americans try to imitate. Latin Americans are aware that they should assimilate European culture, but feel uncertainty as to their capacities. Latin Americans, Zea insists, are not heirs of American indigenous cultures, but at the same time European culture is felt by them as alien, although meaningful. Many Latin Americans tried to forget about their specific reality in order to become Europeans. This situation, according to Zea, recalls a situation of a son, who would like to be his own father.[58]

Although critical of many aspects of Western civilization, Zea used to emphasize that Latin Americans were descendants of European culture. From

Europe comes their language, religion, customs and vision of the world; Latin Americans cannot deny these roots, but should preserve their own personality different from Europe, much the same way children are different from their parents. Latin Americans, as heirs to the European culture, should take the separate position in it, of responsible co-creators.

Latin Americans are conscious of the position of their countries as peripheral in relation to the West and as dependant on more developed countries. Although the degree of subjugation is not so great as in the colonial times, Latin Americans still preserve their feeling of having been damaged and of inferiority.[59] There have been various types of subordination of Latin American thought and reality to the European norm, but not all philosophers see it as an evil. According to Celina A. Lértora de Mendoza, "mimesis" and imitative attitudes are as equally valid as other options and do not mean devaluating oneself or negating one's identity. The present planetary process of universalization favors this.[60]

Europeans rarely included Latin America to the Western world. For Hegel, South America still belonged to geographical space, not to conscious history. According to him, the spirit did not enter either South America or even Eastern Europe. The Slavic countries appeared late in human history and were connected with Asia. Hegel did not take into his historiosophical considerations either Slavic or South American nations or "human masses" since they did not act as an independent force in history. Slavic nations were engaged mostly in agriculture based on lord and servant relations. Natural forces, says Hegel, play a predominant role in agriculture, not cleverness and subjective activity. For that reason, in Hegel's view, the Slavs developed tardily their subjective self and state power. They could not therefore, participate in the development of spiritual freedom.

Latin America even in the 20th century was excluded from the concept of the West by Spengler and some other thinkers, but many included it in the far, but not necessarily wild, West.

From a different point of view, leftist thinkers of Latin America used to accentuate the singularity of their countries, the specific aspects of the *mestizo* continent. They used to perceive positive elements in indigenous elements, rehabilitating thus the person of Caliban who was a symbol of the savage creatures inhabiting Latin America.

From the above, we can conclude that both East Europeans (especially Russians) and South Americans (especially Argentinians) had some similar patterns of thought in relation to the West. The Russians like Peter the Great and his followers and the Argentinians like Sarmiento wanted to lead their countries out from the traditional barbarity of Asian or Indian origin. Peter the Great wanted to negate old Slavic barbarism in order to make possible a Europeanization of Russia. According to Zea, it is "the same 'nordomanía' of which the Latin American José Enrique Rodó will speak and which implies the recognition of values that are not their own, and along with it a subordination to the creators of those values. Peter the Great of Russia, by imposing European civilization on his people, subordinated it, even unwittingly, to the new power of the peoples who created, acknowledged and accepted that civilization. It was not that of the Europe of Europe of the Holy Roman Empire, but of the new Europe of which England was the head."[61]

Among the Russian thinkers it was first of all Aleksander Herzen, the continuator of the tradition of the Decembrists, who considered the Russian pattern to be one of savage barbarity. He chose Western liberties, but was not uncritical of the West European deficiencies. He was confident that in Russia freedom and civilization would triumph after the example of Europe and the United States. According to Herzen, Russia seemed Asiatic as seen from the European point of view and European from the Asian perspective. He thought Russia could serve as a civilizational bridge between Europe and Asia.

There was a somewhat similar situation in Spanish America, which has sought her identity since the period of independence. The famous Liberator Simón Bolivar wrote: "We are, moreover, neither Indian nor European, but a species midway between the legitimate proprietors of this country and the Spanish usurpers. In short, though American by birth we derive our rights from Europe, and we have to assert these rights against the rights of the natives, and at the same time we must defend ourselves against the invaders. This places us in a most extraordinary and involved situation."[62]

The problems involved in East European and Latin American Westernism and a kind of universalism could be better understood if one tried to enter their peculiar or even nationalistic thought, which is so important in the intellectual history of both regions.[63]

NOTES

1 The pride of place in that respect goes to novel studies by Ryszard Stemplowski: *Zależność i wyzwanie - Argentyna wobec rywalizacji mocarstw anglosaskich i III Rzeszy* (Warsaw: KiW, 1975); "Chile y las compañías petroleras, 1931-1932. Contribución al estudio del entrelazamiento dominación-dependencia," *Ibero-Amerikanisches Archiv*, 1 (978).

2 Marian Małowist, *Wschód i Zachód Europy w XIII - XVI wieku* (Warsaw, 1973); see also his comprehensive interview in *Estudios Latinoamericanos*, Ossolineum, 12 (1989): 11-55.

3 Ryszard Stemplowski, "Modernizacja - teoria czy doktryna", *Kwartalnik Historyczny* 1 (1980), 754.

4 Such schematism is visible in the article by Dagnino: "Zależność kulturowa. Próba ujęcia kulturowego", in: *Ameryka Łacińska - dyskusja o rozwoju*, Ed. by R. Stemplowski (Warsaw: Czytelnik, 1987): 183-225.

5 Thus far it was observable at least in one essay by J.C. Nyiri, "Ehrenfels und Masaryk: Űberlegungen an der Peripherie der Geshichte", in: idem, *Am Rande Europas. Studien zur österreichisch-ungarischen Philosophiegeschichte* (Budapest, 1988). Nyiri drew attention to the fact that Wallerstein has forerunners, next to Małowist, also in the Hungarian historian Zsigmund Pach.

6 We disregard here the characteristics of the worldview of pre-Christian Slavs, which have some importance in the eyes of certain philosophers. By analogy, some contemporary Latin American philosophers attach much importance to the thought of the Indians in pre-Christian America.

7 Zdzisław Kuksewicz, *Zarys filozofii średniowiecznej* (Warsaw: PWN, 1979), 396.

8 Cf. *Man, State and Society in East European History*, ed. by S. Fischer-Galati (London, 1970), VI-VII.

9 Quoted after Leopoldo Zea, ed., *Antología de la filosofía americana contemporánea* (México, 1968), 31-32.

10 Władysław Tatarkiewicz, "Między oświeceniem a mesjanizmem", introduction to *Jakiej filozofii Polacy potrzebują* (Warszawa: PWN), XXIV.

11 *Cf.* Andrzej Wierzbicki, *Wschód - Zachód w koncepcjach dziejów Polski* (Warsaw, 1985) 7; Jerzy Jedlicki, *Jakiej cywilizacji Polacy potrzebują* (Warsaw: PWN, 1988), 31.

12 D.F. Sarmiento, *Facundo, o civilización y barbarie en las pampas argentinas* (Santiago de Chile, 1845).

13 Leopoldo Zea, *Filosofía de la historia americana* (Mexico: Fondo de Cultura Económica, 1978).

14 Interesting comments on that issue are to be found in: M.F. Sciacca, ed., *Les grands courants de la pensée mondiale contemporaine* (vol. II, Milano, 1959), 1236-1244. It is the first integrated presentation of world philosophical thought. It is interesting to note that while one comprehensive chapter on the whole of Latin America was prepared by Francisco Romero and José Luís Romero, Central and Eastern Europe (Austria, Bulgaria, Hungary, Poland, Romania, Russia, Czechoslovakia, Yugoslavia) have separate authors quite independent of one another, who even do not try to look for common elements in the history of philosophy of that region. It is likewise in the case of the J.R. Burr, ed., *Handbook of World Philosophy. Contemporary Developments Since 1945* (Westport: Conn., 1980), where the chapter on Latin America (with a special consideration of Mexico) was written by Arthur Berndson, while Eastern Europe (Czechoslovakia, Eastern Germany, Poland, Romania, the Soviet Union) in the interpretation of various authors forms only a a certain political whole. One of the first presentations of philosophy in Slavic countries (Russian, Ukrainian, Polish, Slovenian, Croatian, Serbian, and Bulgarian) is to be found in the collective work: Weingart, ed., *Současna filosofie u Slovanu* (Prague, 1932).

15 Similar formulations occur in the works of Mexican Leopoldo Zea and Brazilian Darcy Ribeiro with reference to Latin Americans.

16 Andrzej Walicki, *Rosyjska filozofia i myśl społeczna od oświecenia do marksizmu* (Warsaw: Wiedza Powszechna, 1973), 132-133.

17 See Thomas G. Masaryk, *The Spirit of Russia. Studies in History, Literature and Philosophy* (London 1919); Janusz Dobieszewski, "Przeciwieństwo między Rosją a Europą jako problem filozoficzny", *Studia Filozoficzne* 8 (1986).

18 See *Seven Centuries of Bulgarian Philosophical Thought* (Sofia, 1973), 82.

19 N.O. Lossky, *History of Russian Philosophy* (London 1952); V. Zenkovsky, *A History of Russian Philosophy* (London, 1953); see also M.A. Maslin, *Sovremenniye burzhuazniye kontseptsii istorii russkoi filosofii* (Moscow, 1988).

20 Andrzej Walicki, *Rosyjska filozofia*, 6.

21 William Rex Crawford, *A Century of Latin American Thought* (New York 1961), 4-5.

22 A. Agh, "The Triangle Model of Society and Beyond", in *State and Civil Society: Relations in Flux*, ed. V. Gathy (Budapest, 1989), 14.

23 Andrzej Walicki, "Historia filozofii polskiej jako przedmiot badań i jako problem kultury współczesnej", *Studia Filozoficzne* 1 (1969): 109-110.

24 Augusto Salazar Bondy, *Sentido y problema del pensamiento filosófico hispanoamericano* (Kansas, 1969).

25 Augusto Salazar Bondy, *Existe una filosofia de nuestra America?* (Mexico: Siglo Veintiuno Editores, 1968), 121.

26 Richard Morse, *El espejo de Próspero* (México: Sglo XXI Editores 1982), 220; quoted after Leopoldo Zea, *Discurso desde la marginación y barbarie* (Barcelona: Anthropos, 1988), 267.

27 See *Edukacja Filozoficzna* 16, 17 (1993, 1994).

28 Andrzej Walicki, *A History of Russian Thought from the Enlightenment to Marxism* (Oxford: Oxford University Press, 1980), 138-139.

29 Andrzej Walicki, *A History of Russian Thought*, 149-150.

30 See Wiktoria Śliwowska, "Rosja - Europa od końca XVIII w. do lat osiemdziesiątych XIX w.", in *Dziesięć wieków Europy. Studia z dziejów kontynentu*, ed. Janusz Żarnowski (Warsaw, 1983), 331-332.

31 R.W. Mathewson, "Russian Literature and the West", *Slavic Review* 3(1962).

32 See Marc Raeff, "Russia's Perception of Her Relatioship with the West", in *The Development of the USSR. An Exchange of Views*, ed. W. Treadgold (University of Washington Press, 1967).

33 Oscar Halecki, *Borderlands of Western Civilization. A History of East Central Europe* (New York, 1952), 3.

34 Omeljan Pritsak and John S. Reshetar, The Ukraine and Dialectics of Nation-Building, in The Development of the USSR, 238; J. Isajewicz, "Na skrzyzowaniu kultur: Ukraina a Europa Środkowo-Wschodnia", *Lithuania*, 2-3 (1994).

35 Henry L. Roberts, "Russia and the West: A Comparison and Contrast", in *The Development of the USSR*, 361.

36 Marc Szeftel, "The Historical Limits of the Question of Russia and the West", in *The Development of the USSR*, 383.

37 Alexy Verizhnikov, "Tradition and Change: the Case of Russia, in *Zeszyty Szkoły Nauk Społecznych* 1 (1996), 301. Note considerations also the reflections of the Russian philosopher Kara-Murza on the barbarization

in Russia (or in "Asiope") of the West European projects of civilization (democracy, socialism, liberalism).

38 *(Un)Civil Societies. Human Rights and Democratic Transitions in Eastern Europe and Latin America*, ed., Rachael A. May and Andrew K. Milton (Lanham, Maryland: Lexington Book, 2005), 209.

39 Interview for the Polish *Gazeta Wyborcza*, 12-13 January, 2002.

40 Jerzy Jedlicki, "Polskie nurty ideowe lat 1790-1863 wobec cywilizacji Zachodu", in *Swojskość i cudzoziemszczyzna w dziejach kultury polskiej*, ed. Zofia Stefanowska (Warsaw, 1973) 196.

41 Ryszard Legutko, "Między papugą a zaściankiem (Polskim liberałom ku przestrodze)", *Znak* 1 (1992).

42 Maria Janion "Rozstać się z Polską?", *Gazeta Wyborcza* 2004, 2-3 October 2004.

43 See Vaclav Černý, *Europejskie źródła czeskiej kultury* (Warsaw: Oficyna Literacka, 1989).

44 Jiři Škvor, "Humanistic and Democratic Thought in Czech Literature", in *The Czechoslovak Contribution to World Culture*, Miloslav Rechcigl, ed. (The Hague - London - Paris: Mouton Co., 1964), 34; see also, Peter Brock and H. Gordon Skilling, eds., *The Czech Renaissance of the Nineteenth Century* ((Univesity of Toronto Press, 1970); *Czech Philosophy in the XXth Century*, ed. L. Novy, J. Gabriel, J. Hroch (Washington, D.C.: The Council for Research in Values and Philosophy, 1994).

45 Karel Čapek, *President Masaryk tells his story* (New York, 1935), 74.

46 Quoted from Thomas Masaryk, *Humanistic Ideals*, foreword by Hubert Humphrey (Lewisburg 1971), 9.

47 See his famous Essay on the tragedy of Central Europe, first published in French and which appeared in Polish for the first time in *Zeszyty Literackie* 55 (1984). Interesting comments on the idea of Central Europe can be found in *Identité(s) de l'Europe Centrale*, ed. Michel Maslowski (Paris: Institut d'Etudes Slaves, 1995); *The Identity of Central Europe*, ed. G. Gorzelak, B. Jałowiecki (Warsaw: University of Warsaw, 1997).

48 Grażyna Szwat-Gobyłowa, "Europa i Orient w świetle bułgarskiej prozy wspomnieniowej XIX stulecia", in Teresa Dąbek-Wirgowa, Andrzej Z. Makowiecki, eds., *Kategoria Europy w kulturach słowiańskich* (Warsaw: Uniwersytet Warszawski - Wydział Polonistyki, 1992).

49 Quoted after Teresa Dąbek-Wirgowa, "Hasła europeizacji dawniej i dziś (na przykładach literatury bułgarskiej)", in *Kategoria Europy w kulturach słowiańskich*, 145. See also E. Draganova-Madelaine, *La Bulgarie face à L'Europe. De la transition à l'integration* (Paris: Éditions l'Harmattan, 2004).

50 See Krzysztof Wrocławski, "Którędy do Europy z Macedonii?", in *Kategoria Europy w kulturach słowiańskich*, 153-160.

51 See H.C.F. Mansilla, "La ensayistica latinoamericana y la cuestión de la identidad colectiva", *Signos. Cuadernos Bolivianos de Cultura* 28 (1989), 14.

52 Juan Bautista Alberdi, *Escritos postumos* (Buenos Aires, 1895), 158.

53 Harold E. Davis, *Latin American Thought: A Historical Introduction* (New York 1974), 78.

54 Quoted after, W. R. Crawford, *A Century of Latin American Thought* (New York, 1961), 51.

55 Quoted after W.R. Crawford, *A Century of Latin American Thought*, 68.

56 Martin S. Stabb, *In Quest of Identity. Patterns in the Spanish American Essay of Ideas, 1890-1960* (Chapel Hill, 1967), 37; see also M.T. Martinez Blanco, *Identidad cultural de Hispanoamerica. Europeismo y originalidad americana* (Madrid 1988).

57 See Leopoldo Zea, *Filosofia de la historia americana* (Mexico, 1978).

58 Leopoldo Zea, "En torno a una filosofia americana", in *Ensayo sobre filosofia en la historia* (México 1948).

59 See V.L. Zemskov, "Ob istoriko-kulturnykh otnosheniakh Latinskoi Ameriki i Zapada", *Latinskaia Amerika* (2,3) 1978.

60 Celina A. Lertora de Mendoza, "European Culture in Argentina", *Dialogue and Humanism,* 1 (1992).

61 Leopoldo Zea , *Discurso desde la marginación y barbarie*, 93.

62 Simón Bolivar, *The Hope of the Universe* (Paris: UNESCO, 1983), 104.

63 See E. Górski, *Dependencia y originalidad de la filosofia en Latinoamerica y en la Europa del Este* (México: UNAM, 1994); id., "Eslavofilia, Eurasia e Indigenismo. (Ideologías nacionalistas en Rusia y en América Latina)", *Con-Ciencia Política*, Veracruz, 2 (2002): 199-210.

Part III

Pluralism and Universalism

Chapter 7

From 'Socialist' to Postmodern Pluralism in Poland

All forms of political pluralism, whatever their specific character, pose the problem of combining diversity with unity. Pluralists by definition, cannot accept a wholly monistic understanding of statehood or nationhood.

-- Frederick M. Barnard, *Pluralism, Socialism and Political Legitimacy*, (Cambridge, 1991), 3.

Over half a century ago communist or socialist Poland had a totalitarian regime that eliminated all forms of political opposition and tried to impose a totalist ideology by monocentric but hardly monolithic power. Pursuing control of society by means of terror and a fully developed secret police, it was obsessed by the superior idea of unity. It should be noted that the key concept of the communist ideology in Poland in the years prior to 1980 was "the moral-political unity of the nation." It is also important, however, to see that the regime began to loosen its strictly totalitarian traits relatively early, soon after 1955, and gradually evolved towards an authoritarian rule marked by limited, lame or "socialist" pluralism.

Classifying Polish socialism under the rubric of authoritarian regimes has a great number of opponents mainly among the radical and stubbornly anti-communist right in Poland, who argue that the regime in spite of its evolution was totalitarian to the very end.

PLURALISM'S POSITION IN POLISH SOCIAL CHANGE – REFLECTION AND ARTICULATION

The most interesting description of Polish socialism under Gierek and especially under Jaruzelski as a form of an authoritarian regime was presented by Andrzej Walicki. He noted that Jaruzelski's regime loosened ideological and economic controls, abandoned the political mobilization of the masses, silently rejected communist ideology, justified pragmatism, "socialist" constitutionalism and pluralism, and granted relative freedom in cultural and academic life.[1]

In the 1970s, the Polish political system evolved from a totalitarian or semi-totalitarian regime to the bureaucratic-authoritarian regime of Edward Gierek and his team. At that time the process of detotalization from above was intensified; the state authorities tried to build a structure characterized by "lame", irresponsible pluralism that simulated various points of view, correcting thus numerous irrationalities of the decision-making process. [2]

At that time new elements not encountered in other socialist countries appeared in Poland: the development of a repressive toleration in which the informal political opposition had a peculiar, a-legal status, but lacked institutional channels of expression. Characteristic of the decade was also the process of further de-ideologization of state activities. The communist utopian ideology was ritualized and eroded with little impact on the authorities and society, "becoming instead a mere verbal façade."[3] According to Jadwiga Staniszkis: "In the cultural sphere, this period was marked by stronger and even more frequent references to such traditional values as the nation and family; a departure from the concept of a separate, socialist culture; and the growing role of elements of mass culture and a pattern of consumption following the more developed Western countries."[4]

Following Juan Linz's early hints that Poland seemed more authoritarian than totalitarian, Jadwiga Staniszkis described the Polish political system of the late 1970s as a typical authoritarian-bureaucratic regime that "contained limited, not responsible political pluralism, without an elaborated and guiding ideology but with distinctive mentalities."[5]

Poland, as is well known, was a specific case in communist Europe. Some elements of political pluralism were present in the Polish socialist system as far back as 1956 and the 1960s, namely, a hegemonic party system, the pluralist structure of the Front for National Unity, active presence of "pressure groups" and Catholic organisations acting as competitive or oppositional ideological forces.[6] In 1965, at a closed seminar in Warsaw Krzysztof Pomian, a famous Polish dissident philosopher, delivered a paper on political pluralism in a socialist society. Probably the first Polish scholarly article on social pluralism was also published that same year. Its author, a Catholic priest, Władysław Piwowarski, acknowledged -- on the basis of Thomist social philosophy -- that all human societies and communities were variegated quantitatively and qualitatatively and were entitled to live and develop independently, although in social order and unity of hierarchical structures.[7]

Yet, it must be stressed that in Poland in the 1960s and 1970s, it was impossible openly to discuss the problems of political pluralism, except for abstract considerations on polycentric and monocentric social systems, and for cultural pluralism.[8]

However, in 1980, a moment before the birth of Solidarity in Poland, a fundamental scholarly monograph on pluralism appeared, written by Stanisław Ehrlich, a world authority in this area.[9] Strangely, his book at first aroused little interest within of the highly pluralistic Polish society of that time.

Ehrlich claims there is no necessary bond between philosophical (ontological) pluralism and the social or political pluralism. He assumes that there can be many pluralisms in society at any given time, each graded on a continuum between extreme totalitarianism and anarchism. For Ehrlich, every movement or trend opposing bureaucratic centralism and uniformity of public life, which can appear in any social and economic system, is pluralistic. He defends the thesis that a pluralistic development of socialist societies is necessary and enumerates important elements of pluralism in Marxism. In his opinion, pluralism is a necessary but not sufficient condition for democracy. He concludes: "Finally, pluralism means also a way of thinking (E. Dupréel's *l'esprit pluraliste*) inspired by tolerance without which there is no social progress, public opinion, humanism, development or intellectual creativity."[10]

The beginning of the 1980s saw the emergence of numerous declarations appraising the value of pluralism. The program of Solidarity, the independent trade union, approved in its first nationwide Congress, accepted broad pluralism as the basis of democracy in the future independent Republic of Poland.

At the same time, many philosophers and sociologists began to speak more and more critically against the one-sided preference of totalitarian unity. Andrzej Nowicki referred to Giordano Bruno's cultural pluralism and to the alleged esteem gained by pluralism in Karl Marx's eyes. He suggested initiating broad interdisciplinary studies on pluralism as a means of preserving and deepening the diversity that in turn favors the development of culture.[11] Andrzej Tyszka discussed the polycentric and pluralistic character of contemporary Polish culture. Its polycentric character was determined by the freedom of initiative and the wide choice of ideas, styles and taste. Tyszka concluded, "Polycentrism is the opposition to monocentrism and totalitarianism, as they are characterized by a restrictive and intervening style of cultural dominance."[12] In his book written in 1982 - 1984, Winicjusz Narojek saw citizens' self-governing organizations as a means to free society of state control even within the framework of socialism by opening certain development alternatives.[13]

THE PRODUCTIVE NAIVETÉ OF "SOCIALIST" PLURALISM

In the years 1982 - 1985, a vivid discussion on pluralism was held in *Nowe Drogi*, *Tu i Teraz*, and other Polish journals. In 1982, Jan Wawrzyniak introduced the term "socialist pluralism"[14] into the official political language of the late semi-communist dictatorship, which at first provoked numerous reservations from the more orthodox positions. Wawrzyniak was attacked for allegedly suggesting the introduction of free interplay of political forces. Wawrzyniak answered that socialist pluralism as he understood it would enable different social groups to formulate their interests clearly.[15]

Terms such as "organised pluralism" and "alliance pluralism" also appeared then.[16] Naive supporters of even a limited, socialist pluralism were defeated by open enemies of any pluralism, who willingly repeated the Soviet ideological arguments. In his speeches Wojciech Jaruzelski criticised political pluralism, for example, "We are undoubtedly taking into consideration the existing differences in the approach towards many issues of our country. However, this does not and cannot have anything in common with the so-called political pluralism, the term which has recently become fashionable. The term provokes close association with bourgeois democracy and the capitalist system. In our conditions, pluralism understood in such a way would mean opening the way for forces opposing the socialist system and pushing our country back to the out-of-date forms and disputes which were concluded long ago."[17]

Two authors who were especially active in fighting the pluralist ideology on the grounds that "pluralism in Poland has not finished its career yet" summed up the first part of the official debate on pluralism: "In principle, the concept of socialist pluralism as introduced by Jan Wawrzyniak in the article published in *Nowe Drogi* was rejected during the discussions. The author gave up the most controversial elements of his concept and participated in the criticism of the conception, according to which pluralistic ideas can be transferred to the socialist political system."[18]

In the mid-980s, pluralistic slogans could only appear in the Catholic press, although the tradition of Polish Catholic thought did not generally favor pluralism.[19] However, the situation soon evolved to favor a pluralism colored by socialist phraseology. For antipluralists, the atmosphere was deteriorating due to the introduction of advanced political reforms in Poland and in the Soviet Union under Gorbachev's *perestroika*. A leftist defender of pluralism wrote, "Attacks against pluralism became less profitable, especially for those who were hoping for a careful and not disinterested guidance on where the wind was blowing."[20] The official ideology began changing at that time. At the end of 1986, Jaruzelski spoke favorably of a "socialist pluralism" and the following year, in Moscow, in favour of a "socialist personalism." [21] Later on, the term "socialist pluralism" appeared in the documents of the 6th Plenary Assembly of the Central Committee of the communist Polish United Workers' Party (PUWP) in 1987. In the Soviet Union, positive opinions on socialist pluralism could already be found in 1987, first in the *Moskovskiie Novosti* newspaper. In his speech delivered on February 18, 1988 Gorbachev said, "This is for the first time within decades that a socialist pluralism of ideas is a real presence."[22] In this situation, some Soviet and Polish antipluralists quickly began to modify their views. Many discussions and press articles praising socialist pluralism followed. However, not everybody accepted the term. The views that were published in the official mass-media led to two principal stands: one of them accepted the irrevocable necessity of political pluralism within the framework of socialism, and the other (represented by Jarosław Ładosz, Włodzimierz Lebiedziński and others) treated pluralism as opposed to Lenin's concept of socialism.[23]

The stand taken by Włodzimierz Lebiedziński characterized a few communist hard-liners of the period who used to complain that the relatively pluralist economic base (the presence of private property in the economy) generates pluralist political opinions. "We are now in a transitional period from capitalism to socialism in Poland."[24] He stated that pluralism in Poland was a fact and its form had the character of transitional pluralism -- not a socialist pluralism, as the socialist contents were not dominant. According to Lebiedziński, socialist pluralism would be possible and justified only in a mature socialist society, "different in form, but homogenous components would then form the socialist society."[25] Note that Lebiedziński never posed the more important question of whether it was possible for transitional socialism to exist on the peripheries of the world system. When the utopian dreams of a reformed socialism collapsed, the transition from the socialist fiction, and also from socialist pluralism, to defective capitalism and pluralism proved inevitable.

However, Poland of the late 1980s witnessed a "happy creativity" of naive followers of socialist pluralism and of equally naive critics of the idea. The former, looking for a magic means to save their privileged positions, managed to defeat the latter. A brochure issued in October 1988 by the Department of Ideology of the Central Committee of the Communist party stated that political pluralism was an element of an all-human political culture and that "People's Poland" has never been a state of rigid homogenous ideas and political institutions. The party document promoted a further deepening of limited pluralism.[26] During his dramatic struggle to maintain the disintegrating socialism one of the ideologists of the times declared that "ideological and theoretical stiffness of most Marxists *vis-à-vis* political pluralism was one of the barriers to achieving a quality enrichment of socialist political structures."[27] However, Andrzej Barcikowski rejected the concept of pluralism with no additional adjectives as excessively one-sided. He added: "Pluralism is not a purely autonomous or independent value in civil axiology. It has a deeper and a more general sense only as a premise for unity in diversity, for a minimum integration, and then for loyal co-operation of different forces in achieving the supreme social goals."[28]

In 1988, the Communist party's journal *Nowe Drogi* organized a discussion on socialist pluralism. It also published, in three subsequent issues, proceedings from a special conference on socialist pluralism. Some illusions of those who not long before trusted the saving power of socialist pluralism are worth quoting. Wiesław Klimczak said that the conditions were sufficiently mature for pluralism not to sound synonymous with antisocialism. Thus the eclectic ideologist of the disintegrating party apparatus had already accepted, just in case, pluralism, socialism, the leading role of the Polish United Workers' party's, "strategic goals of Marxism-Leninism", pragmatism, positivism, tolerance and compromise at the same time.[29] Mariusz Gulczyński, a more learned participant in the discussion also stated that "if we take on pluralism and precisely socialist pluralism, this gives us certain hopes for benefits of two kinds. Firstly, it takes into consideration the reality of our society just the way it is. Secondly, it is a more elastic way of organizing social life -- reorganizing our social life."[30] Elsewhere, Gulczyński talked about pluralism in socialism,[31] i.e., about a slightly broader form of a narrowly understood socialist pluralism. Nevertheless, he insisted on shaping a pro-socialist character of pluralism through limiting the "aggressive antisocialist attitude." Other participants in the discussion (e.g, Karol B. Janowski) connected their unclear hopes for pluralism with a new "articulation and negotiation model."[32] of organizing and managing power. It was to substitute for the previous "mobilization and transmission model."

Generally speaking, political pluralism was already accepted in the Polish ruling spheres in 1988, although two years before, in 1986, it had been said that pluralism could not go hand in hand with socialism. Soon afterwards, in 1987, the general postulate of pluralism, but still not political pluralism, was accepted. Later it too was accepted, but without the "free interplay of political forces."

It is interesting to consider here the reactions of authoritarian regimes confronted with extensive social and political pluralization of society. Thanks to the previous de-ideologization and acceptance of political clubs and associations,[33] "liberalising authoritarianism gave way to a negotiated movement toward post-communist pluralism" in Poland.[34]

One should bear in mind that full pluralism and free interplay of forces were opposed to for quite a long time - not only among communist authorities, who finally went bankrupt, ceding political power to Solidarity in 1989, but also among some representatives of the postsocialist establishment, for whom the drive towards a new monopoly was not unfamiliar (some political leaders of Solidarity initially dreamt of democracy based only on civic committees without political parties). In the new political situation after the Round Table had resulted in an acceptance of trade union pluralism and soon the creation of a Solidarity government, some organisations tried to continue the struggle for the deepening of pluralism.

In Poland in the late 1980s, general problems of pluralism were also addressed, in spite of the strictly political context of discussion on the most necessary system changes. The proceedings of a conference on pluralism in the Polish cultural tradition organized at Jagiellonian University in 1986 are most interesting in this respect. The openness of Polish culture which had its roots in the *sacrum*, but also in the *profanum*, was underlined in the papers.[35] It was shown that pluralism, tolerance, intellectual curiosity, and a desire for diversity were synonyms of freedom in the Polish tradition.

Poland's place between the East and the West and the problems with cultural identity favored, it was argued, seeing Polish neighbors and the whole world in the perspective of civilizational pluralism. In Poland, the perception of civilisation differences was consistently described not in the categories of inspiring and exotic, but as a fundamental difference in existential, political and spiritual forms of organizing human cooperation.[36]

UNIVERSAL TRUTHS AND POSTMODERN DIFFERENCES

Within the new framework of thought, Janusz Kuczyński tried to prove pluralism necessary in order to ensure the authenticity of a new universalism.[37] According to Kuczyński, as pluralism without universalism leads to eclecticism, and "universalism is an indispensable framework and the horizon of pluralism."[38]

At the beginning of the 1990s, after the downfall of communism, any broader discussion on the needs of pluralism in postcommunist Poland disappeared.[39] Some authors thought that it was due to the fact that real pluralism in social, political and economic life had begun. In fact, new important symptoms of pluralization in postcommunist Poland did arise: the establishment of new parties, societies, corporations, initiatives and organizations no longer subject to any state control.[40] An incipient spirit of multiculturalism also contributed to the rediscovery of pluralism.[41] New, less serious life styles and ways of behaviour appeared. The present state of pluralism, however, seems far from perfect. Andrzej Walicki has defined Poland as a country of selective tolerance, not yet of pluralism.[42] Many authors have stressed that pluralist structures in politics and economics are slow in forming and weak.[43] It has often been said that a pluralistic social order cannot be taken for granted[44] and that our democratic institutions are fragile.

Anticommunist Solidarity did pave the way for Polish democracy, but it did little to achieve a genuine tolerant pluralism, since it expressed more often traditionalist, organic and collectivist values than liberal and individualist ones. "Influenced, then, by Polish national and Catholic religious traditions, and by the logic of mobilization against an enemy, the morality of Solidarność emphasized unity, loyalty, and solidarity of vast scope."[45] It did not know how to handle the troublesome problem of living with differences.

Pluralism and the celebration of differences are, however, the hallmarks of a liberal postmodernism, at present in vogue almost everywhere.[46] Its Polish disseminators underline that the category of pluralism is of utmost importance for the postmodern turn. The new quality of that pluralism with its new ways of thinking and new styles of life implies loosing the ideal of an integral whole and unity. The new pluralism "has blown up all unities", expressing "joy and optimism."[47] For its followers, the victory of postmodernism means that the loss of unity does not sadden and need not be negative. This new philosophy demonstrates that all unity, exclusion, Rightness, Truth and Justice led to totalitarianism. Postmodernism is possible and fulfilled only when the obsessive longing for unity is replaced by the relish for plurality of truths and languages, by the "joy of pluralism."[48]

The reception of postmodernism in Poland was rather late and met with serious obstacles coming not from communist or postcommunist forces, but from Solidarity and Roman Catholic fundamentalism. Postmodernism spread throughout Poland and Eastern Europe in the 1990s.[49] Some elements of this philosophical attitude and literary sensibility had been present, in fact, in the region long before the demise of Marxism and communism. The work of some Polish *emigré* thinkers like Witold Gombrowicz and Zygmunt Bauman, may be considered forerunners or near classics of postmodernism. Polish and Central European writers had contributed something to postmodernism *avant la lettre*. Postmodern anti-foundationalism, opposed to all political and religious dogmatism, was widely present in the *emigré* and underground literatures of Central Europe in the 1980s. This literature played a considerable role in the deconstruction and final destruction of the totalitarian ideology of communism and of some other totalising or authoritarian discourses.

It happened, however, that the official reception of postmodernism coincided with the sudden collapse of real and "utopian" socialism. In Eastern Europe the phenomenon of postmodernism is, therefore, closely connected with the postcommunist consciousness of crisis, liberation, exhaustion, void,[50] and with unsuccessful modernization.[51] It became evident that the post-totalitarian chaos somehow corresponded with fashionable Western ideas.

Characteristic for both postmodernism and postcommunism was a loosening of official political structures.[52] In Poland a socialist or postsocialist version of postmodernism (*soc-postmodernizm*), with its extreme relativism and bitter irony widespread especially among "fallen Marxists", was singled out.[53] Such postmodernism combines allegedly destructive elements of western culture with moral and cognitive remnants of the "real socialism": cynicism, lack of responsibility, and questioning of truths and other values.[54] Postmodernism is also connected with the consciousness of shock after the downfall of communism, strongly felt especially in Russia and the Balkan countries.

In Central and Eastern Europe postmodernism means the victory of "weak thought" which is conscious of its limitations and the victory of pluralism over foundationalism; it expresses new feelings of relativism, demystification, endism, chaos, nihilism, decadence, and a loss of values.[55] An appropriate theoretical ground for this kind of philosophy in Central Europe was not prepared and its future is not secure.[56]

In Poland postmodernism met with distrust and opposition coming from the conservative circles of the Roman Catholic Church and from those representing the tradition of Lvov-Warsaw School of logical philosophy (Jerzy Pelc, Andrzej Grzegorczyk, Jan Woleński), which never displayed much tolerance.[57] Also some literary critics try to demostrate an incompatibility of western postmodernism - in which nothing matters, anything goes - with the deeply rooted Polish tradition of meaningful and genuinely engaged literature that prefers reconstruction to deconstruction.[58] Postmodernism is being criticized for its real or alleged propensity towards hedonism, extreme permissiveness, cult of superficiality, and moral and political nihilism. It is being criticized for its speedy farewell to metaphysics with its expression of the "unbearable heaviness of being" and for accepting instead the "unbearable lighteness of being".[59]

It was noticed that in the Polish Catholic and conservative press the label "postmodernism" had lost its neutral and descriptive character and turned into an invective directed against liberals, atheists, adherents of abortion, etc.[60] Postmodernism was also held responsible for abandoning the truth and the authorities, for favoring religious sectarianism,[61] spreading narcotics and underming the mental health of the nation.[62] Postmodernism, allegedly unaccepted by Polish elites, flirts with mass culture and produces a chaotic, "useless void", a "cultural pulp - of liberty, pluralism, and tolerance in caricature."[63]

It is now said that genuine postmodernism is possible only in countries abounding in consumer goods. This type of civilization does not yet exist either in Poland or anywhere else in Eastern Europe. So the countries of this region should not accept uncritically the ideas of modernity, modernization, and postmodernism coming from the advanced West.

The Polish critique of postmodernism is more often associated with the critique of tolerance, liberalism and, democracy -- especially liberal democracy -- than with outright rejection of pluralism. Polish conservative Catholics are longing for traditionalist or fundamentalist unity, prefer to concentrate their attacks on liberalism than on pluralism and human rights which, though efficient tools in the recent struggle against communism, but have never been conceived as autonomous goals. Almost all observers of social reality acknowledge that pluralism is a reality that cannot be ignored, since Polish citizens form a plural society, but only postmodern liberals openly accept it as a model for peaceful coexistence. For example Andrzej Szahaj, a Polish critic of fundamentalism, considers liberal democracy the best means of coping with social, cultural and religious diversities. He underlines that liberalism requires moderation or even a certain restraint in public life,[64] whereas many Catholics strongly oppose separating private from public convictions. For them, in a community where the Catholic Church is clearly a dominant religion and moral force, political and non-political spheres of human life are one.[65] Pluralism is thus viewed as an open expression of imperfection, incomprehension and even vice or sin. The State should therefore exact fundamental truth and unity. Pluralism for Polish fundamentalists means giving consent to spreading evil and is seen as a sign of a creeping cultural conquest of Poland by the West, the "liberal totalitarianism." Polish fundamentalists wish to restrict individual liberties, to impose one religion on all members of society, and to achieve a nationalist unity based upon Catholic principles. They equate pluralism with an extreme relativism, with tolerance of evil and ignorance. It is interesting to see that even for some Polish liberals (conservative liberals), it is difficult psychologically to accept a situation in which their own strongly held opinions may not arouse any vivid interest or may be met with widespread indifference.[66]

Some independent Polish critics of postmodernism with its impossible "radical pluralism"say that postmodern philosophy underestimates the need to "anchor man in history." According to Tadeusz Szkołut, postmodern thought should, instead of deepening axiological confusion, search for models of pluralist order that do not exclude some fundamental values. A more efficient defence of pluralism requires finding in the tradition of European culture (the Enlightenment included) those rational currents that would be helpful today in shaping positive tolerance.[67]

Ryszard Legutko, a Cracow professor of philosophy, has become a main representative of Polish conservatism, relatively enlightened and independent of the Catholic hierarchy. Under late communism he advocated liberal ideas, but after its downfall he became a severe critic of "homo liberalis", as well as of the modern and postmodern tolerance principle and liberal pluralism. He defined his mission as a struggle against the "culture of relativism and nihilism", against various deviations, including the "false concept of tolerance" that transcends the realm of religion. According to Legutko, contemporary tolerance undermines the moral cohesion of democracy and civil society, as it requires simultaneous attitudes of disapproval and respect. He declared himself against the autonomy of the individual and against the pluralism of incommensurable values.[68]

Another professor, Marian Grabowski, a fervently Catholic Physicist declared himself against tolerance and homosexuality: "Tolerance which constitutes a necessary condition for plural societies not only advocates the coexistence of differences and openness to others, but also excessively handicaps fundamental human behaviours and choices. The religious fervor, a passionate service to values, a compulsion to preach faith -- all these are derided and caricatured. Emotional iciness, intellectual distance, indifferent forbearance to everything are praised as virtues. That is when the axiological and religious ´cooling` of society takes place. Tolerance comes not only from a fascination with another human being, from opening to him, but also from fear. Faith which wants to transform reality, truth which declares its unquestionable veracity are eliminated, since they endanger the pluralist order by opposed choices, that is by conflict."[69]

Similar views are presented by Zdzisław Krasnodębski, who feels no anxiety about the persistent lack of tolerance and respect for diversity, but worries about an allegedly excessive pluralism in Poland.[70] With a certain reserve he accepts the rules of procedural democracy for Poland, but at the same time he undermines them on behalf of a superior morality. Criticizing those views, Andrzej Walicki argues that political liberalism respects moral values and even the pursuit of moral perfection. That, however, does not give anybody a licence to impose "comprehensive" moral systems or to negate freedom of conscience. In his rational opinion "the Polish collectivist right sees in liberalism a disastrous relativisation of morality, thus paving the way for totalitarianism; liberals, on the other hand, see the sources of totalitarianism in the tendencies to support various policies with the authority of absolute values' and absolute truth."[71]

More extreme representatives of the conservative right openly criticize liberal democracy and pluralism, saying that the "objective interests" of the nation are more important than the interests of a social, "mathematical" or "fortuitous" majority. Cezary Michalski, for example, opposes "harmful" pluralism in the realm of culture and advocates a State of one Truth.[72] He reduces democracy to "soulless" procedures, to moral relativism and the "rule of falsehood and sin". For Jarosław Zadencki it is "democratic fanaticism, the fanaticism of freedom" and the "despotism of freedom"[73] that is most harmful. He does not perceive any fundamental difference between democracy and dictatorship and proposes limiting citizens` rights within a constitutional dictatorship.[74] His limited perception blinds him to serious pluralism under liberal democracies: "The only pluralism that the present-day man knows from experience is a dualism of a universal producer and a universal consumer. The rest is an unwanted, dangerous, and perplexing prejudice."[75] For Wojciech Chudy, it is pluralism of good and evil that is unwanted: "Pluralism is a cultural fact, but not an aim of culture. The aim for culture is unity based upon the value of truth."[76]

Declarations fully accepting the value of pluralism and tolerance came both from the representatives of classical liberalism and present-day postmodernism. Leszek Kołakowski, a grand master for Polish liberal intellectuals, said once that tolerance and pluralist order do not mean moral neutrality or indifference to values, since they are deeply rooted in open social philosophy.[77] And Janusz Lewandowski, one of the leaders of the first liberal party after communism, *Congress Liberalno-Demokratyczny* (KLD), stated much later that it is essential for Poland to create institutional and material guarantees of pluralism, tolerance, and freedom of conscience. Liberalism, as he put it, is "a sober art of organizing freedom and improving it ever since the times of Locke and Montesquieu. Liberalism is not a program which embraces 24 hours of human life. On the contrary, the point is to guarantee everybody possible, the broadest scope of privacy and free choice, including religious choice."[78] According to Lewandowski, liberalism in postcommunist Poland means laying the foundations for a plural and open society.

Another representative of the same party distinguishes three liberalisms: economic, political and cultural. Economic and political liberalism can easily be reconciled with the social doctine of the Catholic Church. Problems arise with cultural liberalism which stresses the absolute liberty of the individual, an alien ideology to the Church.[79]

Adam Michnik's essays provide the most convincing defense of the value of liberal democracy for Poland and for Central Europe. Michnik was among the enthusiasts for Central Europe's aspirations for liberty and diversity, opposed to Soviet bloc unity. In his opinion, absolute moral values directed against communism proved effective in the victorious struggle, but a search for a similar moral absolutism under democratic rule is futile. Democracy is not infallible, it is not a remedy for all human sins - only for dictatorships. "Democracy is neither black nor white, or red. Democracy is grey; it arises with difficulties, it is a continuous articulation of particular interests and a search for moral compromises between them; it is a market place of passions and emotions, of envy and hope, it is an eternal imperfection, a confusion of sin with virtue, of sanctity with sordidness,"[80] and, Michnik concluded, it is therefore stigmatized by all kinds of fundamentalists. In another essay, he wonders why the Catholic Church is in trouble with Polish democracy and vice versa, why nowadays democracy is being criticized more sharply than the communist dictatorship ever was, and why even tolerance has been branded as an empty and suspicious word.[81]

Adding his voice, Professor Świeżawski, a senior Polish Catholic philosopher, has defended the value of pluralism and tolerance. Resorting to the historic examples of mediaeval conciliatory spirit of Spanish Toledo and Polish Cracow and to the modern spirit of Vaticanum II, he has expressed his conviction in a tolerant and pluralist vocation of Christianity that tells us to be full of sympathy, kindness and love for everybody. According to Świeżawski, a "genuine tolerance follows from a deep conviction that the whole of reality is characterized by an astounding variety, and the human world is characterized by various categories of otherness. Every human being should not only perceive it, but also is morally obliged practically to accept the rights vested in others."[82]

IN SEARCH OF POLAND'S TRANSCENDENT PLURALISM

The first effort to reconcile liberalism and Catholicism and to create a Christian version of liberalism in present-day Poland was made by Cracow professor of philosophy Mirosław Dzielski (1941-1989). Combining liberal principles with the values of Christian ethics, Dzielski maintained that liberalism is a profoundly religious doctrine. His purpose was to overcome the initial hostility between the two visions of the world, to reconcile liberal free market with moral rules, pluralist ideals of open society with the monist, religious conception of truth and good. In articles frequently published in the Polish Catholic press, Dzielski wanted to make Catholicism more similar to Protestantism with its capitalist ethos, religious pluralism and approval of independent human search for God. Christians do not value pluralism itself, but should accept it as a result of a divine will manifested in the imperfect earthly life. Dzielski wanted to integrate liberal and religious visions of life into one ethico-institutional system. Both visions should complement and control each other in one organic whole.[83] Not only is pluralism not an end in itself, but also freedom should serve the realization of higher values of good, truth and beauty. Dzielski's eclectic efforts were not fully successful, since the differences between Catholics and Liberals in Poland are still profound in such matters as the scope of human liberty, the shape of political and economic society, the social and religious (supranatural) meaning of truth.

A more recent effort to reconcile Christianity with liberalism was undertaken by the Reverend Józef Tischner (1931-2000), a leading Polish Catholic philosopher. He announced the emergence of a new version of liberalism -- a Christian version, connected with the renaissance of the idea of freedom in Christianity. Liberalism has not been held in good repute among theologians and vice versa, he added.[84] Professor Tischner noticed that some Poles had fallen victim to a new, hitherto unknown fear, the fear of freedom. They still do not understand the meaning and value of Christian liberalism, seeing it as an enlightened cult of absolute freedom. The new situation of broad civil liberties, presented as a hell even worse than communism, is accused of being guilty of abortion, pornography, and the rejection of moral duties, law and religion.

Professor Tischner proved to be one of the most prestigious critics of the new fundamentalism in Poland, a fundamentalism understood as a denial of pluralism. According to this very enlightened Catholic priest, pluralism means multiplicity in unity and unity in diversity. And unity can also be achieved by acknowledging the existence of necessary differences. Pluralism consists in mutual recognition of differences between human individuals, while fundamentalism means unity achieved by erasing manifest differences. Fundamentalism understood as a negation of pluralism is strictly connected with the will to exercise power and to implement force in order to promote one's own reasoning and experience of truth.[85]

Another open-minded Catholic priest noted an irony in the fact that when the detested communism was politically overcome in Poland in 1989, fundamentalists of the communist era (i. e., those who wished to impose one dogmatic ideology and an official monopoly of "right" opinions) found intellectual acceptance among a significant number of anti-communists -- those who were profoundly religious.[86] A postmodern liberal Andrzej Szahaj has detected among Polish conservatives who usually long for commonly accepted opinions, another yearning for "a moral-political unity of the nation" characteristic of the early communist epoch.[87]

Somewhat more ambiguous, situated between Catholic fundamentalism and the clear liberalism of the Reverend Józef Tischner, is the attitude towards pluralism presented by the Archbishop Józef Życiński, who strongly critiqued Polish post-modernists and post-socialist liberals. Opposed to many traditional Catholics, who long for a simply ordered vision of the world, he does not treat pluralism and diversity of social opinions as redundant or as a necessary evil, but as a consciousness of diverse ways leading to one truth that comprises absolute and relative aspects. Pluralism is not, therefore, a renunciation of absolute truth, but a deep consciousness of its complexity and of the difficulty of every inquiry. Cautiously following the liberal German theologian Hans Urs von Balthasar, professor Życiński maintains that a pluralism that is clearly limited, not though by force, may be understood as a symphony of values, and that the universal Christian teachings cannot be fully expressed in only one system of thought. Contrary to widespread Catholic opinion, this semi-liberal official representative of Polish Catholicism has proclaimed that pluralism does not necessarily lead to moral relativism.[88]

Stanisław Kowalczyk, another eminent Catholic philosopher, following the ambiguous - as we shall see - pronouncements of John Paul II, appreciates a friendly dialogue between Christianity and liberal thought, but does not neglect their axiological differences: the dominance of individual freedom in liberal doctrines, their naturalist interpretation of religion, ethical relativism, distorted, grotesque, and even "farcical" understanding of pluralism and tolerance.[89] Fortunately, at least the word pluralism (like democracy) is not being rejected by Professor Kowalczyk and the majority of Polish Catholics.

The idea of pluralism and postmodernism also appears in the widespread Polish discourse on Europe and on the need to integrate with it, especially with the economic structures of the European Union. Generally speaking, liberals exhibit euro-optimistic views, whereas conservatives are more cautious and even skeptical in their European discourse, resorting rather to the concept of a Europe embracing separate fatherlands than to a united Europe of regions. Some innovative authors show, however, that the process of European integration requires new theoretical tools that cannot be reduced to a simple principle. Stanisław Konopacki, for example, draws attention to the transition from one-dimentional concepts of integration to multidimentional projects of radical pluralism and diversification in postmodern time.[90] The process of European integration should, therefore, be exposed step by step to the discourse of postmodernism. This transition to multidimentional models of integration implies a deconstruction of the hitherto fundamental categories of central management, national economy, and national state, national and European identity -- all so important to the Polish tradition. The process requires more pluralism, more of a dialogue with diversity and differences, a dialogue inspired by postmodern thought rather than in the Polish (religious) Solidarity tradition.

All Polish Catholic intellectuals -- liberal and conservative -- refer with profound reverence to the ambiguous social thought formulated by Pope John Paul II. He was very critical of all existing political systems, since they do not ensure a possibility of integral development of man and larger communities. At the same time, he strongly stated that his teaching is not a third option, somewhere between liberal capitalism and Marxist collectivism. It is not a new ideology, but a moral and theological reflection about human existence in society.

The relatively recent stage of the discussion on the poor condition and quality of liberal democracy in postcommunist Poland was initiated at the beginning of 2000 by professor Zdzisław Krasnodębski.[91] In his lengthy essay published in *Znak*, an increasingly conservative Cracow monthly, Krasnodębski analyzes various models of western democratic philosophy, criticizes "Polish liberals", and proposes to strengthen democracy by resorting to numerous elements of "the Polish tradition." The Polish philosopher and sociologist from the University of Bremen in Germany is greatly annoyed at the strong appeal of the ideas of pluralism and religious neutrality of the state to Polish liberals, who -- in his opinion -- adhere to American political correctness rather than to European patterns of thought.[92] Krasnodębski deems that democracy in Poland would be more consolidated, if it emphasized Polish religious, national and ethical traditions. The conservative-minded Krasnodębski is convinced that a chaotic acceptance by the state of "many truths" does a moral and cognitive wrong to its citizens.

In his discussion with Krasnodębski, Jerzy Szacki, a leading Polish historian of ideas, differs, doubting whether politics can realize absolute truths.[93] More arguments in favor of the public sphere's independence from politics and for pluralism are raised by Wiktor Osiatyński, who defends the idea of tolerance, often ridiculed by the Polish adherents of a religious state and by Catholic conservatives.[94] According to Osiatyński, the tolerance of minorities is a foundation of any pluralist society. In such a society, the state does not impose on its citizens any outlooks or values, but rather presents them in a public debate in which moral, not administrative authorities usually participate. Wiktor Osiatyński along with Karol Modzelewski postulates that the state not grants special privileges to adherents of any one system of values.

Father Maciej Zięba, a more enlightened representative of the church, formally accepts the postulate, but emphasizes that the state does not exist in a historical and axiological void, that it needs an ethos, and that some values stemming from the tradition of the Solidarity movement should be introduced into its constitution. He also warned against the danger of relativism for Poland and the present-day world. Acknowledging the existence of a religious fundamentalism, he draws attention to a liberal version of fundamentalism, aggressive and intolerant toward religion, idealizing democratic liberties.[95]

Roman Graczyk, a representative of the consistently liberal daily *Gazeta Wyborcza*, notices, in his review of *Znak's* special issue, *Democracy after Communism*, that the Cracow *Znak* group shifts from Christian liberalism to Christian conservatism.[96] The monthly's authors regard democracy as not axiologically self-sufficient, because it lacks immutable and binding absolute moral values. Without "strong" moral fundamentals -- they believe -- every political system is doomed to decadence and disintegration. In their opinion, as liberal democracy is not underpinned by any broader philosophical or religious vision of the world, only by electoral procedures and the pluralism of ideas, its structure is fragile and hollow, and must be reconstructed and incorporated into democratic institutions. They maintain that the Catholic Church in Poland, not universal human rights and liberties, is a keystone of democracy, a natural reservoir of lasting political values that should be present in the law, public life, and mass media (e.g. the notorious regulation commanding public television's respect for Christian values).

Roman Graczyk, unlike Jarosław Gowin, does not believe in what Gowin calls a "natural alliance" of democracy with religion. He is, however, convinced that a reconciliation between the two forces is possible. Unable to accept relativism, the church should accept pluralism, concludes Graczyk in his recently published collection of essays.[97]

Summing up the discussion provoked by his article, Krasnodębski asked once again the fundamental question, "what is the place for truth, good, and justice in democracy, or in other words, what is really meant by pluralism of views in democracy."[98] He upheld his criticism of 'Polish liberals", who in his opinion care little for common principles. "Anxious about pluralism, terrified at the vision of a religious state and of nationalists lurking at the corner, Polish liberals do not ask what is integrating, what would unite a radically plural society. Preaching the neutrality of the state, concentrating on cultural and religious diversification, they overlook the questions of unity and the question of principles joining all members of society."[99]

Poland is still at the beginning of a long road leading to democratic consolidation and a relative secularization of society, whereas more advanced countries of liberal capitalism in Europe have reached its end.[100] The recent debate, discussions between the above mentioned authors show that present-day Poland has serious problems in considering the relations between religion and democracy in postmodern plural societies, in showing how to make pluralism integral to cultural and political life.

NOTES

1 Andrzej Walicki, *Zniewolony umysł po latach* (Warsaw: Czytelnik, 1993), 352-353.

2 Jadwiga Staniszkis, *Poland's Self-Limiting Revolution* (Princeton, N.J.: Princeton University Press, 1984), 165.

3 Ibid., 168.

4 Ibid., 169.

5 Ibid., 206.

6 Jerzy Wiatr, "Elements of the Pluralism in the Polish Political System", *Polish Sociological Bulletin* 1 (1966): 19-26.

7 Władysław Piwowarski, "Filozoficzne aspekty pluralizmu społecznego", *Roczniki Filozoficzne KUL* 13:2 (1965): 83-97. Soon after the first innovative article on pluralism was published - abroad - by Stanisław Ehrlich, "Il problema del pluralismo", *Storia e Politica* 3 (Luglio-Settembre, 1969).

8 See Stanisław Ossowski, "O osobliwościach nauk społecznych", in his *Dzieła*, vol. IV (Warszawa: PWN, 1967), 175-178; Zygmunt Komorowski, "Pluralizm - wielokulturowość – diaspora", *Kultura i Społeczeństwo* 1-2 (1975): 259-263.

9 Stanisław Ehrlich, *Pluralism on and off Course* (Oxford - New York: Pergamon Press, 1982); Stanisław Ehrlich and Graham Wootton, eds., *Three Faces of Pluralism: Political, Ethnic, and Religious* (Farnborough, UK.: Gower, 1980); Stanisław Ehrlich, "The Many Shapes of Pluralism and Uniformism, and their Limits", *Revue Internationale de Sociologie* 1 (1988): 71-88. See also the special issue of *International Political Science Review* (3, July 1996), "Traditions in Pluralist Thought", edited by Luigi Graziano and dedicated to Stanisław Ehrlich.

10 Stanisław Ehrlich, *Oblicza pluralizmów* (2nd enlarged ed., Warszawa: PWN, 1985), 404; see also id., "Pluralizm - paradygmatem nauk społecznych?", *Studia Socjologiczne* 4 (1988): 11-25; see also an interview with Ehrlich in Zbysław Rykowski, Wiesław Władyka, eds., *Sposób myślenia* (Warszawa: MAW, 1985). It should be added that before Ehrlich's book, Stanisław Ossowski and other Polish sociologists wrote a little on the subject of pluralism and interest groups, but vigilant censorship did not allow much to be written on the subject matter.

11 Andrzej Nowicki., "Aksjologiczne aspekty pluralizmu", in , Józef Lipiec, ed., *Człowiek i świat wartości* (Kraków: KAW, 1982), 505-517; see also id., "Pluralizm światopoglądowy w kulturze socjalistycznej", *Euhemer* 2 (1981): 117-130; and id., "Perspektywy rozwoju pluralizmu w obrębie polskiej katolickiej filozofii kultury", *Studia Religioznawcze* 21 (1987): 151-166.

12 Andrzej Tyszka, "Policentryzm i pluralizm kultury", *Kultura i Społeczeństwo* 1 (1983): 49-60.

13 Winicjusz Narojek, *Perspektywy pluralizmu w upaństwowionym społeczeństwie* (London: Aneks, 1986).

14 Jan Wawrzyniak, "W sprawie pluralizmu", *Tu i Teraz* 14 (1982): 3-4; also in a modified form in *Nowe Drogi* 9 (1982): 116-132.

15 Jan Wawrzyniak, "Odpowiedź nie tylko na list do redaktora naczelnego", *Nowe Drogi* 4 (1983): 147-151.

16 An orthodox neo-Stalinist criticism of the early forms of pluralistic thinking was presented by Tadeusz Wrębiak, "Socjalizm a pluralizm", *Nowe Drogi* 8 (1983): 115-123; and by Henryk Chołaj, "Pluralizm w kon-

cepcjach antymarksistowskiej opozycji intelektualnej", *Myśl Marksistowska* 5 (1985): 135-146.

17 Wojciech Jaruzelski, *Przemówienia* (Warszawa: Książka i Wiedza, 1983), 124.

18 Mirosław Karwat, Włodzimierz Milanowski, *Pluralizm: mity a rzeczywistość* (Warszawa: Wyd. MON, 1985), 60; see also a series of essays criticizing pluralism, published in 1987 in the weekly *Sprawy i Ludzie*. Leszek Grzybowski, "Kontrowersje wokół pluralizmu" in *Milczenie ideologów* (arszawa: Książka i Wiedza, 1985), 32-67 recommended to avoid using the concept of political pluralism in relation to socialism.

19 Cf. Piotr Szydłowski, *Katolicka filozofia kultury w Polsce 1918-1935* (Warszawa: PWN, 1981); Andrzej Nowicki, "Perspektywy rozwoju pluralizmu", 151; Przemysław Fenrych, "Pluralizm - zagrożenie czy szansa", *W Drodze* 6 (1989): 79-84.

20 Ludwik Hass, "Pluralizm jako zjawisko polityczno-społeczne i problem ruchu zawodowego", *Kwartalnik Historii Ruchu Zawodowego* 2 (1988), 7.

21 See Wiesław Górnicki, *Teraz już można* (Wrocław: Wydawnictwo Dolnośląskie, 1994), 349-351; Edward M. Swiderski, "From Social Subject to the Person. The Belated Transformation in Latter-Day Soviet Philosophy," *Philosophy of the Social Sciences*, 2 (1993): 199-227; Tadeusz Płużański, "U źródeł wartości ludzkich (Wprowadzenie do marksistowskiego personalizmu)", *Studia Filozoficzne* 5 (1987): 3-15.

22 Mikhail Gorbachev, "Rewolucyjna przebudowa i ideologia odnowy", *Trybuna Ludu*, 19th February, 1988.

23 See more on the subject in Jerzy Jaskiernia, "Spór o istotę polskiego pluralizmu socjalistycznego", *Ideologia i Polityka* 2 (1988): 64-77; Leszek Grzybowski, "Pluralizm polityczny w socjalizmie", *Ideologia i Polityka* 12 (1988): 37-52; Władysław Jaworski, Andrzej Lech, *Pluralizm polityczny* (Łódź: Uniwersytet Łódzki, 1991).

24 Włodzimierz Lebiedziński, "Czy możliwy jest socjalistyczny pluralizm", *Myśl Marksistowska* 5 (1987), 72.

25 Ibid, 74.

26 Andrzej Barcikowski, ed., *Pluralizm i porozumienie narodowe* (Warszawa: Książka i Wiedza, 1988); see also Marian Stępień, "Pluralism", *Polish Perspectives* 3 (1988): 5-8; and for a distinction between democratic and non-democratic pluralism, see introduced by Jerzy Gaul, "Pluralizm - zasada czy fasada", *Przegląd Powszechny* 3 (1987): 425-430.

27 Andrzej Barcikowski, "Siedem dylematów pluralizmu politycznego w Polsce", *Ideologia i polityka* 11 (1988), 39.

28 Ibid., 42.

29 *Nowe Drogi* 6 (1988), 61.

30 Ibid., 92.

31 *Nowe Drogi* 7 (1988), 26.

32 Ibid., 42.

33 See Jan Skórzyński, *Ugoda i rewolucja. Władza i opozycja 1985-1989* (Warszawa: Presspublica, 1995).

34 Andrzej Walicki, "From Stalinism to Post-Communist Pluralism: The Case of Poland", *New Left Review* 185 (January/February 1991), 107.

35 Introduction to Franciszek Adamski, ed., *Pluralizm w kulturze polskiej* (Kraków: Zeszyty Naukowe UJ, 1988), 7; more monolithic aspects of the Polish traditional culture (the canon of Catholicism and romanticism) were exhibited in Marian Kempny et al., *U progu wielokulturowości. Nowe oblicza społeczeństwa polskiego* (Warszawa: Oficyna Naukowa, 1997).

36 Zbigniew Pucek, *Pluralizm cywilizacyjny jako perspektywa myśli socjologicznej* (Kraków: WSE, 1990).

37 Janusz Kuczyński, *Uniwersalizm jako metafilozofia*, vol. I (Warszawa: UW, 1989), 34.

38 Janusz Kuczyński, "Pluralism and Universalist Socialism", *Dialectics and Humanism. The Polish Philosophical Quarterly* 1 (1989), 221.

39 The only booklet on the value of pluralism, published in Poland at the beginning of 1990s, was written by the Polish American sociologist Feliks Gross, *Tolerancja i pluralizm* (Warszawa: IFiS Publishers, 1992). There was also a brief, superficial discussion in the Polish press on pluralism in 1990. The emotional and chaotic discussion was in fact related to a short-term struggle for power within two factions of Solidarity (the supporters of Wałęsa and Mazowiecki), hence it did not bring serious, far-reaching results. See I. Pańków, "Debata o pluralizmie w 'wojnie na górze' ", in *Władza i struktura społeczna*, ed. A. Jasińska-Kania, K. Słomczyński (Warsaw: IFiS Publishers, 1999).

40 A detailed analysis can be found in *Democracy, Civil Society and Pluralism in Comparative Perspective: Poland, Great Britain and the Netherlands*, Ed. by Christopher G. A. Bryant and Edmund Mokrzycki (Warszawa: IFiS Publishers, 1995), 166-167.

41 See Joanna Kurczewska, "Odkrywanie wielokulturowości i współczesne ideologie", in Marian Kempny et al., *U progu wielokulturowości*, 32-50. Some argue that the velvet revolutions in Poland and Central Europe were in fact a realization of Hannh Arend's vision of politics and of political pluralism. See W. Heller, *Hannah Arendt: Zródła pluralizmu politycznego* (Poznań: UAM, 2000), 160.

42 See Zdzisław Sadowski, ed., *Post-totalitarian Society. The Course of Change* (Warsaw: IFiS Publishers, 1993), 108-109.

43 Włodzimierz Wesołowski, "Challenges to Pluralism in Eastern Europe," *Transition to Democracy: The Role of Social and Political Pluralism*, a special issue of *Sisyphus. Sociological Studies*, ed. Władysław Adamski et al. (Warsaw: IFiS Publishers, 1991): 79-81.

44 Ibid, 7

45 Martin Krygier, "Virtuous Circles: Antipodean Reflections on Power, Institutions, and Civil Societies", *East European Politics and Societies,* 1(1997), 74.

46 The Polish sociologist Zygmunt Bauman writes about "acceptance of irredeemable plurality of the world" and about "the celebration of pluralism" in his book *Modernity and Ambivalence* (Cambridge: Polity Press, 1993), 97, 157.

47 Krystyna Wilkoszewska, "O pojęciu postmodernizmu uwag kilka", in Alicja Zeidler-Janiszewska, (ed.), *Oblicza postmoderny* (Warszawa: Instytut Kultury, 1992): 9-10.

48 Paweł Lisiecki, "Błogosławiona wielość języków", *Więź* 6 (1995): 44.

49 The first translations into Polish of some postmodern authors (Irrving Howe, John Barth, Jean-Francois Lyotard, Richard Rorty, Ihab Hassan and others) had appeared in the 1980s. See, for example, Zbigniew Lewicki, ed., *Nowa proza amerykańska. Szkice krytyczne* (Warszawa: Czytelnik, 1983); Marcin Giżycki, ed., *Postmodernizm - kultura wyczerpania?* (Warszawa: Akademia Ruch, 1988).

50 Those feelings were well seen in the ephemeral Polish journal *Xuxem*: "Is that the end then? Is it possible to find any support? Is art, philosophy, science, and, first and foremost, life not a visible proof of this? Are the dreams in 20th century doomed to failure?!! What else can inspire hope...? Maybe a denial of dreams about redemption means a passage to 21 century; the age of life careless about illusion which could conceal the taste of the present ? The age of life dispassionate in its rootlessness, life passed by without regret and pain of existence...?" Jacek Alexander Sikora, "Perception Pre-Feeling of Oversublimation of the European Culture. Assemblage of Fragments", *Xuxem* 2 (Spring 1992), 16.

51 See Zdzisław Krasnodębski, "Waiting for Supermarkets or: the Downfall of Communism Seen in Postmodern Perspective", *The Polish Sociological Bulletin* 4 (1991): 281-287; Aldona Jawłowska, Marian Kempny, eds., *Cultural Dilemmas of Post-Communist Societies* (Warsaw: IFiS Publishers, 1994).

52 Paweł Konic in the discussion "Czy postmodernizm jest dobry na postkomunizm?", *Dialog* 11 (1991), 114.

53 The term was coined by Father Maciej Zięba in an interview, published in *Słowo - Dziennik Katolicki*, 29 November 1996. See also his book *Demokracja i antyewangelizacja* (Poznań: Wyd. "W drodze", 1997), 137-140.

54 See "Postmodernizm w Kusiętach Dużych", *Tygodnik Powszechny,* 20 April 1997; Ryszard Legutko, "Postmodernizm", *Życie,* 1-2 March, 1997; Jarosław Gowin, "Kościół przyszłości", *Życie,* 22-23 March, 1997. The Polish quarterly *FA-Art* has presented a milder, anti-nihilistic version of a "postmodernism with human face"

55 Halina Janaszek-Ivaničkova, "Paradoksalny żywot postmodernizmu w krajach słowiańskich Europy Środkowej i Wschodniej", in *Postmodernizm w literaturze i kulturze krajów Europy Środkowo-Wschodniej* , 79; id., *Od modernizmu do postmodernizmu do postmodernizmu* (Katowice:

Wyd. UŚ, 1996); E.G. Trubina, "Posttotalitarna kultura: vsie dozvoleno ili ničego nie garantirovano?", *Voprosy Filosofii* 3 (1993): 23-27.

56 Marek Kwiek, "Polski postmodernizm?", *Kultura współczesna,* 3-4 (1996), 10.

57 For a severe critique of the Polish opponents of postmodernism, see Marek Wilczyński, "Antypostmodernizm polski", *Czas kultury* 5-6 (1994): 4-7; Marek Wiczyński, "Egzorcyści i demaskatorzy. Neokonserwatyści wobec kultury ponowoczesnej", *Czas kultury* 1 (1996): 4-9; Cezary Wodziński, "W trybach zmory. O polskich krytykach postmodernizmu uwag kilka", *Odra,* 10 (1997): 55-63.

58 See Włodzimierz Bolecki, "Polowanie na postmodernistów w Polsce", *Teksty Drugie* 1 (1993): 7-24; id., "Postmodernizowanie modernizmu", *Teksty Drugie* 1-2 (1997): 31-45; Grzegorz Wołowiec, "Recepcja postmodernizmu w polskiej krytyce i publicystyce literackiej", *Kultura Współczesna* 3-4 (1996): 11-42; Agnieszka Izdebska, Danuta Szajnert, eds., *Postmodernizm po polsku?* (Łódź: Wydawnictwo Uniwersytetu Łódzkiego, 1988).

59 Jadwiga Mizińska, "Cóż po filozofie w czasie marnym?, Głos w dyskusji na temat filozofii postmodernistycznej", in Alicja Zeidler-Janiszewska, (ed.), *Oblicza postmoderny*, 30-31.

60 Lidia Burska, "Inkwizytorzy i sarmaci", *Gazeta Wyborcza*, 19-20 August, 2000, 19.

61 Paweł Bortkiewicz, "Mentalność sekty a ideologia postmodernistyczna", *Ethos* 9, 1-2 (1996), 165.

62 See Zbigniew Sareło, *Postmodernizm w pigułce* (Poznań: Pallotinum, 1998), 28.

63 Marzenna Guzowska, "W sztuce: nadzieja czy wyczerpanie", *Więź* 6 (1995):72.

64 Andrzej Szahaj, "Jednostka czy wspólnota? O sporze pomiędzy liberałami a komunitarystami w najnowszej filozofii polityki", in *Liberalizm u schyłku XX wieku*, ed. Justyna Miklaszewska (Kraków: Meritum, 1999), 170; see also his recent book: *Jednostka czy wspólnota? Spór liberałów z komunitarianami a „sprawa polska"* (Warszawa: Fundacja Aletheia, 2000).

65 See, for example, Marian Grabowski, "Trzy mowy przeciwko tolerancji", *Znak* 6 (1993): 37-47; Jan Maria Jackowski, *Bitwa o Polskę* (Warszawa: Inicjatywa Wydawnicza «ad astra», 1993).

66 Marcin Król, *Liberalizm strachu czy liberalizm odwagi* (Kraków: Wydawnictwo Znak, 1996), 100.

67 Tadeusz Szkołut, "Spór o sens pluralizmu w kulturze i sztuce postmodernistycznej", in Tadeusz Szkołut, ed., *Aksjologiczne dylematy epoki współczesnej* (Lublin: Wyd. UMCS, 1994), 117.

68 See his books: *Nie lubię tolerancji* (Cracow: Wydawnictwo Arka, 1993), *Tolerancja. Rzecz o surowym państwie, prawie natury, miłości i sumieniu* (Cracow: Wydawnictwo Znak, 1997) and numerous articles published in the Polish conservative press and in the American *Critical Review*. See also his recent polemic "Nadal nie lubię liberalizmu. Odpowiedź moim po-

lemistom", *Europa* 38 (2005) and "Dlaczego nie lubię liberalizmu", in: *Raj przywrócony* (Cracow, 2005), 11-25. For a critique of his views see, among others, Roman Graczyk, "Jak filozofuje się młotem", *Gazeta Wyborcza*, 10 February 2000.

69 Grabowski, "Trzy mowy," 47.

70 Zdzisław Krasnodębski, "Polityka i moralność - w ogóle, u nas i gdzie indziej", *Znak* 7 (1997), 11.

71 Andrzej Walicki, "Moralność polityczna liberalizmu, narodowa moralistyka i idee kolektywistycznej prawicy", *Znak* 7 (1997). The article is included in his excellent collection of political essays: *Polskie zmagania z wolnością* (Kraków: Universitas, 2000), 187-204.

72 Cezary Michalski, *Powrót człowieka bez właściwości* (Warszawa: Biblioteka Debaty, 1997).

73 Such is the title of Zadencki's ill-famed book: *Wobec despotyzmu wolności* (Kraków: Platan, 1995).

74 Jarosław Zadencki, "Oswajanie dyktatury", *Nowa Res Publica* 60:1(1993): 52-54.

75 Jarosław Zadencki, *Lewiatan i jego wrogowie. Szkice postkonserwatywne* (Kraków: Wydawnictwo Arcana, 1998), 23.

76 Wojciech Chudy, "Katolik na arenie współczesnego społeczeństwa", *Arcana* 3 (1997), 157.

77 Leszek Kołakowski, *Czy diabeł może być zbawiony i 27 innych kazań* (London: Aneks, 1984), 215-216.

78 Janusz Lewandowski, "Jaki liberalizm jest Polsce potrzebny?", in Donald Tusk, ed., *Idee gdańskiego liberalizmu* (Fundacja Liberałów, 1998), 137; see also Wojciech Sadurski, *Moral Pluralism and Legal Neutrality* (Dordrecht: Kluwer Academic Publishers, 1990).

79 Lech Mażewski, "Thatcheryzm po polsku", in Tusk, ed., *Idee gdańskiego* liberalizmu, 139.

80 Adam Michnik, "Szare jest piękne", *Gazeta Wyborcza,* 4-5 January 1997.

81 Adam Michnik, *Kościół, lewica, dialog* (Warszawa: Świat Książki, 1998), 313.

82 Stefan Świeżawski, "O właściwe rozumienie tolerancji", *Znak* 6 (1993): 5.

83 See Adam Samojłowicz, "Mirosława Dzielskiego chrześcijański liberalizm", *Archiwum historii myśli politycznej* VII (1998), 52.

84 Józef Tischner, *Nieszczęsny dar wolności* (Kraków: Wydawnictwo Znak, 1997): 10.

85 Ibid., 151.

86 Jan Kracik, "Chrześcijaństwo a pokusa fundamentalizmu", *Znak* 3 (1998), 19.

87 Andrzej Szahaj, *Jednostka czy wspólnota? Spór liberałów z komunitarianami a "sprawa polska"*, 273-274.

88 Józef Życiński, *Ziarno samotności* (Kraków: Wydawnictwo Znak, 1997): 113-116.

89 Stanisław Kowalczyk, *Liberalizm i jego filozofia* (Katowice: Wydawnictwo Unia, 1995): 201, 216. See also Stanisław Olejnik, *Jedność Kościoła a pluralizm życia chrześcijańskiego* (Warsaw: ATK, 1982) and essays in German and in Polish: *Pluralistische Gesellschaft. Herausforderung an Kirche und Theologie*, ed. Stefan Knobloch, Piotr Tarlinski (Opole, 2001).

90 Stanisław Konopacki, *Integracja Europy w dobie postmodernizmu* (Poznań: UAM, 1998):137-138; see also "The Future of Europe: Universal Values and Postmodernism", *Dialogue and Universalism* 12 (2000): 71-80.

91 Zdzisław Krasnodębski, "O czym można dyskutować w demokracji?", *Znak* 1 (2000):10-42.

92 The imitation of American patterns of thought and behaviour in the present-day Poland is criticized also by Ryszard Legutko, *Czasy wielkiej imitacji* (Kraków, Wydawnictwo Arcana, 1998).

93 Jerzy Szacki, 'Przeciw, a nawet za tezami Krasnodębskiego", *Znak* 1 (2000): 43-52. Szacki's reasonable defence of political correctness was critized by Paweł Paliwoda ("Przeciw tezom Szackiego", *Życie,* 27 April 2000), for whom the state should not defend conflicts and controversies destibilizing social order, and should not support allegedly opressed minorities.

94 Znak 1 (2000): 74.

95 Ibid., 119-120.

96 Roman Graczyk, "Demokratyczna asceza i jej wrogowie", *Gazeta Wyborcza*, 12-13 February, 2000. See also the polemical voices of Jarosław Gowin, Zbigniew Stawrowski and Roman Graczyk, in *Gazeta Wyborcza*, 28 February, 2000.

97 Roman Graczyk, *Polski Kościół, polska demokracja* (Kraków: Universitas, 1999), 187.

98 Zdzisław Krasnodębski, "Czego nie chcą widzieć «polscy liberałowie»", *Znak* 5 (2000): 110.

99 Ibid.

100 See a commmentary by Adam Szostkiewicz, "Spór o stosunek Kościoła do wolności. Miejsce dla ołtarza", *Polityka* 8 (2000): 64-66.

Chapter 8

The Idea of Universalism in Poland and in the Americas [1]

Un fantasma recorre nuestra época llamada posmoderna: él de la universalidad.

-- Fernando Savater, *Diccionario filosófico* (Barcelona 1995), 400.

Al final del siglo XX parecemos immersos y a veces perdidos en una conciencia paradójica de globalidad y universalismo, por una parte, y de diferencias y de particularidad por otra.

-- Carlos Thibaut, en *Modernidad y posmodernidad* (Cuenca 1999), 61.

In the history of human thought, various writers have called their philosophies universal, universalistic or simply 'universalism'. Almost every philosophical or scientific theory claims to be of universal importance, to be a generalization and universality, but relatively few have believed that the term "universalism" to be the only adequate, and therefore only viable, description of their own thought system or newly constructed theory. Efforts to construct, develop or reconstruct a theory, viewpoint, vision or universalistic attitude — or merely to reinforce universalistic postulates — have long been undertaken in many different countries. Such attempts include those that implicitly assume or imply some sort of universalism. I would like to emphasize that I am principally interested in the visions, frequently appearing both in Poland and the Americas, whose authors, and not merely commentators, have defined their own philosophy, more or less refined, as universalism. Most often, the word "universalism" has been used in conjunction with the adjective "Christian" to denote Catholicism (from the Greek *katholikós* — "universal") or, more broadly, Christianity. Christian universalism "may be understood as: (1) having the ability to embrace all people in the hope of salvation, or (2) having the ability to be embraced by all people", or even as "Christianity's openness to all truths".[2]

Christian universalism has been closely tied to the concept of universalism that was related to the Pope and imperial Rome,[3] or even to Byzantium.[4] Quite frequently, the word "universalism" has been used in a political context during lively discussions on human rights, as well as in the framework of Marxism and more recently Western liberalism's claims to universality.[5]

FROM TRENTOWSKI TO SMOLIKOWSKI

Within Polish culture, the first attempt to create a synthetic "universal" philosophical system (sometimes referred to as "universalism") was made by the renowned philosopher, pedagogue and publicist, Bronisław Ferdynand Trentowski (1808–1869). Significant universalistic themes had also appeared much earlier, from the Middle Ages to the Enlightenment.[6]

According to Trentowski, the task of Polish (and Slavic) philosophy was to overcome the one-sidedness, extremes in thought and action and dualism of philosophy at that time. Its goal was a synthesis — *Concordia* — a unity of elements drawn from other philosophies; a unity and synthesis of the social and empirical thought of ancient Rome and speculative German thought; a unity of realism ("rehabilitation of matter") and idealism in the world of the human self; an agreement and unity of experience and reason, of thesis and antithesis, of subject and object. The universal system of Trentowski's "real idealism" (*Real-Idealismus*) included elements of all possible philosophical systems, although he did not want it to be described as a "final" philosophy, and even less as syncretic or eclectic.[7]

Polish philosophy, aspiring to universality, rejects nothing from the rich European and world experience in this field; all development should incorporate the achievements of previous epochs and other cultures. Such a philosophy, in order to reveal the truth completely, should draw upon various systems of partial truths, methods and styles of philosophical discourse. According to Trentowski, in its style true philosophy should encompass all manner of human speech: "if necessary, it can be poetic and metaphysical, or dry and empirical", it must be "noble, like eternity, and, like omnipresence, always authentic. In order to capture diversity, it must master the entire kingdom of speech. The style must let the precious gems of reality shine with all their radiance and colors. Emeralds should always be green, rubies red, and diamonds transparent! Since the style of discourse makes the gems of reality shine in the realm of nature, it should also make them shine in the realm of philosophy! Sometimes, it should ring out with a blazing word of incitement, other times, with a soothing word of comfort. In it, the Aeolian harp of the West should blend its sounds with the harmonious sounds of the East."[8] Trentowski strives to merge contradictory forces and unite researchers in all fields. According to him, "universal philosophy promises eternal peace in the realm of scholarship because it reconciles contradictory academic disciplines and all their various contradictory elements. In the realm of academia, there are no borders. Hence — *concordia*, o, world of learning! Today, Apollo weds Minerva and the Muses join hands with the Graces in a joyous wedding dance. O, scholars, you are more akin to each other than you might think! Indians — Trentowski solemnly continues — call the Earth their mother, the wind-their father, the water-their sister, and the fir — their brother. If body and soul, experience and reason comprise a unity, you are even more a unity. Hence — Trentowski concludes, brimming with optimism — peace, peace in the brotherly realm of academia."[9]

Trentowski did not look to the espousers of absolute idealism or realism for inspiration (Leibniz, Locke, Kant, Fichte or Hegel), but rather to those philosophers who understood philosophy as self-knowledge of universal wholeness and combined idealism with realism. Such philosophers included

Spinoza, "who brought Descartes the spiritualist and Bacon the materialist into one",[10] and, to an even greater extent, Schelling, "Germany's first real philosopher",[11] who then achieved the most perfect synthesis of idealism and realism. Trentowski, in his universal philosophy, wanted to achieve a real, and not merely formal, union of realism and idealism; he wanted "to blend the subject-objectivity of natural philosophers with that of Hegel".[12]

Trentowski's concept of "unity in diversity", best described by the term "multi-oneness," was not related to totalitarianism or "Asian" mysticism, but rather to pro-Western liberalism.

Other Polish Romantic thinkers who shared the same foundations of this unique brand of universalism were generally opposed to the abstract universalism of the Enlightenment. Andrzej Walicki notes, "The ideal of the Enlightenment's rational universalism was uniformity, the leveling of differences to fit one commonly accepted norm of the enlightened mind, while the ideal of Romantic universalism (with its references to Herder) was diversity, universality and wholeness, and the celebration of pluralism and national cultures as unique and irreplaceable individualizations of humanity".[13]

Various twentieth-century thinkers have evoked Trentowski's idea of universalism and synthesis. Adam Zieleńczyk (1880–1943), for example, appreciated the precursory pragmatism and the spirit of Trentowski's[14] original humanistic and sweeping synthesis of three truths (the truths of cognition, emotion and will), which had also been present in Polish Romanticism. This striving to attain synthesis in the theoretical and practical spheres is also evident in the humanism and pragmatism of Władysław Mieczysław Kozłowski (1858–1935) and Florian Znaniecki (1882–1958). Recently, Janusz Kuczyński, an heir and independent continuator of the Promethean-heroic tradition of Romantic universalism at the turn of 20th and 21th century, as well as a spokesperson for this new synthesis, alludes to Trentowski's thought, to his faith in philosophy's mission, to the solemnity of his universal philosophy, and in particular, to the concept of "multi-oneness".[15]

Before discussing the concept of universalism in twentieth-century Polish thought, a closer look at the works of Seweryn Smolikowski (1850-1920) is appropriate. All but forgotten today, he used the term "universalism" interchangeably to describe his own spiritualistic monism. According to his philosophy, "dividing the realms of matter and spirit leads to dualism, in the face of which our fragmented thought strives in vain to reach the source of existence and for some kind of foothold: this philosophy runs down two parallel lines, which disappear into infinity, never finding a point at which they can meet."[16]

In his work, Smolikowski referred to the writings of Leibniz, Schopenhauer and Hartmann; he was also interested in Comte's philosophy. According to Smolikowski, universalism was the only way to achieve a truly synthetic philosophy, one which would succeed in uniting matter and spirit, science and metaphysics. His universalism assumed that there exists a unity of thought and being. He asserted that the absolute lies at the basis of every philosophy, with the divine spirit bringing together world's various elements.

In Smolikowski's vision, universalism is "idealism transferred from our mind to that of the Absolute, i.e. idealism merged with ideal empiricism."[17]

The metaphysical idea of the Absolute is inherent to human mind; it manifests itself in our striving for the ideal, for subjective and objective truth in all scientific and philosophical investigation. Smolikowski assumes the existence of a single building block of spiritual - rational harmony, inherent in the infinity of the entire Universe, as well as in human thought.

THE INTERWAR PERIOD AND THE SECOND WORLD WAR

During the inter-war period, the positions of Jan Nepomucen Miller (1890–1977)[18], a socialist, and Władysław Leopold Jaworski (1865–1930), a Cracow conservative thinker can best be described as universalistic.

Miller was a literary critic and essayist affiliated with the Polish Socialist Party and its journal *Robotnik* [Worker], an author who towards the end of his life was involved with the democratic opposition to the communist regime in Poland. In the 1920's and 1930's, Miller won renown as a critic of the Polish romantic and individualistic tradition in the name of a "new universalism". He was known, for example, for his attack on Adam Mickiewicz's glorification of provincialism, the traditionalism and "sybaritism" of the nobility in *Pan Tadeusz,* which, however, did not, apply to his *Liryki lozańskie* [Lausanne Poems].

Beyond the extremes of early twentieth-century mutually exclusive literary and artistic trends, Miller discerned the emergence of a more general pattern, one "connecting the contradictions contained within the established directions through a synthesis made possible by an all-encompassing *universalism*" (emphasis by J. N. Miller). "In its staggering consequences, this current bridges seemingly incompatible movements such as, for example, cubism and classicism."[19] Miller's universalistic views were set against sterile individualism in the name of the collective force of the laboring masses, the foundation of societal existence. This new brand of universalism was based on the conviction that "a collective, as a particular kind of a totality, antecedes and determines the inner reality of a human being".[20] However, the author notes that setting individualism and universalism against each other is not absolute; "they are not fundamentally impervious to each other. Of course, they represent mere points of view, not a phenomenon's actual characteristics; in order to grasp the totality of some phenomenon, one should consider it from these two complementary points of view. As Miller points out, "these two concepts are inversely proportional. The more universalistic features a given phenomenon has, the fewer individualistic ones it will have. The line between these concepts becomes blurred in its highest, most extreme manifestations, and they unite, as in a Hegelian dialectic trinity, in a synthetic harmony. Extreme individualism (in a monistic vision of reality) inevitably verges on universalism. In those special moments of individualistic initiation, one eventually merges with Being, God, the Absolute, Unity, or whatever we choose to call this fundamental power in the world."[21]

Miller's universalistic theory was expounded in a separate book, in which he expresses his view that universalism is a system of broad concepts, one, which grasps reality, and its various spheres of existence through different totalities rather than through a single dogmatically understood metaphysical or Romantic totality.[22] Miller perceives reality in a pluralistic and positivistic manner, at least at his point of departure; thus, he relinquishes any chances of reaching the ultimate and absolute foundation for all inquiry.

In order to become acquainted with and master the largest possible range of reality in practice, various methods and sources of cognition are admissible. Various forms of universalism are also possible (empirical, Romantic, communist and religious), but for Miller, the most appropriate is that which "transcends this reality yet does not sever its connection with it, has no delusions of attaining the absolute and does not limit itself to an investigation of the realm embracing the reality that is accessible to us. The concept of totality — Miller adds — should demonstrate its practical value when applied to the full range of phenomena accessible to us".[23]

Miller dreamed that the foundations of a new Polish and universalistic culture, understood holistically, could be established in the socialist system of the future. This new culture would be built by class-less and nation-less 'worker-artists,' understood to represent the fullest possible union of human beings with the Earth and the Cosmos. In this political system, the objective of culture and art would not be the emphasis on particular class differences, social injustice or local patriotism. Man and his new art would have far more serious challenges to meet.

In addition, Miller made interesting observations about social and economic topics, which he approached in a utopian spirit of socialism, internationalism and universalism, as well as globalism. The latter is particularly relevant today, and is perhaps a harbinger of new forms of socialization. He believed that "individual economies of various countries will become increasingly wasteful and senseless viewed from the perspective of the economic life of humanity as a whole. Therefore, attempts will be made to restructure the world economy within the framework of a future socialist system or the present one — either through the League of Nations or the United States of Europe."[24]

In the 1920's, Władysław Jaworski, a lawyer, thinker, and conservative politician, defined his worldview by means of universalism. At times, he would replace universalistic concepts with non-historical Romantic or religious ones.[25] For Jaworski, universalism was a metaphysical system, embracing the world in its totality; it represented an orientation within social and natural sciences, which assumed the primacy of the whole over its constituent parts, and would lead to the highest totality, which was God.[26] Thus, universalism defied individualism of any kind. However, as in Miller's thought, universalism was understood as a harmony between an individual, conceived as a totality, and a larger societal whole.

Jaworski noted the opposition between universalistic and individualistic thought, and between rationalistic and religious thought, which was later referred to as organic and universalistic. He believed that the dominant rationalistic thought should be balanced with universalistic thought. The rationalistic mode of thought dominates in industrialized countries and universalistic is prevalent in agrarian societies. Jaworski wanted to harmonize both types. Universalistic thought has its roots in the enduring ideas of Plato; it takes into account the importance of irrational factors in human life, and in particular the importance of Christian love. In addition, it employs a holistic approach to social phenomena by postulating the gathering of atomized individuals into organic labor unions.[27]

Towards the end of his life, the conservative Jaworski was inspired by Othmar Spann (1878–1950), an Austrian proponent of an authoritarian, etatist "universalism", of conservative Romanticism and a corporate system. "Compared to Spann", one researcher writes, "Jaworski was not a harsh critic of liberalism, especially in terms of economics, nor was he such a strong opponent of legal neo-Kantian normativism."[28]

In interwar Polish philosophy, universalistic themes, conveyed programmatically and explicitly, albeit not entirely free of nationalistic tendencies, appeared in such periodicals as *Marchołt, Prosto z mostu, Zet* nd *Myśl Narodowa.*[29] Those motives were also present in Jerzy Braun's national messianism and his idea of philosophy as *scientia universalis*, a concept directly related to Józef M. Hoene-Wroński's "absolute philosophy".[30]

In prewar articles Braun called for „thinking with the universal categories of history", preached messianism as the highest of the Polish national genius, of the eternal and immortal Poland. He believed in the Polish mission, in the possibility of engendering a universal idea that would overcome egoistic inclinations. On the eve of the Second World War he forecast: „A new Poland will bring to the divided West new rules of moral and political order in the place of the bankrupt League of Nations. Poland will go to the East with the idea of Liberty and Christian Reconstruction. Poland will defend the South against conquering powers and will contribute to overcoming Nordic myths".

In a book written during the war he envisaged a „unionist era", he sought how Poland could heighten the Christian civilization to a universal level, how to pass from the nation to humanity, to the unity of humankind, to a genuine universal community. He looked for a new organization of economic life, criticizing both the communist enslavement with production and omnipresent capitalist rule of profit. He opposed to them the Polish unionist rule which synthesizes modern humanism, the idea of creative freedom and moral Christianity. In a programic work written towards the end of the war he defended the Polish unionism „as a method of uniting nations and of overcoming contradictions". He presented this current as genuinely Polish, international and all-human. He supported all efforts to develop the human personality and to create politico-economic unions (for example the Central European Union) and finally an all-human Union in a higher synthesis. A road to this should lead through the solution of the Europe-Asia antinomy. In Braun's words, unionist thought synthesizes the whole of humanity, harmonizes unity with multitude, tends to an „all-human love". This would be a new culture of unification, opposed to the idea of hatred, violence and struggle.

Recently a new, modernized interpretation of Braun's philosophy, and especially of his idea of universal society, overcoming the limits of socialism and liberalism, has appeared.[31] Braun's vision embraced some elements of myth and utopia. His idea of universal society was based upon the work and creativity (he even envisaged a future possibility of supplanting work with creativity) and was associated with the idea of peace, justice, truth, morality and beauty. The characteristic for Braun's universalist aspiration for unity should not be achieved at the expense of diversity, but should rather be based upon it.

Braun's idea of a universal society has recently been compared to the conception of civil society, fashionable after the collapse of communism. It was concluded that Braun's program of social reconstruction is not opposed to it, but complimentary. Their common motifs are the superiority of society over the state, respect for the rules of law and for self-government. A difference is seen in a greater attachment of the „creative citizen" to culture and metaphysics than to mere economics.

Jerzy Braun organized in 1940 a clandestine organization named UNIA. This Union, to which young Karol Wojtyła belonged, presented a vision of a postwar democratic state of Poland without ethnic, religious and class conflicts, the state that would overcome both individualism and totalitarianism. UNIA announced the epoch of synthesis, postulated the rule of moral law over politics and economy. According to George Weigel, American biographer of John Paul II, „UNIA was a pioneering effort to build what a later generation would call 'civil society' from under the rubble of totalitarianism. Its principles of 'self-government' and 'union' were an attempt to marry the Polish passion for freedom ('Nothing about us without us') to a Catholic inspired communitarian concept of the common good. History, in the person of Stalin, would determine that UNIA's dreams for postwar Poland were dashed at the time. But its communitarian ideas about a just modern society and a reconstituted European community remained part of the intellectual architecture of Karol Wojtyła for life".[32]

Other writers, such as Erazm Majewski, Feliks Młynarski and Jacek Woroniecki broached the theme of the struggle between universalism and individualism as well. Universalistic thinking was diversified; it took both moderate and extreme forms, focused on the idea of humanity and/or God and challenged not only individualism but also collectivism and totalitarianism.[33] In particular, the universalism of Christian philosophy placed itself above any form of individualism, collectivism, nationalism, fascism or racism.

Various writers derived universalism from the Aristotelian thesis of the primacy of the whole before its constituent parts[34] and associated it with moderation and solidarity. Universalism defined in this way denounced national and class struggle; it was not only a logical concept, but also a territorial one, which embraced and cherished all of humanity. In the German tradition (Adam Müller, Othmar Spann), on the other hand, there appeared a combination of universalism and nationalism, with a preponderance of nationalistic elements, which also made a marginal appearance in Poland, particularly in *Ruch Młodych* [Youth Movement].[35]

Teodor Seidler concluded that the coup d'état of May 1926 led the Polish political system and philosophy toward universalistic elements and ideas. For him, of fundamental importance were principles such as the individual's organic relationship to the state, limited individual freedom, the civil right of equality and respect for the state. "Only Polish society", Seidler complained, "stumbles for the most part in the wasteland of any possible kind of individualism" and remains far from thinking in universalistic terms.[36]

In 1942, *Konfederacja Narodu* [Confederation of the Nation] published a book in Warsaw entitled *Universalizm: Zarys narodowej filozofii społecznej* [Universalism: Outline of a National Social Philosophy].[37] Its author, Józef Warszawski, was a Jesuit priest known as Father Paul, served also as the Home Army chaplain during the Warsaw Uprising in 1944. In a note from the publisher in the second edition issued in the *Biblioteka Postscriptio* series in 1997, Bogdan Byrzykowski drew the readers' attention to those neglected accomplishments in Polish philosophy whose roots had been in Catholicism and nationalism, but which had nevertheless succeeded in attaining universal ideas. Byrzykowski called for the further cultivation and development of these ideas, and hoped that they would provide inspiration, since they could constitute "our contribution to history and our mission".[38]

According to Józef Warszawski (1903–1997), universalistic ideas had their origins in Polish blood. Polish Hegelianism played an important role in their formation, since it managed to avoid totalitarianism and "was transformed in the Polish soul into a universalistic theme *za waszą wolność i naszą* [for your freedom and ours]. Polish universalism produced a great many thinkers and philosophical ideas (Hoene-Wroński, Trentowski, Libelt, Mochnacki)."[39]

Father Paul, criticizing individualism's one-sidedness, liberal democracy and the unilateralism of all totalitarian systems (fascism and Bolshevism), was convinced that he would bring about a successful synthesis of individual and society (and vice versa), which he christened 'universalism'. The following is his most complete definition of this concept: "Universalism as a philosophical mode of thought conveys and signifies the tendency of the human mind to encompass all, while avoiding one-sidedness. In its final form, it should be united with wisdom as a holistic science, as opposed to knowledge, which is particular, fragmented and partial. As a system, it is a direct source of knowledge about society, which is perceived as a totality consisting of supra-organic constituent parts. Indirectly, it constitutes a worldview, encompassing all spheres of life and existence with all their scientific representations, which creates the impression of a concise, harmonious synthesis and general uniformity."[40]

Warszawski's universalism, like Jaworski's, attempts to reconcile the whole with its Strona: 12 parts, and social factors with those that are individualized and personalized; it also strives to achieve a totality of the "global *universum*". According to this Polish Jesuit, universalism represents a natural and harmonious union of an individual and society, which at the same time maintains the primacy of the latter. According to Father Paul, it makes no sense to ask what takes precedence for an individual, his or her nation or humanity as a whole, since it is clear that humanity must be placed higher in an individual's hierarchy than his or her own nation, although the person may feel a stronger personal link with the latter. The author adds that "one cannot be a good constituent part in the body of humanity without being a good son of his homeland; one cannot serve his homeland adequately without striving to reach goals shared by all humanity."[41]

Father Warszawski's bibliography (published in Rome in 1985 in honor of his eightieth birthday), notes that the Polish Jesuit continued vigorously to promote the theme of universalism even in the very unfavorable conditions that prevailed in Poland after 1942. In 1943, he published in the underground monthly *Sztuka i Naród* [Art and Nation], and then in the hand-copied periodical *Polska Myśl Uniwersalistyczna* [Polish Universalistic Thought], which was published in a camp for prisoners of war. After the war, in exile, he gave various lectures and also published in *Universum,* a journal published in Munich, London and Paris.

The editors of *Art and Nation* were young and courted nationalism under the influence of Father Warszawski's universalism, though they did not hesitate to criticize him as well. One of them, a prominent poet, Andrzej Trzebiński (1922–1943) organized *Studium Kultury* [Cultural Studies], where universalism as a new synthesis was discussed. According to Tadeusz Sołtan's personal testimony, most participants were of the opinion that accepting the primacy of the whole over its parts should not necessarily lead to the abolishment of personal liberties.[42] In 1943, Trzebiński published an interesting article under the pen name of Stanisław Łomień, in which he referred to a brochure published anonymously by Father Warszawski a year earlier. In universalism, Trzebiński discerned "a new and revolutionary way of thinking", "a blueprint for peace of mind", "a philosophy of balance", and the triumph over "philosophies of extremes".

It did not represent a cool detachment to everything, a shunning of the perils posed by extremism, or a philosophy of "the golden mean", but rather it was about the challenge of earnest engagement, of a difficult spiritual adventure. According to Trzebiński, universalism was not a means of attaining the golden mean, but rather the "golden peak", a chance to reach the summit "through struggle, drama and madness," the poet wrote, "to finally conquer the golden peak. We shall not travel easily and safely on the highway of the golden mean with muddy ditches on both sides."[43]

The universalism of Trzebiński and other young writers of the wartime generation "never constituted a well-defined philosophical system; it was more a proposition, an attempt to gather some thoughts and subject them to one overriding, unifying principle, which for young intellectuals took the form of a certain directional systematization."[44]

Although the monthly *Art and Nation* had its roots in an extremely nationalistic tradition, the *Confederation of the Nation*, associated with it, underwent a significant ideological evolution and severed its ties with *Obóz Narodowo-Radykalny* [National Radical Camp], emphasizing its Catholic and Christian Universalism roots instead. Its activists and writers each conceived of universalism in his own way.[45] Trzebiński was influenced by the neo-Aquinist Józef Warszawski and probably by the socialist Jan Nepomucen Miller, as well, since he professed that "this man (Miller) has a devilish charm" that is "difficult to shake off," and that his words contained "a certain intellectual beauty and a disquieting, truly metaphysical maturity and wisdom."[46]

The universalism of the young Polish wartime generation definitely dissociated itself from Italian[47] and German totalitarianism as well as from the principle of leadership and the individuals' absolute submission to power structures; occasionally, it also distanced itself from the hierarchical Thomistic worldview of Father Warszawski. Many years later, a participant of those discussions wrote: "I could not consent to a simplified hierarchical way of seeing and ordering the world, to a relinquishing of the entire legacy of theoretical assertions (frequently of real practical import) that belong to the canon of secular thought and have largely shaped my personal, and rather convoluted path of intellectual and ideological development."[48] Tadeusz Sołtan stated that certain ideas and discussions of this intellectual movement, which was not always sufficiently mature, "had their own point and meaning and deserve to be mentioned if only briefly."[49] Andrzej Mencwel in his highly valued book on Polish attitudes in the 20th century saw that vague universalism as protecting many thinkers and poets of the war generation against extreme nationalism.[50]

MODERN POLISH AND AMERICAN UNIVERSALISM

For several decades after the war, no attempts were made to return to the universalism of Trentowski, Jaworski, Warszawski, Trzebiński or Miller. Universalism was rather one-sidedly associated with either Christianity or Marxism-Leninism. In the late 1970's, Trentowski's *Podstawy filozofii uniwersalnej* [Foundations of a Universal Philosophy] was published in Polish and a timid reminder of the intellectual significance of universalism during the Second World War was offered. Later, Marxist-Christian dialogue intensified and there was a search for common values. Janusz Kuczyński, an original philosopher and materialistic "creationist", who would later be the founding father and leading member of the International Society for Universalism (ISU), offered the latest vision of universalism without adjectives. He has made a significant contribution to the development of modern universalism in Poland.

The election of Karol Wojtyła as Pope in 1978 contributed to the strengthening of the position of Christian universalism. In addition, the rise of "Solidarność" [Solidarity], which can be interpreted as a Romantic-universalistic movement, contributed to a solidary universalism[51] and to a gradual end to Marxist-Leninist and Marxist-socialist claims to universality.

Intellectual historians should note a shift away from local perspectives towards a more universalistic one in Eastern European countries, and vice versa. "The golden mean", Tyszka wrote recently, "may only be a *coincidentia oppositorum*: universalism imbued in that which is local, and universalism grafted onto that which is local, which is not that xenophobic and closed attitude that is hostile towards everything foreign, nationalistic in the traditional sense".[52]

Janusz Kuczyński has developed the most extensive vision of universalism yet, which has been quite widely publicized in both Polish and English.[53] Kuczyński's universalism is an independent and original crowning achievement of virtually all universalistic views discussed above. In his interpretation, universalism has many meanings. Above all, it is a meta-philosophy and meta-theory of humanity that transcends a state of consciousness that can be described as "in itself" to a higher one that can be described as "for itself". This springs from an awareness of the crisis of all philosophies to date. In a synthetic form, it contains the entire wealth of cultures, their uniqueness and diverse approaches to reaching a universal unity. Moreover, universalism forms an intellectual basis for genuine tolerance, openness, holistic integration, synergic cooperation and a promise for the global emergence of a universalistic society in the wake of communism, whose erosion, it will be recalled, first began in Poland.[54]

Within the milieu of the University of Warsaw Center for Universalism, the ISU Polish and the Polish Life Federation, many original collaborative works on ecological thinking and universalistic ecology have been published.[55]

Polish scholars have recently and wisely reflected on forgotten aspects of Christian and soteriological universalism, close to liberal-democratic post-Protestant universalism. For example, Waclaw Hryniewicz has developed more amply the content of the Gospel of hope.[56]

A Polish-American sociologist, Felix Gross, has formulated a vision of a future system similar to that outlined above, which would integrate many modern ideological and cultural orientations while upholding a set of basic common norms. It would be a "universal, higher-order regulatory mega-ethos, an executive instrument or a system for organizing humanity that would be placed higher than any other value systems. Such a system, since it is fundamental, would be kept to the most basic, essential values. It would represent tolerance and dialogue. Undoubtedly there still would be a differentiation of value systems among various groups. Moreover, such differentiation is not contrary to the idea of human unity."[57]

Another Polish-American author has presented a general system of civilization, developed an original dynamic and quantitative model of civilization, distinguished between global and the universal civilization (supra-civilization) understood as a set of autonomous civilizations. Those considerations based upon cybernetics and information sciences enable comparisons between civilizations.[58]

Universalism, now reborn, reformed and institutionalized in the form of International Society for Universalism and International Society for

Universal Dialogue and their local branches (the organization was registered in Boston in 1989, but its basic framework had been set up earlier) has been met with great interest in both North and South Americas, particularly in North America, since in some Latin American countries the word "universalism" is still strongly associated with Western European and U.S. claims to world domination. The relative ease with which reference can be made to universal ideas in North and South America lies in with the special character of American cultures, which have been melting pots for different races, ethnic groups and cultures. For Latin America, the conflict between particularism and aspirations to universality has always been as vital as the striving for an all-encompassing cultural synthesis. It should be added that Poland, too, has been considered a viable intermediary between different civilizations, lying as it does at the cultural crossroads between East and West, and as a driving force behind the new universalist civilization.

America, in the universalistic meaning of this word, encompasses not only the United States of America, but also a vast diversified "unity in plurality", stretching from Alaska to Tierra del Fuego. If one attempts to consider this historic and geographic area in synthetic terms, considerable problems arise. This area, after all, is far larger than Europe and encompasses the entire Western Hemisphere. Ever since 1492, both Europeans and Americans have been confronted with this dilemma in their reflections on the subject.

The idea of America as the New World may be examined from the perspective of historical and cultural philosophy, philosophical anthropology, ontology and political philosophy. Edmundo O'Gorman, a Mexican historian and philosopher, believes that the essence of America's existence, concealed at first from European awareness, must be clarified, and that this represents a task of fundamental importance. America's true existence is genetically derived from its mother, Europe. While examining America's ontology, O'Gorman concludes that America enjoys a special, peculiar existence, one, which is culturally and historically dependent on Europe.[59] The fact that at one time America lived a veiled existence, as a continent situated between Asia and Europe, then discovered accidentally by Christopher Columbus, and thus coming into contact with Europe, serves here as a point of departure for a philosophical discussion on the idea of Europe's discovery and launching of the New World.

At first, the idea that the New World would become a second Europe was considered a serious possibility. Edmundo O'Gorman describes not only the process of discovering America in a physical sense, but also of its "creation" in the image and likeness of the old continent that had discovered it.[60] This was particularly evident in Anglo-Saxon America. Over the years, rather than contrasting the New World with the Old World, an idealistic perception strove to create a Euro-America with the Atlantic as *Mare Nostrum*.

The idea of America as an independent whole often took the shape of the concept of a "Western Hemisphere". This concept, which emerged in the late eighteenth-century, assumed that there existed special ties that united the inhabitants of that hemisphere and set them apart from Europe and the rest of the world. The Enlightenment and Positivist periods encouraged the conceptualization of America as a whole. The Western Hemisphere idea, sometimes referred to as pan-Americanism, found its political expression in the Monroe Doctrine, first outlined by U.S. president James Monroe in 1823, during an address to the nation. The aim of the Monroe Doctrine was to prevent Europe from intervening in the Americas and to perpetuate the dominant presence of the United States in the Americas. In 1889, Saenz Peña, an Argentinian, tried to replace the regional and exclusionist slogan "America for Americans" that had grown out of the Monroe Doctrine, with the more universalistic motto, "America for humanity".

The Left of Latin America, inspired by various dependency theories, has long analyzed the unfair relations between the two Americas — the poor South, and the rich North. They strove to understand the processes that had led one group of people to full-fledged development, while bringing others to ruin. The subsequent outcry did not prove constructive. At present, a search in the spirit of the new universalism is underway for a more conciliatory vision to include both Americas.

Searching for an inter-American frame of mind and "inter-American system"[61] constitutes an important element in the intellectual and political efforts being made on both sides of Rio Grande, despite socioeconomic barriers and cultural and psychological contrasts.[62]. This search is considered to be one of many important components of "building a world community on the basis of nations' voluntary cooperation and political pluralism."[63] At present, after the collapse of the communist system, which had been quite influential in Latin America, a true pan-Americanism or inter-American unity based on democracy, dialogue and generally accepted values seems more realistic.[64] Latin Americans, though still disheartened by their misfortunes, are inclined to accept broad cooperation with the powerful northern neighbor perhaps more today than before.

Waldo Frank (1889–1967), a leftist writer and an essayist in the American tradition of prophetism and messianism (Emerson, Whitman, and others), during the interwar period was one of the first to advance the idea of mutual understanding of all inhabitants of both Americas, as a re-discovery of America.[65] His program for an American alliance and his idea of an American "commandment" encouraged a positive attitude toward the people of Latin America. Waldo Frank was an ardent advocate of broad cultural and intellectual cooperation among Americans. His philosophical views reflected his desire to bring about a harmonious whole. He considered Latin America to be an important element in the development of American unity.

After the war, discussions about the shape of the future world civilization intensified, especially in the United States. Some intellectuals emphasized that the input of many nations and cultures would be necessary for future unity and universality; others foresaw the clear domination of a single center. A frequent question was whether "this would be a total universalism leaving no room for diversity, or would it be a universalism that has its roots in diversity?"[66] In the United States, the model world society has been equated quite often with the North Atlantic Community or even the USA itself, since it has been a multi-ethnic melting pot and a "nation of many nations". The world has become increasingly uniform thanks to similar technological, communication and cosmopolitan trends. In the 1950's, an American political scientist Quincy Wright, and later the Canadian Herbert Marshall McLuhan, who was one of the authors of the "global village" theory, paid close attention to the processes that were forming universal culture. Universalism has not taken issue recently with pluralism as such, and "pluralistic unity" is seen in America as a potential role model for the world.[67]

Latin America and its Anglo-Saxon northern neighbor seem to represent two different versions of Western civilization, two different sides of one global civilization in the Western Hemisphere.[68] Many attempts have been made to reconcile these two sides. Filmer Northrop, a North American philosopher, has emphasized the fusion of Latin American and Anglo-Saxon cultures as a key issue. According to Northrop, the goal of pan-Americanism has universal significance — in order to express world unity, it will facilitate the creation of a universal philosophy: "the goal of uniting aesthetic, affective and religious values with scientific, doctrinal and pragmatic ones would be the same as uniting East and West safely and appropriately."[69] Similarly, the Mexican author Leopoldo Zea believed that the American philosophy that would subsequently arise from the union of Anglo-American and Latin American cultural values would become a universal philosophy, capable of eliminating differences between East and West and expressing the world's unity.[70]

THE LATIN AMERICAN CONTRIBUTION

Great masters of Mexican thought, such as Antonio Caso (1883–1946) and Alfons Reyes (1889–1959), have included certain elements of universalism in their work. According to Reyes, the mission of the New World is to overcome ecumenically cultural and racial differences between all peoples and nations. He saw precisely this type of cultural synthesis in America, which is larger than the sum of its parts. Reyes emphasized the fact that the fulfillment of the American dream and its destiny are closely tied with Europe; as a philosopher, however, he was interested in humanity as a whole. Reyes wrote of the "inherent internationalism of Latin American culture".[71] He proposed a synthesis whose aim was to reconcile Hindu, ancient Greek and Chinese wisdom with Western European culture and science.

His compatriot Antonio Caso noted in his writings on the Iberian sources of Mexican culture that "the Latin spirit does not mean unification, but rather universalism, which is at once both unity and synthesis, unity and diversity".[72]

Latin American thinkers understand the concept of universalism in a variety of ways. The outstanding Peruvian philosopher, Francisco Miró Quesada has noted the dilemma posed by the peculiar understanding of universalism and historicism in Latin American thought.[73] Phenomenologists, for example, representing one such group, believe that the mission of Latin American philosophy should be to engage itself in all topics of universal importance that have held the attention of Western philosophers. Others maintain that authenticity in philosophy can be reached only when philosophers consider topics originating in their own historical experience. Miró Quesada has attempted to reach a middle ground, making a conciliatory gesture in the dispute between abstract universalism and philosophical historicism, nationalism and regionalism. At one point, he believed Latin American philosophy to be not very original, "eccentric" (looking up to the West) and "prospective" (looking toward the future) and warned about its consequent risks. With time, he admitted that "authentic Latin American philosophy is not as much an opportunity for the future as it is an already implemented, fully-blown reality, enriching the treasury of world thought.

As Latin American philosophy has matured, long-running polemics on the issue of Americanization and universalism have played an important role among Latin American philosophers, who have had doubts as to whether they are actually capable of creating an authentic philosophy. Latin American philosophy (*filosofia de lo americano*) has garnered recognition of the need in Latin America to gain some degree of independence from the dominant giants. Philosophy first began to be transformed into a "philosophy for the Third World", and through it into a philosophy of liberation, and then became an intercultural philosophy. These efforts have led to the creation of true humanism, that is universally applicable to people of all races and creeds.

Miró Quesada maintains that Latin American philosophy realizes itself both on a universal and continental level, and its shortcomings and limitations, which can be overcome, are similar to those inherent in the philosophies and the natural powers of the mind anywhere else in the world.[74] Miró Quesada, an optimist, contends that "the Latin America of today is clearly participating in an Odyssey which imparts character and meaning to human history."[75] Recently, the Peruvian philosopher argued that this debate between the universalists and Latin Americanists is of central importance on his continent. Still optimistic, he asserted that Latin America is capable of creating a new synthetic and universalistic philosophy during the twenty-first century which will represent the culmination of necessary philosophical analyses. This new philosophy will "facilitate the merging of theoretical cognition with *wisdom*, i.e. morality based on human dignity, freedom and creativity."[76]

Two other outstanding Argentinian thinkers, a Christian spiritualist, Alberto Caturelli, and an existential Marxist, Carlos Astrada, have raised the problem of the universality of philosophy and Latin American culture. The former recognized this universal heritage first and foremost in Europe, in its Greek, Latin and Christian *logos*, which "enlightened" and imparted an original form of expression to the "wonderful world of the native Americans" and its "lesser civilization".[77] In Europe, this view also helped give a new meaning and character to universal "eternal philosophical reflection". In this sense, this reflection accepts these new, somewhat particularistic self-manifestations. These manifestations emerged from the old universal Greek and Latin *logos* and are present in Latin American philosophies, which are being subject to universalization.[78]

Astrada had a more favorable view of the native American heritage, as is apparent from his study on universalism and the autonomy of what he often called *Amerindia*, i.e. Latin American culture. As early as 1967, Astrada observed a "universalistic calling", a striving for a "universalistic integration" of his dual, heterogeneous America with the world as a whole. "On its way to cultural autonomy", Astrada wrote, "this America will even overcome its own dualism in order to gain universalistic dimensions, i.e. ones that are pluralistic and have been the result of factors contributing to its cultural integration".[79]

Many unorthodox Latin American Marxists defend their particular brand of universalism by linking it to pluralism and the right to "otherness".

Moreover, Christian thinkers, especially those associated with liberation theology, which exhibited Marxist leanings, have renounced their own dogmatic universalism, while disregarding their region's peculiarities.

Michael Lowy, a French Marxist who has connections with Brazil, admitted that "a creative application of Marxism to the Latin American reality means transcending both tendencies, an *Aufhebung* of the dilemma between a hypostatic particularism and dogmatic universalism; it means the formation of a dialectic unity of the particular and universal in a given situation".[80]

Pope Paul II also noted the universality of knowledge about an "integral human being" and Spanish universalism, "which for a long time has been a characteristic of your culture, enriched by many discoveries and many explorers, as well as the profound influence of countless missionaries around the world. Your nation has been a melting pot, in which so many rich traditions melted into one cultural synthesis. The Arab world's historic contributions enriched the salient features of Spanish communities – your harmonious language, art and terminology best attest to this fact. They melt into Christian civilization, which is wide open to everything that is universal. Equally within its borders as well as outside of them, Spain has shaped itself, accepting the universalism of the Evangel and all great cultural movements of Europe and the world"[81]

Enrique Rivera de Ventosa, the great Spanish philosopher, believed that the greatest contribution of hispanic thought to culture was its universalistic meaning and expression.[82] Rivera de Ventosa noted this characteristic already in the humanistic works of Francisco Vitoria (1480–1546), who defended the universality of human rights, which he believed should be recognized without exception in the case of the newly encountered native Americans as well. Vitoria contributed to the secularization of Christian universalism's earlier medieval version and pursued a broader universalism based on human rights and international law in a differentiated world.

The famous Mexican philosopher José Vasconcelos (1882–1959) expanded this anti-racist position in the twentieth century and developed a universalistic theory of a "cosmic race".[83] He regarded Latin America's destiny with great hope, just as he did future generations and the prospect of joining all races into one universal "cosmic race" of the future. In his opinion, Latin

America, especially Amazonia in Brazil, is the best place for the emergence of such a clear-cut, synthetic race on Earth, incorporating humanity's best features. His noble vision of solving racial problems in the tropics is an important example of Latin American universalism, messianism, and prophetism.

It is often emphasized that when the Spaniards came into contact with America, a new shared history was inaugurated.[84] From that moment, the Spanish-speaking world has been made up of Europeans, Indians and Africans. Vasconcelos' planetary universalism, referring to the whole of humanity, is interpreted as a refined continuation of earlier Spanish universalism, integrating various races and cultures.

"Hence, it is here, on our continent, that we hold all components of the new humanity in our grasp", according to the Mexican visionary.[85] The "world's fifth era, one of universalism and cosmic feeling" would begin there.[86]

Leopoldo Zea argued that Vasconcelos' views had become even more timely during the celebration of the five-hundredth anniversary of the discovery of America. His worldview was perceived as key to a new interpretation of the Spanish adventure that had been undertaken so boldly over five hundred years before, as well as now, as North America and Europe are becoming more "Latin Americanized" due to the tangible presence of different races and cultures there, and as the search for universal solutions for the modern world is intensifying.[87] He recognized the spread of cultural universalism and racial intermingling in both Americas. According to Zea, the racial and cultural melting pot of America, from Alaska to Tierra del Fuego is increasingly apparent not only in the New World, but also in the Old, and is thus, the core of the new "cosmic race" once envisioned by Vasconcelos.[88]

At the eleventh Inter-American Philosophical Congress, Lepoldo Zea noted that it was philosophy that could serve as a tool to help bring about inter-American understanding, for example by attempting to establish the general and universal meaning of America in its constituent parts. Zea noted that pan-Americanism could not be based on a unilaterally beneficial linking of one part of America to another. Zea pointed out that analogous integrational tendencies are currently taking place in Europe; he wrote about the aspiration to build a common European home. Such a home, he added, as a nation of nations, must include significant non-European populations within its European identity, in addition to the Eastern part of the continent, which had previously been marginalized. According to Zea, like America, Europe, too, is gradually transforming itself into a "vast melting pot of races and cultures, embracing the whole planet".[89]

The Argentinian writer Alberto Buela has placed great emphasis on America's fusion and symbiosis, on its "welcoming existence," rather than on the ethnic intermingling in both North and South America.[90] Presently, one often hears the opinion that in the twenty-first century, the "Latin American synthesis, based on patterns of fusion and amalgamation, could contribute to a model worthy of global application."[91]

Recently, attempts to construct an inter-cultural philosophy based on a solidary dialogue of all cultures, equally treated, have brought interesting results. This philosophy draws on the Latin American and non-European experience. For Raúl Fornet-Betancourt, a Cuban émigré in Aachen (Germany), inter-cultural philosophy opposes the neo-liberal, homogenizing globalization of the planet, and the rash attempt to create one uniform world culture. Intercultural philosophy strives for universality not by means of unification by force, but by multilateral communication between humanity's various cultures.[92]

FINAL REMARKS

At present, a neo-liberal, abstract and technocratic version of universalism prevails in both North and South America, particularly among those in power. Considered to be the highest expression of universalism, its proponents want to change Latin American culture radically and make it more pragmatic and compatible with Western demands. The politicians who are introducing neo-liberal methods in Latin America (as in Poland and Eastern Europe) have promised to modernize their countries, bringing them to the "First World", the West, (North) America and (Western) Europe. Mario Vargas Llosa, the outstanding Peruvian author and former presidential candidate, supports these changes and has admitted that growing numbers of people in Latin American want a free market economy, rationality, freedom and integration with the rest of humanity.[93]

However, Latin American intellectuals usually prefer versions of universalism that reject one-sidedness and take into account pluralism and different life styles, a factor which is vital to the character of the "*mestizo* continent". Fearful of being crushed by outside powers, they approach universalism, which is inevitable, and the global dimensions of the modern world from their own particularistic perspective.[94]

Some US scholars have also criticized Western universalism, which they believe poses a threat to the world. Imperialism, they say, is the "inevitable logical consequence" of Western universalism.[95] The false western universalism is also criticized in Poland in behalf of the idea of dialogue among civilizations. This looks at all civilizations as equal and valuable and "requires from the Westerners a liberation from contemptuous attitudes towards other civilizations and paternalism towards non-Western nations."[96]

Many American thinkers, especially those associated with the *Council for Research in Values and Philosophy*, the *International Society for Universalism* and *International Society for Universal Dialogue*, emphasize that humanity needs a truly universal philosophy in order to survive, not a parochial one; it needs a philosophy that seeks out what is common to all human beings.[97] Such a philosophy will be the result of cooperation between many peoples and cultures.[98] It will promote the world's cultural diversity, and attempt to understand world history in all its "complexity and cultural richness as a dynamic, creative process."[99] According to Michael H. Mitias, universalism is an open and cooperative philosophy that recognizes different concepts and standpoints, "manages to grasp the human universal in the different fruits of human civilizations."[100] This philosophy will also try to enrich current concepts of democracy and liberalism.[101]

George F. McLean and the teams of the Council for Research in Values and Philosophy have launched a universal philosophical dialogue "to search out new elements of unity, cultural diversity and intercultural cooperation which constitute the architectural elements of our age."[102]

Their approach is to look not for the abstract and universal principles from which to deduce all in the rigorous and restrictive "top-down" procedures of modernity, but to invert that process. That is, to begin from the civil societies of many cultures as they draw upon their heritages and apply them in new ways in facing their present challenges. This constitutes rather a "bottom-up" process which in global times is interrelational, holistic or global for the radically new times into which we now enter. For this the new paradigm is neither the One of antiquity nor the many individuals of modernity, but the whole constituted of free persons living socially.

Immanuel Wallerstein shows that European, scientific universalism of the powerful has been partial and distorted. He proposes as a real alternative to the existing world-system a universal or global universalism beyond the European universalism. According to this famous American sociologist, "the struggle between European universalism and universal universalism is the central ideological struggle of the contemporary world."[103]

Modern universalism does not oppose pluralism;[104] it embraces the old saying: *E pluribus unum*. What it does object to are the extremes embodied in postmodernist nihilism and any authoritarian or totalitarian tendencies which have appeared under the cloak of universalism within fascism and communism, in some versions of authoritarian and dogmatic globalism, and in hegemonic liberalism.[105]

NOTES

1 This text is an elaborated version of a paper delivered at Warsaw University during the 50th International Congress of Americanists (July 10–14, 2000) entitled "The Americas' Universal Messages for the Twenty-First Century." The paper was presented in Spanish at the "Filosofia e interculturalidad: una perspectiva universalizable desde las Américas" session. An earlier version of this Essay was published in *Dialogue and Universalism*, 11-12 (2001), 51-74.

2 Fr. Z. Wolak, *Uniwersalizm chrześcijaństwa a logika, filozofia i nauka* [Christian Universalism and Logic, Philosophy and Science], in *Uniwersalizm chrześcijaństwa a pluralizm religii: Materiały z sympozjum* [Christian Universalism and Religious Pluralism: Symposium Materials], eds. S. Budzik and Z. Kijas (Tarnów, 2000), 213, 222; see also: H. Mourier, *Antropologia misyjna: Religie i cywilizacje w zderzeniu z uniwersalizmem* [Missionary Anthropology: Religions and Civilizations in a Clash with Universalism] (Warsaw, 1997).

3 Compare definitions of this topic in *Encyklopedia szkolna: Historia* [Student Encyclopedia: History] (Warsaw, 1993), 648–649. In the United States, even a Universalist Church exists, which is a liberal Protestant religious denomination; for a detailed definition of universalism, see *Universalism in America. A Documentary History of a Liberal Faith.* Edited by Ernst Cassara (Boston: Skinner House Books, 1997).

4 H. Grala, "Uniwersalizm wschodni (idea Cesarstwa Powszechnego w kręgu cywilizacji bizantyjskiej)" [Eastern Universalism – The Idea of a Universal Empire within Byzantine Civilization], in *Pamiętnik XV Powszechnego Zjazdu Historyków Polskich* [Fifteenth General Congress of Polish Historians Commemorative Volume], Vol. 1, ed. J. Staszewski (Toruń, 1996).

5 See materials from the conference "Uniwersalizm praw człowieka. Idea a rzeczywistość w krajach pozaeuropejskich" [Universalism of Human Rights: Idea Versus Reality in Non-European Countries], ed. K. Tomala (Warsaw, 1998), and K. Gawlikowski, "The 'Asian Values' Problem and Western Universalism," in *Dialogue and Universalism*, 1–2 (2000); id, "From False 'Western Universalism' Towards True 'Universal Universalism'", *Dialogue and Universalism* 10-12 (2004).

6 J. Domański, "Swoistość i uniwersalizm polskiej myśli średniowiecznej" [The Special Characteristics and Universalism of Polish Medieval Thought], in *700 lat myśli polskiej* [*700 Years of Polish Thought*], vol. 1 (Warsaw, 1978), 1–38; J. Maciejewski, "Uniwersalność i swoistość polskiego Oświecenia" [Universality and specificity of Polish Enlightenment], in *Uniwersalizm i swoistość kultury polskiej* [The Universalism and Special Characteristics of Polish Culture], vol. 1 (Lublin, 1989), 271–297.

7 B.F. Trentowski, *Grundlage der Universellen Philosophie* (Karlsruhe, 1837); Polish edition, *Podstawy filozofii uniwersalnej: Wstęp do nauki o naturze* [Foundations of Universal Philosophy: Introduction to the Science of Nature] (Warsaw, 1978), 300.

8 B.F. Trentowski, *Podstawy...* [Foundations…], 310. It is interesting to note that it was Trentowski who was first to establish an opposition, long lasting in the Polish history, between the foreign state apparatus of partitioning powers and a moral, clandestine civil society of independent associations.

9 Ibid., 322–323

10 Ibid., 35

11 Ibid.

12 Ibid., 52

13 A. Walicki, "Uniwersalizm i narodowość w polskiej myśli filozoficznej i koncepcjach mesjanistycznych epoki Romantyzmu (po roku 1831)" [Universalism and Nationality in Polish Philosophical Thought and Messianic Tradition of Romanticism (after 1831)] in *Uniwersalizm i swoistość kultury...* [Universalism and the Special Characteristics of Polish Culture…], vol. 2, 36–37; see also "The Idea of Universalism in the Polish Romantic Tradition", in *Dialogue and Universalism,* 4 (1993).

14 See his work *Filozofia uniwersalna Trentowskiego* [The Universal Philosophy of Trentowski] (Warsaw, 1913).

15 J. Kuczyński, *Wstęp do uniwersalizmu* [Introduction to Universalism], vol. I (Warsaw, 1998), 206.

16 S. Smolikowski, *Filozofia wyzwolenia* [The Philosophy of Liberation] (Warsaw, 1883), 104–105; see also Barbara Skarga's brief note on Smolikowski in *Zarys dziejów filozofii polskiej 1815–1918* [A Brief History of Polish Philosophy] (Warsaw, 1983), 243–244; and J. R. Błachnio, *Filozofia Seweryna Smolikowskiego a uniwersalizm końca XX wieku* [The Philosophy of Seweryn Smolikowski and Late Twentieth-Century Universalism] (Bydgoszcz, 2000). Błachnio situates Smolikowski's philosophy within the field of metaphysics (Aristotle, Thomas Aquinas, M. A. Krąpiec), demonstrating his search for permanent principles, values and the unyielding truth about being.

17 S. Smolikowski, *Filozofia* ...[Philosophy…], 106.

18 S. Frankiewicz, "Jan Nepomucen Miller", *Więź*, 12 (1977); G. Ratajska, "Jan Nepomucen Miller: Krytyk i publicysta zapomniany" [Jan Nepomucen Miller – A Forgotten Critic and Publicist], *Zeszyty Naukowe Instytutu Nauk Społecznych WSI* [Publication of the Institute of Social Sciences, WSI] vol. 6, part II (Koszalin, 1986).

19 J. N. Miller, *Zaraza w Grenadzie: Rzecz o stosunku nowej sztuki do romantyzmu i modernizmu w Polsce* [The Plague in Granada: About New Art Attitude towards Romanticism and Modernism in Poland] (Warsaw, 1926), 24; The chapter "Od indywidualizmu do uniwersalizmu" ["From Individualism to Universalism"] reprinted in J. N. Miller, *Bez kropki nad "i"* [Without Dotting the I's] (Warsaw, 1964). Miller's articles and books on universalism were a subject of heated debate in 1925–1926, as well as in later years.

20 J. N. Miller, *Na gruzach Granady: Studium krytyczne* [In the Ruins of Granada – A Critical Study] (Warsaw, 1933), 13–14.

21 J. N. Miller, *Zaraza*... [The Plague...], 66.

22 J.N. Miller, *Na gruzach Granady: Studium krytyczne* [In the Ruins of Grenada – A Critical Study] (Warsaw, 1933), 13–14.

23 Ibid., 20.

24 Ibid., 113.

25 M. Jaskólski, *Między normatywizmem i uniwersalizmem: Myśl prawno-polityczna Władysława L. Jaworskiego* [Between Normativism and Universalism: Władysław L. Jaworski's Legal and Political Thought] (Wrocław, 1988), 38–39.

26 W. L. Jaworski, *Projekt Konstytucji* [The Project for the Constitution] (Kraków, 1928), 13–14; Ibid., *Notatki* [Notes] (Cracow, 1929), 138.

27 See the writings of K. Michalski, *O rozwoju religijno-filozoficznym W. L. Jaworskiego* [On the Religious and Philosophical Development of W. L. Jaworski], and A. Benis, "Wł. L. Jaworski jako filozof i ekonomista" [W. L. Jaworski as Philosopher and Economist], in the collective work, *Wl.*

L. Jaworskiego życie i działalność [The Life and Work of W. L. Jaworski] (Kraków, 1931).

28 S. Borzym, "Dwa 'uniwersalizmy': Jaworskiego i Spanna" [Two Universalisms: Those of Jaworski and Spann], *Archiwum historii filozofii i myśli społecznej,* vol. 44 (1999), 211; the following authors wrote about Spann's universalism in Poland: S. Druks, "Typy myślenia w filozofii prawa (dokończenie)" [Types of Thought in the Philosophy of Law – Conclusion], *Kwartalnik Filozoficzny*, no. 26 (1926): 139–141; F. Zweig, *Cztery systemy ekonomii: Uniwersalizm – nacjonalizm – liberalizm – socjalizm* [Four Economic Systems: Universalism – Nationalism – Liberalism – Socialism] (Kraków, 1932); T. Seidler, *Jednostka, państwo, rząd: Próba syntezy* [Individual, State, Government – An Attempt at Synthesis] (Warsaw, 1934); L. Caro, "Liberalizm a kapitalizm" [Liberalism and Capitalism], *Ateneum Kapłańskie,* bulletin 4 (1937); see also K. Maurin in "Albo albo" (2000/2001).

29 In particular, see a series of misleading articles on universalism of 'totality', 'history', and the 'collective', by Karol Ludwik Koniński, published under the collective title, "Universalism-Individualism-Personality," in *Myśl Narodowa*, nos. 29, 30, 31 and 32 (1934).

30 S. Borzym, *Filozofia polska 1900–1950* [Polish Philosophy in 1900–1950] (Wrocław, 1991), 115–116, 185–186.

31 Lucyna Wiśniewska-Rutkowska, *Mesjanizm Jerzego Brauna. Myślenie w perspektywie Józefa Marii Hoene-Wrońskiego* (Kielce: Wyd. AŚ), 2004.

32 George Weigel, *Witness to Hope. The Biography of Pope John Paul II* (New York: Harper Collins Publishers, 1999), 67.

33 More on this topic can be found in B. Truchlińska, *Antropologia i aksjologia kultury: Koncepcje podmiotu kultury i hierarchii wartości w polskiej myśli filozoficzno-społecznej 1918–1939* [The Anthropology and Axiology of Culture: The Concepts of the Cultural Subject and Value System in Polish Philosophical and Social Thought, 1918–1939] (Lublin, 1998), particularly Chapter 3, "W kręgu myśli uniwersalistycznej" [Within the Realm of Universalistic Thought], 83–130.

34 F. Zweig, *Cztery...* [Four...], 50; T. Seidler, *Jednostka...*[Individu al…], 24.

35 It combined Catholic universalism, as opposed to cosmopolitanism, with 'Catholic nationalism'. See J. J. Lipski, *Katolickie państwo narodu polskiego* [The Catholic State of the Polish Nation] (London, 1994), 86. During the war, an anti-individualistic, "civilizational" universalism was associated with pagan nationalism and totalitarianism. J. Stachniuk, *Zagadnienie totalizmu* [The Problem of Totalitarianism] (Warsaw, 1943), 16–21, 33–34, 67.

36 T. Seidler, *Jednostka*..., 61, 94.

37 Recently an attention has been devoted to an interesting fact: „It is not accidental that in the midlle of the furious Second World War under German occupation in 1942 there appeared independently from each other three centers of future social thought. In Wilno, in the illegal Catholic Institute the priest Józef Wojtukiewicz on behalf of a conspiratory group elaborated

a programatic document *Universalist Poltical System*. In Warsaw the Jesuit priest published a pamphlet *Universalism*. However Jerzy Braun formed the organization UNIA. All three circles envisaged the collapse of both fascism and bolshevism and postulated the initiation of an epoch of synthesis". Leon Brodowski, „Unia, czyli wyższa synteza", in Jerzy Braun, *Unionizm* (Warszawa: Fronda, 1999), 16.

38 J. Warszawski, *Uniwersalizm: Zarys narodowej filozofii społecznej* [Outline of Social Philosophy (in Poland)] (Warsaw: Pressto Agency, 1997), 4.

39 Ibid., 30.

40 Ibid., 38.

41 Ibid., 67.

42 T. Sołtan, *Z rachunków mego pokolenia* [From My Generation's Conscience] (Warsaw, 1988), 43; see also Urbanowski's introduction to A. Trzebiński, *Aby podnieść różę: Szkice literackie i dramat* [To Pick Up a Rose: Essays and Plays] (Warsaw, 1999), 13–15.

43 S. Łomień, "Metoda 'złotego szczytu' (głosy na temat 'uniwersalizmu')" [Method of the 'Golden Peak': Voices on Universalism], *Sztuka i Naród*, no. 7 (1943); reprint in A. Trzebiński, *Kwiaty z drzew zakazanych: Proza* [Flowers from Forbidden Trees: Prose], Z. Jastrzębski, ed. and foreward (Warsaw, 1972), 44.

44 L. M. Bartelski, *Genealogia ocalonych: Szkice o latach 1939–1944* [The Genealogy of Survivors: Essays on the Years 1939–1944] (Kraków, 1963), 114. The political implications of Trzebiński's work provoke strong arguments, which have no simple solutions. See A. Kopiński, *Ludzie z charakterem. O okupacyjnym sporze Czesława Miłosza z Andrzejem Trzebińskim* (Warsaw: Fronda, 2004).

45 Józef Szczypka, ed., *W gałązce dymu, w ogniu blasku... Wspomnienia o Wacławie Bojarskim, Tadeuszu Gajcym, Onufrym Bronisławie Kopczyńskim, Wojciechu Menclu, Zdzisławie Stroińskim, Andrzeju Trzebnickim* [In a Swirl of Smoke, in the Light of Fire… Memories of Wacław Bojarski, Tadeusz Gajcy, Onufry Bronisław Kopczyński, Wojciech Mencel, Zdzisław Stroiński, Andrzej Trzebiński] (Warsaw, 1977); see also J. Tomaszkiewicz, ed., *Portrety twórców 'Sztuki i Narodu'* [Portraits of the Founders of 'Art and Nation'] (Warsaw, 1983), 146; Z. Kobylańska, Konfederacja narodu w Warszawie [Confederace of the Nation in Warsaw] (Warsaw, 1999), 30.

46 A. Trzebiński, *Kwiaty...*, 132–133. Jan Józef Lipski, ill-disposed toward nationalistic organizations, has maintained that some of them, such as the Polish Organization for Cultural Action, achieved certain successes: the success of POCA lay in the fact that many outstanding intellectuals took part in discussions organized by POCA, among them not only those who were periodically close to Falanga, such as F. Goetel, but also those completely alien to fascist ideology (K. Irzykowski, J. N. Miller, etc.). J. J. Lipski, *Katolickie państwo...* [Catholic State…], 16.

47 The Italian influence was visible in 'universalism' of some Polish nationalists, and in Latin America, in Peron's populism. Two years before his

death, Peron stated: "Yesterday was the era of the United Nations; today is the era of Continentalism, which will soon be followed by that of Universalism. We must be united, organized in the spirit of solidarity, always respecting the customs and sovereignty of other peoples, and seeking a proper solution to the urgent problems for the cause of Common Unity, and perhaps one day we will all be able to grant ourselves the honorary title of 'Citizen of the World'." See F. Chavez, *Perón y el justicialismo* (Buenos Aires, 1984), 124.

48 T. Sołtan, "Sens uniwersalizmu" [The Meaning of Universalism], in *Motywy i fascynacje* [Motifs and Fascinations] (Warsaw, 1978), 106.

49 Ibid, 111; see also M. Gutowska, "Sztuka i naród a uniwersalizm" [Art and Nation and Universalism], *Zeszyty Naukowe WSP w Bydgoszczy* 5 (1979): 91–102.

50 Andrzej Mencwel, *Przedwiośnie czy potop* (Warszawa 1997), 203.

51 See: T. Grabińska and M. Zabierowski, *Aksjologiczny krąg solidarności: Rekonstrukcja uniwersalizmu solidarnościowego i jego uzasadnienie w nauce społecznej Jana Pawła II* [Axiological Domain of Solidarity: Reconstruction of the Universalism of Solidarity and its Legitimation in the Social Teachings of John Paul II] (Wrocław, 1998). Cited there: "Solidarity's initiation of social support for egalitarian changes was a symbol of Polish (Catholic) Universalism; after 1989, its citizens were persuaded that their chief concern was self-interest and not the concern for each other. In reality, Solidarity was a universalistic movement, and not, as some tried to falsely diagnose, a xenophobic one", 61. They continued: "The Romanticism Solidarity was accused of was the basis for a world-formulating attitude of assessing each event through the filtration principle of universalism's cognitive apparatus", 78.

52 A. Tyszka, "Rodzimość i uniwersalizm śródkontynentu" [Local Perspectives and Central European Universalism], in *Róża wiatrów Europy* [The Rose of the Winds of Europe], A. Tyszka, ed. (Warsaw, 1999), 137; cf. J. Minkievičius, "Zbieżność idei uniwersalizmu w historii polskiej i litewskiej myśli filozoficznej" [Convergence of Universalistic Ideas in Polish and Lithuanian Philosophical Thought], *Lithuania*, 1 (1995).

53 This theory was expounded in the columns of *Dialogue and Universalism* (earlier called *Dialectics and Humanism* and then later *Dialogue and Humanism*), in the extensive work of J. Kuczynski, *Dialogue and Universalism as a New Way of Thinking* (Warsaw: Warsaw University, 1989), and in the consecutive, two-volume works by the same author, *Uniwersalizm jako metafilozofia* [*Universalism as Metaphilosophy*] (Warsaw, UW, 1989–90), and in *Wstęp do uniwersalizmu* (Introduction to Universalism) (Warsaw, 1998–99).

54 Today, in the ISU Polish Division, post-communists, Marxists, liberals, proponents of analytical philosophy, Catholics, Protestants and followers of other religions cooperate harmoniously. Universalistic elements inherent in Eastern religions and Judaism are emphasized. See J. Chodorowski, "Uniwersalizm religii żydowskiej a polityczna integracja Europy" [The

Universalism of Judaism and the Political Integration of Europe], *Nomos*, 24/25 (1998/99).

55 For example: *Ziemia domem człowieka* [The Earth, Home for Man] (1997); *Szkoła przeżycia cywilizacyjnego* [School of Civilizational Survival] (1997); *Ekologia ducha* [Ecology of the Spirit] (1999); *Hipoteza ekologii uniwersalistycznej* [Universalistic Ecology Hypothesis] (1999).

56 See W. Hryniewicz, We Are All the People of the Beginning, *Dialogue and Universalism,* (9-10) 2003: 37-40; id., „Hope for Man and the Universe. On some forgotten Aspects of Christian Universalism", *Dialogue and Universalism*, (10-12) 2004: 9-23.

57 F. Gross, *Tolerancja i pluralizm* [Tolerance and Pluralism] (Warsaw, 1992), 7.

58 See, for example, Andrew Tarkowski's recent paper „The Civilization Index", *Dialogue and Universalism* (10-12) 2004: 71-86.

59 E. O'Gorman, *La idea del descubrimiento de América* (México, 1976), 9.

60 E. O'Gorman, *La invención de América* (México, 1977), 152; see also passages in Polish in a bi-lingual edition of *'Wynalezienie' Ameryki* [The 'Discovery' of America] (Warsaw: CESLA, University of Warsaw, 1999).

61 H. Berstein, *Making an Inter-American Mind* (Gainsville, FL, 1961); A. Stepan, ed., *Americas: New Interpretative Essays* (New York: Oxford Univ. Press, 1992); G. Pope Atkins, *Encyclopedia of the Inter-American System* (Westport, CT, 1997).

62 G. C. Dilly, *The Latin Americans: Spirit and Ethos* (San Francisco: Oxford Univ. Press, 1992).

63 L. R. Scheman, *The Inter-American Dilemma: The Search for Inter-American Cooperation at the Centennial of the Inter-American System* (New York, 1988), 2.

64 Howard J. Wiarda, *Democracy and its Discontents: Development, Interdependence, and U.S. Policy in Latin America* (Lanham – New York – London, 1995).

65 W. Frank, *The Rediscovery of America: An Introduction to a Philosophy of American Life* (New York – London, 1929).

66 K. Krzysztofek, *Uniwersalistyczne i pluralistyczne wizje pokojowego świata* [Universalistic and Pluralistic Visions of World Peace] (Warsaw: PISM, 1990), 40.

67 R. Cornelison, "E pluribus unum: Universalism and Particularism in American Civil Religion", *Dialogue and Universalism*, 7 (1995), 58.

68 J.P. Gillin, "Modern Latin American Culture," in *Man, State and Society in Latin American Culture*, S. B. Liss & P. K. Liss, eds. (London, 1972), 326–327; R. Morse, *El espejo de Próspero: Un estudio de la dialéctica del Nuevo Mundo* (México, 1982), 7.

69 F. Northrop, *The Meeting of East and West: An Inquiry Concerning World Understanding* (New York, 1946), 436.

70 L. Zea, *La esencia de lo americano* (Buenos Aires, 1971), 29.

71 Quoted after, J. Wojcieszak, *Dylemat uniwersalizmu i partykularyzmu w hispanoamerykańskiej filozofii kultury lat 1900–1960* [Dilemma of Universalism and Particularism in Hispanic American Cultural Philosophy, 1900–1960] (Warsaw: CESLA, 1989), 130.

72 Ibid., 99.

73 F. Miró Quesada, "Historicismo y universalismo en la filosofía", in *Relativismo cultural y filosofía: Perspectivas norteamericana y latinoamericana*, ed. , M. Dascal (México, 1992), 206–209.

74 F. Miró Quesada, "Posibilidad y limites de una filosofia latinoamericana", *Revista de Filosofia de la Universidad de Costa Rica*, no. 43 (1978): 80.

75 Ibid, 82; Miró Quesada gives a detailed analysis of Latin American philosophy problems in his book *Proyecto y realización del filosofar latinamericano* (México, 1981).

76 F. Miró Quesada, "Universalismo y latinoamericanismo," *Isegoría* 19 (1998): 77.

77 A. Caturelli, "Filosofías latinoamericanas y filosofía universal," *Convivium: Investigaçao e cultura,* no. 4 (1974): 307.

78 Ibid., 310–311

79 C. Astrada, "Autonomia y universalismo de la cultura latinoamericana", *Revista de Filosofia Latinoamericana y Ciencias Sociales,* 14 (1989), 149.

80 M. Lowy, *Le marxism en Amérique Latine* (Paris: Maspero, 1980), 11.

81 In "Przemówienie do przedstawicieli świata nauki i kultury w Hiszpanii" [Speech to the Representatives of the Spanish Cultural and Academic World], in *Jan Paweł II w Portugalii, Hiszpanii i Lourdes: Przemówienia i homilie* [Pope John Paul II in Portugal, Spain and Lourdes: Speeches and Homilies] (Warsaw, 1986), 265.

82 E. Rivera de Ventosa, "Máxima aportación del pensamiento hispánico a la cultura: el sentido universalista", *Revista de Filosofía,* 51 (1984). Also J. M. Aznar has recently paid attention to the fact that Spanish culture should not be afraid of globalization and universalization, that it has a strong component of universal vocation and that Spain was first to make a kind of globalization as early as 16th century. See J.M. Aznar, *Ocho años de gobierno. Una visión personal de España* (Barcelona: Planeta, 2005), 37-38.

83 E. Rivera de Ventosa, "Universalismo planetario de José Vasconcelos", *Cuadernos Salmantinos de Filosofia,* 9 (1982); Ibid, "Lo vivo y lo muerto del pensamiento hispánico en el problema de America", *Naturaleza y Gracia,* 1 (1994); see also B. Díaz, *El internacionalismo de Vitoria en la era de globalización* (Pamplona: Universidad de Navarra, 2005).

84 See also special issue of *Dialogue and Universalism,* 1 (1992).

85 J. Vasconcelos, *Rasa kosmiczna (wybór)* [Cosmic Race: Selected Writings] (Warsaw: CESLA, 1993), 27.

86 Ibid, 23; also see M. J. Gracía Puig, *Joaquin Torres y el Universalismo Constructivo* (Madrid, 1990).

87 See Zea's introduction to the Polish selection of Vasconcelos' writings cited above.

88 L. Zea, "Sentido y proyección del descubrimiento de América", *Cuadernos Americanos*, 21 (1999), 114.

89 L. Zea, "Filosofar desde la realidad americana", *Cuadernos Americanos,* 22 (1990), 48.

90 A. E. Buela, *El sentido de América* (Buenos Aires, 1990), 85-88; compare his article "Czas amerykański" ["American Time"], *Ameryka Łacińska* [Latin America, 1 (1997).

91 R. S. Hillman, ed., *Understanding Contemporary Latin America* (Boulder: Co., 1997), 346.

92 R. Fornet-Betancourt, "Lateinamerikanische Philosophie zwischen Inkulturation und Interkulturalität", in *Interculturalidad y globalización* (Frankfurt-San José, 2000).

93 M. Vargas Llosa, "The Culture of Liberty", *Journal of Democracy,* 1 (1992).

94 E. Lander, "Retos del pensamiento critico latinoamericano en la década de los noventa", in E. Lander, ed., *Modernidad & universalismo* (Caracas, 1991), 145–177.

95 S. Huntington, *Zderzenie cywilizacji* [Clash of Civilizations] (Warsaw, 1997), 478.

96 K. Gawlikowski, „From False 'Western Universalism' Towards True 'Universal Universalism' ", *Dialogue and Universalism* 10-12 (2004), 56.

97 Albert A. Anderson, in *Quo vadis, Philosophie? Antworten der Philosophen: Dokumentation einer Weltumfrage*, R. Fornet-Betancourt, ed. (Aachen, 1999), 31–32.

98 C. Brown, "The University, Dialogue and Universalism", *Dialogue and Humanism,* 2–3 (1994): 157.

99 M. Mitias, "Challenges of Universalism", *Dialogue and Humanism,* 1 (1991): 14.

100 M. Mitias, „Universalism as Metaphilosophy", *Dialogue and Universalism,* 10-12 (2004): 101.

101 J. Riser, "Democracy as a Reflection of Principles of Universalism", *Dialogue and Humanism,* 2–3 (1994); K. A. Appiah, "How to Universalize Liberalism?" *Dialogue and Universalism,* 10 (1998).

102 G. McLean, „Architectural Elements of the Dialogue of Civilizations in a Global Age", *Dialogue and Universalism* 5 (2003), 10; id., „The Universal and the Particular: Dialogical System and Creative Freedom", *Dialogue and Universalism*, 9-10 (2003), 33.

103 I. Wallerstein, *European Universalism: The Rhetoric of Po*wer (New York: The New Press, 2006), XIV.

104 See P.C. Bori, *Universalismo come pluralità delle vie* (Genova: Marietii, 2004); S. Ihingran, *Ethical Relativism and Universalism* (Delhi, 2001); T. Masuzawa, *The Invention of World Religions or, How European*

Universalism Was Preserved in the Language of Pluralism (Chicago and London: The University of Chicago Press, 2005).

105 J. Kuczyński discusses the differences between globalism and universalism in his article: "Metaphilosophy, Science and Art as the Foundation of Wisdom: The Co-creation of a Rational and Ethical Universal Society", *Dialogue and Universalism*, 7–8 (2001), 5.

Chapter 9

John Paul II - Christian and Civil Universalism

It will take strength
to raise up this world;
The strength that will come with the Slavic Pope,
The people's son...
He will cleanse the world's wounds, and rid it
of all its depravity, worms and reptiles,
Bringing health and love,
He will redeem the world;

-- Juliusz Słowacki, 1848

I have carried with me the history, culture, experience and language of Poland. Having lived in a country that had to fight for its existence in the face of the agresssions of its neighbors, I have understood what exploitation is. I put myself immediately on the side of the poor, the disinherited, the oppressed, the marginalized and the defenseless.

-- John Paul II, *Time*, 26 December 1994, 60.

John Paul's universalism is a continuation of a tradition of universalist thinking lasting two thousands years. It makes it possible to look at the reality of the individual man and of the whole of humanity in their personalistic and communitarian dimensions at one time.

John Paul's thought brings a universal message, it embraces both abstract philosophical questions and specific socio-economic problems, strictly connected with the citizens' life. The Encyclical *Redemptoris missio* (1990) presented a program of a new evangelization, of conquering „new Areopaguses", especially the world of mass media, science, culture, politics, and economy. It is a new program of conquering the dominion over the souls, the conquest of the present-day world spirit, of attaining - in Antonio Gramsci's words - moral and intellectual hegemony.

John Paul II's socio-economic views are of a synthetic and conciliatory character. The Pope's message, ambiguous and directed to broad masses of recipients, does not accept definitely any classical type of political thought. It can be said that John Paul II bases his thought on a broader vision of Christian and humanist universalism, transcending the particular economic, national or cultural interests. "So, opposed to purely economic and political universalisms, it is a universalism at its roots, based upon philosophical premises."[1]

Starting from his profound Polishness John Paul II defends strongly universalism, among others in his speech to Polish pilgrims: „Universalism means a membership in the inclusive human community, broader than particular nations. At the same time it is a specific maturity of the nation which gives full citizenship among all nations of the world. Universalism has a deeply humanistic character, and at the same time a peculiar feature of Christianity is revealed in it that strives to unite peoples and nations on the basis of a full respect for their dignity, subjectivity, liberty and rights."[2]

IS THE SOCIAL TEACHING OF THE CHURCH POSSIBLE?

Pope John Paul II made a considerable contribution to the social teaching of the Catholic Church, which came into being together with the intensification of the so-called social question during the nineteenth century. Papal teaching is based on social-economic principles developed by Pope Leo XIII in his celebrated encyclical *Rerum novarum* (1891), as well as on slight modifications proposed by his successors—both the conservative and traditionally inclined Piuses, and the reformers John XXIII and Paul VI. A characteristic feature of John Paul II was the continuum of fundamental moral principles, together with a discernible evolution of the language and manner of interpreting particular problems[3].

The social teaching of the Church was in crisis as seen in John XXIII encyclical *Mater et Magistra* and during Vaticanum II. The teaching was criticized and silenced many times in Europe and in Latin America. It has been successfully promoted by John Paul II already during his first visit to Mexico in 1979.[4] Indirectly at least it was a reaction to the Latin American liberation theology. Many times the Pope warned against resorting to violence.

Progressive Church teaching on the economy concentrates on man as an economic subject, and presumes that by striving towards assorted goals he should wield power over economic goods. In other words, this is a doctrine suffused with anthropological and ethico-economic elements. Representatives of this trend criticize the axiology of Enlightenment liberalism, oppose "the illusion that such values as freedom or pluralism can be separated from the entire hierarchy of values, sanctified by tradition",[5] and are convinced that "today, the most outstanding economists develop their reflection in such way as to take into consideration, as completely as possible, both moral and social reality, perceived as an integral factor of economic processes. In the face of these tendencies, discernible in contemporary economy, the economic teaching of the Church appears to be valuable proposal worthy of attention, even more so considering that it has its own extensive and developed tradition".[6]

The concrete shape of the socioeconomic views of John Paul II was influenced to a considerable degree by the general transformations which occurred in the world during the twentieth century, and especially the dramatic conditions in Poland during the so-called sanacja period, Nazi occupation, and the communist epoch. The Pope also inclines towards profound reflection on the disturbing state of the postmodern world and the post-communist end of the 20th century.

A review of the socioeconomic views of John Paul II and their synthetic-conciliatory nature should begin with a presentation of the social-philosophical and ethical thought of Cardinal Karol Wojtyła, since his teaching retains a certain continuum: numerous later encyclicals develop thoughts that had been expressed earlier. The most important text of interest to us, dating from the pre-pontifical period, is the extremely extensive interview entitled *Is the social teaching of the Church possible?*, which appeared in 1978 in the quarterly "Il Nuovo Aeropago".[7] Cardinal Wojtyła, a former professor of Catholic social ethics at the Catholic University in Lublin, placed particularly strong emphasis on the importance of this question, and the significance of socio-moral principles in the pastoral work performed by the Church, which remain obligatory regardless of changing historical and political conditions.

In the opinion of Wojtyła, the social teachings of the Church are based on the Gospel, with social theology at the very foundation, containing the "divine-human" eschatological and temporal dimension decisive for man's development. Here, social order is perceived in terms of justice, freedom and social love. The specificity and originality of the Gospel and the ensuing social teachings of the Church do not consist of retaining the "golden mean" between liberalism and Marxism; but rather going beyond all materialism and economism.[8] Catholic doctrine subjugates the human being not to things, but to the spiritual factor and divine transcendence.

HUMAN LABOR AS CREATION

In September 1981, upon the ninetieth anniversary of *Rerum novarum*, John Paul II published *Laborem exercens*, his first social encyclical dealing with labor, capital, and ownership, as well as an analysis of numerous symptoms of injustice and alienation in the contemporary world. It presents a creationist interpretation of labor and its dignity as an injunction of God and man's continuation of the effort of creation. In abandoning the penitentiary interpretation of work as penance for original sin, this was particularly innovative against the background of the earlier teachings of the Church. In this new meaning, "labor constitutes the fundamental dimension of man's existence on Earth".[9] It is thus not punishment for sin, but the eternal calling of man.

Work also plays an essential part in shaping communal interpersonal links.[10] Here, the Pope develops his theory of participation presented in his well-known study entitled *Osoba i czyn* [The Person and Action] (1969). This postulates the need for labor as socializing and favors striving towards co-participation in work performed whether within "rigid" capitalism and bureaucratic collectivism.

Through work we realize that divine command to rule over the Earth as well as man's planned and purposeful activity pursued as a person. The Pope drew attention not so much to the objective aspects of labor and its evaluation as to its basic ethical value, "which is directly connected with the fact that the person who performs it is a conscious and free subject, who decides about himself".[11] Christian truth about labor opposes the materialistic-economic treatment of work as a "commodity" or a "labor force", sold to the owner of capital. John Paul II criticizes the mistake of "primary capitalism" embedded in assorted forms of neo-capitalism and collectivism, which reify man and degrade him to the role of an instrument on par with material means of production.[12]

The Pope accentuates the need to ground the principle of the primacy of human labor in relation to capital in the process of production. One should not counterpoise concrete persons concealed within the concepts of labor and capital. A system of work which overcomes those antinomies and aims at "the subjectivity of human labor and its causal participation in the process of production" is morally appriopriate. It also differs from the program launched by collectivism and liberal capitalism. Christian tradition understands the right of ownership differently than does liberalism; it does not comprehend it in an exclusivistic manner, but as the right to a universal destination of goods[13] and the real ability of benefiting therefrom. The economism, which lies at the basis of liberalism is the reason for numerous social and class conflicts.

The noblement of labor as a divine command and a social obligation presumes the need to respect personalist norms in socioeconomic relations. The performance of work should be accompanied by suitable means of security in the form of wages (especially those paid to the head of a family), combating unemployment, the protection of health and the right to join trade unions. The latter should be of a corporate rather than a class nature, in order to avoid the threat of class war.

The battle conducted by working men for their rights led to numerous symptoms of solidarity within human labor. In his "gospel of labor" the Pope expressed his own solidarity with "the poor", declaring that the realization of social justice in various parts of the world, in different countries, and in mutual relations requires ever new fronts of solidarity between workers as well as solidarity with workers. Such solidarity, he added, should occur constantly whenever it is demanded by the social degradation of the laboring subject, the exploitation of the workers, growing regions of poverty and sometimes outright hunger.[14]

Father Maciej Zięba is deeply convinced that the vision of the system depicted in the discussed encyclical evades all traditional classifications, and delineates only the fundamental and necessary conditions which should be met by every just socio-political system, based on the personalist vision of human life.[15] Nonetheless, the application of pseudo-Marxist vocabulary, the rather harsh criticism of the West, a division of the world into poor and rich countries, reflections on the conflict between labor and capital, and animosity towards private property, which outright emanate from this encyclical, are the reason why certain conservative Catholics, for example the American Senator James P. Lucier, described its author in the following words: "The Pope originates from a social democratic system. He was brought up in a Marxist country and himself did not understand capitalism satisfactorily. Thus, he derived all his imagery from Marx's *Capital*. We, in the United States, see capitalism in a different way".[16]

THE DRAMA OF THE CONTEMPORARY WORLD: NEITHER COLLECTIVISM NOR LIBERALISM

A global analysis and assessment of evil existing in the contemporary world are to be found in *Sollicitudo rei socialis*, the second social encyclical by John Paul II, published at the beginning of 1988 upon the twentieth anniversary of *Populorum progressio*, the encyclical of Paul VI. It was a disappointment for those overly optimistic regarding progress and the socioeconomic development of the entire world. *Sollicitudo rei socialis* (the seventh encyclical by John Paul II and the seventh social encyclical in the history of the Church), has been described by commentators, in a rather exaggerated manner, as an "encyclical of defeat". For it presents a rather pessimistic evaluation of the present-day world, and declares that the hope for development, so lively at the time of Paul VI, "today, appears to be extremely distant from being implemented".[17] Both Paul VI and John Paul II recognized that in contemporary times the "social question" assumes a global dimension and depends upon the impact of supranational factors. Today, the number of poor countries has grown in relation to those that are developed, as has the number of people "deprived of the goods and services produced by development"; the unequal division of indispensable means has grown even more distinctively.[18] Furthermore, the Pope drew attention to the increasing division and distance between the developed North, with its plentiful goods, and the backward South. By resorting to a vocabulary close to the theology of liberation, he drew attention to the situation of people who carry the unbearable burden of poverty within "structures of sin".[19] This situation is the reason why the unity of the world and mankind is becoming seriously endangered: within a single world there come into being three or even four worlds, which differ as regards the material and cultural conditions of man's existence. The Pope shifts responsibility for the resultant situation primarily onto the developed nations and economic-financial mechanisms (international debt), which augment the riches of the few and the poverty of the majority. John Paul II believes that true development must encompass all countries of the world, or moral , economic and civilizational regress will result.

The Pope underlines that the purely economic conception of development is undergoing a severe crisis, and that the realization of the happiness of mankind and its liberation can no longer be achieved by "the amassing of goods and services, even those profitable for the majority".[20] We need the cultural, religious and moral development of mankind. The poverty of under-development is morally intolerable; and the same is true for "overdevelopment", which leads to pure consumption and a surplus of material goods for those few who become slaves of their possession. John Paul II emphasizes that economic development in a situation in which natural resources are becoming limited must take into consideration moral requirements, while ruling over Nature does not signify unhampered exploitation, arbitrary usage of things, or absolute power over them.[21]

Heretofore the remarks pertained to the papal criticism of the chasm between the economic development of capitalism in the North and the South. It must be added that the Pope drew attention to the negative consequences of tension between the East and the West, which presented two different conceptions of development. The Pope used a mild description: "Both are imperfect and call for thorough correction".[22] The collectivist countries of the East, dominated by a bureaucratic apparatus, restrict the right to economic initiative, and ruin entrepreneurship and the subjective creativity of the citizen. The population of those countries, frustrated and subjugated to "decision-makers", brings to mind the old, capitalist dependence of the proletarians. Tension and rivalry between the East and the West have moved to countries of the South, thus rendering the already existing problems even more intense. The encyclical once again states that the social teaching of the Church "is critical both as regards capitalism and Marxist collectivism", since the latter two do not guarantee the possibility of an integral development of man and community. Herein lies the ideology of the cult of money, technology and class. Each of the blocs contains an inclination towards imperialism and neo-colonialism. It is precisely this division of the world which causes excessive armament and the absence of joint efforts for the welfare of mankind as a whole.

The need for such solidarity, however, is paving a road in the contemporary world, encompassed by an ecological awareness of the limited nature of available resources as well as an awareness of the radical co-dependence of all parts of the world. The inimical attitude towards both dominating blocs was the reason why the Pope spoke rather positively about the international movement of non-aligned countries, and its concern for the independence, identity, security and regional co-operation of those countries which relatively recently had gained their independence.

Critical towards the dominant political systems, the Pope emphasized that the social teaching of the Church does not constitute a third path between liberal capitalism and Marxist collectivism. It is by no means a new ideology, but a moral-theological reflection on human existence in society.

Despite numerous negative and pessimistic assessments of the contemporary world, the encyclical ends with rather optimistic accents.[23] The Pope expressed the conviction that it is possible to overcome evil, and that there still exists hope for a true liberation of humankind. Trusting in God and man's capabilities (and stressing his dignity), the Pope called for facing the challenge made at the end of the millennium, for disentangling ourselves from the embrace of despair, pessimism and passivity, and for renouncing the sins of egoism and cowardice. We should all face the great dangers hovering over mankind, and in particular oppose the possibility of a global economic crisis and universal war. "In view of such perils", the Pope concluded, "the differentiation between rich countries and people and poor countries and people is of slight significance, although greater responsibility encumbers those who have more and are capable of more".[24]

CHRISTIAN LIBERALISM ?

On 1 May 1991, the hundredth anniversary of the encyclical *Rerum novarum*, John Paul II issued a third social encyclical opening with the words *Centesimus annus*. In it, he pursues the reflection contained in the two previous encyclicals, refers to the "unexpected" events of 1989, in which communism in Europe collapsed, renders a profound criticism of socialism, and considerably alleviates his previous reservations towards victorious liberal capitalism. The encyclical contains a perceptible acceptance of the market economy and democratic capitalism, and a Catholic response to the defeat of Marxism (including the failure of so-called socialism with a human face) as well as "the excesses of extreme liberalism".[25] Others see in the encyclical elements which at first glance appear contradictory, and thus they describe it as "schizoidal". A closer examination of the last two encyclicals indicates that as late as 1988 the Pope, like many secular observers, did not notice the approaching fall of communism.[26] In 1988, he criticized predominantly the deviations of capitalism, and treated socialism rather leniently, not only for reasons of courtesy or diplomacy. The encyclical of 1991 already criticizes primarily real socialism, which at that time was no longer existent in Central-Eastern Europe, and praises the qualities of the market economy. This change of accents reflected a more general shift of moods and political opinions, which took place throughout the world at the beginning of the 1990s.

Turning his attention towards the "new things" of the present, John Paul II, in the spirit of his source of inspiration, Leo XIII, underlined the fundamental, "anthropological" error committed by socialism, which subjugates the individual to economic and social mechanisms, and ignores him as the subject of independent moral decisions, depriving him of all private property. In the opinion of both popes, the foundation of the mistakes made by socialism is composed of atheism and the theory of class struggle.

John Paul II added that the ultimate source of the crisis undergone by Marxism were new forms of workers' consciousness, which demanded justice and the recognition of the dignity of labor, whereas socialism amplified alienation by means of an insufficient and ineffective economy. The Pope stressed, however, that the present-day crisis of Marxism "does not signify liberating the world from a situation of injustice and oppression, from which Marxism, which treated them instrumentally, drew sustenance".[27] The phenomena of marginalization, exploitation, extreme material and moral poverty still occur, especially in the so-called Third World.

Rejecting purely liberal and socialist solutions, the Pope expressed his approval for such types of society, existing since the end of the world war, which contain an expanded social security system and a structure of participation, in which work ceases to be a "commodity", and the healthy mechanisms of the free market are controlled by social forces and the state. Such control could implement the "principle of the universal destination of the goods of land".[28] This is by no means a ready-made model nor a compromise between the free market, Marxism and Christianity. Nonetheless, the

Pope ceased speaking about the "structures of sin" and "option for the poor", and he rejected theories about the need to isolate the poor countries from the world markets. Furthermore, he advised Latin American countries and the so-called Third World seeking paths of development to draw conclusions from the experiences of the downfall of real socialism in 1989. They should accept the principles of the free economy or "market economy", free initiative in the economy based on private ownership, and the ensuing responsibility for means of production. In this encyclical, John Paul II confirmed the value of the integral vision of man and the "authentic theology of the holistic emancipation of man", contained in the famous Instruction about Christian Freedom and Liberation, published earlier in 1986 by the Congregation of the Faith.

Numerous liberals acknowledged that in *Centesimus annus* the Pope praised the institution of democratic liberalism more distinctly than had been the case up to now by declaring that: "The free market is the most effective tool for making use of resources and for fulfilling needs".[29] He praised the positive role played by the market, the contemporary economy of the enterprise, which recognizes the freedom and qualifications of man as the decisive production factor. Nevertheless, he added that the striving towards profit should not consist of its absolute maximalization, and should not be the only indicator or regulator of the work performed by an enterprise. Alongside profit one should take into consideration concern for the welfare of the workers, their development, the observance of principles of remuneration and the safety of labor, concern for the universal destination of goods, "human and moral factors, which from a longer perspective prove to be at the very least equally essential for the life of the enterprise".[30]

Diligent Catholic researchers emphasize the Pope's attachment to political-economic modernity; according to Michael Novak, just as the Second Vatican Council brought religious freedom, so John Paul II introduced economic freedom (and democracy) into the social teaching of the Catholic Church.[31] According to Jarosław Gowin, "it is precisely John Paul II who among all popes went furthest in the acceptance of democracy and the free market—the two pillars of modernity".[32] Father Zięba wrote that on the hundredth anniversary of *Rerum novarum* John Paul II presented a pro-community, communitarian and Catholic version of liberalism, different from its individualistic version, based on the concept of negative liberty.[33] Also the expression civil society has been found in Centesimus annus.[34]

The Pope also appreciated authentic democracy as a political system in the state of law, which retains unshaken values of "Christian truth", the subjectivity of society, and the "correct conception of the human being". He recognized, however, that "democracy without values easily becomes open or camouflaged totalitarianism".[35] This thesis produced controversies not only among agnostics and postmodern sympathizers of skeptical relativism. Milton Friedman, an outstanding representative of classical liberalism and a Nobel Prize winner, reacted to John Paul II's statements about the absolute truth of the Church and the necessity of obedience towards the truth about God and man as the first condition of freedom: "Whose truth? Established by whom?

Are these the echoes of the Spanish inquisition?".[36] But even the "pope of liberalism" (as Friedman is frequently described), who perceives a "Marxist impact upon the Polish Pope", discovers in this document numerous praiseworthy elements (the acceptance of private ownership, the free market, and profit; respect for the autonomy of democratic order; a decisive rejection of totalitarianism). This encyclical, he maintains, is able to satisfy almost everyone "with the exception of Marxists, communists and supporters of abortion".[37]

THE STRIVING TOWARDS A SYNTHESIS OF CONCEPTIONS OF SOCIETIES

In order to understand the sociopolitical views held by the Pope, essential significance must be ascribed to the famous interview held in November 1993 by J. Gawroński for the Italian journal *La Stampa.* In the wake of a rather decisive and acute condemnation of Marxism and communism, expressed in the encyclical *Centesimus annus*, the interview contains rather astounding statements about "seeds of truth" found even in Marxism, the socialist program and communism (the struggle against unemployment, concern for the poor, social welfare), seeds which should not be destroyed. Herein lies the "oscillating" nature of the socioeconomic and political thought of the Pope who, while remaining loyal to the leitmotif, each time accentuates different aspects of the rather ambiguous social teaching of the Church. Upon this particular occasion, emphasis on the "pro-social" and not the pro-capitalist aspects of papal teaching followed from the disillusionment of Latin American Catholic masses with the decisive defense of private property and the free market, carried out in accord with the official neo-liberalism of those countries, especially considering that quite recently the Pope had expressed compassion for the repressed of the world. Growing disappointment with the first effects of the construction of "wild" and untamed capitalism in Central and Eastern Europe, which led to numerous election victories of the post-communists, contributed to a greater condemnation of the assorted abuses of capitalism and its "degenerate" symptoms in different parts of the world. The Pope opposed such a conception of the Europeanization of Poland which would signify a blind and uncritical acceptance of the "whole ultra-liberal and consumerist system, deprived of all value, and forcefully introduced by propaganda".[38] This is not to say that the Pope seeks some sort of a third way between capitalism and socialism; once again, he confirmed that such a path is "another utopia".[39]

The above mentioned interview, containing a rather emotional critique of the negative aspects of capitalism, produced considerable unrest and even consternation among Polish Catholic circles. Attempts were made to diminish its significance, since it is not an official document in the manner of an encyclical, and assurances were made that in no case does it constitute a rehabilitation of communism. Some even tried—a rather rare situation in Poland—to criticize the Pope with distinct resentment (but also with openly declared "humility") for numerous ambiguities and the absence of precision in his assessments of communism.[40]

Western authors, such as the well-known French publicist Bernard Guetta, are of the opinion that the Pope "proposes a social democratic hue for free economy"[41]. Orthodox liberals are upset by the populist-gnostic declarations made by the Pope about the particular qualities of the poor, and by his suggestions that all workers are people of good will, etc. —these pronouncements were made either due to the Pope's attachment to tradition or for more down-to-earth socio-technical reasons. Mirosław Dzielski (1941–1989), a Catholic reviver of liberalism in Poland, accused the Pope of a logical confusion—characteristic of the left wing—of mutually exclusive (according to Hayek) concepts of justice and so-called social justice.[42] Dzielski wrote that "for us, liberals, the social thought of John Paul is by no means an easy problem to tackle. It is presented in a language different from the one to which we—brought up on the classics of the free market—are accustomed. Many of us are irritated by certain formulations, which appear to be derived from the language of a pro-Marxist left wing. Frequently, we feel incorrectly accused by the Pope for being ideologues and consumptionists driven by a primitive economism desire for profit".[43] Dzielski maintained that the Pope understands liberalism rather narrowly, in its French mode, i.e. as moral permissivism, tolerance for debauchery, and the non-recognition of religious norms and natural law. Dzielski wrote: "The Pope is certainly not a liberal", but added that "he does not prohibit being a liberal in the pro-liberty meaning of the word".[44]

We can see, therefore, that the papal style of making ambiguous and rather Pythic announcements cannot be easily subjected to simple interpretation. Documents signed by John Paul II, similarly to other well-balanced political statements, must be addressed to the largest possible number of people; this is the reason for the absence of unambiguous and decisive ideological opinions, which would *a priori* exclude potential opponents. Various commentators who do not notice this feature, and are attached to sentences taken out of their context, describe the Pope as a social democrat, an egalitarian, and even a socialist, a supporter of the third path, a messianist, a universalist, a moral rigorist, and a supporter of democratic capitalism, ordoliberalism, of community liberalism as well as of the American idea of religious and economic liberty, a traditionalist, a conservative, a fundamentalist, and a reactionary.

The Maciej Zięba OP, cited above, is firmly convinced that "the Pope consistently refuses to outline a completed, cohesive and closed description of social reality, since it always carries the threat of ideologization".[45] The papal project of sociopolitical and economic life is anti-ideological and hostile towards all rigid ideologies. John Paul II supports projects of democratic capitalism, and at the same time shows—according to an interesting but not quite proven interpretation proposed by the above cited author—that "it is possible to build a liberal society which respects values of the absolute; this could be even seen as a condition necessary for the survival of free society".[46] The warning against the supposedly destructive elements of agnosticism and liberal culture is excessively dramatic, and nothing indicates that freedom deprived of foundations embedded within dogmas of absolute Christian truth would inevitably lead to fatal annihilation. Apparently, men and even more so humankind of the postmodern epoch will no longer accept without outer coercion any sort of a system of steadfast principles.

There exists yet another reason why John Paul II does not unambiguously accept any of the classical types of political thought (liberalism, socialism, conservatism). Today, in the wake of a thorough re-evaluation and blend of classical principles, and a rapprochement of left and right-wing economic and social programs,[47] the Pope is not the only one to find it difficult to analyze the new reality by applying classical and rather rigid divisions. In 1978, the year when Karol Wojtyła ascended the papal throne and two years prior to the birth of socio-liberalconservative "Solidarity", Leszek Kołakowski formulated an enthralling "catechism" prophetically entitled: *How To Be a Conservative-Liberal Socialist*?[48] It follows that one can accept simultaneously regulative ideas derived from three political currents: "It is possible to be a conservative-liberal-socialist or—and this comes down to the same thing—those three words no longer constitute options capable of living and mutually excluding themselves".[49] We can agree with the opinion that Leszek Kołakowski, who attained a moral and intellectual hegemony in the Polish civil society, was also a "founder of a new universal ideology of intellectuals – conservative-liberal socialism"[50]. Nonetheless, Kołakowski claimed that no great and powerful International would ever emerge upon the basis of conservative-liberal socialism, because it cannot promise people happiness. Does its spiritual form, namely the Universal Church, not tower upon a similar foundation? The Church is a significant international force, which has preserved considerable vitality, proclaims respect for the family and tradition, promises freedom, social justice and even eternal happiness, while its recent superior is an unsurpassed master at being a conservative-liberal socialist.

The contribution of John Paul II to the philosophy of peace and world unity is very important. It calls for an opening for the cause of the whole of humankind, understanding mutual connections between all nations of the world. In his address of December 2004 and also in previous declarations the Pope called for international solidarity, for the mobilization in favor of preferential love for the poor and for consequent application of the „world citizenship". The Pope has noted universalizing trends, has appealed to the unity of humankind and to civilizational universalism. „The civilisational universalism", according to one of his commentators, „similar to cultural universalism, in the thought of John Paul II does not acquire a form of uniformization or an expansion of one particular civilization. Thus, it is a pluralistic universalism, which rather than one global civilization recognizes particular varieties."[51]

The Father Oszajca noted in the Pope's social views a divine and universalistic ability „to combine water with fire"[52], Leszek Kołakowski has seen in his messsage universal questions of the Good and Evil, of God and Man, Life and Salvation,[53] but the Pope himself has modestly declared in a conversation with Vittorio Messori that the master of philosophical and theological universalism is first of all Saint Thomas.

After John Paul II's death in April 2005 there has begun in the Polish press an interesting discussion on the possibility of renovation and moral awakening of Poland based on the spiritual heritage of the Pope and on the unusual climate of community created during the deep and long lasting mourning.

NOTES

1 Arkadiusz Modrzejewski, „Uniwersalizm w myśli filozoficzno-społecznej Jana Pawła II", *Krakowskie Studia Małopolskie* 6(2002), 446. See also Garry O'Connor, *Universal Father. A Life of Pope John Paul II* (London: Blumsbury, 2005).

2 Jan Paweł II, *Przemówienia do Polonii i Polaków za granicą 1979-1987* (London 1978), 151; Interesting words on the close connection between universalism, Catholicism and patriotism were uttered by the Pope also during his encouter with the Episcopate of Argentina.

3 See: *Dokumenty nauki społecznej Kościoła* [Documents of the Social Teaching of the Church], ed. M. Radwan et al., part 1 and 2 (Rome—Lublin 1987); P. Laubier, *Myśl społeczna Kościoła katolickiego od Leona XIII do Jana Pawła II* [The Social Thought of the Catholic Church from Leo XIII to John Paul II] (Warszawa—Kraków: Michalineum, 1988); *Ewolucja nauki społecznej Kościoła. Od Rerum novarum do Centesimus annus* [The Evolution of the Social Teaching of the Church. From *Rerum novarum* to *Centesimus annus*], ed W. Piątkowski (Łódź, 1997).

4 John Paul II's visits to Mexico have been interestingly commented by the famous Mexican philosopher Lepoldo Zea (1912-2004): L. Zea, „Polonia al filo de nuestro tiempo", in *Ameryka Łacińska rozumem i sercem*, ed. F. Rodriguez (Warsaw: CESLA, 2003).

5 F. Kampka, *Antropologiczne i społeczne podstawy ładu gospodarczego w świetle nauczania Kościoła* [The Anthropological and Social Foundations of Economic Order in the Light of The Teaching of the Church] (Lublin: Wyd. KUL, 1995), 7.

6 Ibid., 273.

7 Jan Paweł II, *Nauczanie społeczne Kościoła integralną częścią Jego misji* [The Social Teaching of the Church as the Integral Part of Its Mission] (Rome: Fundacja Jana Pawła II, Ośrodek Dokumentacji Pontyfikatu, 1996), 11–91.

8 Ibid, 20.

9 *Laborem exercens. Tekst i komentarz* [*Laborem exercens*. Text and commentary] (Cracow: Polskie Towarzystwo Teologiczne, 1983), 16.

10 See the commentary by Rev. W. Gubała on 126–131 in the above cited edition.

11 *Laborem*...,21.

12 Ibid., 36.

13 Bronisław Łagowski interprets with certain exaggeration this particular aspect of papal teaching as a collectivist and socialist principle and as a mistaken defense of common ownership. See: *Servo veritatis II. Spotkanie naukowe poświęcone myśli Jana Pawła II* [*Servo veritatis II.* A Scientific Meeting Devoted to the Thought of John Paul II], ed. A. Pelczar and W. Stróżewski (Cracow: Universitas, 1996), 163–164, 168.

14 *Laborem...*, 26.

15 M. Zięba, *Papieże i kapitalizm. Od Rerum novarum po Centesimus annus* [Popes and capitalism. From Rerum novarum to Centesimus annus] (Cracow: Wyd. "Znak", 1998), 49.

16 Quoted after A. Domosławski, *Chrystus bez karabinu. O pontyfikacie Jana Pawła II* [Christ without a Machine Gun. On the Pontificate of John Paul II] (Warsaw: Prószyński i S-ka, 1999), 191.

17 *Sollicitudo rei socialis*, in: *Encykliki Ojca Świętego Jana Pawła II* [The Encyclicals of His Holiness John Paul II] (Cracow: Wyd. "Znak", 1997), 447.

18 Ibid., 443.

19 Ibid., 448, 483.

20 Ibid., 469.

21 Ibid., 481.

22 Ibid., 459.

23 In a reference to those who perceive in the encyclical only pessimistic tones, Rev. Józef Majka declared: "No Christian can be a pessimist and the Pope even more so. And he is not". Commentary to *Sollicitudo rei socialis* (Wrocław: Wydawnictwo Wrocławskiej Księgarni Archidiecezjalnej, 1994), 129.

24 *Encykliki Ojca Świętego...*, 503.

25 George Weigel in a block of statements entitled *Papież, wolność i kapitalizm* [The Pope, Freedom and Capitalism] (Cracow: Wyd. "Znak") 11 (1991), 118.

26 It is interesting that a swift decline of "real socialism" was predicted only by neo-Marxists from the dependency school—pessimistically inclined theoreticians who perceived the growing, structural dependency upon the capitalist Center of all of its peripheries, i.e. countries of the former Third World and former Communist Bloc.

27 *Centesimus annus*, in: *Encykliki Ojca Świętego...*, 655.

28 Ibid., 646.

29 Ibid., 666. The Latin American liberals saw in that encyclical a significant presence of Michael Novak's views, a US liberal-conservative theologian. See P.A. Mendoza, C.A. Montaner, A. Vargas Llosa, *Fabricantes de miseria. Las verdaderas causas de la pobreza en el Tercer Mundo* (Barcelona: Plaza & Janés Editores, 1999), 135. Somewhat similarly theologians of liberation and the Latin American Left saw in the official Church social doctrine "an apologetic ideology of liberal capitalism". See A.M. Ezcurra, *Doctrina social de la Iglesia. Un reformismo antisocialista* (México 1986); G. Giraldi,

La túnica rasgada. La identidad cristiana hoy, entre liberación y restauración (Santander 1991).

30 Ibid., 668; in a commentary on the views of John Paul II a celebrated historian of economic thought stated: "The world of values should comprise the basis of shaping a positive economic order. This goal should be served by assorted instruments, in the most general meaning of the term—the system of property, the market and the state. These tools should be functional in relation to the world of values. They are valuable not as such, but only owing to their function in realizing values associated with the essence of man. I believe"—he added—"that this is the stand of John Paul II" —W. Piątkowski, *Etyczne podstawy gospodarki w świetle encyklik Jana Pawła II* [The ethical foundations of the economy in the light of encyclicals by John Paul II], in *Myśl społeczna Jana Pawła II*. ed. W. Piątkowski (Warsaw - Łódź: PWN, 1999), 165.

31 *Znak* 11 (1991), 109; Michael Novak's views, especially his conservative effort to establish a "Catholic liberalism", have been criticized by F.J. Mazurek, "Czy jest możliwy 'katolicki liberalizm' ", *Społeczeństwo* 1 (1996).

32 J. Gowin, *Kościół po komunizmie* [The Church after Communism] (Cracow: Wyd. "Znak", 1995), 286–287. A bit later, in 2002 Gowin acknowledged that the present day Poland, in which the synthesis of capitalism and solidarity failed and even disgraced itself, "is a country hurting the Pope's expectations".

33 M. Zięba OP, *Kościół wobec liberalnej demokracji* [The Church and Liberal Democracy], in: M. Novak, A. Rauscher SJ, M. Zięba, *Chrześcijaństwo, demokracja, kapitalizm* [Christianity, Democracy, Capitalism] (Poznań: Wydawnictwo "W drodze", 1993), 134–136. Some authors underline the concurrence of the social teaching of the Church with the German ordoliberalism. See K.-U. Bartels, *Katolische Soziallehre und Ordnungskonzeption. Eine ordnungspolitische Analyse der Enzyklika Centesimus Annus* (Frankfurt am Main 1997).

34 John Paul II sponsored as early as 1989 a very important symposium in Vatican on the idea of civil society. For more information on the topic, see John A. Coleman, S.J., "A Limited State and a Vibrant Society: Christianity and Civil Society", in *Civil Society and Government*. Edited by Nancy L. Rosenblum and John A. Hall (Princeton: Princeton University Press, 2002): 223-254; Dominique Colas, *Civil Society and Fanaticism* (Stanford: Stanford University Press, 1997), especially its chapter entitled: "The Catholic Church and its Will to Control Civil Society". See also numerous favorable references to civil society and pluralism in the official *Compendium of the Social Doctrine of the Church* (Washington, D.C.: United States Conference of Catholic Bishops, 2005).

35 Ibid., 683.

36 The Polish translation in the cited block of statements: *Papież, wolność i kapitalizm* (Cracow: Wyd. "Znak", 1991), 94.

37 Ibid., 93.

38 "Jestem papieżem dwóch światów: Zachodu i Wschodu" [I am the Pope of two Worlds: the West and the East], *Więź*, February (1994), 33.

39 Ibid., 36.

40 See: the discussion held by the editorial board concerning the interview published in *Więź*, February (1994), 10–31.

41 *Znak* 11(1991), 121.

42 M. Dzielski, "Odrodzenie ducha—budowa wolności. Pisma zebrane" [The Rebirth of the Spirit—the Construction of Freedom. Collected Writings] (Cracow: *Znak*, 1995) 131; other Polish authors, by no means left-wing, clearly support the defense of the principle of social justice in the conditions of systemic transformations and the thought of John Paul II, e.g. Rev. J. Kondziela, "Solidarność i wolny rynek. Perspektywy rozwoju społeczno-gospodarczego w świetle encykliki Centesimus annus" [Solidarity and the free market. Perspectives of socioeconomic development in the light of the encyclical *Centesimus annus*], *Ethos* 21/22 (1993), 172.

43 Ibid., 166.

44 Ibid., 167–168; another author declares: "For a liberal freedom is the target, and for the Church it is but a means which can be utilized in assorted ways", and adds: "It would seem the right thing to agree with Rev. Tischner considering that the teaching of John Paul II exceeds liberalism, but does not reject it. It utilises its potential although it criticizes it. One can be the enemy of liberalism, but this teaching cannot be used as a mallet against liberals " —E. Skalski, "Czy Jan Paweł II jest liberałem?" [Is John Paul II a liberal?], *Gazeta Wyborcza*, no. 16–17 August 1997. The Pope's critique of liberalism, of liberty without truth and responsibility, strongly exposed by foreign commentators, was present in his speeches and homilies during his last visit to Poland in 2002. This critique contributed to John Paul's popularity among populists, anti-globalists, and even to Fidel Castro's tribute.

45 M. Zięba, *Papieże...,* 103.

46 M. Zięba, *Papieże ...,* 190.

47 For an interesting discussion on this topic see: D. Zagrodzka (*Gazeta Wyborcza*, 10–11 July 1999) and B. Łagowski (*Polityka*, 24 July 1999), who analyzed the so-called social democratic manifesto of Tony Blair and Gerhard Schröder, the program of the supposed third path or the new mean, resembling the election program of... the Christian democratic CDU/CSU, Catholic social teaching and the so-called social market economy.

48 This text was first published in the *Encounter* of October 1978.

49 L. Kołakowski, *Czy diabeł może być zbawiony i 27 innych kazań* [Can the Devil be Saved and 27 Other Sermons] (Londyn: "Aneks", 1984), 205. B. Łagowski draws attention to an earlier attempt at a synthesis of conservatism, liberalism and socialism in the thought of August Cieszkowski, and to the relation between the views of the Pope and Polish Romantic thought, in: *Servo veritatis II...*, 161, 168; J. R. Błachnio perceives other concurrences between the thought of Cieszkowski and Wojtyła. See his monographic study *Polskie inspiracje i wartości w nauczaniu Jana Pawła II* [Polish Inspirations and Values in the Teaching of John Paul II] (Bydgoszcz, 1995), 46. Also J.

Kuczyński, who notices in the thought of John Paul II a striving towards a conciliation of the world of labor and the world of capital sees an attempt at a synthesis of the free market, planning and self-government, i.e. the bases of universal society and a universal manifesto, see: J. Kuczyński, *Wstęp do uniwersalizmu* [Introduction to Universalism], vol. I, *Ogrodnicy świata* [Gardeners of the World] (Warsaw, 1998), 206, 214.

50 C. Michalski, *Powrót człowieka bez właściwości* (Warsaw 1996), 230; see also D. Colas, *Civil Society and Fanaticism* (Stanford: Stanford University Press, 1997), 87.

51 Arkadiusz Modrzejewski, *Uniwersalizm w myśli filozoficzno-społecznej Jana Pawła II*, 443.

52 *Gazeta Wyborcza*, 2002, 24-25 August.

53 *The Independent* 2005, 4 April.

About the Author

Professor Eugeniusz Górski is Senior Research Fellow at the Institute of Philosophy and Sociology of the Polish Academy of Sciences in Warsaw and Professor of Political Ideas at the Świętokrzyska Academy in Kielce (Poland). He is the author of over 150 works, predominantly on Spanish and Latin American thought (Miguel de Unamuno, José Ortega y Gasset, Fernando Savater, José Martí, José Carlos Mariátegui, and others).

Professor Górski was engaged in various comparative research projects and has taken part in numerous international conferences and seminars, chiefly in Poland, Spain and the America. Recently he took part in the 10 week seminar on “History and Cultural Identity” at The Catholic University of America, Washington, D.C. (September 20-November 20, 2006).

Index

E

F

G

H

K

L

M

O

P

T

THE COUNCIL FOR RESEARCH IN VALUES AND PHILOSOPHY

PURPOSE

Today there is urgent need to attend to the nature and dignity of the person, to the quality of human life, to the purpose and goal of the physical transformation of our environment, and to the relation of all this to the development of social and political life. This, in turn, requires philosophic clarification of the base upon which freedom is exercised, that is, of the values which provide stability and guidance to one's decisions.

Such studies must be able to reach deeply into one's culture and that of other parts of the world as mutually reinforcing and enriching in order to uncover the roots of the dignity of persons and of their societies. They must be able to identify the conceptual forms in terms of which modern industrial and technological developments are structured and how these impact upon human self-understanding. Above all, they must be able to bring these elements together in the creative understanding essential for setting our goals and determining our modes of interaction. In the present complex global circumstances this is a condition for growing together with trust and justice, honest dedication and mutual concern.

The Council for Studies in Values and Philosophy (RVP) unites scholars who share these concerns and are interested in the application thereto of existing capabilities in the field of philosophy and other disciplines. Its work is to identify areas in which study is needed, the intellectual resources which can be brought to bear thereupon, and the means for publication and interchange of the work from the various regions of the world. In bringing these together its goal is scientific discovery and publication which contributes to the present promotion of humankind.

In sum, our times present both the need and the opportunity for deeper and ever more progressive understanding of the person and of the foundations of social life. The development of such understanding is the goal of the RVP.

PROJECTS

A set of related research efforts is currently in process:

1. *Cultural Heritage and Contemporary Change: Philosophical Foundations for Social Life*. Focused, mutually coordinated research teams in university centers prepare volumes as part of an integrated philosophic search for self-understanding differentiated by culture and civilization. These evolve more adequate understandings of the person in society and look to the cultural heritage of each for the resources to respond to the challenges of its own specific contemporary transformation.

2. *Seminars on Culture and Contemporary Issues*. This series of 10 week cross-cultural and interdisciplinary seminars is coordinated by the RVP in Washington.

3. *Joint-Colloquia* with Institutes of Philosophy of the National Academies of Science, university philosophy departments, and societies. Underway since 1976 in Eastern Europe and, since 1987, in China, these concern the person in contemporary society.

4. *Foundations of Moral Education and Character Development*. A study in values and education which unites philosophers, psychologists, social scientists and scholars in education in the elaboration of ways of enriching the moral content of education and character development. This work has been underway since 1980.

The personnel for these projects consists of established scholars willing to contribute their time and research as part of their professional commitment to life in contemporary society. For resources to implement this work the Council, as 501 C3 a non-profit organization incorporated in the District of Colombia, looks to various private foundations, public programs and enterprises.

PUBLICATIONS ON CULTURAL HERITAGE AND CONTEMPORARY CHANGE

Series I. Culture and Values
Series II. Africa
Series IIA. Islam
Series III. Asia
Series IV. W. Europe and North America
Series IVA. Central and Eastern Europe
Series V. Latin America
Series VI. Foundations of Moral Education
Series VII. Seminars on Culture and Values

****

Series I. Culture and Values

I.1 *Research on Culture and Values: Intersection of Universities, Churches and Nations.* George F. McLean, ed. ISBN 0819173533 (paper); 081917352-5 (cloth).
I.2 *The Knowledge of Values: A Methodological Introduction to the Study of Values;* A. Lopez Quintas, ed. ISBN 081917419x (paper); 0819174181 (cloth).
I.3 *Reading Philosophy for the XXIst Century.* George F. McLean, ed. ISBN 0819174157 (paper); 0819174149 (cloth).
I.4 *Relations Between Cultures.* John A. Kromkowski, ed. ISBN 1565180089 (paper); 1565180097 (cloth).
I.5 *Urbanization and Values.* John A. Kromkowski, ed. ISBN 1565180100 (paper); 1565180119 (cloth).
I.6 *The Place of the Person in Social Life.* Paul Peachey and John A. Kromkowski, eds. ISBN 1565180127 (paper); 156518013-5 (cloth).
I.7 *Abrahamic Faiths, Ethnicity and Ethnic Conflicts.* Paul Peachey, George F. McLean and John A. Kromkowski, eds. ISBN 1565181042 (paper).
I.8 *Ancient Western Philosophy: The Hellenic Emergence.* George F. McLean and Patrick J. Aspell, eds. ISBN 156518100X (paper).
I.9 *Medieval Western Philosophy: The European Emergence.* Patrick J. Aspell, ed. ISBN 1565180941 (paper).
I.10 *The Ethical Implications of Unity and the Divine in Nicholas of Cusa.* David L. De Leonardis. ISBN 1565181123 (paper).
I.11 *Ethics at the Crossroads: 1.Normative Ethics and Objective Reason.* George F. McLean, ed. ISBN 1565180224 (paper).
I.12 *Ethics at the Crossroads: 2.Personalist Ethics and Human Subjectivity.* George F. McLean, ed. ISBN 1565180240 (paper).
I.13 *The Emancipative Theory of Jürgen Habermas and Metaphysics.* Robert Badillo. ISBN 1565180429 (paper); 1565180437 (cloth).
I.14 *The Deficient Cause of Moral Evil According to Thomas Aquinas.* Edward Cook. ISBN 1565180704 (paper).
I.15 *Human Love: Its Meaning and Scope, a Phenomenology of Gift and Encounter.* Alfonso Lopez Quintas. ISBN 1565180747 (paper).
I.16 *Civil Society and Social Reconstruction.* George F. McLean, ed. ISBN 1565180860 (paper).
I.17 *Ways to God, Personal and Social at the Turn of Millennia: The Iqbal Lecture, Lahore.* George F. McLean. ISBN 1565181239 (paper).
I.18 *The Role of the Sublime in Kant's Moral Metaphysics.* John R. Goodreau. ISBN 1565181247 (paper).

I.19 *Philosophical Challenges and Opportunities of Globalization.* Oliva Blanchette, Tomonobu Imamichi and George F. McLean, eds. ISBN 1565181298 (paper).
I.20 *Faith, Reason and Philosophy: Lectures at The al-Azhar, Qom, Tehran, Lahore and Beijing; Appendix: The Encyclical Letter: Fides et Ratio.* George F. McLean. ISBN 156518130 (paper).
I.21 *Religion and the Relation between Civilizations: Lectures on Cooperation between Islamic and Christian Cultures in a Global Horizon.* George F. McLean. ISBN 1565181522 (paper).
I.22 *Freedom, Cultural Traditions and Progress: Philosophy in Civil Society and Nation Building, Tashkent Lectures, 1999.* George F. McLean. ISBN 1565181514 (paper).
I.23 *Ecology of Knowledge.* Jerzy A. Wojciechowski. ISBN 1565181581 (paper).
I.24 *God and the Challenge of Evil: A Critical Examination of Some Serious Objections to the Good and Omnipotent God.* John L. Yardan. ISBN 1565181603 (paper).
I.25 *Reason, Rationality and Reasonableness, Vietnamese Philosophical Studies, I.* Tran Van Doan. ISBN 1565181662 (paper).
I.26 *The Culture of Citizenship: Inventing Postmodern Civic Culture.* Thomas Bridges. ISBN 1565181689 (paper).
I.27 *The Historicity of Understanding and the Problem of Relativism in Gadamer's Philosophical Hermeneutics.* Osman Bilen. ISBN 1565181670 (paper).
I.28 *Speaking of God.* Carlo Huber. ISBN 1565181697 (paper).
I.29 *Persons, Peoples and Cultures in a Global Age: Metaphysical Bases for Peace between Civilizations.* George F. McLean. ISBN 1565181875 (paper).
I.30 *Hermeneutics, Tradition and Contemporary Change: Lectures In Chennai/ Madras, India.* George F. McLean. ISBN 1565181883 (paper).
I.31 *Husserl and Stein.* Richard Feist and William Sweet, eds. ISBN 1565181948 (paper).
I.32 *Paul Hanly Furfey's Quest for a Good Society.* Bronislaw Misztal, Francesco Villa, and Eric Sean Williams, eds. ISBN 1565182278 (paper).
I.33 *Three Theories of Society.* Paul Hanly Furfey. ISBN 978-1565182288 (paper).
I.34 *Building Peace In Civil Society: An Autobiographical Report from a Believers' Church.* Paul Peachey. ISBN 978-1565182325 (paper).

Series II. Africa

II.1 *Person and Community: Ghanaian Philosophical Studies: I.* Kwasi Wiredu and Kwame Gyeke, eds. ISBN 1565180046 (paper); 1565180054 (cloth).
II.2 *The Foundations of Social Life: Ugandan Philosophical Studies: I.* A.T. Dalfovo, ed. ISBN 1565180062 (paper); 156518007-0 (cloth).
II.3 *Identity and Change in Nigeria: Nigerian Philosophical Studies, I.* Theophilus Okere, ed. ISBN 1565180682 (paper).
II.4 *Social Reconstruction in Africa: Ugandan Philosophical studies, II.* E. Wamala, A.R. Byaruhanga, A.T. Dalfovo, J.K.Kigongo, S.A.Mwanahewa and G.Tusabe, eds. ISBN 1565181182 (paper).
II.5 *Ghana: Changing Values/Chaning Technologies: Ghanaian Philosophical Studies, II.* Helen Lauer, ed. ISBN 1565181441 (paper).
II.6 *Sameness and Difference: Problems and Potentials in South African Civil Society: South African Philosophical Studies, I.* James R.Cochrane and Bastienne Klein, eds. ISBN 1565181557 (paper).
II.7 *Protest and Engagement: Philosophy after Apartheid at an Historically Black South African University: South African Philosophical Studies, II.* Patrick Giddy, ed. ISBN 1565181638 (paper).
II.8 *Ethics, Human Rights and Development in Africa: Ugandan Philosophical Studies, III.* A.T. Dalfovo, J.K. Kigongo, J. Kisekka, G. Tusabe, E. Wamala, R. Munyonyo, A.B. Rukooko, A.B.T. Byaruhanga-akiiki, M. Mawa, eds. ISBN 1565181727 (paper).

II.9 *Beyond Cultures: Perceiving a Common Humanity: Ghanian Philosophical Studies, III.* Kwame Gyekye ISBN 156518193X (paper).
II.10 *Social and Religious Concerns of East African: A Wajibu Anthology: Kenyan Philosophical Studies, I.* Gerald J. Wanjohi and G. Wakuraya Wanjohi, eds. ISBN 1565182219 (paper).
II.11 *The Idea of an African University: The Nigerian Experience: Nigerian Philosophical Studies, II.* Joseph Kenny, ed. ISBN 978-1565182301 (paper).
II.12 *The Struggles after the Struggles: Zimbabwean Philosophical Study, I.* David Kaulemu, ed. ISBN 9781565182318 (paper).

Series IIA. Islam

IIA.1 *Islam and the Political Order.* Muhammad Saïd al-Ashmawy. ISBN ISBN 156518047X (paper); 156518046-1 (cloth).
IIA.2 *Al-Ghazali Deliverance from Error and Mystical Union with the Almighty: Al-munqidh Min Al-dalil.* Critical edition of English translation with introduction by Muhammad Abulaylah and Nurshif Abdul-Rahim Rifat; Introduction and notes by George F. McLean. ISBN 1565181530 (Arabic-English edition, paper), ISBN 1565180828 (Arabic edition, paper), ISBN 156518081X (English edition, paper)
IIA.3 *Philosophy in Pakistan.* Naeem Ahmad, ed. ISBN 1565181085 (paper).
IIA.4 *The Authenticity of the Text in Hermeneutics.* Seyed Musa Dibadj. ISBN 1565181174 (paper).
IIA.5 *Interpretation and the Problem of the Intention of the Author: H.-G.Gadamer vs E.D.Hirsch.* Burhanettin Tatar. ISBN 156518121 (paper).
IIA.6 *Ways to God, Personal and Social at the Turn of Millennia: The Iqbal Lecture, Lahore.* George F. McLean. ISBN 1565181239 (paper).
IIA.7 *Faith, Reason and Philosophy: Lectures at The al-Azhar, Qom, Tehran, Lahore and Beijing; Appendix: The Encyclical Letter: Fides et Ratio.* George F. McLean. ISBN 1565181301 (paper).
IIA.8 *Islamic and Christian Cultures: Conflict or Dialogue: Bulgarian Philosophical Studies, III.* Plament Makariev, ed. ISBN 156518162X (paper).
IIA.9 *Values of Islamic Culture and the Experience of History, Russian Philosophical Studies, I.* Nur Kirabaev, Yuriy Pochta, eds. ISBN 1565181336 (paper).
IIA.10 *Christian-Islamic Preambles of Faith.* Joseph Kenny. ISBN 1565181387 (paper).
IIA.11 *The Historicity of Understanding and the Problem of Relativism in Gadamer's Philosophical Hermeneutics.* Osman Bilen. ISBN 1565181670 (paper).
IIA.12 *Religion and the Relation between Civilizations: Lectures on Cooperation between Islamic and Christian Cultures in a Global Horizon.* George F. McLean. ISBN 1565181522 (paper).
IIA.13 *Modern Western Christian Theological Understandings of Muslims since the Second Vatican Council.* Mahmut Aydin. ISBN 1565181719 (paper).
IIA.14 *Philosophy of the Muslim World; Authors and Principal Themes.* Joseph Kenny. ISBN 1565181794 (paper).
IIA.15 *Islam and Its Quest for Peace: Jihad, Justice and Education.* Mustafa Köylü. ISBN 1565181808 (paper).
IIA.16 *Islamic Thought on the Existence of God: Contributions and Contrasts with Contemporary Western Philosophy of Religion.* Cafer S. Yaran. ISBN 1565181921 (paper).
IIA.17 *Hermeneutics, Faith, and Relations between Cultures: Lectures in Qom, Iran.* George F. McLean. ISBN 1565181913 (paper).
IIA.18 *Change and Essence: Dialectical Relations between Change and Continuity in the Turkish Intellectual Tradition.* Sinasi Gunduz and Cafer S. Yaran, eds. ISBN 1565182227 (paper).

Series III.Asia

III.1 *Man and Nature: Chinese Philosophical Studies, I.* Tang Yi-jie, Li Zhen, eds. ISBN 0819174130 (paper); 0819174122 (cloth).
III.2 *Chinese Foundations for Moral Education and Character Development: Chinese Philosophical Studies, II.* Tran van Doan, ed. ISBN 1565180321 (paper); 156518033X (cloth).
III.3 *Confucianism, Buddhism, Taoism, Christianity and Chinese Culture: Chinese Philosophical Studies, III.* Tang Yijie. ISBN 1565180348 (paper); 156518035-6 (cloth).
III.4 *Morality, Metaphysics and Chinese Culture (Metaphysics, Culture and Morality, I).* Vincent Shen and Tran van Doan, eds. ISBN 1565180275 (paper); 156518026-7 (cloth).
III.5 *Tradition, Harmony and Transcendence.* George F. McLean. ISBN 1565180313 (paper); 156518030-5 (cloth).
III.6 *Psychology, Phenomenology and Chinese Philosophy: Chinese Philosophical Studies, VI.* Vincent Shen, Richard Knowles and Tran Van Doan, eds. ISBN 1565180453 (paper); 1565180445 (cloth).
III.7 *Values in Philippine Culture and Education: Philippine Philosophical Studies, I.* Manuel B. Dy, Jr., ed. ISBN 1565180412 (paper); 156518040-2 (cloth).
III.7A *The Human Person and Society: Chinese Philosophical Studies, VIIA.* Zhu Dasheng, Jin Xiping and George F. McLean, eds. ISBN 1565180887.
III.8 *The Filipino Mind: Philippine Philosophical Studies II.* Leonardo N. Mercado. ISBN 156518064X (paper); 156518063-1 (cloth).
III.9 *Philosophy of Science and Education: Chinese Philosophical Studies IX.* Vincent Shen and Tran Van Doan, eds. ISBN 1565180763 (paper); 156518075-5 (cloth).
III.10 *Chinese Cultural Traditions and Modernization: Chinese Philosophical Studies, X.* Wang Miaoyang, Yu Xuanmeng and George F. McLean, eds. ISBN 1565180682 (paper).
III.11 *The Humanization of Technology and Chinese Culture: Chinese Philosophical Studies XI.* Tomonobu Imamichi, Wang Miaoyang and Liu Fangtong, eds. ISBN 1565181166 (paper).
III.12 *Beyond Modernization: Chinese Roots of Global Awareness: Chinese Philosophical Studies, XII.* Wang Miaoyang, Yu Xuanmeng and George F. McLean, eds. ISBN 1565180909 (paper).
III.13 *Philosophy and Modernization in China: Chinese Philosophical Studies XIII.* Liu Fangtong, Huang Songjie and George F. McLean, eds. ISBN 1565180666 (paper).
III.14 *Economic Ethics and Chinese Culture: Chinese Philosophical Studies, XIV.* Yu Xuanmeng, Lu Xiaohe, Liu Fangtong, Zhang Rulun and Georges Enderle, eds. ISBN 1565180925 (paper).
III.15 *Civil Society in a Chinese Context: Chinese Philosophical Studies XV.* Wang Miaoyang, Yu Xuanmeng and Manuel B. Dy, eds. ISBN 1565180844 (paper).
III.16 *The Bases of Values in a Time of Change: Chinese and Western: Chinese Philosophical Studies, XVI.* Kirti Bunchua, Liu Fangtong, Yu Xuanmeng, Yu Wujin, eds. ISBN 156518114X (paper).
III.17 *Dialogue between Christian Philosophy and Chinese Culture: Philosophical Perspectives for the Third Millennium: Chinese Philosophical Studies, XVII.* Paschal Ting, Marian Kao and Bernard Li, eds. ISBN 1565181735 (paper).
III.18 *The Poverty of Ideological Education: Chinese Philosophical Studies, XVIII.* Tran Van Doan. ISBN 1565181646 (paper).
III.19 *God and the Discovery of Man: Classical and Contemporary Approaches: Lectures in Wuhan, China.* George F. McLean. ISBN 1565181891 (paper).
III.20 *Cultural Impact on International Relations: Chinese Philosophical Studies, XX.* Yu Xintian, ed. ISBN 156518176X (paper).
III.21 *Cultural Factors in International Relations: Chinese Philosophical Studies, XXI.* Yu Xintian, ed. ISBN 1565182049 (paper).

III.22 *Wisdom in China and the West: Chinese Philosophical Studies, XXII.* Vincent Shen and Willard Oxtoby †. ISBN 1565182057 (paper)
III.23 *China's Contemporary Philosophical Journey: Western Philosophy and Marxism ChineseP hilosophical Studies: Chinese Philosophical Studies, XXIII.* Liu Fangtong. ISBN 1565182065 (paper).
III.24 *Shanghai : Its Urbanization and Culture: Chinese Philosophical Studies, XXIV.* Yu Xuanmeng and He Xirong, eds. ISBN 1565182073 (paper).
IIIB.1 *Authentic Human Destiny: The Paths of Shankara and Heidegger: Indian Philosophical Studies, I.* Vensus A. George. ISBN 1565181190 (paper).
IIIB.2 *The Experience of Being as Goal of Human Existence: The Heideggerian Approach: Indian Philosophical Studies, II.* Vensus A. George. ISBN 156518145X (paper).
IIIB.3 *Religious Dialogue as Hermeneutics: Bede Griffiths's Advaitic Approach: Indian Philosophical Studies, III.* Kuruvilla Pandikattu. ISBN 1565181395 (paper).
IIIB.4 *Self-Realization [Brahmaanubhava]: The Advaitic Perspective of Shankara: Indian Philosophical Studies, IV.* Vensus A. George. ISBN 1565181549 (paper).
IIIB.5 *Gandhi: The Meaning of Mahatma for the Millennium: Indian Philosophical Studies, V.* Kuruvilla Pandikattu, ed. ISBN 1565181565 (paper).
IIIB.6 *Civil Society in Indian Cultures: Indian Philosophical Studies, VI.* Asha Mukherjee, Sabujkali Sen (Mitra) and K. Bagchi, eds. ISBN 1565181573 (paper).
IIIB.7 *Hermeneutics, Tradition and Contemporary Change: Lectures In Chennai/ Madras, India.* George F. McLean. ISBN 1565181883 (paper).
IIIB.8 *Plenitude and Participation: The Life of God in Man: Lectures in Chennai/ Madras, India.* George F. McLean. ISBN 1565181999 (paper).
IIIB.9 *Sufism and Bhakti, a Comparative Study.* Md. Sirajul Islam. ISBN 1565181980 (paper).
IIIB.10 *Reasons for Hope: Its Nature, Role and Future.* Kuruvilla Pandikattu, ed. ISBN 156518 2162 (paper).
IIB.11 *Lifeworlds and Ethics: Studies in Several Keys.* Margaret Chatterjee. ISBN 9781565182332 (paper).
IIIC.1 *Spiritual Values and Social Progress: Uzbekistan Philosophical Studies, I.* Said Shermukhamedov and Victoriya Levinskaya, eds. ISBN 1565181433 (paper).
IIIC.2 *Kazakhstan: Cultural Inheritance and Social Transformation: Kazakh Philosophical Studies, I.* Abdumalik Nysanbayev. ISBN 1565182022 (paper).
IIIC.3 *Social Memory and Contemporaneity: Kyrgyz Philosophical Studies, I.* Gulnara A. Bakieva. ISBN 9781565182349 (paper).
IIID.1 *Reason, Rationality and Reasonableness: Vietnamese Philosophical Studies, I.* Tran Van Doan. ISBN 1565181662 (paper).
IIID.2 *Hermeneutics for a Global Age: Lectures in Shanghai and Hanoi.* George F. McLean. ISBN 1565181905 (paper).
IIID.3 *Cultural Traditions and Contemporary Challenges in Southeast Asia.* Warayuth Sriwarakuel, Manuel B.Dy, J.Haryatmoko, Nguyen Trong Chuan, and Chhay Yiheang, eds. ISBN 1565182138 (paper).
IIID.4 *Filipino Cultural Traits: Claro R.Ceniza Lectures.* Rolando M. Gripaldo, ed. ISBN 1565182251 (paper).
IIID.5 *The History of Buddhism in Vietnam.* Chief editor: Nguyen Tai Thu; Authors: Dinh Minh Chi, Ly Kim Hoa, Ha thuc Minh, Ha Van Tan, Nguyen Tai Thu. ISBN 1565180984 (paper).

Series IV.Western Europe and North America

IV.1 *Italy in Transition: The Long Road from the First to the Second Republic: The Edmund D. Pellegrino Lectures.* Paolo Janni, ed. ISBN 1565181204 (paper).
IV.2 *Italy and The European Monetary Union: The Edmund D. Pellegrino Lectures.* Paolo Janni, ed. ISBN 156518128X (paper).

IV.3 *Italy at the Millennium: Economy, Politics, Literature and Journalism: The Edmund D. Pellegrino Lectures.* Paolo Janni, ed. ISBN 1565181581 (paper).
IV.4 *Speaking of God.* Carlo Huber. ISBN 1565181697 (paper).
IV.5 *The Essence of Italian Culture and the Challenge of a Global Age.* Paulo Janni and George F. McLean, eds. ISBB 1565181778 (paper).
IV.6 *Italic Identity in Pluralistic Contexts: Toward the Development of Intercultural Competencies.* Piero Bassetti and Paolo Janni, eds. ISBN 1565181441 (paper).

Series IVA. Central and Eastern Europe

IVA.1 *The Philosophy of Person: Solidarity and Cultural Creativity: Polish Philosophical Studies, I.* A. Tischner, J.M. Zycinski, eds. ISBN 1565180496 (paper); 156518048-8 (cloth).
IVA.2 *Public and Private Social Inventions in Modern Societies: Polish Philosophical Studies, II.* L. Dyczewski, P. Peachey, J.A. Kromkowski, eds. ISBN.paper 1565180518 (paper); 156518050X (cloth).
IVA.3 *Traditions and Present Problems of Czech Political Culture: Czechoslovak Philosophical Studies, I.* M. Bednár and M. Vejraka, eds. ISBN 1565180577 (paper); 156518056-9 (cloth).
IVA.4 *Czech Philosophy in the XXth Century: Czech Philosophical Studies, II.* Lubomír Nový and Jirí Gabriel, eds. ISBN 1565180291 (paper); 156518028-3 (cloth).
IVA.5 *Language, Values and the Slovak Nation: Slovak Philosophical Studies, I.* Tibor Pichler and Jana Gašparíková, eds. ISBN 1565180372 (paper); 156518036-4 (cloth).
IVA.6 *Morality and Public Life in a Time of Change: Bulgarian Philosophical Studies, I.* V. Prodanov and M. Stoyanova, eds. ISBN 1565180550 (paper); 1565180542 (cloth).
IVA.7 *Knowledge and Morality: Georgian Philosophical Studies, 1.* N.V. Chavchavadze, G. Nodia and P. Peachey, eds. ISBN 1565180534 (paper); 1565180526 (cloth).
IVA.8 *Cultural Heritage and Social Change: Lithuanian Philosophical Studies, I.* Bronius Kuzmickas and Aleksandr Dobrynin, eds. ISBN 1565180399 (paper); 1565180380 (cloth).
IVA.9 *National, Cultural and Ethnic Identities: Harmony beyond Conflict: Czech Philosophical Studies, IV.* Jaroslav Hroch, David Hollan, George F. McLean, eds. ISBN 1565181131 (paper).
IVA.10 *Models of Identities in Postcommunist Societies: Yugoslav Philosophical Studies, I.* Zagorka Golubovic and George F. McLean, eds. ISBN 1565181211 (paper).
IVA.11 *Interests and Values: The Spirit of Venture in a Time of Change: Slovak Philosophical Studies, II.* Tibor Pichler and Jana Gasparikova, eds. ISBN 1565181255 (paper).
IVA.12 *Creating Democratic Societies: Values and Norms: Bulgarian Philosophical Studies, II.* Plamen Makariev, Andrew M.Blasko and Asen Davidov, eds. ISBN 156518131X (paper).
IVA.13 *Values of Islamic Culture and the Experience of History: Russian Philosophical Studies, I.* Nur Kirabaev and Yuriy Pochta, eds. ISBN 1565181336 (paper).
IVA.14 *Values and Education in Romania Today: Romanian Philosophical Studies,* Marin Calin and Magdalena Dumitrana, eds. ISBN 1565181344 (paper).
IVA.15 *Between Words and Reality, Studies on the Politics of Recognition and the Changes of Regime in Contemporary Romania.* Victor Neumann. ISBN 1565181611 (paper).
IVA.16 *Culture and Freedom: Romanian Philosophical Studies, III.* Marin Aiftinca, ed. ISBN 1565181360 (paper).
IVA.17 *Lithuanian Philosophy: Persons and Ideas Lithuanian Philosophical Studies, II.* Jurate Baranova, ed. ISBN 1565181379 (paper).

IVA.18 *Human Dignity: Values and Justice: Czech Philosophical Studies, III*. Miloslav Bednar, ed. ISBN 1565181409 (paper).
IVA.19 *Values in the Polish Cultural Tradition: Polish Philosophical Studies, III*. Leon Dyczewski, ed. ISBN 1565181425 (paper).
IVA.20 *Liberalization and Transformation of Morality in Post-communist Countries: Polish Philosophical Studies, IV*. Tadeusz Buksinski. ISBN 1565181786 (paper).
IVA.21 *Islamic and Christian Cultures: Conflict or Dialogue: Bulgarian Philosophical Studies, III*. Plament Makariev, ed. ISBN 156518162X (paper).
IVA.22 *Moral, Legal and Political Values in Romanian Culture: Romanian Philosophical Studies, IV*. Mihaela Czobor-Lupp and J. Stefan Lupp, eds. ISBN 1565181700 (paper).
IVA.23 *Social Philosophy: Paradigm of Contemporary Thinking: Lithuanian Philosophical Studies, III*. Jurate Morkuniene. ISBN 1565182030 (paper).
IVA.24 *Romania: Cultural Identity and Education for Civil Society*. Magdalena Dumitrana, ed. ISBN 156518209X (paper).
IVA.25 *Polish Axiology: the 20th Century and Beyond: Polish Philosophical Studies, V*. Stanislaw Jedynak, ed. ISBN 1565181417 (paper).
IVA.26 *Contemporary Philosophical Discourse in Lithuania: Lithuanian Philosophical Studies, IV*. Jurate Baranova, ed. ISBN 156518-2154 (paper).
IVA.27 *Eastern Europe and the Challenges of Globalization: Polish Philosophical Studies, VI*. Tadeusz Buksinski and Dariusz Dobrzanski, ed. ISBN 1565182189 (paper).
IVA.28 *Church, State, and Society in Eastern Europe: Hungarian Philosophical Studies, I*. Miklós Tomka. ISBN 156518226X (paper).
IVA.29 *Politics, Ethics, and the Challenges to Democracy in 'New Independent States'*. Tinatin Bochorishvili, William Sweet, Daniel Ahern, eds. ISBN 9781565182240 (paper).
IVA.30 *Comparative Ethics in a Global Age*. Marietta T. Stepanyants, eds. ISBN 978-1565182356 (paper).
IVA.31 *Lithuanian Identity and Values: Lithuanian Philosophical Studies, V*. Aida Savicka, eds. ISBN 9781565182367 (paper).
IVA.32 *The Challenge of Our Hope: Christian Faith in Dialogue: Polish Philosophical Studies, VII*. Waclaw Hryniewicz. ISBN 9781565182370 (paper).
IVA.33 *Diversity and Dialogue: Culture and Values in the Age of Globalization: Essays in Honour of Professor George F. McLean*. Andrew Blasko and Plamen Makariev, eds. ISBN 9781565182387 (paper).
IVA.34 *Civil Society, Pluralism and Universalism: Polish Philosophical Studies, VIII*. Eugeniusz Gorski. ISBN 9781565182417 (paper).

Series V. Latin America

V.1 *The Social Context and Values: Perspectives of the Americas*. O. Pegoraro, ed. ISBN 081917355X (paper); 0819173541 (cloth).
V.2 *Culture, Human Rights and Peace in Central America*. Raul Molina and Timothy Ready, eds. ISBN 0819173576 (paper); 0-8191-7356-8 (cloth).
V.3 *El Cristianismo Aymara: Inculturacion o Culturizacion?* Luis Jolicoeur. ISBN 1565181042.
V.4 *Love as theFoundation of Moral Education and Character Development*. Luis Ugalde, Nicolas Barros and George F. McLean, eds. ISBN 1565180801.
V.5 *Human Rights, Solidarity and Subsidiarity: Essays towards a Social Ontology*. Carlos E.A. Maldonado ISBN 1565181107.

Series VI. Foundations of Moral Education

VI.1 *Philosophical Foundations for Moral Education and Character Development: Act and Agent.* G. McLean and F. Ellrod, eds. ISBN 156518001-1 (cloth) (paper); ISBN 1565180003.
VI.2 *Psychological Foundations for Moral Education and Character Development: An Integrated Theory of Moral Development.* R. Knowles, ed. ISBN 156518002X (paper); 156518003-8 (cloth).
VI.3 *Character Development in Schools and Beyond.* Kevin Ryan and Thomas Lickona, eds. ISBN 1565180593 (paper); 156518058-5 (cloth).
VI.4 *The Social Context and Values: Perspectives of the Americas.* O. Pegoraro, ed. ISBN 081917355X (paper); 0819173541 (cloth).
VI.5 *Chinese Foundations for Moral Education and Character Development.* Tran van Doan, ed. ISBN 1565180321 (paper); 156518033 (cloth).
VI.6 *Love as theFoundation of Moral Education and Character Development.* Luis Ugalde, Nicolas Barros and George F. McLean, eds. ISBN 1565180801.

Series VII. Seminars on Culture and Values

VII.1 *The Social Context and Values: Perspectives of the Americas.* O. Pegoraro, ed. ISBN 081917355X (paper); 0819173541 (cloth).
VII.2 *Culture, Human Rights and Peace in Central America.* Raul Molina and Timothy Ready, eds. ISBN 0819173576 (paper); 0819173568 (cloth).
VII.3 *Relations Between Cultures.* John A. Kromkowski, ed. ISBN 1565180089 (paper); 1565180097 (cloth).
VII.4 *Moral Imagination and Character Development: Volume I, The Imagination.* George F. McLean and John A. Kromkowski, eds. ISBN 1565181743 (paper).
VII.5 *Moral Imagination and Character Development: Volume II, Moral Imagination in Personal Formation and Character Development.* George F. McLean and Richard Knowles, eds. ISBN 1565181816 (paper).
VII.6 *Moral Imagination and Character Development: Volume III, Imagination in Religion and Social Life.* George F. McLean and John K. White, eds. ISBN 1565181824 (paper).
VII.7 *Hermeneutics and Inculturation.* George F. McLean, Antonio Gallo, Robert Magliola, eds. ISBN 1565181840 (paper).
VII.8 *Culture, Evangelization, and Dialogue.* Antonio Gallo and Robert Magliola, eds. ISBN 1565181832 (paper).
VII.9 *The Place of the Person in Social Life.* Paul Peachey and John A. Kromkowski, eds. ISBN 1565180127 (paper); 156518013-5 (cloth).
VII.10 *Urbanization and Values.* John A. Kromkowski, ed. ISBN 1565180100 (paper); 1565180119 (cloth).
VII.11 *Freedom and Choice in a Democracy, Volume I: Meanings of Freedom.* Robert Magliola and John Farrelly, eds. ISBN 1565181867 (paper).
VII.12 *Freedom and Choice in a Democracy, Volume II: The Difficult Passage to Freedom.* Robert Magliola and Richard Khuri, eds. ISBN 1565181859 (paper).
VII 13 *Cultural Identity, Pluralism and Globalization* (2 volumes). John P. Hogan, ed. ISBN 1565182170 (paper).
VII.14 *Democracy: In the Throes of Liberalism and Totalitarianism.* George F. McLean, Robert Magliola, William Fox, eds. ISBN 1565181956 (paper).
VII.15 *Democracy and Values in Global Times: With Nigeria as a Case Study.* George F. McLean, Robert Magliola, Joseph Abah, eds. ISBN 1565181956 (paper).
VII.16 *Civil Society and Social Reconstruction.* George F. McLean, ed. ISBN 1565180860 (paper).
VII.17 *Civil Society: Who Belongs?* William A.Barbieri, Robert Magliola, Rosemary Winslow, eds. ISBN 1565181972 (paper).

VII.18 *The Humanization of Social Life: Theory and Challenges.* Christopher Wheatley, Robert P. Badillo, Rose B. Calabretta, Robert Magliola, eds. ISBN 1565182006 (paper).
VII.19 *The Humanization of Social Life: Cultural Resources and Historical Responses.* Ronald S. Calinger, Robert P. Badillo, Rose B. Calabretta, Robert Magliola, eds. ISBN 1565182006 (paper).
VII.20 *Religious Inspiration for Public Life: Religion in Public Life, Volume I.* George F. McLean, John A. Kromkowski and Robert Magliola, eds. ISBN 1565182103 (paper).
VII.21 *Religion and Political Structures from Fundamentalism to Public Service: Religion in Public Life, Volume II.* John T. Ford, Robert A. Destro and Charles R. Dechert, eds. ISBN 1565182111 (paper).
VII.22 *Civil Society as Democratic Practice.* Antonio F. Perez, Semou Pathé Gueye, Yang Fenggang, eds. ISBN 1565182146 (paper).
VII.23 *Ecumenism and Nostra Aetate in the 21st Century.* George F. McLean and John P. Hogan, eds. ISBN 1565182197 (paper).
VII.24 *Multiple Paths to God: Nostra Aetate: 40 years Later.* John P. Hogan and George F. McLean, eds. ISBN 1565182200 (paper).
VII.25 *Globalization and Identity.* Andrew Blasko, Taras Dobko, Pham Van Duc and George Pattery, eds. ISBN 1565182200 (paper).

The International Society for Metaphysics

ISM.1. *Person and Nature.* George F. McLean and Hugo Meynell, eds. ISBN 0819170267 (paper); 0819170259 (cloth).
ISM.2. *Person and Society.* George F. McLean and Hugo Meynell, eds. ISBN 0819169250 (paper); 0819169242 (cloth).
ISM.3. *Person and God.* George F. McLean and Hugo Meynell, eds. ISBN 0819169382 (paper); 0819169374 (cloth).
ISM.4. *The Nature of Metaphysical Knowledge.* George F. McLean and Hugo Meynell, eds. ISBN 0819169277 (paper); 0819169269 (cloth).
ISM.5. *Philosophhical Challenges and Opportunities of Globalization.* Oliva Blanchette, Tomonobu Imamichi and George F. McLean, eds. ISBN 1565181298 (paper).

The series is published and distributed by: The Council for Research in Values and Philosophy, Cardinal Station, P.O.Box 261, Washington, D.C.20064, Tel./Fax.202/319-6089; e-mail: cua-rvp@cua.edu (paper); website: http://www.crvp.org. All titles are available in paper except as noted. Prices: $17.50 (paper).

THE COUNCIL FOR RESEARCH IN VALUES AND PHILOSOPHY

CULTURAL HERITAGE AND CONTEMPORARY CHANGE

Series IVA. Eastern and Central Europe

Vol.IVA. 2 *Public and Private Social Inventions in Modern Societies, Polish Philosophical Studies II*
Leon Dyczewski, Paul Peachey and John Kromkowski, eds.
ISBN 1-56518-050-x (cloth); ISBN 1-56518-051-8 (paper).

Vol.IVA. 19 *Values in the Polish Cultural Tradition, Polish Philosophical Studies, III*
Leon Dyczewski, ed.
ISBN 156518-142-5 (paper).

Vol.IVA. 20 *Liberalization and Transformation of Morality in Post-Communist Countries, Polish Philosophical Studie*
Tadeusz Buksinski
ISBN 1-56518-178-6 (paper).

Vol.IVA. 21 *Islamic and Christian Cultures: Conflict or Dialogue, Bulgarian Philosophical Studies, III*
Plament Makariev, ed.
ISBN 1-56518-162-X (paper).

Series VII. Seminars on Culture and Values

Vol.VII. 11 *Freedom and Choice in a Democracy, Volume I: Meanings of Freedom*
Robert Magliola and John Farrelly, eds.
ISBN 1-56518-186-7 (paper).

Vol.VII. 13 *Cultural Identity, Pluralism, and Globalization*
John P. Hogan, ed.
ISBN 1-56518-217-0 (paper).

Vol.VII. 14 *Democracy: in the Throes of Liberalism and Totalitarianism*
George F. McLean, Robert Magliola and William Fox, eds.
ISBN 1-56518-195-6 (paper).

Vol.VII. 15 *Democracy and Values in Global Times: With Nigeria as a Case Study*
George F. McLean, Robert Magliola and Joseph Abah, eds.
ISBN 1-56518-195-6 (paper).

Vol.VI I. 16 *Civil Society and Social Reconstruction*
George F. McLean, ed.
ISBN 1-56518-086-0 (paper).

Vol.VII. 17 *Civil Society: Who Belongs?*
William A. Barbieri, Robert Magliola and Rosemary Winslow, eds.
ISBN 1-56518-197-2 (paper).

Vol.VII. 22 *Civil Society as Democratic Practice*
Antonio F. Perez, Semou Pathé Gueye, Yang Fenggang, eds.
ISBN 1-56518-214-6 (paper).

The series is published and distributed by:
The Council for Research in Values and Philosophy
Cardinal Station, P.O. Box 261
Washington, D.C. 20064
Tel./Fax. 202/319-6089
E-mail: cua-rvp@cua.edu
Website: http://www.crvp.org
Price: $17.50